Challenging Clitics

Linguistik Aktuell/Linguistics Today (LA)

Linguistik Aktuell/Linguistics Today (LA) provides a platform for original monograph studies into synchronic and diachronic linguistics. Studies in LA confront empirical and theoretical problems as these are currently discussed in syntax, semantics, morphology, phonology, and systematic pragmatics with the aim to establish robust empirical generalizations within a universalistic perspective.

For an overview of all books published in this series, please see
http://benjamins.com/catalog/la

Volume 206

Challenging Clitics
Edited by Christine Meklenborg Salvesen and Hans Petter Helland

Challenging Clitics

Edited by

Christine Meklenborg Salvesen
Hans Petter Helland
University of Oslo

John Benjamins Publishing Company
Amsterdam / Philadelphia

The paper used in this publication meets the minimum requirements of the American National Standard for Information Sciences – Permanence of Paper for Printed Library Materials, ANSI Z39.48-1984.

Library of Congress Cataloging-in-Publication Data

Challenging clitics / Edited by Christine Meklenborg Salvesen, Hans Petter Helland.
p. cm. (Linguistik Aktuell/Linguistics Today, ISSN 0166-0829 ; v. 206)
Includes bibliographical references and index.
1. Grammar, Comparative and general--Clitics I. Salvesen, Christine Meklenborg.
P288.C43 2013
415'.92--dc23 2013008964
ISBN 978 90 272 5589 1 (Hb ; alk. paper)
ISBN 978 90 272 7194 5 (Eb)

John Benjamins Publishing Co. · P.O. Box 36224 · 1020 ME Amsterdam · The Netherlands
John Benjamins North America · P.O. Box 27519 · Philadelphia PA 19118-0519 · USA

Table of Contents

Acknowledgements

This present volume is the offspring of the Challenging Clitics workshop, held at the University of Oslo from October 27th–October 28th 2011. The general idea of the workshop was to gather researchers investigating clitics from different angles and perspectives without restricting the discussion to a particular framework. This aspect also characterises the present volume, which presents a selection of the papers presented at the workshop. The 11 peer-reviewed papers in this book cover a variety of fields and languages. Our aim is that this selection will provide a deeper insight into the nature and diversity of clitics.

Organising a workshop and editing a book require help at so many levels, and we wish to thank everyone involved with the project. Our mentor all the way has been Terje Lohndal, who has been a most valued discussion partner. The scientific committee did an excellent job assessing the papers to be presented at the workshop, and we would like to thank Terje Lohndal, Jan Terje Faarlund, Atle Grønn, and Chantal Lyche for their contribution. Synnøve Midtbø Myking and Anne-Kathrine Woldsnes did a wonderful job helping us with all practical matters on the days of the workshop. Our warmhearted thanks go to everybody who assisted us in the work on the present volume (in alphabetical order): Laura Bafile, Luc Baronian, Wayles Browne, Jennifer Culbertson, Hanne Martine Eckhoff, Kristine Gunn Eide, Pål Kristian Eriksen, Effi Georgala, Marie Labelle, Terje Lohndal, Chantal Lyche, Marios Mavrogiorgos, Genoveva Puskas, Bridget Samuels, Manuela Schönenberger, Ur Shlonsky, Arhonto Terzi, and Harold Torrence. There would have been no book without you! Finally, we would like to thank Bridget Samuels, who has proof-read the entire volume.

We would also like to express our gratitude to the the Department of Literature, Area Studies and European Languages at the University of Oslo, which provided us with the financial support we needed to pursue this project.

Oslo, January 2013
Christine Meklenborg Salvesen
Hans Petter Helland

Why challenging clitics?

Some introductory remarks

Christine Meklenborg Salvesen & Hans Petter Helland
University of Oslo

Linguists have been drawn to the intriguing nature of clitics ever since the golden age of philology in the 19th century. In this paper we aim to provide a brief history of different approaches to clitics, from Wackernagel's law to modern theories that link clitics to phases. We also present the papers that follow in this volume and show how they fit into the overall picture of research done on clitics in the 21st century.

1. Introduction[1]

In the introductory remarks of his state of the art report on clitics from 1999 (405–31), Henk van Riemsdijk claims that the '*syntax*' [our emphasis] of clitics has been providing us with a considerable challenge and still is.' Van Riemsdijk then goes on to cite Richard Kayne's 1975 book on French Syntax as 'one of the first major contributions to the analysis of clitics in generative grammar' (van Riemsdijk 1999: 406). Between these two dates of publication, while not forgetting that Kayne's seminal work was based on his research from the mid-sixties and onwards, there had been a huge interest in what had been known as 'clitics,' and not only on the *syntax* of clitics, but also on issues related to their morphological and phonological analysis. And the degree of interest in clitics has of course far from stopped since 1999. There have been major contributions within the domain since that date. For example, one must mention Anderson's book from 2005 and the extensive overview given by Spencer and Luis in 2012 on a steadily increasing number of publications on the clitics. What these latter works have in common is that they handle clitics not only from a syntactic viewpoint, but take into account both phonological, morphological and syntactic dimensions of their treatment, at

1. We would like to thank Terje Lohndal and Marios Mavrogiorgos for their insightful comments and suggestions. All mistakes are our own.

the interface of different linguistic core components. It is interesting to note that Spencer and Luis (2012: 12–13), while surveying major works on clitics, focusing mainly on publications from 1970 until the present, do not even mention Kayne's book among those seen by the authors as 'particularly influential.' This means of course that the Kaynian and purely syntactic method of treating clitics is by now only one among many other theoretical perspectives on the market. Moreover, Spencer and Luis' book from 2012, quite independently of particular linguistic theories and frameworks, shows that clitics still are 'challenging' even if by now they have already been 'challenged' a great deal in the past years. In this chapter, we will use some of these major contributions in the linguistic literature to draw a picture of why clitics still are, and will be, challenges, and how they have been and continue to be challenged.

This chapter is organised as follows: We start out with some well known, but still widely accepted, hugely influential approaches in the field of clitics: Kayne (1975) and Zwicky (1977). In Section 2.3 we look at the position of clitics and present Wackernagel's law (Wackernagel 1892) and the Tobler-Mussafia law, two observations from the 19th century that are still influential. In Section 2.4 we present fundamental theoretical issues linked to the nature of clitics and the way clitic structures are derived. In order to look at empirical data about clitics, we present the grammaticalisation cycle (van Gelderen 2011) in Section 3. We close the chapter in Section 4 with some remarks on the structure of this particular book and its main contributions.

2. Clitics as a linguistic object

2.1 Words, clitics and affixes

In the standard literature, clitics are most often seen as linguistic elements which are neither independent words nor fully integrated parts of words like affixes. In this sense clitics are negatively defined (neither words nor affixes) though a continuum of being more or less word-like or affix-like is still invoked. Like affixes, clitics need an element to which they can attach, called the clitic's *host*. This kind of attachment can be to the right edge of the host (*enclisis*) or to the left edge of the host (*proclisis*).[2] Like words, clitics have their own forms that in written material can even be detached from other (forms of) words. In the standard definition of

2. The third kind of possible attachment, not before or after but within the host (*endoclisis*), is rare and will not concern us here. See Zwicky (1977: 7–9) for early comments.

a clitic in the syntactic sense, the underlined forms (1) are detached from their verbal host, but still seen as clitics because they are not autonomous:

(1) *Je ne leur en ai pas parlé.*
I NEG them.DAT of-it have NEG talked
'I haven't talked to them about it.' (French)

In the Kaynian tradition, these forms, whether they are pronominals (*je*, *leur*, *en*) or not (the negative particle *ne*), meet a certain number of criteria for clitichood (i–v) (Kayne 1975: 66–92).

i. They often appear in special positions compared to full phrases. Thus, the pronominals *leur* and *en* in (1) have corresponding prepositional phrases in the postverbal position, respectively 'à mes amis' and 'de mes problèmes':

(2) *Je n' ai pas parlé de mes problèmes à mes amis.*
I NEG have NEG talked of my problems to my friends
'I haven't talked to my friends about my problems.' (French)

ii. None of the underlined forms in (1) can be stressed:

(3) *JE ne leur en ai pas parlé.

(4) *Je NE leur en ai pas parlé, etc.

iii. They cannot be separated from their verbal host by constituents except other clitics:

(5) **Je aussi ne leur en ai pas parlé.*
I also NEG them.DAT of-it have NEG talked
'Me too, I haven't talked to them.' (French)

iv. They cannot be modified:

(6) **Même je ne leur en ai pas parlé.*
even I NEG them.DAT of-it have NEG talked
'Not even I have talked to them.' (French)

v. They cannot be coordinated:

(7) **Je et il ne leur en avons pas parlé.*
I and he NEG them.DAT of-it have NEG talked
'I and he haven't talked to them.' (French)

One of the characteristics of this type of identification (to which we return below in Section 2.2) is that the clitic form is typically in complementary distribution with a non-clitic form. For the French case above, there are 'strong' forms of the pronouns that appear in the canonical syntactic positions and otherwise act as (non-clitic) nominals. Thus, the strong form 'eux' corresponding to 'leur' in (1) can indeed be stressed in its canonical syntactic position within the PP:

(8) *Je n' ai pas parlé de mes problèmes à EUX.*
I NEG have NEG talked of my problems to them
'I haven't talked about my problems with THEM.'

Strong forms also readily appear in the clauses above, where the clitic counterparts are impossible, even if the strong forms strongly tend to prefer dislocation structures, as in examples (9)–(11).

(9) *Moi aussi (, je) ne leur en ai pas parlé.*
me too (, I) NEG them.DAT of-it have NEG talked
'Me neither, I haven't talked about it with them.'

(10) *Même moi (, je) ne leur en ai pas parlé.*
even me (, I) NEG them.DAT of-it have NEG talked
'Not even I have talked about it with them.'

(11) *Moi et lui (, nous) ne leur en avons pas parlé.*
me and him (, we) NEG them.DAT of-it have NEG talked
'Me and him have talked about it with them.'

One of the major challenges in the literature has been to define the clitic forms with respect to independent words and affixes. A very good illustration of this is seen in Zwicky and Pullum's classic 1983 paper where the authors discuss contrasting properties of inflectional affixes and cliticised word forms in English.

Zwicky and Pullum (1983: 502–6) take as their starting point auxiliary verb forms of English such as *is*, *has* and *have* which attach to preceding words of different kinds, in this case to pronominals:

(12) She's gone = She is/has gone

(13) They've all seen this movie before = They have all seen this movie before.

Using the terminology from Zwicky's own work from 1977 (3–9), Zwicky and Pullum label the underlined forms in (12) and (13) *simple clitics* as variants of the corresponding full forms. Simple clitics are then contrasted with affixes on the basis of a set of criteria (i–vi):

i. Unlike affixes, clitics exhibit a low degree of selection with respect to their hosts, illustrated by attachment to pronouns in (12) and (13) and a preposition in (14):

(14) The person I was talking to's going to be angry with me.

Inflectional affixes, however, such as plural endings for nouns or past endings for verbs, are restricted to specific (nominal or verbal) stems for their attachment.

ii. Clitics exhibit no arbitrary gaps in the array of hosts to which they can attach (they attach freely to pronouns, prepositions, verbs, etc.) whereas gaps in inflectional paradigms do occur. The example given by Zwicky and Pullum (1983: 505) is the English verb *stride*, which lacks a past participle.

iii–iv. There are no morphophonological or semantic idiosyncrasies in clitic-host combination while this is quite common for inflectional affixes. There is thus no unexpected morphological host-clitic combination in the *'s* and *'ve-no* cases above with semantic correlates whereas the adjectival inflection of comparatives and superlatives show arbitrary gaps like *good/ better/best* (and not **gooder/*goodest*) (morphological idiosyncrasy). And the morphological superlative *last* from *late* in 'last words' is not necessarily the 'last word' in a temporal sense, but can rather be the 'final word' (showing semantic idiosyncrasy).

Criterion (v) of Zwicky and Pullum states that clitics do not necessarily form a syntactic unit with their host. In this sense, the clitics in (12–13) still belong syntactically to the verb phrase while they attach morphophonologically to the subject pronouns. And finally, criterion (vi) says that clitics can attach to material that already contains another clitic, like the combination between a cliticised modal 'could' and an auxiliary verb 'have' in (15).

(15) I'd've done it = I could have done it.

Inflected material, however, cannot attach to an already established clitic-host combination.

Zwicky and Pullum (1983) use these criteria to investigate the affix(-like) properties of the contracted negator *n't* in English. For our purposes, the Zwicky-Pullum example contrasted with the ones from the Kaynian tradition in (1)–(10) give us the starting point for a standard typology of clitics that has been adopted in some form or another by most followers.

2.2 Simple clitics and special clitics

In the original Zwicky (and Pullum) sense of the term, simple clitics were unaccented variants of full words, meaning that they appear in the same syntactic environment as their lexical counterpart, but in a phonologically reduced form (*is* vs *'s*, etc.). Anderson (2005: 22–30) takes the Zwicky typology a point further by showing that there are indeed phonologically dependent forms that should be treated as (simple) clitics without having non-clitic lexical counterparts. Examples are taken, for instance, from the Wakashan language Kak̓ala (spoken in the British

Columbia) where first and second person pronouns have clitics and full forms as optional variants whereas in the third person only the clitic form is found (Anderson 2005: 23). Thus, the (independent) first person pronoun *nug*^{w}*a* ('me') could correspond to the clitic *qs*, and the second person *qsu* ('you') to *us*, while third person *s* ('him') only has the clitic form. The definition from Anderson (2005: 23) in (16) reflects the purely phonological properties of deficiency of simple clitics, relabeling them as phonological clitics.

(16) **Phonological clitic**: A linguistic element whose phonological form is deficient in that it lacks prosodic structure at the level of the (Prosodic) Word. (Anderson 2005: 23)

Phonological (or simple) clitics are then contrasted with special clitics in the Kaynian sense above. Special clitics are of course not 'special' in the phonological sense because they are prosodically deficient just like simple clitics. However, they are special in the sense that they display unusual morphosyntactic properties. This was the initial assumption made by Zwicky from his 1977 paper, corresponding to the Kaynian definition of clitics, and pursued in the tradition ever since. In Anderson's treatment this category defines the second main type of clitics, where the label 'special' is replaced by 'morphosyntactic':

(17) **Morphosyntactic clitic**: a linguistic element whose position with respect to other elements of the phrase or clause follows a distinct set of principles, separate from those of the independently motivated syntax of free elements in the language. (Anderson 2005: 31)

What is missing from the original Zwicky definition of special clitics in Anderson's treatment is that special clitics in the original sense, just like simple clitics, were related to non-cliticized forms, but in the case of a special clitic, the full lexical alternate form occupies another (canonical) syntactic position. This was seen most clearly with the pronominal complements *leur* 'them' and *en* 'of-them' in example (1) above, with the cliticized forms occupying an obligatory preverbal position and the prepositional phrases the postverbal position. Anderson's point is that there are many examples of 'special' clitics where there are no possible lexical counterparts in a 'canonical' syntactic position. Take as an example the ethical dative *te* 'you' in (18). On all accounts, *te* 'you' is a clitic but there is no corresponding prepositional phrase introduced by à 'to' that could appear in the postverbal position.

(18) *Je vais te lui dire la vérité.*
I go you.DAT him.DAT say the truth
'I will tell him the truth, I tell you.'

The verb *dire* 'say' already subcategorizes for a dative complement (*lui*) and the non-lexical ethical dative, in informal usage, just adds to the structure as a preverbal clitic with no postverbal alternant, as in (19).

(19) **Je vais lui dire la vérité à toi.*
I go him tell the truth to you

On this basis, we adopt the classical typology of two main types of clitics, either 'simple' or 'special.' Clitics in general share the properties in (20).

(20) i. Clitics are non-accentuated elements (both simple and special clitics).
ii. Clitics are independent elements that need a host to attach to.
iii. Clitics may have a lexical alternant in another (canonical) syntactic position. In this sense, they are (morphosyntactically) special. They may also have a lexical alternant in the same syntactic position (simple clitics). Or they may have no lexical alternants at all, as seen in Anderson's cases (both simple and special clitics).

Clitics in the broad sense are seen as an 'umbrella' (Nevis et al. 1992) covering a wide set of phenomena which have sparked research in different theoretical directions.

2.3 The position of clitics

Besides the typologically based questions about (simple and special) clitics in the Zwicky sense, some approaches, being essentially 'non-syntactic' in nature, focus mainly on positional issues. These works emerge to a large extent from Wackernagel's pioneering monograph from 1892, which is often seen as the first serious attempt to investigate the position of clitics in Indo-European. Starting with data from Classical Greek, he examined different old Indo-European languages and concluded that these languages all had in common what he called enclitic pronominals (*enklitische Pronominalformen*) and particles occurring in second position of the clause, elements which nowadays are called 2nd position *(2P) clitics.*[3] This had already been noted for Sanskrit by Delbrück and Windisch (1878) and for Classical Greek by Bergaigne (1877),[4] but Wackernagel extended these observations to the whole Indo-European area. In Latin, the clitic could

3. There has of course been much refinement in later years of Wackernagel's initial proposals. For instance, now a distinction is often made between 2P(osition) clitics (placed after the first word in the clitic's domain) and more common 2D(omain) clitics (placed after the first phrase in the clitic's domain). See Spencer and Luis (2012:39–41).

4. Bergaigne (1877): *Memoires de la Societe de Linguistique* III, quoted by Wackernagel 1892.

come between the first and the second noun in a coordinated nominal phrase (21), a construction that was preferred, according to Wackernagel.

(21) *Iuppiter te di-que perdant*
Jupiter you gods-and lose
'May Jupiter and the gods destroy you!'
(Plautus, cited by Wackernagel 1892: 410)

Slightly prior to Wackernagel's influential work, Romance philologists Adolf Tobler and Adolfo Mussafia independently of each other discovered that clitics in Old Romance behaved in a particular way. If the clitics otherwise would appear in first position of the clause, the clitics are enclitic on the verb rather than proclitic. This is known as the *Tobler-Mussafia law*. The alternation between proclitic and enclitic constructions may be observed in a language such as Old French until the beginning of the 13th century (Skårup 1975, quoted by Hirschbühler & Labelle 2000). In (22), Old French still obeys the Tobler-Mussafia law. In a yes/no question, the verb occurs in first position of the clause, and proclisis would entail that the clitics occur clause-initially. Instead, the clitics occur as enclitics. Later in the history of French, however, the rule no longer comes into play (23), and (object) clitics are preverbal also in interrogative contexts.

(22) *Renart, di le me tu por voir?*
Renard, say it me you for real
'Renard, are you telling me this for real?' (Old French, 12th c.)

(23) *Les me fault-il laver trestous?*
them me must-he wash all
'Is it necessary for me to wash them all?' (Middle French, 16th c.)

Wackernagel as well as Tobler and Mussafia all described clitic placement without taking syntax into account. Zwicky (1977) gave these observations a theoretical frame which, as we have seen, has been enormously influential. Zwicky's theory was further developed by Klavans (1985). Klavans distinguishes the parameter of 'dominance' (whether the clitic is placed at the beginning or at the end of its domain) and the parameter of phonological attachment (the proclitic/enclitic dimension). More recently this approach has been used in the morphologically based Optimality Theory framework of Anderson (2005). On the other hand, there have been a large number of pure syntactic treatments of clitics which emphasize other research questions.

In more recent approaches of this kind it is not the linear order of the clitics that has attracted interest, but their distribution in light of independent syntactic principles.

2.4 Thematic arguments or functional heads?

Special clitics are often analysed as arguments, and in general a special clitic is incompatible with a syntactically equivalent full DP argument (other than in cases of dislocation), as in (24).

(24) *Maria (*lo) legge il giornale.*
Mary it reads the paper
'Mary reads the paper.' (Italian)

However, in Spanish, an indirect object clitic may co-occur with a full PP in argument position, as in (25), a phenomenon known as *clitic doubling.* In Greek, both direct and indirect objects may be doubled, as in (26). In fact, both the accusative and the dative clitic may be doubled, as in (27). Note that no preposition is involved in the doubled dative structure, something which distinguishes Greek from Spanish clitic doubling.

(25) *Miguelito le regaló un caramelo a Mafalda*
Miguelito it.CL.DAT gave a candy to Mafalda
'Miguelito gave Mafalda (a piece of) candy.' (Spanish, from Jaeggli 1982: 12)

(26) *Ton idha ton Jani.*
Him.CL.ACC saw the Jani
'I saw Janis.' (Greek, from Mavrogiorgos 2010)

(27) *Tu to edhosa to vivlio tu Kosta*
him.CL.DAT it.CL.ACC gave.1SG the book.ACC the Kosta.DAT
'I gave it to him, the book to Kostas.'
(Modern Greek, from Mavrogiorgos, p.c.)

In (25) the dative object clitic *le* co-occurs with the PP *a Mafalda* 'to Mafalda.' In (26) the direct object clitic *ton* appears in front of the finite verb even though the object is realised with a full accusative DP, *ton Jani* 'the Janis.' These constructions are unexpected, as classical θ-theory predicts that two elements may not carry the same θ-role.

Observations such as the one in (25) and (26) led to a major question that may not have been sufficiently answered, and which is also at the core of this book, namely *What are clitics?* We hope that the contributions to this volume may shed light on this question.

The question may be rephrased as follows: How can an element which is normally analysed as the bearer of a θ-role at the same time incorporate into a head in the sense of Baker (1988)? In the syntactically oriented literature on clitics, two major lines of thought have dominated: One suggests that special clitics are base-generated in a θ-position and then moved to their final positions

(Kayne 1975). The other views clitics as heads merged in the position in which they occur (Jaeggli 1982) and linked to a null argument in the θ-position (Sportiche 1996). The question may thus be reformulated: Is cliticisation related to movement or to Agree? In the following section we will look at the different analyses.

2.4.1 *Clitics as D^0s*

The first point of view is the classical one stating that clitics start out as the head D^0 of a DP, and that this DP is in a θ-position (Kayne 1975; Rizzi 1993; Uriagereka 1995; Chomsky 1995; Cardinaletti & Starke 1999; Matushansky 2006; Mavrogiorgos 2010).[5] At some point in the derivation the clitic head is extracted from the DP in order to adjoin to its host by head-to-head-movement. A major problem is how to explain the movement. What triggers the clitic to move? Different explanations have been given, both syntactic and phonological (see Mavrogiorgos 2010 for a presentation of the different lines of analysis).

Uriagereka (1995) suggests that in Western Iberian, clitics move to a head F^0, situated above AgrSP (which presumably would correspond to TP in current theories). Uriagereka also discusses Spanish doubling constructions such as the one in (25), and suggests that *a Mafalda* 'to Mafalda' is base-generated in the specifier position of the DP in which the clitic is the head.

(28) $[_{DP}$ a Mafalda $[_{D^0}$ le$]]$

When the clitic moves to its landing site in F^0, the PP *a Mafalda* 'to Mafalda' is stranded, which yields the clitic doubling structure.

2.4.2 *Clitics as functional heads*

The opposite stand is that clitics are functional heads, base-generated in the position in which they occur, without any movement, and standing in some relation to the position of the full DP (Jaeggeli 1982; Borer 1983, 1986; Roberge 1990). This was of course the starting point for treating clitics as agreement markers (see Girard this volume), and also the analysis proposed by Sportiche (1996), who nevertheless maintained a movement analysis. According to Sportiche, clitics were merged as functional heads, and the clitic was co-referential with an XP in VP. This XP would then move to the specifier position of the head in which the clitic was merged (Clitic Voice) by either overt or covert movement. In cases where only the clitic appears in the clause structure, this XP would be a *pro*. A clause such as

---

5. We leave aside the distinction between transitive and intransitive DPs. An intransitive DP does not contain any material other than the clitic in its D^0, whereas a transitive DP may contain a NP as its complement or in its specifier. For an in-depth discussion of this problem, see Mavrogiorgos (2010).

the one in (24), repeated as (29), would have the structure in (30). The verb moves to Cl^0, where the clitic incorporates into it by head adjunction. *Pro* is moved from SpecVP to SpecClP (using ClP as shorthand for Clitic Voice Phrase).

(29) *Maria lo legge.*
Mary it reads
'Mary reads it.'

(30) [$_{ClP}$ pro [$_{Cl^0}$ lo + legge [$_{VP}$ pro [$_{V^0}$ leggere]]]]

In the Spanish doubling cases, such as Jaeggli's example in (25), the XP *a Mafalda* 'to Mafalda' would move by covert movement to the specifier position. Sportiche's analysis implies that the clause would have a different structure at LF and PF, which we could represent by the structures in (31) and (32) (our interpretation). We leave aside irrelevant details.

(31) PF: [$_{ClP}$ [$_{Cl^0}$ le + regaló [$_{VP}$ un caramelo [$_{V^0}$ regalar a Mafalda]]]]

(32) LF: [$_{ClP}$ a Mafalda [$_{Cl^0}$ le + regaló [$_{VP}$ un caramelo [$_{V^0}$ regalar a Mafalda]]]]

Sportiche's analysis has had a strong impact, as he presupposed the existence of a clitic field. The existence of such a field has been important in the cartographic project (Manzini & Savoia 2004; Poletto & Pollock 2004a, b).

2.5 Clitics and phases

Earlier research had proposed that clitics move to a host – for instance, the verb in the Romance languages – generally situated somewhere in the IP field. During the last decade this conception has been challenged by new research, which links clitic movement to the existence of phases (Chomsky 2001, 2008). This is the essence of two important volumes that appeared almost simultaneously: Roberts (2010) (for Romance languages) and Mavrogiorgos (2010) (for Modern Greek). The idea is that clitics move to the edge of a phase – in other words, they will target the phase head. The phase head will be v*, V, T (if TP is to be regarded as a phase) or C, depending on language specific constraints (Mavrogiorgos 2010: 131).[6] A consequence of this analysis is that the cliticisation point may be very different from what was assumed in previous research. If Roberts and Mavrogiorgos are on the right track, the cliticisation point of Romance and Greek is the v*P and not

6. Note that in Chomsky's first analysis, only CP and vP were considered phases (Chomsky 2001). Later Svenonius (2003) proposed that DP too is a phase. Although it has been claimed that there may be more phases, the claim that VP and TP are phases is controversial.

the TP as previously assumed. The link between cliticisation and phases is further pursued in this volume by Fernández-Rubiera, who examines data from Asturian.

3. The subject cycle

Another question to consider is where clitics come from. Within the grammaticalisation framework, clitics represent a stage on the grammaticalisation cline, where an element starts off as a full word and becomes an affix, before fading out altogether, as illustrated in (33) (from Hopper & Traugott 1993).

(33) content item > grammatical word > clitic > inflectional affix

3.1 The subject pronoun in French

The evolution of subject pronouns in French may illustrate this. In this section we will show the changes that have affected the French subject pronoun and describe what van Gelderen (2011) calls the *Subject Agreement Cycle* or simply the *Subject Cycle*. Whereas Latin was a *pro* drop language, as are still the majority of Romance languages, subject pronouns appear regularly in Old French. However, unlike object pronouns, subject pronouns are not clitics in the earliest texts. Using Kayne's (1975) tests of clitichood (see Section 2.1 above), we see that subject pronouns act as full words. In (34) the subject is separated from the finite verb by a long apposition. In (35) it is modified by *meismes* 'self,' and in (36) and (37) it is coordinated with other words.

(34) *je, Luces, chevaliers et sires del Chastel del Gat,*
I Luke knight and sire of-the castel of-the Gat
voisin prochien de Salesbieres, cum chevaliers amoreus et
neighbour near of Salisbury how knight loving and
envoisiez, enpreing a translater une partie de ceste estoire.
gay try to translate a part of this story
'I, Luke, knight and sire of the Castel of Gat, close neighbour of Salisbury, as a loving and joyful knight, I try to translate a part of this story.'
(Old French, 13th c.)

(35) *Il meismes fist ensi que je di.*
he self did such that I say
'He himself did exactly that what I say.' (Old French, 13th c.)

(36) *Nous parlerons ensamble, je et mi conpaignon*
we speak together I and my companions
'We will speak together, I and my companions.' (Old French, 13th c.)

(37) *Bon ami seron je et tu.*
good friends are I and you
'You and I are good friends.' (Old French, 12th c.)

From the 13th century, subject pronouns start losing their independent status, and from the late 14th (Adams 1989) or 15th (Dufresne & Dupuis 1994) century subject pronouns are clitics. At the same time the systematic use of strong forms arises so that the pronominal system of French contains a set of strong and weak forms (clitics) that have two separate usages. The clitic form appears in front of the finite verb, as the first member in the sequence of clitics. In contexts such as dislocation (38) or modification of the subject (39), one uses the strong form of the pronoun.

(38) *Moi, je n' ai rien fait.*
Me I NEG have nothing done
'I haven't done anything.'

(39) *Je l' ai fait moi-même.*
I it have done me-self
'I've done it myself.'

However, even though the pronoun is a clitic, it is not incorporated into the verb in the sense of Baker (1988).[7] When the finite verb raises to C^0, the subject does not move along with it, unlike object clitics. The question in (41), corresponding to the declarative clause in (40), shows this difference between subject and object pronouns. This observation leads us to postulate that the pronominal subject occupies a distinct specifier position, more specifically SpecTP.

(40) *Tu l' as fait.*
you it have done
'You have done it.'

(41) *L' as-tu fait?*
it have you done
'Have you done it?'

(42) $[_{CP}\ [_{C^0}$ L'as $[_{IP}$ tu $[_{VP}\ [_{V^0}$ fait$]]]]]$

In colloquial French, inversion is hardly ever in use, at least not in informal registers. In addition, the subject pronoun needs to be repeated in front of every verb when verbs are coordinated (43). In Standard Modern French this is not necessary, and the subject pronoun may be omitted in co-ordinated structures (44).

7. This might imply that the subject, at least in earlier stages, was a weak pronoun in the sense of Cardinaletti and Starke (1999).

(43) *Elle chante et elle danse.*
she sings and she dances
'She sings and dances.' (Colloquial French)

(44) *Elle chante et danse.*
she sings and dances
'She sings and dances.' (Standard French)

The fact that the subject pronoun may not be omitted in colloquial contemporary French has led Roberge (1990), Zribi-Hertz (1994) and Auger (1995, 2003) to propose that the subject has become an affix and an agreement marker. Van Gelderen (2011) concludes that French is in the process of turning subjects into agreement markers and that 'different varieties of French are in different stages' of this process (van Gelderen 2011:38).

Languages which may have undergone a full process of pronouns > affixes are the polysynthetic languages. In a language such as Mohawk, Baker (1996) shows that no noun phrases are exterior to the clause proper; in other words, they must be regarded as dislocated elements. Inside the clause, affixes on the verb express the syntactic roles corresponding to the dislocated elements. In (45) the three noun phrases 'Sak,' 'pencil' and 'Mary' are all situated outside the clause. The verbal complex *washakóyune* has an infix (or 'endoclitic') expressing a masculine singular subject and a feminine singular object (*shakóy*), whereas its prefix *wa-* expresses the factual tense and *-u* expressing the verbal root.

(45) *Sak ye-hyantú-hkw-a' wa-shakóy-u'- ne Uwári*
Sak FsS-write-INSTR-HAB FACT-MsS/FsO-give-PUNC NE Mary
'Sak gave Mary a pencil.' (Mohawk, from Baker 1996: 100, his example 11a)[8]

Baker argues that arguments in Mohawk are expressed as affixes on the verb, and that all full noun phrases are situated outside this verbal complex. Interestingly, he compares this construction in Mohawk to the Clitic Left Dislocation in the Romance languages. Pronominal clitics in these languages have indeed been described as affixes rather than clitics (see Miller & Monachesi for an overview of all Romance languages). In his conclusion, Baker claims that phonological change may in fact change a configurational language into a head-marking language, as has been proposed for the Gunwinjguan languages of Northern Australia (see Baker 1996: 503 and references therein). Baker, however, proposes that a language needs to have a certain macroparameter in place in order for such a fundamental

8. The abbreviations are taken from Baker (1996) and should be read as follows: FsS = feminine, single subject; INSTR = instrumental; HAB = habitual; FACT = factual ('aorist'); MsS = masculine singular subject; FsO = feminine singular object; PUNC = punctual.

change to take place. In other words, French is in no way necessarily becoming a polysynthetic change. In fact, a different change may take place, namely the reanalysis of other sentential elements as pronouns.

If we return to French and the status of subjects, these may then be comparable to the infixes of Mohawk. As an affix, the subject does not occupy a specifier position (which it most probably does in Standard French), and it has not been moved to its surface position. Rather, it has merged in the head hosting the finite verb (Rowlett 2007). In a clause such as the one in (46) it is not the pronoun clitic *je* 'I' but the strong form *moi* 'me' that has to be analysed as the subject (irrelevant details omitted), as schematized in (47). This is a new development from the language as it was in the Classical or Modern periods, where *moi* 'me' would have to be interpreted as a left dislocated element, as in (48).

(46) *Moi je n' ai rien fait.*
me I NEG have nothing done
'I have done nothing.'

(47) $[_{\text{SpecTP}}$ Moi $[_{\text{T}^0}$ je n'ai ... rien fait$]]$

(48) $[_{\text{SpecCP}}$ Moi $[_{\text{TP}}$ je $[_{\text{T}^0}$ n'ai ... rien fait$]]$

In this way we can distinguish the following path of the subject pronoun in the history of French. If the reanalysis we saw in (47) leads to a reanalysis of *moi* from a strong form to an ordinary weak subject pronoun, we may be witnessing the emergence of a new set of personal pronouns in French.

This is a process which in many respects resemble Jespersen's cycle, but which affects pronouns. Van Gelderen (2011) describes the *Subject Agreement Cycle* in (49). As for French, we have not shown evidence for the origin of the subject pronouns, but we have seen examples of the rest of the cycle. With the possible reanalysis of strong pronouns (emphatic use) as subjects, the cycle may be starting over, as this reanalysis would represent van Gelderen's first point.

(49) *The Subject Agreement Cycle* (van Gelderen 2011: 54) noun/oblique/ emphatic > first/second person pronoun > clitic > agreement > zero

These changes strongly resemble the grammaticalisation cline, and may be accounted for in different frameworks (see van Gelderen 2004, 2011). Van Gelderen (2011) suggests that the mechanism behind the change described in this section is what she calls Feature Economy.

(50) *Feature Economy (from van Gelderen 2011: 41)*

Adjunct	> Specifier	> Head	> affix
emphatic	> full pronoun	> head pronoun	> agreement
[semantic]	> [i-phi]	> [u-1/2] [i-3]	>[u-phi]

In other words, there is a change from a semantically full adjunct, which in turn becomes the specifier of a projection. As such, it is a full pronoun with interpretable φ-features. The next step is that the pronoun becomes a head pronoun, or a clitic as we refer to it in this volume. A clitic has either uninterpretable φ-features (1st and 2nd persons) or interpretable φ-features (3rd person). In the final step in the cycle the head becomes an affix and an agreement-marker, with uninterpretable φ-features.

4. The interest of this volume

From this presentation we have shown different approaches to clitics, such as the truly descriptive ones of Wackernagel, Tobler and Mussafia, to the theoretical discussions, either purely syntactic (such as Kayne 1975; Sportiche 1986; Roberts 2010 and Mavrogiorgos 2010) or morphosyntactic, phonological and interface-based (like Zwicky 1977 & Anderson 2005). Still, there are numerous aspects of clitics that have not been addressed in the presentation so far. This volume presents both cutting-edge theoretical papers as well as meticulous descriptive papers that present new data. The papers are not limited to one particular approach, but discuss clitics from very different sides. All in all we hope this array of different approaches will provide the reader with insight into the complex nature of clitics.

4.1 The derivation of clitic structures

If clitics are indeed base-generated as phrases, it is essential to know more about the movement processes that might affect them. This is an important question in the literature on clitics. There are two different approaches to the movement of clitics. One emphasises PF when it comes to clitic placement (Barbosa 1996; Bošković 2004; Franks 2008; Samuels 2009). The other is to claim that clitic movement is syntactically motivated (see among others Kayne 1991; Rivero 1994; Benincà 1995; Dimitrova-Vulchanova 1995; Uriagereka 1995; Tomić 1996 & Shlonsky 2004).

4.2 Finiteness and phases

In his paper, Mavrogiorgos examines both finiteness-sensitive languages and Tobler-Mussafia languages and argues that it is not possible to see enclisis and proclisis as the result of either PF or syntactic requirements. Rather, it is the interaction between the two that gives rise to the proclisis-enclisis alternation. He also proposes that finiteness should be linked not only to syntax but also to PF. In this way proclisis, enclisis and finiteness are all linked to the syntax-PF interface.

In addition, the notion of phases is essential in understanding the cliticisation processes. Mavrogiorgos describes three different ways in which proclisis may be derived, and four different types of enclisis. In this way he shows how structures that bear resemblance to one another may be derived in very different ways.

Just like Mavrogiorgos, Fernández-Rubiera links cliticisation to phases, even though the analysis is somewhat different. Fernández-Rubiera examines Asturian, a Western Iberian Romance language which has been poorly studied. Asturian shows an alternation between enclisis and proclisis in declarative clauses, both matrix and embedded. In some cases an XP-V structure yields proclisis, in other cases enclisis. Fernández-Rubiera relates this to the different status of the preverbal elements and to verb movement. Under Fernández-Rubiera's analysis, Fin^0 is a phase head in all of Western Iberian, and it carries an edge condition which implies that it must be filled. The edge condition can be satisfied by A' movement of a phrase, something which yields proclisis. If no other element moves to FinP, the finite verb moves, which results in enclisis. A prerequisite to make this analysis work is to view all preverbal non-quantified subjects as topics, an approach which has been proposed for other Iberian languages (see *inter alia* Barbosa 1995, 2000 and Raposo 2000). As such, they are base-generated in the left periphery and are unable to satisfy the edge condition.

4.3 Clitics in LFG

A very different take on the problems linked to the position of clitics is taken by Dione, who suggests that clitics don't move at all, and that they are merged in their surface position. Dione, discussing clitics in Wolof, uses a Lexical Functional Grammar (LFG) framework (Kaplan & Bresnan 1982; Bresnan 2001; Dalrymple 2001). This is a new approach to the analysis of these clitics, which principally have been studied within a Chomskyan generative framework (Dunigan 1994; Torrence 2003; Russell 2006). Clitics in Wolof are sensitive to a number of factors, such as the inflectional status of their host, clause type and prosodic domain, so they have proven difficult to describe within a traditional generative framework. Zribi-Hertz and Diagne (2002) have proposed that clitics in Wolof are sensitive both to PF and syntax and as such represent the most radical of the transformative analyses discussing clitics in this language. Dione proposes that clitics preserve their lexical integrity and that they are generated in their surface position.

4.4 Clitics in Distributed Morphology

The derivation of clitic structure is also a major question in Sandalo & Galves' paper. Working within the framework of Distributed Morphology (Embick & Noyer 2001), they examine proclisis and enclisis in Modern Portuguese. They endorse the analysis that enclisis in Modern Portuguese is affix-like in nature, both from a syntactic and phonological point of view (see *inter alia* Klavans 1985; Zwicky 1977; Spencer 1991; Halpern 1995; Duarte & Mattos 1995, 2000; Rouveret 1999). Whereas proclisis occurs when the clitic is adjoined to T′ or TP, enclisis is derived by Lowering, a post-syntactic incorporation process. In Classical Portuguese the state of affairs was different, and Sandalo and Galves argue that enclisis was derived by Prosodic Inversion, a very different process from Lowering. They identify this shift as a step in a grammaticalisation process.

4.5 Slavic clitics and the TP projection

While the study of Romance languages dominated for a long time, there has been an increased interest in Slavic clitics since the late 1990s (Franks & King 2000). Slavic clitics typically fall into two groups: verb adjacent clitics (Bulgarian and Macedonian) and clause-second clitics (Czech, Slovak, Slovene, Bosnian-Croatian-Serbian, and to a certain extent Polish). There has been an important discussion in the literature as to the original placement of clitics in Slavic (Wayles Browne, p.c). Were clitics in Proto-Slavic verb-adjacent or second position clitics, and to what extent do the earliest written documents (Old Church Slavonic) reflect the original Slavic position (Progovac 1993, 1996; Tomić 1996; Franks 1998; Franks & King 2000; Bošković 2001; Pancheva 2005)?

Migdalski takes the stand that they were verb-adjacent, and that this property was lost over the course of time as the languages lost morphological tense. Furthermore, Migdalski suggests that this loss has led to the loss of TP projection. When clitics could no longer adjoin to TP, they had to find other landing sites above VP. The position that the TP layer is not universally available was proposed by Bošković (2010), who also linked this to the loss of the DP layer.

4.6 Interrogative clitics

Fine-grained studies of the linguistic hierarchy have been very important in the linguistic literature, and no less so when it comes to the placement of clitics. Since Pollock (1989) and Rizzi (1997), IP and CP have not been seen as distinct projections, but as *fields* of projections, and the study of these fields has been known as cartography (see among numerous others Rizzi 2004, 2006; Benincà & Poletto 2004, and, with a slightly different approach É. Kiss 1994, 2002). Dalmi's article adds to the research on the left periphery as she examines the interaction between the interrogative clitic *-e* and the weak erotetic *vajon* 'if … at all'.

Just like the South Slavic languages, Hungarian is a multiple *wh*-fronting language (Surányi 2002, 2004). In interrogative contexts, the clitic *-e* appears, and this element is merged in Fin^0. *Vajon* 'if ... at all' and *-e* may co-occur, but the order between them is not fixed. Dalmi suggests that in the cases where the clitic *-e* precedes *vajon*, it is due to remnant VP movement to a position situated higher than *vajon*, thus creating a complex CP structure. In this way, the clitic *-e* is used as a diagnostic for verb placement. Dalmi also points out that long *wh*-movement out of a subordinate interrogative clause is impossible if *vajon* occurs in the context. Dalmi suggests that *vajon* simply indicates that the INT operator and the clitic *-e* have created an OP chain that blocks long *wh*-movement and creates freezing effects.

4.7 Clitics or affixes?

As we have seen in the discussion above (Sections 2.1 and 3), it is necessary to distinguish between clitics and affixes, a distinction which is not always an easy one. In French, there has been a long-standing debate as to the status of different pronouns: Are they clitics, or should they be regarded as affixes?

Girard discusses changes in the French pronominal system as it is observed in Cajun French, e.g. the variety of French spoken in Louisiana in the USA. Girard's paper fills a gap in research done on other varieties of French such as Quebec French and Picard (Brasseur 2001; Auger 2003), and it relates to colloquial French as it is spoken in France. On one hand there is a discussion on the status of pronominal clitics in colloquial French. Have they indeed turned into affixes (Roberge 1990; Zribi-Hertz 1994 and Auger 1995, 2003), or must they still be regarded as clitics (Côté 2001 and De Cat 2005)? On the other hand there is the observed difference between standard French and other varieties, both dialectal and non-metropolitan. Girard shows how Cajun French in some respects patterns with other non-metropolitan varieties of French. Her conclusion is that clitics in Cajun French has come a lot further than the other varieties of colloquial French in the process of grammaticalization from independent morphemes towards affixes.

The evolutionary path from lexical item to affix, as described in Section 3, may not be the only one that can explain the occurrence of clitics. One very interesting question is whether clitics or clitic-like elements could be borrowed from other languages. This is the possibility explored by Pavlou and Panagiotidis, who discuss the element *-nde* in Cypriot Greek. Pronominal clitics in Cypriot Greek have been subject to extensive studies (Terzi 1999a, 1999b; Grohmann 2011; Grohmann et al. 2012), but their distribution with Cypriot Greek *-nde* has not yet been described. *-Nde* however also exists in Standard Modern Greek. Pavlou and Panagiotidis compare the distribution of *-nde* in Cypriot Greek and in Standard Modern Greek and show that the distribution is very different in the two languages. Instead of drawing the link between the two varieties of Greek, the authors propose that *-nde* has in fact been borrowed from neighbouring Turkish, more specifically from the clitic dA. They analyse the function of *-nde* in Cypriot Greek and propose that its behaviour is that of a validational marker, building on the terminology of Weber (1986).

Pavlou and Panagiotidis also discuss whether *-nde* is an affix or a clitic and show that *-nde* competes with postverbal clitics for the same position. *-Nde* in Cypriot Greek is moribund, but the article sheds interesting light on the possibility of clitics being borrowed into a language through language contact.

4.8 The acquisition of clitics

How are clitics acquired? Studies of Italian, French and Spanish speaking children have shown that clitics typically occur from the age of 20 months. These forms are enclitics, most often attached to an imperative verb (Cipriani et al. 1993; Hamann et al. 1995: 92; Antelmi 1997; Montrul 2004). In her study of the emergence of clitics in the language of a tri-lingual child, Khachaturyan finds that the acquisition of clitics took place somewhat later. The child, who learned Italian, Russian and Norwegian, started using Italian clitics at about 26 months. Just as the studies of monolingual children show, the clitics were enclitic forms with imperatives. At a later stage, the child replaced clitics of the 1st and 2nd person forms with strong forms. Interestingly, the child kept using 3rd person clitics, which most often occurred in right dislocation constructions. Khachaturyan proposes that it is interference from Norwegian and Russian that led to the use of strong forms instead of clitics in the 1st and 2nd persons. The fact that the child does not exchange 3rd person clitics for tonic forms may have to do with the frequency of the input.

4.9 Clitic clusters

So far we have seen how the placement of clitics may be approached from different angles. However, cliticisation has several other sides, such as phonological and morpho-phonological aspects. Pescarini discusses the morpho-phonological aspect of Italo-Romance clitic clusters. Two major points of view have been proposed in the literature: One that sees clitic clusters as a series of prosodic words (Nespor & Vogel 1986), and one that analyses the clusters as an autonomous prosodic constituent that forms the foot of a prosodic word (Peperkamp 1995, 1996, 1997; Monachesi 1996, and Selkirk 1995). Pescarini discusses various phonetic and prosodic patterns in Italian and suggests that Modern Italian has two types of clitic clusters. The first contains a single morphosyntactic constituent, which he calls a *true cluster*. The other has a sequence of separate units, which Pescarini labels a *split cluster*. Pescarini links the diachronic phonetic and linear changes in clitic clusters in Italian to a change from split clusters to true clusters.

Just like Pescarini, Salvesen is concerned with the internal organisation of clitic clusters in Old Romance, more specifically in Old French. As is well known in the literature on Old Romance, the internal order of clitic clusters changed towards the late medieval ages. Salvesen suggests that the catalyst for this process in Old French was the increased use of the reflexive pronoun. This line of thought was first presented by Brusewitz (1905), but Salvesen provides statistical material and elaborates on the analysis, which is presented in a generative framework using insight from Laenzlinger (1993), Kayne (1994) and Pescarini (2012).

5. Conclusion

We have seen that clitics have been the interest of study for at least 150 years. While philologists in the late 19th century described the placement of clitics, modern linguists seek to understand clitic behaviour with respect to syntax, phonetic requirements (PF), morphosyntax or grammaticalisation. The most recent development in our understanding of clitics is to link them to the existence of phases, as is also reflected in this volume (Mavrogiorgos and Fernández-Rubiera).

The major strength of this volume is that it deals with multiple sides of cliticisation, from different theoretical frameworks and with data from a number of different languages. Unlike many other books on clitics, we do not only consider them from merely a syntactical point of view; we also give accounts of the acquisition of clitics, of PF's role in cliticisation, of morpho-phonological aspects and historical change – to name but a few of the approaches presented in this volume. Taken together, the contributions in this volume not only provide insight into the nature of clitics, but into derivations and structures in language that go beyond the study of clitics themselves.

It is our belief that this way of presenting clitics will give the reader insight into the extremely complex nature of clitics. We have challenged clitics, but in many respects they are still challenging.

References

Adams, Marianne. 1989. Verb second effects in Medieval French. In *Studies in Romance Linguistics: Selected Papers from the Seventeenth Linguistic Symposium on Romance Languages (xvii. lsrl), Rutgers University, 27–29 March 1987*, Carl Kirschner & Janet de Cesaris (eds), 1–33. Amsterdam: John Benjamins.

Anderson, Stephen. 2005. *Aspects of the Theory of Clitics*. Oxford: OUP.

Antelmi, Donella. 1997. *La prima grammatica dell'italiano*. Bologna: Il Mulino.

Auger, Julie. 1995. Les clitiques pronominaux en français parlé informel: Une approche morphologique. *Revue Québécoise de Linguistique* 24(1): 21–60.

Auger, Julie. 2003. Les pronoms clitiques sujets en picard: Une analyse au confluent de la phonologie, de la morphologie et de la syntaxe. *French Language Studies* 13(1): 1–22.

Baker, Mark C. 1988. *Incorporation: A Theory of Grammatical Function Changing*. Chicago IL: University of Chicago Press.

Baker, Mark C. 1996. *The Polysynthesis Parameter* [Oxford Studies in Comparative Syntax]. Oxford: OUP.

Barbosa, Pilar. 1995. Null Subjects. Ph.D. dissertation, MIT.

Barbosa, Pilar. 1996. Clitic placement in European Portuguese and the position of subjects. In *Approaching Second: Second Position Clitics and Related Phenomena*, Aaron Halpern & Arnold Zwicky (eds), 1–40. Stanford CA: CSLI.

Barbosa, Pilar. 2000. Clitics: A window into the null subject property. In *Portuguese Syntax: New Comparative Studies*, João Costa (ed.), 31–93. Oxford: OUP.

Benincà, Paola & Poletto, Cecilia. 2004. Topic, focus, and V2. In *The Structure of CP and IP.* [Oxford Studies in Comparative Syntax], Luigi Rizzi (ed.), 52–75. Oxford: OUP.

Benincà, Paola. 1995. Complement clitics in medieval Romance: The Tobler-Mussafia law. *In Clause Structure and Language Change*, Adrian Battye & Ian Roberts (eds), 325–344. Oxford: OUP.

Borer, Hagit. 1983. *Parametric Syntax*. Dordrecht: Foris.

Borer, Hagit. 1986. Introduction. In *The Syntax of Pronominal Clitics* [Syntax and Semantics 19], Hagit Borer (ed.), 1–11. Orlando FL: Academic Press.

Bošković, Željko. 2001. *On the Nature of the Syntax-Phonology Interface. Cliticization and Related Phenomena*. Amsterdam: Elsevier.

Bošković, Zeljko. 2004. On the clitic switch in Greek imperatives. In *Balkan Syntax and Semantics* [Linguistik Aktuell/Linguistics Today 67], Olga Tomić (ed.), 269–291. Amsterdam: John Benjamins.

Bošković, Željko. 2010. On NPs and Clauses. Ms, University of Connecticut.

Brasseur, Patrice. 2001. *Dictionnaire des régionalismes du français de Terre-neuve*. Tübingen: Max Niemeyer.

Bresnan, Joan. 2001. *Lexical-Functional Syntax*. Oxford: Blackwell.

Brusewitz, Victor. 1905. Étude historique sur la syntaxe des pronoms personnels dans la langue des Félibres. Ph.D. dissertation, Uppsala University.

Brusewitz, Victor. 1905. Étude historique sur la syntaxe des pronoms personnels dans la langue des Félibres. Ph.D. dissertation, Uppsala University.

Cardinaletti, Anna & Starke, Michael. 1999. The typology of structural deficiency: A case study of the three classes of pronuns. In *Clitics in the Languages of Europe*, Henk van Riemdsijk (ed.), 145–233. Berlin: Mouton de Gruyter.

Chomsky, Noam. 1995. *The Minimalist Program* [Current Studies in Linguistics Series 28]. Cambridge MA: The MIT Press.

Chomsky, Noam. 2001. Derivation by phase. In *Ken Hale: In A Life in Language*, Michael Kenstowicz (ed.), 1–52. Cambridge MA: The MIT Press.

Chomsky, Noam. 2008. On phases. In *Foundational Issues in Linguistic Theory: Essays in Honor of Jean-Roger Vergnaud*, Robert Freidin, Carlos P. Otero & Maria Luisa Zubizarreta (eds), 133–166. Cambridge MA: The MIT Press.

Cipriani, Paola, Chilosi, Anna Maria, Bottari, Piero & Pfanner, Lucia. 1993. *L'acquisizione della morfosintassi in italiano. Fasi e processi.* Padova: Unipress.
Côté, Marie-Hélène. 2001. On the status of subject clitics in child French. In *Research on Child Language Acquisition*, Margareta Algren, Andoni Barreña, Maria-José Ezeizabarrena, Itziar Idiazabal & Brian MacWhinney (eds), 1314–1330, Sommerville, MA: Cascadilla Press.
Dalrymple, Mary. 2001. *Lexical-Functional Grammar* [Syntax and Semantics 34: Syntax and Semantics]. San Diego CA: Academic Press.
De Cat, Cécile. 2005. French subject clitics are not agreement markers. *Lingua* 115: 1195–1219.
Delbrück, Berthold & Windisch, Ernst. 1878. *Syntaktische Forschungen.* Waisenhauses: Halle. Open library: ⟨http://openlibrary.org/books/OL24129485M/Syntaktische_forschungen⟩ (15 January 2013).
Dimitrova-Vulchanova, Mila. 1995. Clitics in Slavic. *Studia Linguistica* 49: 54–92.
Duarte, Inês & Gabriela Matos, 2000. Romance clitics and the minimalist program. In *Portuguese Syntax,* João Costa (ed.), 116–142. Oxford: OUP.
Dufresne, Monique & Dupuis, Fernande. 1994. Modularity and the reanalysis of the French subject pronoun. *Probus* 6: 103–123.
Dunigan, Melynda B. 1994. On the clausal structure of Wolof. Ph.D. dissertation, The University of North Carolina at Chapel Hill.
É.Kiss, Katalin. 1994. Sentence structure and word order. In *The Syntactic Structure of Hungarian* [Syntax and Semantics 27], Ferenc Kiefer & Katalin É. Kiss (eds), 1–84. New York: Academic Press.
É.Kiss, Katalin. 2002. *Hungarian Syntax.* Cambridge: CUP.
Embick, David & Noyer, Rolf. 2001. Movement operations after syntax. *Linguistic Inquiry* 32(4): 555–596.
Franks, Steven & King, Tracy Holloway. 2000. *A Handbook of Slavic Clitics.* Oxford: OUP.
Franks, Steven. 1998. Clitics in Slavic. Paper presented at Comparative Slavic Morphosyntax Workshop, Bloomington IN.
Franks, Steven. 2008. Clitic placement, prosody, and the Bulgarian verbal complex. *Journal of Slavic Linguistics* 16: 91–137.
van Gelderen, Elly. 2004. *Grammaticalization as Economy* [Linguistik Aktuell/Linguistics Today 71]. Amsterdam: John Benjamins.
van Gelderen, Elly. 2011. *The Linguistic Cycle: Language Change and the Language Faculty.* Oxford: OUP.
Grohmann, Kleanthes K. 2011. Some directions for the systematic investigation of the acquisition of Cypriot Greek: A new perspective on production abilities from object clitic placement. In *The Development of Grammar: Language Acquisition and Diachronic Change* [Hamburg Studies on Multilingualism 11], Esther Rinke & Tanja Kupisch (eds), 179–203. Amsterdam: John Benjamins.
Grohmann, Kleanthes K., Theodorou, Eleni, Pavlou, Natalia, Leivada, Evelina, Papadopoulou, Elena, & Martínez-Ferreiro, Silvia. 2012. The development of object clitic placement in Cypriot Greek and the Romance connection. In *Selected Proceedings of the Romance Turn IV*, Sandrine Ferré, Philippe Prévost, Laurie Tuller & Rasha Zebib (eds), Newcastle-upon-Tyne: Cambridge Scholars.
Halpern, Aaron. 1995. *On the Placement and Morphology of Clitics.* Stanford: CA: CSLI.

Hamann, Cornelia, Rizzi, Luigi & Frauenfelder, Uli. 1995. On the acquisition of the pronominal system in French. In *Recherches Linguistiques de Vincennes* 24: 83–101.

Hirschbühler, Paul & Labelle, Marie. 2000. Evolving Tobler-Mussafia effects in the placement of French clitics. In *New Approaches to Old Problems. Issues in Romance Historical Linguistics* [Current Issues in Linguistic Theory 210], Steven N. Dworkin & Dieter Wanner (eds). Amsterdam: John Benjamins.

Hopper, Paul J. & Traugott, Elizabeth Closs. 1993. *Grammaticalization.* Cambridge: CUP.

Jaeggli, Osvaldo. 1982. *Topics in Romance Syntax* [Studies in Generative Grammar 12]. Dordrecht: Foris.

Kaplan, Ronald M., & Bresnan, Joan. 1982. Lexical-functional grammar: A formal system for grammatical representation. In *The Mental Representation of Grammatical Relations*, Joan Bresnan (ed.), 173–281. Cambridge MA: The MIT Press.

Kayne, Richard S. 1994. *The Antisymmetry of Syntax* [Linguistic Inquiry Monographs 25]. Cambridge MA: The MIT Press.

Kayne, Richard. 1975. *French Syntax: The Transformational Cycle.* Cambridge MA: The MIT Press.

Klavans, Judith. 1985. The independence of syntax and phonology in cliticization. *Language* 61(1): 95–120.

Laenzlinger, Christopher. 1993. A syntactic view of Romance pronominal sequences. *Probus* 5(3): 241–270.

Manzini, M. Rita & Savoia, Leonardo M. 2004. Clitics: Cooccurrence and mutual exclusion patterns. In *The Structure of CP and IP* [Oxford Studies in Comparative Syntax], Luigi Rizzi (ed.), 211–250. Oxford: OUP.

Matushansky, Ora. 2006. Head movement in linguistic theory. *Linguistic Inquiry* 37: 69–109.

Mavrogiorgos, Marios. 2010. *Clitics in Greek: A Minimalist Account of Proclisis and Enclisis* [Linguistik Aktuell/Linguistis Today 160]. Amsterdam: John Benjamins.

Miller, Philip & Monachesi, Paola. 2003. Les pronoms clitiques dans les langues romanes. In *Les langues romanes, problèmes de la phrase simple*, Danièle Godard (ed.), 67–123. Paris: Editions du CNRS.

Monachesi, Paola. 1996. On the representation of Italian clitics In *Interfaces in Phonology* [Studia Grammatica 41], Ursula Kleinhenz (ed.), 83–101. Berlin: Akademie Verlag.

Montrul, Silvina A. 2004. *The Acquisition of Spanish. Morphosyntactic Development in Monolingual and Bilingual L1 Acquisition and Adult L2 Acquisition* [Language Acquisition and Language Disorders 37]. Amsterdam: John Benjamins.

Nespor, Marina & Vogel, Irene. 1986. *Prosodic Phonology*. Dordrecht: Foris.

Nevis, Joel Ashmore, Joseph, Brian D. & Wanner, Dieter. 2011. *Clitics. A Comprehensive Bibliography 1892–1991* [Library and Information Sources in Linguistics 22], Arnold M. Zwicky (ed.). Amsterdam: John Benjamins.

Pancheva, Roumyana. 2005. The rise and fall of second-position clitics. *Natural Language and Linguistic Theory* 23: 103–167.

Peperkamp, Sharon. 1995. Enclitic stress in Romance. In *Papers from the 31st Regional Meeting of the Chicago Linguistic Society,* Vo. 2: *The Parasession on Clitics*, Audra Dainora, Rachel Hemphill, Barbara Luka, Barbara Need & Sheri Pargman (eds), 234–249. Chicago IL: Chicago Linguistic Society.

Peperkamp, Sharon. 1996. On the prosodic representation of clitics. In *Interfaces in Phonology* [Studia Grammatica 41], Ursula Kleinhenz (ed.), 102–127. Berlin: Akademie Verlag.

Peperkamp, Sharon. 1997. Prosodic words [HIL Dissertations 34]. The Hague: HAG.

Pescarini, Diego. 2012. Prosodic restructuring and morphological opacity. The evolution of Italo-Romance clitic clusters. Lingbuzz/001477.
Poletto, Cecilia & Pollock, Jean-Yves. 2004a. On Wh-clitics and WH-doubling in French and some North Eastern Italian Dialects. *Probus* 16(2): 241–272.
Poletto, Cecilia & Pollock, Jean-Yves. 2004b. On the left periphery of some Romance Wh-questions. In *The Structure of CP and IP* [Oxford Studies in Comparative Syntax], Luigi Rizzi (ed.) 211–250. Oxford: OUP.
Pollock, Jean-Yves. 1989. Verb movement, universal grammar, and the structure of IP. *Linguistic Inquiry* 20(3): 365–424.
Progovac, Ljiljana. 1993. Locality and subjunctive-like complements in Serbo-Croatian. *Journal of Slavic Linguistics* 1: 116–144.
Progovac, Ljiljana. 1996. Clitics in Serbian/Croatian: Comp as the second position. In *Approaching Second: Second Position Clitics and Related Phenomena*, Aaron Halpern & Arnold Zwicky (eds), 411–428. Stanford CA: CSLI.
Raposo, Eduardo P. 2000. Clitic positions and verb movement. In *Portuguese Syntax: New Comparative Studies*, João Costa (ed.), 266–298. Oxford: OUP.
van Riemsdijk, Henk. 1999. Clitics: A state-of-the-art report. In *Clitics in the Languages of Europe*, Henk van Riemdsijk (ed.), 1–30. Berlin: Mouton de Gruyter.
Rizzi, Luigi. 1993. Some notes on Romance cliticization. Eurotyp Group on Clitics. Ms, University of Geneva.
Rizzi, Luigi. 2004. On the cartography of syntactic structures. In *The Structure of CP and IP*, Vol. 2, Luigi Rizzi (ed.), 3–17. Oxford: OUP.
Rizzi, Luigi. 1997. The fine structure of the left periphery. In *Elements of Grammar*, Liliane Haegeman (ed.), 281–337. Dordrecht: Kluwer.
Rizzi, Luigi. 2006. On the form of chains. Criterial positions and chain effects. In *Wh-movement: Moving on*, Lisa Cheng & Nigel Corver (eds), 97–134. Cambridge MA: The MIT Press.
Roberge, Yves. 1990. *The Syntactic Recoverability of Null Arguments*. Kingston: McGill-Queen's University Press.
Roberts, Ian. 2010. *Agreement and Head Movement: Clitics, Incorporation and Defective Goals* [Linguistic Inquiry Monographs 59]. Cambridge MA: The MIT Press.
Rouveret, Alain. 1999. Clitics, subjects and tense in European Portuguese. In *Clitics in the Languages of Europe*, Henk van Riemdsijk (ed.), 1–30. Berlin: Mouton de Gruyter.
Rowlett, Paul. 2007. *The Syntax of French* [Cambridge Syntax Guides]. Cambridge: CUP.
Russell, Margaret A. 2006. The Syntax and Placement of Wolof Clitics. Ph.D. dissertation, University of Illinois at Urbana-Champaign.
Samuels, Bridget. 2009. The Structure of Phonological Theory. Ph.D. dissertation, Harvard University.
Selkirk, Elisabeth. 1995. The prosodic structure of function words. In *Papers in Optimality Theory*, Jill Beckman, Laura Walsh Dickey & Suzanne Urbanczyk (eds), 439–70. Amherst, MA: GLSA. Also in *Signal to Syntax: Bootstrapping from Speech to Grammar in Early Acquisition*, James L. Morgan & Katherine Demuth (eds), 187–214. Mahwah NJ: Lawrence Erlbaum Associates.
Shlonsky, Ur. 2004. Enclisis and proclisis. The *Structure of CP and IP. The Cartography of Syntactic Structures*, Luigi Rizzi (ed.), 329–353. Oxford: OUP.
Spencer, Andrew & Luís, Ana R. 2012. *Clitics. An Introduction*, Cambridge: CUP.
Spencer, Andrew. 1991. *Morphological Theory. An Introduction to Word Structure in Generative Grammar*. Oxford: Blackwell.

Sportiche, Dominique. 1996. Clitic constructions. In *Phrase Structure and the Lexicon*, Laurie Zaring & Johan Rooryck (eds), 213–276. Dordrecht: Kluwer.
Surányi, Balázs. 2002. Multiple operator movements in Hungarian. Ph.D. dissertation, University of Utrecht.
Surányi, Balázs. 2004. The left periphery and cyclic spell-out: The case of Hungarian. In *Peripheries: Syntactic Edges and their Effects*, David Adger, Cécile De Cat & George Tsoulas (eds), 49–73. Dordrecht: Kluwer.
Svenonius, Peter. 2004. On the edge. In *Peripheries: Syntactic Edges and their Effects*, David Adger, Cécile de Cat & George Tsoulas (eds), 259–287. Dordrecht: Kluwer.
Terzi, Arhonto. 1999a. Clitic combinations, their hosts and their ordering. *Natural Language and Linguistic Inquiry* 17: 85–121.
Terzi, Arhonto. 1999b. Cypriot Greek clitics and their positioning restrictions. In *Studies in Greek Syntax*, Artemis Alexiadou, Geoffrey Horrocks & Melita Stavrou (eds), 227–240. Dordrecht: Kluwer.
Tomić, Olga. 1996. The Balkan Slavic clausal clitics. *Natural Language and Linguistic Theory* 14: 811–872.
Torrence, Harold. 2003. Verb movement in Wolof. *UCLA Working Papers in Linguistics*, 1–31.
Uriagereka, Juan. 1995. Aspects of the syntax of clitic placement in Western Romance. *Linguistic Inquiry* 26: 79–124.
Wackernagel, Jacob. 1892. Über ein Gesetz der Indogermanischen Wortstellung. *Indogermanische Forschungen* 1: 333–436.
Weber, David. 1986. Information perspective, profile, and patterns in Quechua. In *Evidentiality: The Linguistic Coding of Epistemology*, Wallace Chafe & Johanna Nichols (eds), 137–155. Norwood NJ: Ablex.
Zribi-Hertz, Anne & Diagne, Lamine. 2002. Clitic placement after syntax: Evidence from Wolof person and locative markers. *Natural language and Linguistic Theory* 20(4): 823–884.
Zribi-Hertz, Anne. 1994. La syntaxe des clitiques nominatifs en français standard et avancé. *Travaux de Linguistique et de Philologie* 32: 131–147.
Zwicky, Arnold & Pullum, Geoffrey. 1983. Cliticization vs. inflection: English N'T. *Language* 59(3): 502–13.
Zwicky, Arnold. 1977. *On Clitics*, Bloomington IN: Indiana University Linguistics Club.

Enclisis at the syntax-PF interface

Marios Mavrogiorgos
University of Ulster

This paper discusses the proclisis-enclisis alternation of object clitics in finiteness sensitive and Tobler-Mussafia languages. I argue that proclisis/enclisis can be derived via the interaction of syntactic and PF operations, at least in a number of environments, although purely syntactic or PF derivations are also possible but rare. I present an outline of how certain proclitic and enclitic structures are derived, using a grammatical model in which syntax feeds PF, and I try to show how much of the alternation is syntactic and how much is PF. The implications for head movement are also discussed.

1. The proclisis-enclisis alternation

1.1 Introduction

Cliticization and the proclisis-enclisis alternation of adverbal object clitics in Indo-European languages is a highly researched and debated issue. Most accounts that have been proposed for different types of clitic languages tend to attribute the alternation primarily to syntax or to PF. They typically postulate the same derivation for enclisis/proclisis across structures or across languages, which appears to be quite a strong claim. In this paper I will propose that an approach that combines syntax and PF is preferable to a purely syntactic/PF account. However, I will argue that more than one PF or syntactic factor may be involved, that syntax may restrict the application of an independent PF operation, and that purely syntactic or PF derivations are also a possibility in a few particular contexts. According to this analysis, both proclisis and enclisis can be the result of different operations/requirements, even if these structures appear identical on the surface across structures and across languages. The implications for head movement will also be discussed.

1.2 Proclisis and enclisis in finiteness sensitive and Tobler-Mussafia languages

1.2.1 *Overview of the data*

Adverbal object clitic pronouns (henceforth, clitics) may precede or follow their verbal host in a number of languages, a phenomenon known as 'proclisis-enclisis alternation.' The following example from Modern Greek illustrates the alternation (= shows directionality of phonological cliticization in this and following examples).

(1) a. *Ton= idha.* [proclisis] [Mod. Greek]
Him.CL saw.1SG
'I saw him.'

b. *Dhes =**ton!*** [enclisis]
See.2SG.IMP him.CL
'Look at him!'

In Modern Greek (as in other clitic languages), the verb is both the morpho-syntactic and the phonological host of the clitic. (2) shows that this is not the only possibility found cross-linguistically (see Klavans 1985):

(2) a. *...ke póte =**to** ethkiavasen?* [Cypriot Greek]
and when it.CL read.3SG
'And when did s/he read it?'

b. *Ne= **go** viždam.* [Bulgarian]
not him see.1SG
'I do not see him.'

Here, both clitics are proclitics, in that they linearly precede the verbal morpho-syntactic host, but they are phonologically attached to a head preceding them.[1]

In this paper, the notions of proclisis and enclisis refer specifically to the linear position of clitics in relation to their verbal host, with no implications regarding phonological directionality. Where directionality is relevant to the discussion, the necessary information will be provided as part of the linguistic data. The discussion will be restricted to finiteness sensitive and Tobler-Mussafia languages only. Nevertheless, my view is that the same approach as the one proposed in this paper could also be extended to second position languages (see Halpern 1995;

1. The same phenomenon can be found in second position languages, like Serbo-Croatian and Ancient Greek (see Halpern & Zwicky 1996).

Halpern & Zwicky 1996; Franks 1998), independently of whether they have inherently enclitic clitics (e.g. Serbo-Croatian) or not (e.g. Slovene).[2]

Two sets of languages can be distinguished descriptively, depending on the factors 'regulating' the proclisis-enclisis alternation: (a) finiteness sensitive languages, and (b) Tobler-Mussafia languages.

Finiteness sensitive languages include, among others, Standard Modern Greek, Standard French, Standard Italian, Catalan, Peninsular Spanish, Romanian, Macedonian, and Albanian. In this language group, the proclisis-enclisis alternation is typically linked to morpho-syntactic properties of the verbal host (tense, mood and/or subject agreement). In particular, enclisis is found when the verbal host lacks tense, mood and/or subject agreement specifications/marking, while the opposite holds for proclisis. This is illustrated below with a subjunctive (marked) and an infinitival (unmarked) verbal host respectively:[3]

(3) *Vreau să **mă** asculte.* (**asculte **mă***) [Romanian]
Want.1sg subj me.cl hears.3sg.subj
'I want that h/she listens to me.'

(4) *Voglio telefonar**gli**.* (*****gli** telefonare*) [Standard Italian]
Want.1sg call.inf.-him.cl
'I want to call him.'

Tobler-Mussafia languages do not allow clitics at the very beginning of the utterance (like second position languages), but clitics are grammatical in any other clausal position as long as they are adjacent to the verb (like finiteness sensitive languages).[4] As a result, clitics in these languages may be preceded by one or more constituents (XPs and/or Xs). This language group is not entirely homogeneous, in that different Tobler-Mussafia languages may display properties that make them more akin to second position or to finiteness sensitive languages, although all of them share the prohibition against 'first position' clitics, at least in most, if not all, contexts. Examples of Tobler-Mussafia languages are Old Romance, Medieval Greek, Modern Cypriot Greek, Western Iberian languages, and Bulgarian. An

2. I would like to thank an anonymous reviewer for pointing out to me that there are Second Position languages (like Slovene, for example), which may allow both enclitics and proclitics.

3. There seem to be a few cases where this descriptive generalization does not hold (e.g. French infinitives), however they can be accounted for independently (see e.g. Mavrogiorgos 2010).

4. Some Tobler-Mussafia languages (e.g. European Portuguese or Old Spanish) may allow clitics to be separated from the verbal host by certain constituents (e.g. adverbs, negation, subjects or other preverbal DPs), a phenomenon known as *interpolation*. Even in these cases, clitics must be as close as possible to the verb (although languages differ in this respect).

example of proclisis-enclisis alternation in a Tobler-Mussafia language is given below from Bulgarian:

(5) a. *****Mi*** ***go*** *dade* *Vera včera.* [Bulgarian]
me.dat it.ACC gave.3SG Vera yesterday

b. Vera **mi go** *dade* včera.

c. Včera Vera **mi go** *dade*.

d. *Dade* **mi go**

e. *Včera **mi go** Vera *dade*.

'(Vera) gave it to me (yesterday).'

(5a–b) show the ban against first position clitics, whereas (5c–d) illustrate the fact that one or more XPs, or a head X, may precede the clitic cluster. Finally, (5e) illustrates the adjacency requirement in Bulgarian.

In these languages, proclisis/enclisis correlates mainly with properties of the left periphery of the clause, such as focus, wh, neg and topic (see examples in (6–10)), and in particular with the presence/absence of an XP/X immediately c-commanding the cliticization site (normally these constituents are CP related) (for a more detailed exposition of the relevant data, see Dimitrova-Vulchanova 1995; Uriagereka 1995a,b; Halpern & Zwicky 1996; Terzi 1999b; Raposo & Uriagereka 2005, among many others). Typically, proclisis obtains if some head or XP is overtly realized in the CP domain. Otherwise, enclisis obtains, where the verb serves as the phonological clitic host. In some languages only certain heads or XPs can trigger proclisis (e.g. Western Iberian and Cypriot Greek), while in other languages any head or XP within the CP can have this property (e.g. Bulgarian and early stages of Old French). Still, both language types can accept an [X Y clitic] construction (where X and Y can be phrases, heads or a combination thereof).

(6) a. *I Maria emilisen* ***tu.*** *(****tu*** *emilisen)* [C. Greek]
The Mary talked.3SG him.dat.CL
'Mary talked to him.'

b. *Ivan* ***go*** *vižda. (*vižda* ***go****)* [Bulgarian]
Ivan him.CL sees
'Ivan sees him.'

c. *Pjos* ***to*** *ethkjavasen? (*ethkjavasen* ***to****)* [C. Greek]
who it.CL read.3SG
'Who read it?'

d. *Quem* ***a*** *viu ontem? (*viu-****a****)* [European Portuguese]
Who her.CL saw.3SG yesterday
'Who saw her yesterday?' (example from Raposo & Uriagereka 2005)

In (6) we see that whereas in Cypriot Greek a c-commanding/preverbal subject topic triggers enclisis, in Bulgarian the opposite happens. Moreover, a c-commanding wh-word triggers proclisis in both Cypriot Greek and European Portuguese. This illustrates the fact that different types of c-commanding XPs may give rise to either proclisis or enclisis depending on the language. (7) illustrates cases of proclisis with a preverbal X and XP (7a; 7d), two preverbal Xs (7b; 7e), and three preverbal XPs (7c; 7f).

(7) a. *...če Ivan **go** vižda.* (**vižda **go***) [Bulgarian]
that Ivan him.CL sees
'That Ivan sees him.'

b. *... če ne **go** vižda.* (**vižda **go***) [Bulgarian]
that not him.CL sees
'That he does not see him.'

c. *Na Ivan knigata az **mu***
To Ivan book-the I him.CL
ja** dadox.* (**dadox **mu ja) [Bulgarian]
it.CL gave
'To Ivan, the book, I gave it to him.'

d. *...que ele **a** vise.* (**vise-**a***) [E. Portuguese]
That he her.CL saw.subj
'that he saw her.'

e. *...que ñao **a** viu.* (**viu-**a***) [E. Portuguese]
That not her.CL saw.3SG
'that he did not see her.'

f. *Esses libros, só o Pedro **os** dei*
These books only the Peter them.CL gives
a Maria. (**dei-**os***) [E. Portuguese]
to Mary
'The books only Peter gives them to Mary.'

In some Tobler-Mussafia languages the presence of multiple XPs may trigger enclisis, as the following example shows (in this case two topic phrases precede the clitic-verb cluster):

(8) *Tu Petru, ta vivlia edhokan*
The Peter.DAT the books.ACC gave.3PL
tu ta. (****tu ta** edhokan*) [C. Greek]
him.CL them.CL
'To Peter, the books, they gave them to him.'

This is expected, if preverbal topics in Cypriot Greek give rise to enclisis. However, in the same example, if a head precedes the clitic-verb cluster, proclisis is obligatory. This is illustrated in (9), where the subjunctive head *na* precedes the cluster (see Terzi 1999b):[5]

(9) *Tu Petru, ta vivlia na* ***tu***
The Peter.DAT, the books.ACC SUBJ him.CL
ta *dhokis.* (**dhokis* ***tu ta***) [C. Greek]
them.CL give.2SG
'To Peter, the books, you should give them to him.'

If two or more *distinct* constituents c-command the cluster, typically the one that is closest (in terms of c-command) to the cluster will decide whether proclisis or enclisis obtains. For example, in the following two examples from Cypriot Greek a wh-phrase triggers proclisis because it is closer to the cluster than the c-commanding topic phrase (10a), while a topic phrase triggers enclisis because it is closer to the cluster than the c-commanding complementizer (10b):[6]

(10) a. *Ta vivlia pjos* ***ta*** *edhoken?* (**edhoken* ***ta***) [C. Greek]
The books who them.CL gave.3SG
'The books, who gave them?'

b. *…an i Maria edhoken*
whether the Mary gave.3SG
tu ta. (*****tu ta*** *edhoken*) [C. Greek]
him.CL them.CL
'…whether Mary gave them to him.'

On the other hand, in languages like Bulgarian or early stages of Old French, where any constituent may trigger proclisis, either a single (preceding) head or XP are sufficient to block enclisis. This is shown below with data from Bulgarian (see e.g. Dimitrova-Vulchanova 1995; Dimitrova-Vulchanova & Hellan 1999):

(11) a. *Ne* ***go*** *viždam.* (**viždam* ***go***) [Bulgarian]
Neg him.CL saw.1SG

b. *Az* ***go*** *viždam.* (**viždam* ***go***)
I him.CL saw.1SG

5. Note that the presence of a c-commanding head does not always trigger proclisis. For example, the complementizer *oti* ('that') may trigger both proclisis and enclisis, with distinct phonological phrasing for each case (see Revithiadou 2006).

6. This would not apply to E. Portuguese, where the presence of a complementizer always triggers proclisis (see example (7d)).

c. *Viždam* **go**. (***go** *viždam*)
Saw.1SG him.CL

d. *Viždam ne **go**.

e. *(Az) viždam (az) **go**.
'I saw/did not see him.'

If no CP-related XP or X is available, enclisis obtains in all Tobler-Mussafia languages, where typically the highest available non-affixal verb hosts the clitic:

(12) a. *Veit* **me** *li reis.* [Old French]
Sees me the king
'The king sees me.'

b. *Četjal* **sum ja** *bil knigata.* [Bulgarian]
Read have.1SG.CL it.CL had book-the
'I have read it, the book.'

Finally, (13–14) illustrate the fact that the CP-related X or XP must c-command the clitic in order for proclisis to obtain:

(13) a. <u>*A muito mestre*</u> **o** *enviaram!'* [E. Portuguese]
To many teacher him.CL they-sent
'Many teachers have they sent him to!'

b. *Enviaram*-**no** a muito mestre.

(14) a. <u>*Que*</u> **me** *valha Deus!* [Galician]
That me.CL may-help God

b. *Valha*-**me** Deus!
'May God help me!'

(both examples taken from Raposo & Uriagereka 2005)

1.2.2 *Past analyses*

Numerous analyses have been proposed to try to capture the properties of the proclisis-enclisis alternation in finiteness sensitive and Tobler-Mussafia languages.

PF-only analyses assume that the prohibition on clause initial clitics (and hence the presence of enclisis) in Tobler-Mussafia languages only stems from the inherent enclitic property of the clitics (see e.g. Barbosa 1996). When syntax cannot provide a prosodic host, a PF operation that corrects/filters out the ungrammatical structure takes place (this takes different forms, e.g. as Prododic Inversion (see Halpern 1995; Condoravdi & Kiparsky 2001), or PF-merger (see Franks 2008), or in the form of spell-out of a lower copy (see Bošković 2001; Revithiadou 2006, 2008; Samuels 2009 although she talks about second position clitics in languages which do not necessarily involve inherent enclitics (e.g. Slovene))). Enclisis, then, at least in these languages, is a PF-product based on a syntactically derived proclitic input. It is much less clear how enclisis in finiteness sensitive languages is derived, but Bošković (2004) for example has proposed that it could also be attributed to host-related PF reasons (and see Raposo & Uriagereka 2005 for a similar intuition regarding Tobler-Mussafia languages).

Syntax-only analyses do not take into consideration the enclitic or proclitic nature of clitics in Tobler-Mussafia languages. Rather, they argue that enclisis is derived by syntactic movement of the (main/auxiliary) verb across the cliticization site to a higher head (see e.g. Kayne 1991; Martins 1994; Rivero 1994; Benincà 1995; Dimitrova-Vulchanova 1995; Rivero & Terzi 1995; Uriagereka 1995a,b; Tomić 1996; Terzi 1999a,b; Shlonsky 2004, among others). Enclisis in finiteness sensitive languages is derived in exactly the same way. The generalization seems to be that verb movement to a C-head, across the cliticization site in T, derives enclisis in both language types.

Syntax-PF analyses also argue that enclisis is syntactically derived via syntactic verb movement across the cliticization site, but the motivation for this movement is phonological/prosodic in Tobler-Mussafia languages (see e.g. Cardinaletti & Roberts 1991). These analyses view the syntax-PF interface in a way that is not compatible with current assumptions in the literature (see e.g. Chomsky 2001), and which would not be compatible with the null hypothesis that syntactic and PF operations are interrelated though independent.

The common property that all these approaches share is that enclisis is analyzed as a uniform phenomenon across the two language types and across constructions. In this paper I will argue that such a conclusion faces theoretical problems, and moreover it cannot adequately account for the data in both language types. My main claim will be that both proclisis and enclisis, in both language types, should be analyzed as the result of the combination of syntactic and PF operations, and that what looks like the same phenomenon might not be derived in the same way in all constructions and all languages. I will follow the basics of the approach proposed by Pancheva (2005) for Bulgarian cliticization, according to which syntactic operations first take place, followed by PF/morphological operations. If syntactic or PF-operations linked to affixal features do not offer a prosodic host for the clitic, PF filters out the input, unless further PF/prosodic operations are available to apply (possibly as a last resort mechanism).

2. V-movement analysis as a purely PF or syntactic account

In this section I will argue that both syntactic and PF operations need to be postulated in order to account for the proclisis-enclisis alternation in finiteness sensitive and Tobler-Mussafia languages.

2.1 Against a pure PF account

According to some pure PF analyses, clitics in Tobler-Mussafia languages are inherently enclitic, so they will phonologically attach to any preceding constituent that meets their prosodic requirements. If no host is offered by the syntax, PF reorders the CL-V cluster, giving rise to finite enclisis. A different version, proposed by Franks (1998), Bošković (2004), and Revithiadou (2006), among others, argues that PF filters out ungrammatical sentences by choosing a lower clitic copy for pronunciation in only those cases where a higher copy would violate a prosodic restriction/rule. According to this view, enclisis may be derived by purely syntactic means, in which case PF spells out the lower clitic copy. For pure PF-analyses, finiteness sensitive enclisis is either syntactically triggered, or linked to PF properties of the host (see Bošković 2004).

There are a number of issues that pertain to pure PF analyses more generally, and to those analyses which make use of the copy theory of movement in particular. First of all, a preceding XP or X cannot always support an inherently enclitic element, as the following example illustrates:

(15) a. *Pjos =**to** ekamen? (*ekamen =**to**)* [C. Greek]
Who it.CL did.3SG
'Who did it?'

b. *O Spiros ekamen =**to**. (***to**= ekamen)*
The Spiros did.3SG it.CL
'Spiros did it.'

(16) a. *Ipen oti ekamen =**to** i Maria. (**to**= ekamen)-see Footnote 5*
Said.3SG that did.3SG it.CL the Mary
'H/she said that Mary did it.'

b. *Otan =**to** ekamen… (*ekamen =**to**)*
when it-CL did-3SG
'When he/she did it…'

In (15) a preceding wh-word triggers proclisis, as opposed to a preceding subject topic. Assuming that clitics require an appropriate prosodic host (see Richards 2004), one could argue that a wh-word can form a prosodic word with the clitic but not with a topic XP (see e.g. Barbosa 1996). However, it is not entirely clear why this should be the case, given that left-dislocated topics may or may not be separated by an intonational break from the rest of the sentence. Moreover, in (16) we see that two tonic complementizers trigger enclisis and proclisis respectively, which is not expected under a prosodic account, without further stipulations.

Second, it is possible to find examples of finite enclisis which involve syntactic V-movement to the front of the clause, as the following example from Bulgarian shows (see Franks 2008):

(17) a. *Pročela* ***mu*** *ja* *beše.*
READ me.CL it.CL had.3SG
'She had READ it to me (and not…)'.

b. *Pročela beše knigite.*
READ had.3SG books-the
'She had read the books.'

(17) illustrates a case of V-moment with a focus effect (long head movement), which takes place independently of the presence of a clause initial clitic. This suggests that enclisis may be the result of an independently motivated syntactic operation in certain languages and contexts, and that the sentence is grammatical if the prosodic requirement against clause initial clitics is satisfied.

A third problem faced by most (although not all) PF-only accounts is that Tobler-Mussafia clitics, like finiteness sensitive clitics, can be both proclitics and enclitics, as the following examples illustrate (see e.g. Fischer 2002 for Medieval Romance; Pancheva 2005 and Franks 2008 for Bulgarian). This means that the ban on first position clitics in these languages is related to an absolute PF requirement that clitics should not appear at the beginning of some prosodic domain (e.g. utterance), and not necessarily to their inherent enclitic nature.

(18) a. *Tharo* *<u>pos</u>* ***tá*** *=fae*
Think.1SG that them.CL ate.3SG
ta pitakja. [Kos, Dodecanese]
the little pies
'I think s/he ate them the little pies.'

b. *…ke* *<u>ná</u>* ***=to*** *pulisum ton,* *na parum*
and na it.CL sale.1PL were.3SG, na get.1PL
lio kirjas. [Ulaghatsh, Cappadocia]
some meat
'We would have sold it to get a little meat.'

c. *Ne* ***=mu*** *kazvaj.* [Bulgarian]
Not him.CL tell.IMP
'Do not tell him!'

d. *Az* ***săm*** *už* ***ti=*** ***go=*** *dala.* [Bulgarian]
I have maybe you.CL it.CL given
'I have maybe already given it to you.'

e. *en* *=**mu*** *ethkiavasen.* [C. Greek]
not me.CL read.3SG
'She did not read to me.'

f. *pos=* ***to=*** *thkiavasen* [C. Greek]
that it.CL read.3SG
'That he read it.'

Although this argument does not disprove the role of prosody, it narrows it down to such an extent that at least some examples would be attributed to the syntactic component.

A fourth argument against the pure PF nature of the alternation is that in very few Tobler-Mussafia languages (mainly Old Romance), clitics may be allowed in clause initial position (see e.g. Fischer 2002; Fontana 1996):

(19) a. *S'=* *est* *il* *donques* *corrouciez* *a* *nos?* [Old French]
'Himself is he then vexed with us'

b. *oy dia* *en* *Grecia:* ***lo=*** *traen* *por...* [Old Spanish]
today in Greece it.CL bring.3PL for...
'Today in Greece they bring it as..." (taken from Fontana 1996)

These examples show that Tobler-Mussafia clitics can be proclitics, and that they may sometimes appear at the beginning of the clause, suggesting that these two prosodic requirements are independent, and that the ban against clause initial clitics may not always be PF-related.

A final point should be raised here with regard to PF accounts which recognize the role of syntax in the alternation, but treat finite enclisis as the product of a PF-filtering operation. I think there are two main problems with these accounts: first, they analyze non-finite enclisis as purely syntactic and finite enclisis as purely PF, which is not necessarily true, as I hope to show later on, at least not in all cases. Second, they postulate massive syntactic movement of clitics and verbs, which provide the necessary copies. This would not be a problem if these copies were accounted for independently (via syntactic and/or semantic means). Unless the copy theory of movement is modified or evidence is given for the presence of all these postulated copies (especially those of clitics), it remains a question whether this particular form of PF filtering is appropriate for all cases. For example, the postulation of one clitic copy in T and another one within the VP complement in finite enclisis (under standard assumptions about cliticization – see Kayne 1991) would either predict massive interpolation (if the lower VP clitic copy is used), or V-movement to a C-head for no obvious reason (if the higher T clitic copy is used). Such hypotheses would need to be independently proved.

All in all, it seems that although PF factors may be related to the distinct properties of the proclisis-enclisis alternation in each language type (e.g. the ban on utterance initial clitics as well as the c-command restriction imposed on XPs and Xs, which would suggest that Long Distance Agree is not a sufficient condition for proclisis), these are not sufficient to account for all cases, and in addition they fail to recognize the importance of syntactic factors. For example, as I hope to show later on, a PF-only analysis misses the generalization that the proclisis-enclisis alternation seems to be related to the presence of a phase head with a PF requirement on its edge (at least in a number of cases, but in both Tobler-Mussafia and finiteness sensitive languages), and that a phase head with such properties is also found in other syntactic contexts, which do not involve cliticization (see e.g. Collins 2007; Nchare & Terzi to appear). More generally, these approaches view the PF-syntax interface as a static process, whereas it appears to be much more dynamic, as I hope to show in the rest of this paper.

2.2 Against a pure syntactic account

According to pure syntactic analyses, enclisis in both language types is derived via syntactic movement of the highest verb across the cliticization site (typically T) to some higher head (typically CP-related). PF does not seem to play any role whatsoever. The role of syntax is based on the claim that both finite and non-finite enclisis is linked to syntactic features, with syntactic and semantic effects. These features reside in a projection that immediately c-commands the cliticization site, and they include, among others, imperative agreement, gerund agreement, focus, negation, wh-features or interrogative (Q) features. PF analyses argue that it is far from clear whether these features have anything in common, and hence a syntactic approach based on the postulation of such features is not tenable (i.e. it is merely a descriptive artifact). However, my view is that this is a rather weak argument, as it is based on a technicality. In fact, within a phase model of derivation, such as the one proposed by Chomsky (2001), all these cases seem to involve a phase head, and phase heads need only contain syntactic and semantic features, along with an EPP and/or PF requirement. Whether a purely syntactic approach works or not should be based on theoretical issues (such as e.g. the postulation of operations/rules and their nature), or on empirical grounds.

An argument in favor of a syntactic approach is the blocking potential of particles/heads with regard to V-movement in both language types. This is a phenomenon that is independent of cliticization, and there are various ways of accounting for it syntactically (e.g. as an intervention effect, or as complementary distribution between particles and v-related features, among others). An example is given below, where the presence of a preverbal particle is in complementary distribution with the [+ imperative] form of the verb in Modern Greek (see Roussou 2000):

(20) **na* *dhine!* *vs.* *na* *dhinis* [Mod. Greek]
subj give.2SG.[+IMP] subj give.2SG.[- IMP]
'Give!'

If this blocking effect is syntactic in nature, it seems possible to assume that enclisis is linked to the presence of a syntactic head/feature in a position where the particle would normally be found in the proclitic cases. That could suggest that enclisis can be derived via syntactic head movement across the cliticization site, at least in certain cases (namely those where V-movement can be independently shown to have taken place).

Moreover, a syntactic approach correctly predicts that phonological proclisis is possible in Tobler-Mussafia languages, provided the clause initial PF requirement is satisfied. This could be done either in the syntax or in the PF (e.g. via a filtering approach, according to some PF analyses) depending on the structure involved:

(21) a. *...pos=* ***mas=*** *ghirevi.* [C. Greek]
that us.CL looks.for
'that s/he looks for us.'

b. *...oti* ***=mas*** *ghirevi.* [C. Greek]
that us.CL looks.for
'that s/he looks for us.'

c. *Pročela* ***mu*** *=* ***ja*** *=* *beše.* [Bulgarian]
READ me.CL it.CL had.3SG
'She had READ it to me (and not...)'.

Although the evidence given above and in Section 2.1 suggests that syntactic factors do have a place in the proclisis-enclisis alternation in both language types, it remains a fact that PF is also part of this alternation, as the section on PF analyses has shown, and that purely syntactic accounts would fail to capture this. In what follows I will argue that PF may have a more complex role that goes beyond a prosodic requirement, and that syntax could be closely linked to this role. This could have important implications for theories of head movement.

2.3 V-movement across the cliticization site: What is syntax and what is PF?

In this section, I will argue that enclisis in finiteness sensitive languages is not purely syntactic, as it is commonly assumed, but the result of the syntax-PF interface. Enclisis will be linked to the presence of syntactic features in a head c-commanding the cliticization site, and to a PF requirement that these must be realized by a non-affixal vocabulary item. On the other hand, proclisis will be linked to merger of syntactic features and their subsequent realization by the PF component.

The main claim of the syntactic approach is that enclisis is the result of syntactic verb movement to a head c-commanding the cliticization site. Proclisis obtains if the verb does not cross the clitic.

(22) Enclisis: … V … CL … (V)

(23) Proclisis: … CL …V … (V)

There are at least two major issues with regard to this analysis. First, in Tobler-Mussafia languages certain XPs or Xs block movement of the verbal host, and as a result proclisis obtains. It is not clear how a purely syntactic head movement approach would capture the blocking effect of an XP.

Moreover, in finiteness sensitive languages V-movement across the cliticization site is not a sufficient condition for enclisis (assuming that the cliticization site stays constant, in that it targets the same set of features in the clause, wherever these are). This is illustrated below:

(24) a. *(*Se*) *Giorgio* *l'* *avesse*
If George it.CL. had
comunicato *al direttore, ….* [Standard Italian]
communicated to-the director
'If Giorgio had told it (the change) to the director….'

b. (**Se*) l'*avesse* Giorgio comunicato al direttore, …
(adapted from Rizzi 1982).

(25) ***Go*** *vide li?* [Macedonian]
Him-acc saw Q
'Did you see him?'

(26) ***Me*** *daste mo ka les medijines enscnoet?* [Marebbe]
me give.SCL mo here the medicines tonight
'Will you give me my medicine tonight?' (from Poletto & Zanuttini 2010)

In (24a–b), *se* in C is in complementary distribution with the CL-V cluster. This means that in (24b) the cluster is in C, and assuming that the cliticization site is in T, movement across the cliticization site has given rise to proclisis. In this example, the proclitic positioning correlates with the finiteness of the verbal host, and not with its position in the clause. The same observation can be made for (25), which also involves finite V-movement to C and proclisis (see Tomić 1996). Finally, in (26) the finite interrogative verbal form precedes the CP particle *mo* but proclisis obtains. The following example from Modern Greek shows that verb movement across the cliticization site may give rise to proclisis, independently of the exact clausal positions targeted by verb movement or cliticization.

(27) a. *Ta kerdhi tu schedhon/idhi* ***ta*** *triplasiase*
The winnings-ACC his.CL almost/already them.CL tripled-3SG
o Jianis. [Mod. Greek]
the John-nom
'John almost tripled/already tripled his winnings.'
b. Ta kerdhi tu **ta** *triplasiase* schedhon/idhi o Jianis.
c. *Ta kerdhi tu *triplasiase* **ta** schedhon/idhi o Jianis.
d. *Ta kerdhi tu *triplasiase* schedhon/idhi **ta** o Jianis.
e. *Ta kerdhi tu **ta** schedhon/idhi *triplasiase* o Jianis.

Assuming that in this language object clitics target the vP periphery (see Mavrogiorgos 2010, and Roberts 2010 for Romance), and that the verb may move to distinct positions within the IP domain (see Ledgeway & Lombardi 2005), proclisis again correlates with the finiteness marking on the verb, and not with its position within the clause. Even if we assumed that clitics can target two distinct positions within the IP domain (one higher and one lower than T), it is not clear why the verb must be next to the clitics. It seems more likely that the clitic piggy-backs on the verb, after having incorporated into it at the vP periphery (see Matushansky 2006).

Directly relevant to the above mentioned observation is the fact that non-finite enclisis (in both language types, modulo some rare exceptions) obtains when the verb moves across the cliticization site to some higher head. Given that here again the outcome of verb movement is contingent on finiteness, it appears that finiteness is an independent factor that cannot be reduced to verb movement. An example of non-finite enclisis is given below:

(28) ***Avendolo*** *Gianni visto...* [Standard Italian]
Having-it.CL John seen
'Having John seen it...'

In what follows I will argue that the role of finiteness, although linked to syntactic features, is also PF-related (in that it involves affixal features that must be supported phonologically), and that finite enclisis seems to share similar properties, at least in some contexts.

3. V-movement to a V-related head: The role of PF

3.1 The finiteness factor in finiteness sensitive languages

It has been proposed that in finiteness sensitive languages the role of finiteness in the proclisis-enclisis alternation correlates with the lack of an unvalued person feature (see Mavrogiorgos 2010 for Modern Greek). The non-finite feature(s) is located in a head immediately c-commanding the cliticization site, is affixal in nature, and must be spelled out in situ (via an agreement morpheme on the verbal host, or via the verbal host itself if an overt exponent is not available). According to this analysis, the presence of such a syntactic feature triggers obligatory realization of the verbal host in the head containing the feature (i.e. verb movement), and this is taken to be the PF/morphological reflex of a syntactic Agree relationship.

In Modern Greek, and other languages, true imperatives cannot be negated (see Han 1998), the standard analysis being that negation blocks some form of syntactic relationship between the lower verb and the higher head that contains the relevant verbal features (see e.g. Roussou 2000). Moreover, as we have seen in Section 2.2., particles block verb movement, giving rise to proclisis. One way to account for this blocking effect is to argue that particles both check and realize the relevant syntactic features (in some form of discontinuous realization of clausal features, which is so often seen in languages with particles, like Irish or Arabic). However, if we look at Bulgarian (see e.g. (29) below) and similar languages, which allow true negated imperatives, we see that long distance Agree between the verbal host and the higher head hosting the imperative features is indeed possible. Assuming that movement is contingent on Agree, this could indicate that the blocking effect in other languages is PF-related, in that it involves a PF requirement that the relevant verbal features are realized in situ. The presence of a negation head would block such morphological realization, and the sentence would be ungrammatical, unless a verbal form with no syntactic features related to this higher position was involved.[7]

(29) *Ne* *=mu* *kazvaj!* [Bulgarian]
Not him.CL tell.2SG.IMP
'Don't tell him!'

For positive suppletive forms, we must assume that the indicative or subjunctive form can spell out the imperative features (if we assume they are present) as elsewhere forms in a CP or IP position (depending on the language) (see Harris 1995). In negative suppletive imperatives, we could either assume that the negation

7. See also Bošković (2004) for the same intuition.

head satisfies the PF requirement, or that there are no special imperative features merged in this particular case.[8]

The important point to keep in mind here is that enclisis in finiteness sensitive languages appears to be linked to syntactic features which are located in a head c-commanding the cliticization site, and which have a PF-requirement that they should be realized phonologically by the verbal host (or, possibly, by a particle if a verbal form is used that does not realize such features). Later on, we will see that the PF requirement may be satisfied by a verb, a particle/non-affixal head or an XP, depending on the language, i.e. it is a requirement that holds for the edge (i.e. head or specifier, following Chomsky 2001) of a projection right above the cliticization site.

As for proclisis, in finiteness sensitive languages it typically correlates with the clitic moving to a TP-internal position that c-commands the verb. Clitic movement is typically taken to be linked to syntactic features (involving either Agree and/or Move), as it gives rise to syntactic and semantic effects (see e.g. Anagnostopoulou 2003 for Greek, Uriagereka 1995a for Romance, and Daskalaki & Mavrogiorgos to appear for Greek resumptive clitics), whereas V-movement to T could be linked to syntax or PF, depending on theoretical assumptions. The status of head movement in this particular case would not play any role in the outcome, namely proclisis.

A more difficult question concerns those cases where the verb has moved across the cliticization site to some higher head, but proclisis obtains (see e.g. (24–26)). One important aspect of these structures is that the verbal host lies within the CP domain (cf. e.g. interrogatives), and that the verbal form used is no different from the forms used within the TP domain (namely, indicatives and subjunctives). This suggests that syntactic features in some C-head are present (cf. interrogative, modal (counterfactual), etc. interpretation), and that these features are not affixal in nature (i.e. they do not involve a morphological affix that may only get phonological support from the verbal host). This is the opposite situation from what we find with non-finite enclisis, and could be related to the proclisis-enclisis switch we find between non-finite enclisis and finite proclisis within the CP domain (or any domain higher than the cliticization site). This in turn would mean that enclisis (at least in these particular structures in finiteness-sensitive languages) is PF related,

8. Although a spell out requirement could be satisfied by any form in principle, it seems that the form must be syntactically linked to the spelled out position (see finite enclisis below). For the purposes of this paper I will not look into the details of the morphological form of the verb (e.g. whether it contains a conjugational vowel or additional morphemes). What is crucial is that the verb spells out a set of features which include imperative (or imperative related agreement) features. Other constituents (e.g. particles) can also spell out these features, if available.

even if it is based on a syntactic configuration (namely an Agree relation between two heads within the extended verbal projection).

Based on these observations, I would like to propose that finite proclisis in CP is an instance of true syntactic head movement. In particular, the features on the T head are re-merged in some position within the CP domain. If an independent 'non-agreement like' head is present in the numeration that can check these features, verb movement does not take place. PF simply spells out those syntactic features that are present in the C-head at Spell-Out. Given that only proclisis is possible in these structures, and that proclisis is related to movement of the verb across the cliticization site for syntactic reasons (and not for PF-related reasons, since the C-head does not contain a verbal affix), one could assume that the clitic and the verbal host in T already form a unit before the verb moves to C, and as a result no reordering is possible. There are different ways of implementing this intuition, but one possibility would be to argue that in enclisis the presence of the higher inflectional head blocks merger between the clitic and T, while in proclisis merger takes place before the verb is syntactically moved to the higher non-inflectional head.[9] Such an analysis would imply that enclisis in these structures is linked to PF/morphology (besides syntax), and that verb movement can be purely syntactic or both syntactic and PF/morphological.

3.2 Non-finite enclisis in Tobler-Mussafia languages

Most Tobler-Mussafia languages have obligatory non-finite enclisis, and in those cases they resemble finite sensitive languages in that enclisis correlates with finiteness and not with the presence/absence of a c-commanding XP or X. This is illustrated in the following example:[10]

---

9. The same reasoning would apply to cases of enclitic non-finite structures, when the verb-CL cluster appears inside the CP.

10. Not all Tobler-Mussafia languages have obligatory non-finite enclisis. For example, Bulgarian, early stages of Old French, and Medieval Greek allow proclisis with imperatives if an XP precedes the clitic-verb cluster:

(i) *aghia* ***tin*** *ipe!* [Medieval Greek]
Holy her.CL call.2SG.IMP
'Call her holy!' (example from Pappas 2004)

Given that in these languages any XP can trigger proclisis, two possibilities arise: either such structures are independently derived in the syntax, and the PF requirement (namely ban on first position clitics) is met; or this a PF phenomenon related to the prosodic requirement against first position clitics in these particular languages. My view is that these structures are derived in the syntax, as they normally involve the syntax and semantics of a topic or focus

(30) a. *To VIVLIO thkiavase* ***tu!*** [C. Greek]
The book read.2SG.IMP him.CL
'Read to him THE BOOK!'

b. *egho thoronda* ***se.*** [Medieval Greek]
I looking you.CL
'I, looking at you.'

c. *min eksevrondas* ***to*** [Medieval Greek]
not knowing it.CL
'Not knowing it...'. (examples (b) and (c) from Pappas 2004)

The simplest hypothesis would be to extend the analysis of non-finite enclisis in finiteness sensitive languages (i.e. as a syntactic and phonological phenomenon involving the features of a head c-commanding the cliticization site) to those cases, as well. What would remain to be explained is finite enclisis in Tobler-Mussafia languages. This task will be undertaken in the following section.

3.3 Finite enclisis in Tobler-Mussafia languages

In this section I will argue that this analysis can be extended to finite enclisis in Tobler-Mussafia languages, although a number of residual cases will need to be accounted for separately. In particular, it will be argued that finite enclisis, which is not found in finiteness sensitive languages, also involves a F(unctional)- head merged above the cliticization site. The main difference between this head and the one found in non-finite enclisis is that while the latter contains features that are linked to subject, tense and/or mood agreement (i.e. agreement normally linked to the TP domain and the notion of finiteness), the former contains CP-related features.[11] On a par with non-finite enclisis, these features are taken to be affixal, triggering reordering of the clitic-verb cluster at PF. This PF requirement, which is distinct from the prosodic ban against first position clitics, will be shown to be satisfied in three distinct ways.

First of all, the existence of such a head in Tobler-Mussafia languages has been proposed by various researchers, who have claimed that it lies above T and contains strong (syntactic) V-features, triggering overt movement under certain

construction which may be independently found in those languages, but more research is required.

11. In a feature inheritance model (e.g. Chomsky 2001), where a CP-related phase head transfers phi-features to the lower T head, these heads would not involve such an operation. This is so because in enclisis the inflectional features are affixal, and hence they must trigger V-movement to the relevant C-head at PF. The role of syntax (presumably in terms of Agree) is to establish a syntactic relationship between the two heads.

conditions (see e.g. Laka 1990; Martins 1994; Uriagereka 1995a,b; Terzi 1999b; Cardinaletti & Roberts 1991; Fischer 2002; Raposo & Uriagereka 2005). This head, and its projection, have been assigned various names (including F, M, Σ, W or CFin), and a number of claims have been made regarding its semantics (see Uriagereka 1995a,b). What remains a fact, though, is that this head is an abstract syntactic category, as it surfaces with such different features as neg, foc, wh, inter, topic, among others. As I have already pointed out in Section 2.2, this fact has been presented as an argument against a syntactic approach to finite enclisis by some PF approaches.

If we look at the properties of the F-head, we can see that it behaves in a way that is similar to imperative and other non-finite heads in finiteness sensitive constructions. For example, it triggers obligatory V-movement resulting in enclisis (the verb cannot be spelled out in the lower T position, unless an appropriate XP or X can satisfy the PF-requirement of the relevant feature(s)). We saw evidence for that in the data section, where it was pointed out that in finite enclisis constructions some overt constituent (either an XP, an X, or the verbal host) must realize some syntactic feature(s) on the F-head. Typically, the XP or X must be related in terms of syntactic features with the feature(s) on the head, and the same would apply to the verbal host, given that both share a V-feature (cf. that they are part of the extended verbal projection). Second, in certain environments a special overt morphology can appear either on the verb or on the projection itself, which is what we also find with imperative and gerunds (e.g. special agreement (31b), or focus particles (31a)).

(31) a. *...depois que aqui* ***er*** *veeres* [Medieval Galician]
after that here FOC came.2SG
'...after here you did come.' (from Uriagereka 1995b)

b. *Convidarmos-**te** para a fiesta seria una*
To-invite.1PL-you.CL for the party would.be a
boa ideia. [E. Portuguese]
good idea
'To invite you to the party would be a good idea.'
(from Raposo & Uriagereka 2005)

Although such overt morphology is rarely found, it strongly suggests that this head contains some syntactic feature which is affixal, on a par with non-finite heads in finiteness sensitive languages. Using Chomsky's (2001) ideas that syntactic derivation proceeds in phases, and that each phase involves a phase head which contains all features related to the phase and which triggers Agree and Merge, I would like to propose that the C-head which is merged above the cliticization site in T, and which is linked to enclisis in both language types, is a phase head.

Accordingly, it triggers Agree (i.e. a syntactic relationship) with T, but also has a PF requirement that may be satisfied by a number of constituents, depending on the syntactic features involved. This is illustrated below:

(32) $F_{[+V]}$...CL-X...T-V//$XP_{[+a]}$...$F_{[+a]}$...CL-X...T-V//$X_{[+a]}$ – $F_{[+a]}$...CL-X...T-V

Since the F-head contains features related to the CP domain (such as wh, neg, foc, etc.), which in most cases are not related to impoverished agreement, the lack of correlation with finiteness would follow. What connects finiteness sensitive enclisis to non-finiteness sensitive enclisis is that both involve the presence of a syntactic feature with a PF requirement.

Finite enclisis allows us to take a better look at this PF requirement, and at how it relates to the independent prosodic requirement that bans first position clitics, as well as to the syntactic Agree relationship established between the F-head and the lower T-head. The main characteristic of finite enclisis is that it is blocked by the presence of an overt head or XP above the cliticization site.[12] When more than one constituent precedes the clitic, it is the one immediately c-commanding the cliticization site that decides whether proclisis or enclisis obtains. This is illustrated in (33):

(33) *Ta vivlia pjos* ***ta*** *edhoken?* (**edhoken* ***ta***) [C. Greek]
The books who them.CL gave.3SG
'The books, who gave them?'

Assuming that in Null Subject Languages, preverbal topics precede wh-words, which immediately precede T (see e.g. Barbosa 2001), it follows that the F-head is what heads the projection that immediately c-commands the cliticization site, and that it is this head that is directly related to the proclisis-enclisis alternation. Particles that realize some syntactic feature of the F-head (e.g. negation) also trigger proclisis. Verb movement is only forced if no XP or X is present (12a), if an XP or X is present that cannot establish a syntactic relationship with the F-head (6a and 16a respectively), or if an XP is present that can establish a syntactic relationship with the F-head but cannot satisfy the PF requirement of the relevant feature as it is not merged at the edge of the F-projection (13b).

12. In non-finite enclisis, no cases of an XP that precedes the cliticization site and which triggers proclisis are to be found, at least to my knowledge. This would be attributed to the fact that XPs with imperative or gerund or infinitival features are not available for independent reasons. Preverbal particles such as negation, subjunctive, or hortative (see e.g. Roussou 2000 for Modern Greek) could be counted as instances of an independent (i.e. non-affixal) X-head that triggers proclisis.

These data show that all the constituents that may satisfy the PF requirement must first establish a syntactic relationship with the F-head. If an XP can be internally merged or if an X can be externally merged to the edge of the F-projection, the PF requirement can be satisfied by merger. If no such constituent is available (either because no such constituent is available in the numeration, or because no syntactic relationship can be established, or because internal merge does not apply), the verb satisfies the requirement. This is possible as both the verbal complex in T and the F-head share a V-feature. Given that the feature on the F-head is affixal (as it must be obligatorily realized by a non-affixal constituent at PF), enclisis is derived via some PF operation that unites the verb and the F-head. This is exactly what we found with non-finite enclisis, which is a welcome result, as it unites enclisis in both language types.[13]

What is important to point out is that in all cases the PF/prosodic requirement is satisfied automatically (i.e. no special operation takes place), and that the actual realization of the F-head by the T-V head could take place via some PF/ morphological operation which 'repairs' the PF representation. If this operation does not take place, the derivation crashes at PF. Finally, the fact that finite enclisis is blocked by an XP or X with appropriate syntactic features clearly captures the PF nature of verb movement in this particular structure, which is that V-movement to the F-head takes place if the PF/morphological requirement imposed by the F-head has not been satisfied in the syntax (see also Raposo & Uriagereka 2005 for a similar intuition). This is a form of a doubly filled comp criterion, which has also been attributed to PF (see e.g. Pesetsky 1998), and it differs from other criteria like the wh-criterion or V2. A similar requirement has been proposed in the literature by Collins (2007) and Nchare and Terzi (to appear) in relation to prepositional phrases, according to which the edge of a projection (strictly speaking, the spec or head) must be phonologically realized. At the moment, it is not clear how such a PF requirement could be related to the EPP requirement of phase heads, as the latter is a requirement that the edge is projected syntactically. Further research is required in this respect.

Three additional points should be made here. First, although the presence of a null affixal head can be argued for independently (cf. e.g. semantic and/or syntactic properties of the structure – and see (14)), this is less clear for other cases

13. An implication of this analysis is that F-head must involve a zero affixal morpheme, and that this morpheme can be supported by an X or an XP constituent. It is not clear to me in what sense these two possibilities could be unified in a way that would make sense morphologically. Presumably, both a phrase and a head can support the affixal edge.

(cf. e.g. simple indicative clauses). Some researchers have proposed that even such full clauses contain a CFin head (see e.g. Roberts 2005), which could be used for our purposes. However, even if such a postulation turned out to be wrong, this would not affect the analysis proposed here for enclisis, as the latter is analyzed as being the outcome of a PF requirement. Although this is often a morphological requirement, nothing in principle prevents a prosodic requirement from yielding the same surface result, namely enclisis. This could be the case, for example, with positive imperatives in languages like Bulgarian, as the latter allows the syntactic realization of imperatives in T.

Second, in some Tobler-Mussafia languages any XP may block enclisis (e.g. Bulgarian), and multiple preverbal XPs are possible (cf. (7c)). One way to deal with this issue would be to claim (following the analysis in Dimitrova-Vulchanova 1995) that in these languages all preverbal XPs are hosted in the F-projection, e.g. as multiple specifiers. One XP would be required for proclisis, but more XPs could be available. Alternatively, in these languages the spell out requirement may not always be contingent on the establishment of a syntactic relationship between the F-head and the constituent that realizes its features.

Third, in languages like Cypriot Greek we find both proclisis and enclisis with certain complementizers, something which is not normally found in other Tobler-Mussafia languages (e.g. E. Portuguese). This is illustrated below:

(34) a. *Ipen oti* ***to*** *ethkiavasen i Maria* [Cypriot Greek]
Said.3SG that it.CL read.3SG the Mary
'H/she said that Mary read it.'

b. Ipen oti ethkiavasen **to** i Maria.

c. Ipen oti i Maria ethkiavasen **to**.

Crucially, this possibility seems to arise mainly with complementizers such as *oti*, which have been found to be able to appear in a higher or lower C-head (cf. recomplementation constructions in Spanish, where a topic phrase is sandwiched between two *que* complementizers – see Demonte & Fernández-Soriano 2009). Accordingly, we could assume that enclisis obtains only if the complementizer does not phonologically realize the F-head,[14] a possibility that would explain (34b).

14. This could be the result of movement or direct base generation.

4. Summary and conclusions

Although the analysis presented in this paper is tentative to some degree, it seems that there is some evidence from different structures from finiteness sensitive and Tobler-Mussafia languages that cliticization and the proclisis-enclisis alternation are the complex result of syntactic and different types of PF operations/ requirements. In this section, as well as in previous ones, we identified at least seven cliticization strategies:

a. proclisis 1: This is the most typical case of proclisis found in finiteness sensitive languages (cf. 1a). Here, the clitic (cluster) targets a position that c-commands the verb (typically within the TP domain), without any further operations applying (modulo incorporation, which is a syntactic or PF operation that mergers the clitic with its verbal host – see Matushansky 2006; Roberts 2010).
b. proclisis 2: This corresponds to finite proclisis within the TP domain in Tobler-Mussafia languages (cf. 2a). Here, the clitic (cluster) targets a position that is immediately c-commanded by a C-head (what I called 'the F-head'). This head carries syntactic features and a PF/morphological requirement, which is satisfied by an XP or X (particle) that is merged (for syntactic reasons) at the edge of the F-head, and which has established a syntactic relationship with it. A prosodic requirement that bans clause initial clitics (if applicable) is also satisfied in this case.
c. proclisis 3: This case corresponds to finite proclisis within the CP domain (cf. 24–26). Here, the clitic incorporates into the verb within the TP domain (as in all other cases of proclisis), and then the whole cluster moves syntactically to a CP head.
d. enclisis 1: This case corresponds to most cases of non-finite enclisis within the CP domain (cf. 1b). Here, the F-head contains syntactic features and a PF/morphological requirement. The latter triggers the spell-out of the verbal host in the F-head and gives rise to enclisis, which is analyzed as a syntax-PF phenomenon.
e. enclisis 2: This case corresponds to finite enclisis within the CP domain (cf. (7)–(14)). The derivation proceeds as in *enclisis 1*. Enclisis 2 is aborted if an appropriate XP or non-affixal X can satisfy the syntactic and PF requirements of the F-head. The presence of such constituents depends on their availability in a certain language or construction, i.e. it is linked to the type of features that the F-head contains (TP vs. CP features).
f. enclisis 3: This case is quite rare and corresponds to non-finite enclisis in the CP domain in those cases where enclisis has already obtained within the TP

domain (cf. e.g. gerunds). The derivation proceeds as in *enclisis 1*. After the clitic-V cluster has been formed, T is attracted to some C-head, leading to syntactic dislocation of the cluster to the CP domain.

g. enclisis 4: This form of enclisis is a residual case, and it involves purely syntactic or PF verb movement to some head preceding the cliticization site. Possible examples would involve Bulgarian V-movement for focus reasons, or Bulgarian V-movement for PF/prosodic reasons (linked to the ban on initial clitics, independently of whether the element in question is an object clitic or some affixal zero V-head).

This picture is quite different from what has been proposed before, and it follows from the nature of the PF-syntax interface. The most important implication for head movement is that it may be related to PF even if semantic/syntactic effects are present. These are the cases where head movement is related to an affixal head (i.e. to a morphological requirement), and where enclisis standardly arises. However, we have also seen cases where head movement is triggered solely for syntactic or PF reasons. As things stand at the moment, it seems that enclisis might, in these cases only, correlate with a syntactic or prosodic requirement (and not a morphological requirement). Although the postulation of enclisis for prosodic reasons may not seem problematic (as enclisis is linked to PF operations in all these cases), syntactically triggered enclisis might turn out to be problematic for our generalization. Such a possibility could be linked to whether and (if so) when clitics incorporate to their verbal host in these structures, or to whether the C-head also has an affix requirement. Further inquiry is required for these cases, and should involve investigation of the presence or absence of syntactic and/or semantic effects that could help us distinguish when movement of syntactic features has taken place and whether such movement ever correlates with enclisis.

References

Anagnostopoulou, Elena. 2003. *The Syntax of Ditransitives. Evidence from Clitics*. Berlin: Mouton de Guyter.

Barbosa, Pilar. 1996. Clitic placement in European Portuguese and the position of subjects. In *Approaching Second: Second Position Clitics and Related Phenomena*, Aaron Halpern & Arnold Zwicky (eds), 1–40. Stanford CA: CSLI.

Barbosa, Pilar. 2001. On inversion in Wh-Questions in Romance. In *Subject Inversion in Romance and the Theory of Universal Grammar*, Aafke Hulk & Jean-Yves Pollock (eds), 20–59. Oxford: OUP.

Benincà, Paola. 1995. Complement clitics in medieval Romance: The Tobler-Mussafia law. In *Clause Structure and Language Change*, Adrian Battye & Ian Roberts (eds), 325–344. Oxford: OUP.

Bošković, Zeljko. 2001. *On the Nature of the Syntax-Phonology Interface: Cliticization and Related Phenomena*. Amsterdam: Elsevier.
Bošković, Zeljko. 2004. On the clitic switch in Greek imperatives. In *Balkan Syntax and Semantics* [Linguistik Aktuell/Linguistics Today 67], Olga Tomić (ed.), 269–291. Amsterdam: John Benjamins.
Cardinaletti, Anna & Roberts, Ian. 1991. Clause structure and X second. Ms.
Chomsky, Noam. 2001. Derivation by phase. In *Ken Hale: A Life in Language*, Michael Kenstowicz (ed.), 1–52. Cambridge MA: The MIT Press.
Collins, Chris. 2007. 'Home sweet home.' *NYU Working Papers in Linguistics* 1: 1–34.
Condoravdi, Cleo & Kiparsky, Paul. 2001. Clitcs and clause structure. *Journal of Greek Linguistics* 2: 1–39.
Daskalaki, Evangelia & Mavrogiorgos, Marios. To appear. Obligatory resumption in Greek free and restrictive relatives. Oxford: OUP.
Demonte, Valentina & Fernández-Soriano, Olga. 2009. Force and finiteness in the Spanish complementiser system. *Probus* 21: 23–49.
Dimitrova-Vulchanova, Mila. 1995. Clitics in Slavic. *Studia Linguistica* 49: 54–92.
Dimitrova-Vulchanova, Mila & Hellan, Lars. 1999. Clitics and Bulgarian clause structure. In *Clitics in the Languages of Europe*, Henk van Riemsdijk (ed.), 469–514. Berlin: Mouton de Gruyter.
Fischer, Suzanne. 2002. *The Catalan Clitic System: A Diachronic Perspective On its Syntax and Phonology*. Berlin: Mouton de Gruyter.
Fontana, Josep. 1996. Phonology and syntax in the interpretation of the Tobler-Mussafia law. In *Approaching Second: Second Position Clitics and Related Phenomena*, Aaron L. Halpern & Arnold Zwicky (eds), 41–83. Stanford CA: CSLI.
Franks, Steven. 1998. Clitics in Slavic. Ms, Indiana University.
Franks, Steven. 2008. Clitic placement, prosody, and the Bulgarian verbal complex. *Journal of Slavic Linguistics* 16: 91–137.
Halpern, Aaron. 1995. *On the Placement and Morphology of Clitics*. Stanford CA: CSLI.
Halpern, Aaron & Zwicky, Arnold. 1996. *Approaching Second: Second Position Clitics and Related Phenomena*. Stanford CA: CSLI.
Han, Chung-hye. 1998. The Structure and Interpretation of Imperatives: Mood and Force in Universal Grammar. Ph.D. dissertation, University of Pennsylvania.
Harris, James. 1995. There is no imperative paradigm in Spanish. In *Issues in the Phonology and Morphology of the Major Iberian Languages,* Fernando Martínez-Gil & Alfonso Morales-Front (eds), 537–557. Washington DC: Georgetown University Press.
Kayne, Richard. 1991. Romance clitics, verb movement and PRO. *Linguistic Inquiry* 22: 647–686.
Klavans, Judith. 1985. The independence of syntax and phonology in cliticization. *Language* 61: 95–120.
Laka, Iziar. 1990. Negation in Syntax. On the Nature of Functional Categories and Projections. Ph.D. dissertation, MIT.
Ledgeway, Adam & Lombardi, Alessandra. 2005. Verb movement, adverbs and clitic positions in Romance. *Probus* 17: 79–113.
Martins, Anna-Maria. 1994. Enclisis, VP deletion and the nature of Sigma. *Probus* 6: 173–205.
Matushansky, Ora. 2006. Head movement in linguistic theory. *Linguistic Inquiry* 37: 69–109.
Mavrogiorgos, Marios. 2010. *Clitics in Greek: A Minimalist Account of Proclisis and Enclisis* [Linguistik Aktuell/Linguistics Today 160]. Amsterdam: John Benjamins.
Nchare, Abdoulaye Naziz & Arhonto, Terzi. To appear. Lisencing silent structure: The spatial prepositions of Shupamem. *Natural Language and Linguistic Theory*.

Pancheva, Roumyana. 2005. The rise and fall of second position clitics. *Natural Language and Linguistic Theory* 23: 103–167.

Pappas, Panayiotis. 2004. *Variation and Morphosyntactic Change in Greek. From Clitics to Affixes.* New York: Palgrave Macmillan.

Pesetsky, David. 1998. Some optimality principles of sentence pronunciation. In *Is the Best Good Enough?*, Pilar Barbosa, Daniel Fox, Paul Hagstrom, Martha McGinnis & David Pesetsky (eds), 337–383. Cambridge M: The MIT Press.

Poletto, Cecilia & Zanuttini, Raffaella. 2010. Sentential particles and remnant movement. In *Mapping the Left Periphery. The Cartography of Syntactic Structures,* Vol. 5, Paola Benincà & Nicola Munaro (eds), 201–227. Oxford: OUP.

Raposo, Eduardo & Uriagereka, Juan. 2005. Clitic placement in Western Iberian. In *The Oxford Handbook in Comparative Syntax*, Guglielmo Cinque & Richard Kayne (eds), 639–697. Oxford: OUP.

Revithiadou, Anthi. 2006. Prosodic filters on syntax: An interface account of second position clitics. *Lingua* 116: 79–111.

Revithiadou, Anthi. 2008. A cross-dialectal study of cliticization in Greek. *Lingua* 118: 1393–1415.

Richards, Marc. 2004. Object Shift and Scrambling in North and West Germanic: A Case Study in Symmetrical Syntax. Ph.D. dissertation, University of Cambridge.

Rivero, Maria-Luisa. 1994. Clause structure and V-movement in the languages of the Balkans. *Natural Language and Linguistic Theory* 12: 63–120.

Rivero, Maria-Luisa & Terzi, Arhonto. 1995. Imperatives, V-movement and logical mood. *Journal of Linguistics* 31: 301–322.

Rizzi, Luigi. 1982. *Issues in Italian Syntax*. Dordrecht: Foris.

Roberts, Ian. 2005. *Principles and Parameters in a VSO language: A Case Study in Welsh.* Oxford: OUP.

Roberts, Ian. 2010. *Agreement and Head Movement: Clitics, Incorporation and Defective Goals.* Cambridge, MA: The MIT Press.

Roussou, Anna. 2000. On the left periphery. Modal particles and complementisers. *Journal of Greek Linguistics* 1: 65–94.

Samuels, Bridget. 2009. The Structure of Phonological Theory. Ph.D. dissertation, Harvard University.

Shlonsky, Ur. 2004. Enclisis and proclisis. *The Structure of CP and IP. The Cartography of Syntactic Structures*, Vol. 2., Luigi Rizzi (ed.), 329–353. Oxford: OUP.

Terzi, Arhonto. 1999a. Clitic combinations, their hosts and their ordering. *Natural Language and Linguistic Theory* 17: 85–121.

Terzi, Arhonto. 1999b. Cypriot Greek clitics and their positioning restrictions. In *Studies in Greek Syntax*, Artemis Alexiadou, Geoffrey Horrocks & Melita Stavrou (eds), 227–240. Dordrecht: Kluwer.

Tomić, Olga M. 1996. The Balkan slavic clausal clitics. *Natural Language and Linguistic Theory* 14: 811–872.

Uriagereka, Juan. 1995a. Aspects of the syntax of clitic placement in Western Romance. *Linguistic Inquiry* 26: 79–124.

Uriagereka, Juan. 1995b. An F position in Western Romance. In *Discourse Configurational Languages*, Katalin É. Kiss (ed.). Oxford: OUP.

Clisis revisited

Root and embedded contexts in Western Iberian

Francisco José Fernández-Rubiera
University of Central Florida

This paper contributes to the literature that discusses the trigger for enclisis and proclisis alternations. Empirically, this article presents new data from Asturian, a Western Iberian Romance language which, unlike Galician and European Portuguese, exhibits enclisis also in finite embedded contexts. I argue that this empirical evidence supports an analysis of enclisis/proclisis alternations in terms of syntactic A′- or X^0-movement to Finiteness^0. I illustrate the different interpretations that enclisis/proclisis alternations give rise to in the finite embedded context in Asturian, and I show how they are naturally captured by the proposed analysis. Moreover, the unavailability of embedded enclisis in Galician and European Portuguese can be easily explained, ultimately relating to differences in the complementizer system in this group of languages.

1. Enclisis and proclisis in Western Iberian Romance languages[1]

1.1 Enclisis and proclisis in the matrix context in Western Iberian Romance languages

One of the properties that distinguishes Western Iberian Romance languages (that is, Asturian, Galician and European Portuguese) from other Romance languages is that in matrix contexts, clitics sometimes appear as enclitic to the verb and sometimes as proclitic. As the examples in (1) show, verb-initial contexts

1. I wish to thank the following people for comments and discussion on this paper: Adolfo Ausín, Héctor Campos, João Costa, Violeta Demonte, Olga Fernández-Soriano, Elena Herburger, Christine Meklenborg Salvesen, Ur Shlonsky, as well as the audiences at the 20th Colloquium on Generative Grammar (Pompeu i Fabra, Barcelona) and the Challenging Clitics Workshop (Oslo). Many thanks also to the two anonymous reviewers for their valuable comments, insights and suggestions, which have definitely improved this work. Usual disclaimers apply.

trigger enclisis obligatorily in Asturian (Ast), Galician (Gal) and European Portuguese (EP).[2]

(1) a. *Téoles* *tayaes* [***Les** teo] Ast
have$_{1SG}$-them$_{CL}$ cut
'I have them (my hands) cut' [Álvarez, *Llames*]

b. *Contoumo* *todo* [***Mo** contou] Gal
told$_{3SG}$-me$_{CL}$-it$_{CL}$ everything
'S/he told me everything' [Álvarez et al. (1986: 183)]

c. *Estudara-o* *a fundo* [***O** estudara] EP
had-studied$_{3SG}$-it$_{CL}$ to depth
'S/he had studied it in depth' [Vázquez Cuesta et al. (1971: 165)]

Proclisis, on the other hand, shows up obligatorily in these three languages in the presence of the negative marker, as illustrated in the examples in (2).

(2) a. *Nun* ***me*** *mancó* [*mancó-**me**] Ast
not me$_{CL}$ hurt$_{3SG}$
'S/he didn't hurt me' [Orton, *Mayordomu*]

b. *Non* ***cho*** *dicía* *por* *iso* [*dicía-**cho**] Gal
not you$_{CL}$-it$_{CL}$ said$_{1SG}$ for that
'I didn't say it to you for that (reason)' [Álvarez et al. (1986: 185)]

c. *Tu* *não* ***lhe*** *telefonaste* *hoje?* [*telefonaste-**lhe**] EP
you not him$_{CL}$ phoned$_{2SG}$ today
'You didn't call him today?' [Vázquez Cuesta et al. (1971: 167)]

In turn, the Topic and Focus articulation of the left-periphery gives rise to different clitic patterns in the matrix context in this group of languages. As shown in (3) and (4), a left-dislocated Topic triggers the same pattern as preverbal non-quantified subjects,[3,4] namely obligatory enclisis.

---

2. Clitics are indicated in bold here and in subsequent examples for the reader's convenience. The abbreviations used in the glosses are: CL (clitic), IND (indicative mood), INF (infinitival), PL (plural), RFL (reflexive), SG (singular), and 1/2/3 for first, second and third person, respectively.

3. It is generally assumed since the seminal work of Contreras (1978) that non-focalized non-quantified preverbal subjects in *pro-drop* languages appear in a left-dislocated (i.e. Topic) position, with focalized/quantified subjects being licensed in a Focus position. As will be laid out in sections §3 and §4, I am assuming that T^0's [EPP] feature is licensed by the verbal head in Western Iberian – following Alexiadou and Anagnostopoulou (1998), with Topic subjects being base generated in [Spec, TopicP] and Focus subjects undergoing A′-movement and reaching [Spec, FocusP] through the proposed phase-edge [Spec, FinP]. The reader is referred to sections §3 and §4 for further discussion on this issue.

4. Consider the following example, which illustrates that a quantified preverbal subject triggers proclisis instead of enclisis:

(3) a. *Eso$_i$ sábeslo$_i$ per lleer les cartes* [****lo** sabes] Ast
that know$_{2SG}$-it$_{CL}$ for read$_{INF}$ the cards
'That, you know it from reading the (tarot) cards' [González, *Comedies*]

b. *Iso$_i$ publicárono$_i$ os críticos insidiosos* [****o** publicaron] Gal
that published$_{3PL}$-it$_{CL}$ the critics insidious
'That, the insidious critics published it' [CORGA (2008)]

c. *isso$_i$ digo-vo-lo$_i$ eu* [****vo-lo** digo] EP
that say$_{1SG}$-you$_{CL.PL}$-it$_{CL}$ I
'That, I say it to you' [O Corpus do Português (2007)]

(4) a. *El xenru matóse nun accidente*
the son-in-law killed$_{3SG}$-rfl$_{CL}$ in-an accident
na mina [****se** mató] Ast
in-the mine
'His son-in-law got killed in an accident in the mine'
[González, *Comedies*]

b. *O veciño tróuxoche estas cereixas* [****che** trouxo] Gal
the neighbor brought$_{3SG}$-you$_{CL}$ these cherries
'The neighbor brought you these cherries'
[Carballo Calero (1968: 227)]

c. *O António leu-o ontem* [****o** leu] EP
the António read$_{3SG}$-it$_{CL}$ yesterday
'Antonio read it yesterday' [Martins (1994: 339, (25))]

In contrast, as shown in (5) and (6), preverbal *wh*- and Focus constituents,[5] even when these are subjects, trigger proclisis exclusively.[6]

(i) *Naide lo sabía* [*sabía**lo**] Ast
Nobody it$_{CL}$ knew$_{3SG}$
"Nobody knew it"

A similar effect of preverbal quantified subject is reported for Galician (Uriagereka 1995a, 1995b) and for European Portuguese (Barbosa 1995, 2000).

5. As is customary, capitals are used to indicate the rising intonation of Focus constituents.

6. All *wh*-words, including those that have been analyzed as "higher" *wh*-words in the sense of Rizzi (2001), exclusively trigger a proclitic pattern. A relevant example is given below:

(i) *Por qué-y lo dixiste?* [*dixíste-**ylo**]
Why-him$_{CL}$ it$_{CL}$ said$_{2SG}$
"Why did you say it to him?"

(5) a. *Cómo t'atreves?* [*atréve**ste**] Ast
how rfl_{CL}-dare_{2SG}
'How dare you?' [Rodríguez Medina, *Gaviotes*]

b. *Onde **os** puxeches?* [*puxeches-**os**] Gal
where them_{CL} put_{2SG}
'Where did you put them?' [Álvarez et al. (1986: 185)]

c. *O que **te** disse ele?* [*disse-**te**] EP
the what you_{CL} say_{3SG} he
'What does he tell you?' [Martins (1994: 358, (64))]

(6) a. *YO MESMA **me** **la** repito un*
I $\text{self}_{\text{[FOC]}}$ me_{CL} it_{CL} $\text{repeat}_{\text{1SG}}$ one
cientu vegaes [*repíto**mela**] Ast
hundred times
'I myself repeat it to myself one hundred times' [de Pablo, *Memoria*]

b. *e NO SEU TRABALLO*
and in-the his $\text{job}_{\text{[FOCUS]}}$
***o** prenderon* [*prendero-**no**] Gal
him_{CL} $\text{caught}_{\text{3PL}}$
'And it was in his job that they caught him' [Álvarez et al. (1986: 184)]

c. *OS TRÊS HOMENS **se** sentaram*
the three $\text{men}_{\text{[FOC]}}$ rfl_{CL} sat_{3PL}
à mesa [*sentáram-**se**] EP
at-the table
'It was the three men who sat at the table"
[Vázquez Cuesta et al. (1971: 166)]

Summarizing, enclisis and proclisis arise uniformly in the same matrix contexts in Western Iberian Romance languages: enclisis in verb-initial contexts and after left-dislocated Topics and preverbal non-quantified subjects, and proclisis after the negative marker and after preverbal *wh-* and Focus constituents. As I will show next, similar enclisis/proclisis alternations can also be found in the finite embedded context in Asturian, a pattern that sets this Western Iberian Romance language apart from Galician and European Portuguese.

1.2 Enclisis and proclisis in the finite embedded context in Asturian

In Asturian, in contrast to Galician and European Portuguese, the articulation of the left-periphery in finite embedded contexts such as those in (7) triggers effects on clitic placement alternations similar to those observed in the matrix context: While only enclisis is acceptable in (7a) after a preverbal non-quantified subject, when the subject bears Focus, proclisis obtains, as in (7b).

(7) a. *Repítote* [*que yo* ***dexélo*** *aquel diecisiete*
repeat$_{1SG}$-you$_{CL}$ that I left$_{1SG\text{-}IND}$-it$_{CL}$ that seventeenth
de mayu] [***lo** dexé]
of May
'I repeat to you that I left it that May seventeenth' [de Pablo, *Memoria*]

b. *Repítote* [*que YO* ***lo*** *dexé* *aquel diecisiete*
repeat$_{1SG}$-you that I$_{[FOC]}$ it$_{CL}$ left$_{1SG\text{-}IND}$ that seventeenth
de mayu] (, non él) [*dexé**lo**]
of May
'I repeat to you that I (, and not him) left it that May seventeenth'

Moreover, in the absence of left-peripheral material, both enclisis and proclisis are grammatical in an embedded clause such as the one in (8), as reported in Viejo (2008).

(8) a. *Digo* [*qu'ayúda**me***]
say$_{1SG}$ that-help$_{3SG\text{-}IND}$-me$_{CL}$

b. *Digo* [*que* ***me*** *ayuda*]
say$_{1SG}$ that me$_{CL}$ help$_{3SG\text{-}IND}$
'I say that s/he helps me out'

In contrast, speakers of the other Western Iberian Romance languages, i.e. Galician and European Portuguese, report the enclitic pattern in (8a) as unacceptable. Moreover, speakers report the enclitic pattern after a preverbal non-quantified subject as either marginal or downright unacceptable – see (9).

(9) a. *Xulia dixo* [*que Mon* ***o*** *dixera*] [??? dixera**o**] Gal
Xulia said$_{3SG}$ that Mon it$_{CL}$ had-said$_{3SG\text{-}IND}$
'Xulia said that Mon had said it'

b. *O Pedro disso* [*que o Paulo*
the Pedro said$_{3SG}$ that the Paulo
o *dissera*] [???/*dissera-**o**] EP
it$_{CL}$ had-said$_{3SG\text{-}IND}$
'Pedro said that Paulo had said it'

Summarizing, the finite embedded context in Asturian may exhibit either optional enclisis in the absence of left-peripheral material, as in (8), or obligatory enclisis after a preverbal non-quantified subject, as in (7a). Interestingly, this clitic pattern is reported to be unacceptable by speakers of Galician and European Portuguese.

This article tackles both the similarities in clitic placement in the matrix environment as well as the crosslinguistic variation that speakers report in the finite embedded context in Western Iberian.

Clitic alternations such as those found in Western Iberian have been a topic of much debate since the eighties. In what follows, I discuss two main trends of analysis proposed in the literature, and I show how they fall short of explaining the enclisis/proclisis alternations found in Asturian.

2. Previous approaches to enclisis and proclisis alternations

Broadly speaking, the body of literature that dwells on clitic placement alternations such as those found in Western Iberian Romance languages may be divided into two types: Those which attribute the enclisis/proclisis alternations to the phonological enclitic nature of clitics, which I call phonological approaches, and those proposals that claim that enclisis/proclisis alternations arise as a result of independently triggered syntactic operations, which I dub syntactic approaches. Some of these proposals are reviewed next. As I will ultimately show, none of these proposals explain the enclisis and proclisis alternations we find in the finite embedded context in Asturian.

2.1 Phonological approaches to enclisis and proclisis alternations

For this group of studies (Rivero 1986 for Old Spanish, Campos 1989 for Galician & Barbosa 1995, 2000 for European Portuguese), clitics in these languages are sensitive to phonological filters such as those in (10).

(10) a. *[$_{CP}$ ø clitic$_{[ENCLITIC]}$], where ø = another clitic or a null element [Rivero]

b. *[$_{IntP}$ cl(itic) V…], where IntP = Intonational Phrase [Barbosa]

The filters in (10) trigger last-resort operations, as a result of which an enclitic pattern obtains. Thus, the enclisis found in a verb initial context such as that in (1)/(11) is derived as shown in (12) and (13).

(11) *Téoles* *tayaes* [*Les teo] Ast
have$_{1SG}$-them$_{CL}$ cut
'I have them (my hands) cut' [Álvarez, *Llames*]

(12) a. [$_{CP}$ [$_{C^0}$ [$_{TP}$ les$_{[ENCLITIC]}$ [$_{T^0}$ teo … ~~les~~ tayaes]]]]
b. *[$_{CP}$ les$_{[ENCLITIC]}$] – ruled out by filter in (10a)
c. [$_{CP}$ [$_{C^0}$ teo [$_{TP}$ les$_{[ENCLITIC]}$ [$_{T^0}$ ~~teo~~ … tayaes]]]] – last resort T^0-to-C^0 as a repair

(13) a. [$_{CP/TP}$ les$_{[ENCLITIC]}$ [$_{T^0}$ teo … ~~les~~ tayaes]]
b. [$_{IntP}$ les$_{[ENCLITIC]}$ teo] → illicit structure *pace* (10b)
c. [$_{IntP}$ ~~les~~ teo les] → Pronounce lower copy → PF-convergence ensured

Given the assumed enclitic nature of the clitic, it requires a phonological host to its left, in the absence of which the filters in (10) are triggered as in (12) and (13). As a repair, last-resort verb-movement to C^0 past the clitic as in (12c) for Rivero, or pronouncing a lower copy of the clitic as a repair as in (13c) for Barbosa, explains the enclisis observed.

Proclisis, on the other hand, comes about for these proposals when the filters in (10) are not triggered, as in the case of preverbal Focus constituents like those in (6)/(14). Focus constituents are assumed to prevent the clitics from appearing in absolute initial position and consequently, the filters in (10) are rendered inert. The details are shown in (15) and (16).

(14) *YO MESMA* ***me*** ***la*** *repito* *un*
I self$_{[FOC]}$ me$_{CL}$ it$_{CL}$ repeat$_{1SG}$ one
cientu vegaes [*repíto**mela**] Ast
hundred times
'I myself repeat it to myself one hundred times' [de Pablo, *Memoria*]

(15) a. [$_{CP}$ yo mesma$_{[FOC]}$ [$_{C^0}$ [$_{TP}$ me$_{[ENCLITIC]}$ la$_{[ENCLITIC]}$ [$_{T^0}$ repito … un cientu vegaes]]]]
b. [$_{CP}$ yo mesma$_{[FOC]}$ me$_{[ENCLITIC]}$ la$_{[ENCLITIC]}$] – (10a) inert and derivation converges

(16) a. [$_{CP/TP}$ yo mesma$_{[FOC]}$ me$_{[ENCLITIC]}$ la$_{[ENCLITIC]}$ [$_{T^0}$ repito … un cientu vegaes]]
b. [$_{IntP}$ yo mesma$_{[FOC]}$ me$_{[ENCLITIC]}$ la$_{[ENCLITIC]}$ …] – (10b) is not triggered

The main problem for these phonological approaches comes from the availability of both enclisis and proclisis in finite embedded contexts in Asturian, as in (8)/(17).

(17) a. *Digo* [*qu'ayúda**me***]
say$_{1SG}$ that-help$_{3SG\text{-}IND}$-me$_{CL}$
b. *Digo* [*que* ***me*** *ayuda*]
say$_{1SG}$ that me$_{CL}$ help$_{3SG\text{-}IND}$
'I say that s/he helps me out'

If enclisis arises as a last-resort mechanism whenever the enclitic fails to have a phonological host to its left, the complementizer in cases such as (17b) would be acting as a host for the enclitic, rendering the filters in (10) inert, which leaves the acceptability of enclisis in cases such as (17a) unexplained. Next, I review what I call syntactic approaches to clitic placement alternations.

2.2 Syntactic approaches to enclisis and proclisis alternations

In contrast to the phonological approaches to enclisis/proclisis alternations just reviewed, what I call syntactic approaches claim that these alternations come about from syntactic mechanisms triggered independently of the phonological status of the clitics.

For Raposo and Uriagereka (2005), following previous work of their own (cf. Uriagereka 1995a, 1995b and Raposo 2000), these alternations are the result of an interaction between a left-peripheral head, which they call F^0, and general conditions on fusion. Summarizing, Raposo and Uriagereka (2005) argue that an intermediate projection between C^0 and T^0, as in (18), interacts with clitic placement alternations in Western Iberian as follows: F^0 bears morphological [+φ] features in this group of languages, these features attract the clitic(s) to the head and spell out, and T^0-to-F^0 is triggered in the absence of an adjacent element either in [Spec, FP] or C^0 for the clitic(s) to fuse to, yielding enclisis as a result.

(18)

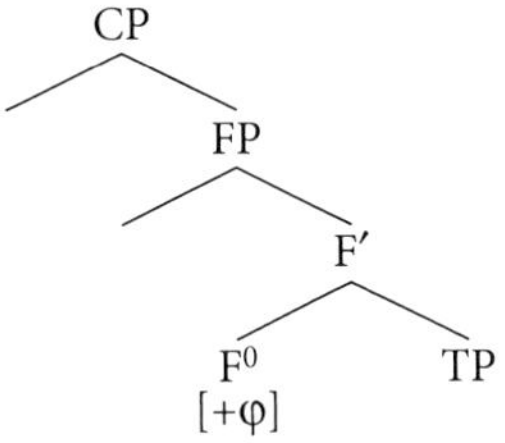

Considering a verb-initial context as those in (1)/(19), the enclisis observed would be derived as shown in (20).[7]

(19) *Téoles* *tayaes* [*Les teo] Ast
have$_{1SG}$-them$_{CL}$ cut
'I have them (my hands) cut' [Álvarez, *Llames*]

(20)

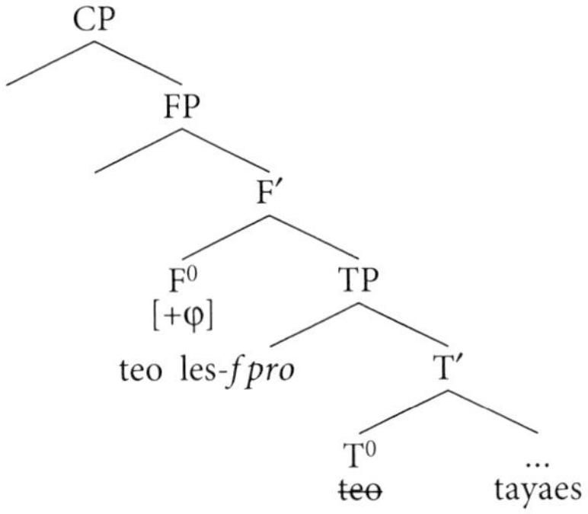

7. Following Raposo and Uriagereka (2005), the feature spell-out is represented by the symbol *f*.

An adjacent element in [Spec, FP] or C^0 would license the clitics in F^0, avoiding last-resort verb-movement and, consequently, enclisis. Thus, the derivation for the proclisis found in cases of A′- (Focus) movement such as those in (6)/(21) would be as in (22).[8]

(21) *YO MESMA* ***me la*** *repito un*
I self$_{[FOC]}$ me$_{CL}$ it$_{CL}$ repeat$_{1SG}$ one
cientu vegaes [*repíto**mela**] Ast
hundred times
'I myself repeat it to myself one hundred times' [de Pablo, *Memoria*]

(22)

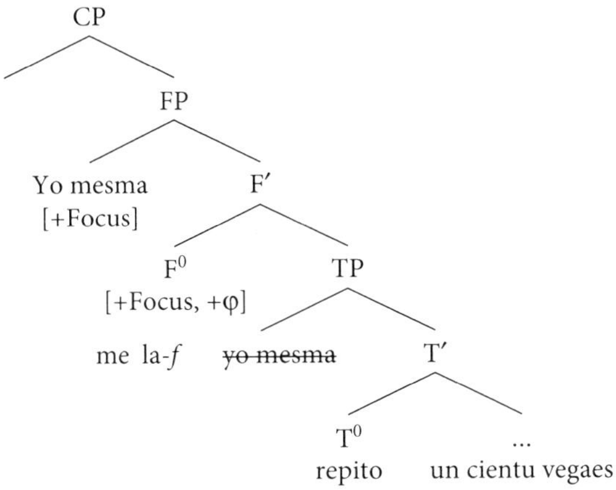

Crucially, Raposo and Uriagereka's (2005) analysis predicts that the presence of an element in C^0 would be adjacent to the clitic(s) in F^0 and consequently, verb-movement and therefore enclisis would be ruled out. Asturian shows that this prediction is not fulfilled, as enclisis is also acceptable even when a complementizer is in C^0, as in (8)/(23).

(23) a. *Digo [qu'ayúda**me**]*
say$_{1SG}$ that-help$_{3SG\text{-}IND}$-me$_{CL}$
b. *Digo [que me ayuda]*
say$_{1SG}$ that me$_{CL}$ help$_{3SG\text{-}IND}$
'I say that s/he helps me out'

8. For Raposo and Uriagereka (2005), F^0 is a syncretic projection which may also bear [Focus] and [Topic] features, thus attracting elements bearing those features to [Spec, FP], as in (22).

Turning now to Shlonsky (2005), his main working hypothesis is that proclisis, and not enclisis, arises as a result of a last-resort operation, whereby proclisis obtains whenever enclisis is ruled out by the grammar. Shlonsky (2005) claims that enclisis obtains when the verb has satisfied all its morphological features and then adjoins to the clitic, which is in turn located in a projection higher in the structure than the one hosting the verb. On the other hand, proclisis obtains when the verb moves past the clitic to satisfy all its morphological features, with subsequent adjunction of the clitic to it resulting in proclisis. The problem for Shlonsky's analysis comes once again from data such as what is shown in (8): Both enclisis and proclisis are grammatical, the verb (i.e. its tense and morphological features) is the same in both cases, and yet both clitic patterns may surface. In short, there is no reason to believe that the verb has not checked all its features and has moved past the clitic in the case of proclisis in (23b), whereas no such verb movement past the clitic is realized in the enclisis found in (23a).

Leaving the review of the relevant literature here, and I before I present my analysis, I next lay out my main assumptions regarding clitics and the clausal structure of Western Iberian Romance languages.

3. The nature of clitics in Western Iberian Romance languages and the role of Finiteness^0 in deriving enclisis/proclisis alternations

In this section, I discuss two assumptions and I lay out the analysis I propose to account for clitic placement alternations in Western Iberian Romance languages. The first assumption relates to the nature of clitics in this group of languages. Following Franco (1994, 2000), Fernández Soriano (1993) and references therein, I analyze clitics in Asturian, Galician and European Portuguese as X^0-agreement affixes[9] which, following Murphy-Armstrong (1986) and Sportiche (1996), are merged in the phrase marker in an extended projection of the TP-domain which I label CliticP. Under this analysis, and in line with Raposo and Uriagereka (2005), I assume that clitics are merged preverbally in Western Iberian Romance languages, with enclisis being the result of an independently triggered verb-movement operation.

The second assumption relates to the status of preverbal subjects in this group of languages. Following Barbosa (1995) and Alexiadou and Anagnostopoulou

9. I take the lack of interpolation (i.e. the presence of an element breaking the adjacency between the clitic and the verb) in Asturian as evidence for the X^0-status of these affixes, with interpolation in regression and considered archaic in the other languages of the Western Iberian family.

(1998), I assume that the verbal head in Western Iberian languages bears nominal features that check T^0's [EPP]. Therefore, and following Barbosa (1995, 2000) and Raposo (2000) for European Portuguese, and Contreras (1978, 1991), Olarrea (1997) and Ordóñez (1998), among others, for Spanish, I analyze preverbal subjects as either A′-moved (i.e. for reasons of Focus; see an example in (21) and in fn. 3) or base-generated elements (i.e. Topics, as in (4) above) licensed in the left-periphery of the clause.

Finally, in line with Chomsky's (2008) phase system, I assume that both CP and v^*P are phases, *"where C is a shorthand for the region that Rizzi (1997) calls 'the left-periphery'"* (Chomsky 2008: 143). Following Rizzi (1997, 2004), I assume a CP-structure as shown in (24).

(24) $[_{ForceP}$ Force^0 $[_{TopicP}$ Topic^0 $[_{FocusP}$ Focus^0 $[_{FinitenessP}$ Finiteness^0 $[_{TP}$ ...]]]]]

I argue for an analysis of enclisis and proclisis alternations that attributes to Rizzi's (1997) Finiteness^0 (Fin^0) the status of what Chomsky (2008) considers the CP-phase. This proposal feeds from Rizzi (1997) and Chomsky (2008) and their proposals for connecting C^0/Fin^0 and T^0 as shown below:[10]

(25) a. Fin^0 shows a strong morphological connection with T^0 (cf. Rizzi 1997).[11]

b. T^0 inherits its agree (φ-) and probe (EPP) features from C^0 (cf. Chomsky 2008).

Entertaining the idea that Fin^0 is a phase-head, I argue that enclisis/proclisis alternations such as those found in Western Iberian can be explained assuming (26).

(26) In Western Iberian, Fin^0 is a phase-head with an edge condition which triggers and ensures the displacement of an element.[12]

10. As an anonymous reviewer points out, choosing Fin^0 as a phase-head raises the question of the status of the higher left-peripheral heads (i.e. Focus^0, Topic^0 and Force^0). Force^0 in matrix environments could be considered a phase-head as it closes the derivation. In turn, a subordinate Force^0 could be considered a constituent of a higher v^0. I believe this is an empirical issue and I do not have the data to test it. However, as I will show, entertaining this idea of Fin^0 as a phase-head allows me to account for enclisis/proclisis alternations and the microparametric variation we find in Western Iberian with the same analysis.

11. Rizzi establishes this connection in relation to the complementizer system of Italian, which is sensitive to the [± finite] morphological specification of T^0, with *che* "that" and *di* "for" matching T^0[+finite] and T^0[-finite] respectively.

12. A more formal way to capture this edge-condition would be to assume that Finiteness^0 has an Internal Merge requirement. The proposed phase-status of Finiteness^0 would in turn explain why elements undergoing A′-movement to the left-periphery must move through the

With (26), I argue that the edge-condition of Fin^{0} can be satisfied either by an element undergoing A′-movement to the left-periphery of the clause, or by the closest available head in the structure. A′-movement gives rise to proclisis uniformly, as the edge-condition of Fin^{0} would be licensed by *wh-* and Focus constituents passing through [Spec, Fin^{0}]. Attracting the closest head in the structure would explain the proclisis we find with the negative marker, as well as the enclisis that results when neither A′-moved elements nor a closer head to Fin^{0} than T^{0} is available, triggering T^{0}-to-Fin^{0} as last-resort movement. Next, I illustrate how the different clitic patterns we find in the matrix context in Western Iberian can be uniformly explained by the analysis I propose.

Summarizing, the clausal structure that I will assume is shown below, with the parentheses indicating that those projections are only present when needed in the structure (cf. Rizzi 1997, 2004 for discussion).

(27)

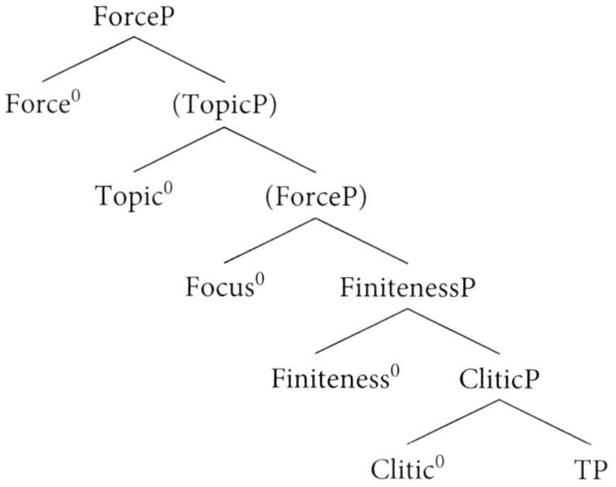

4. The edge-condition of Fin^{0} and its role in deriving enclisis/proclisis alternations in the matrix environment in Western Iberian Romance languages

4.1 Enclisis and the edge-condition of Fin^{0}

On the analysis I propose, enclisis arises in the absence of A′-movement or a closer head to Fin^{0} than T^{0}. Under those circumstances, the verb moves to Fin^{0} to satisfy the edge condition I propose in (26), with the verb picking up the clitic(s) on its way up to Fin^{0}. Let me illustrate the analysis proposed with the data discussed in

---

phase-edges (in this case, [Spec, Finiteness^{0}]), which act as escape-hatches for elements with unchecked features.

section §1 above. Recall that enclisis arises in Western Iberian when no preverbal element appears, as in (1)/(28).

(28) *Téoles* *tayaes* [*Les teo] Ast
have$_{1SG}$-them$_{CL}$ cut
'I have them (my hands) cut' [Álvarez, *Llames*]

The enclisis we find in (28) is analyzed as in (29). As argued in section §3, I assume that the verb in Western Iberian checks T^0's [EPP] when it moves to T^0.[13] Next, the clitic is merged in CliticP, followed by merge of Fin^0. Under the assumption that Fin^0 is a phase-head with an edge condition, I argue that the licensing requirements of Fin^0 trigger last-resort verb-movement of T^0 to Fin^0 picking up the clitic(s) in $Clitic^0$ on its way up.[14] The resulting structure, irrelevant details omitted, is shown in (29).[15]

13. In line with approaches to clitics as agreement-morphemes (cf. Franco 1997, 2000, Fernández-Soriano 1993, and references therein), I assume object-*pro* fills the object slot of the predicate *teo* "I have." As for subject-*pro*, I do not commit to whether it is necessary as argued in Alexiadou & Anagnostopoulou 1998, so I put it in parentheses here and subsequently.

14. A caveat is in order at this point. As the structures show, $Clitic^0$ is closer to Fin^0 than T^0, so an explanation as to why clitics fail to license Fin^0's edge-condition is required. Two reasons may prevent the clitic from moving to Fin^0 to license its edge-condition: Either clitics are defective elements of sorts (as argued in Fernández-Soriano 1993 and in Vulchanova 2011) which makes them unsuitable constituents to license (26), or as argued in Shlonsky (2011), clitics carry a criterial feature that is satisfied in $Clitic^0$ and are therefore subject to criterial freezing (cf. Rizzi 2006, 2007 and Rizzi & Shlonsky 2005 for criterial freezing effects). An anonymous reviewer points out that Fin^0 could bear a [-N] feature, triggering verb-movement to license it and accounting for the enclisis observed. However, that analysis would wrongly predict generalized verb-movement (i.e. enclisis) in cases of A′-movement, as in (33) below.

15. As João Costa (p.c.) pointed out to me, the difference between enclisis and proclisis in coordinated structures such as those in (ia) and (ib) respectively would also follow from the analysis proposed. Consider the following data:

(i) a. *Esti artículu, escribilu y reescribi*(lu) once vegaes*
this article wrote$_{1SG}$-it$_{CL}$ and re-wrote(it$_{CL}$) eleven times
'This article, I wrote and rewrote it eleven times'

b. *Esti artículu, nun lu escribí y (lu) reescribí once vegaes*
this article, not it$_{CL}$ wrote$_{1SG}$ and it$_{CL}$ re-wrote eleven times
'This article, I didn't write and rewrite it eleven times'

In short, when T^0 moves to $Clitic^0$, picking up the clitic(s) on its way to Fin^0, as I claim to be the case in (ia), the resulting T^0+$Clitic^0$ does not allow excorporation, rendering

(29)

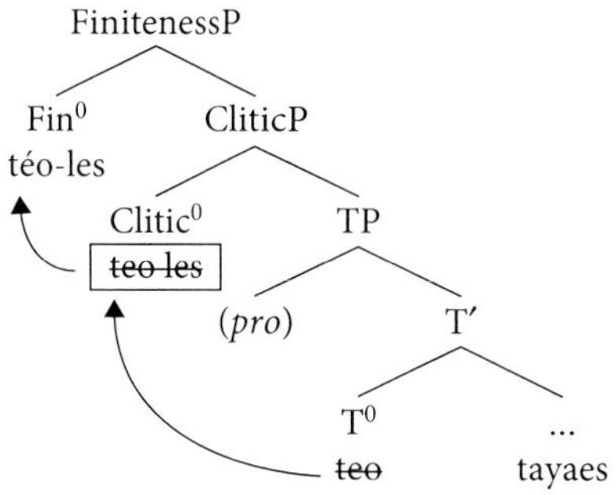

Another matrix environment that exhibits enclisis obligatorily in Western Iberian is with left-dislocated Topics and preverbal non-quantified subjects, as in (3)/(30) and (4)/(31).

(30) *Eso$_i$ sábes**lo**$_i$ per lleer les cartes* [*lo sabes] Ast
that know$_{2SG}$-it$_{CL}$ for read$_{INF}$ the cards
'That, you know it from reading the (tarot) cards' [González, *Comedies*]

(31) *El xenru matóse nun accidente*
the son-in-law killed$_{3SG}$-rfl$_{CL}$ in-an accident
na mina [***se** mató] Ast
in-the mine
'His son-in-law got killed in an accident in the mine' [González, *Comedies*]

Assuming in line with Barbosa (1995, 2000) and Raposo (2000), among others, that preverbal non-quantified subjects are Topic elements licensed in the left-periphery of the clause, the similar clitic pattern we find with Topics other than subjects is expected, and the enclisis in both (30) and (31) can be given a uniform explanation. I follow Barbosa and Raposo and argue that Topics are base-generated in a Topic position in the left-periphery.[16] Thus, since these preverbal elements do

---

the clitic invisible for future operations. This explains why the clitic must obligatorily be repeated in both conjuncts in (ia). On the other hand, as the verb has not incorporated on to the clitic in proclitic structures such as the one in (ib), the clitic may or may not be repeated in the second conjunct, ultimately depending on what the coordinated structure is, i.e. Clitic^0 or T^0.

16. I take *wh*-extraction in (i) below as evidence for the lack of A′-movement properties of the Topics in (30) and (31):

(i) a. *Eso, nun sé quién lo dixo*
that not know$_{1SG}$ who it$_{CL}$ said$_{3SG}$
'That, I don't know who said it"

not involve A′-movement, Fin^0 must satisfy its edge condition by attracting the closest available element in the structure, namely the verb in T^0. This results in the following derivation for (30).

(32)

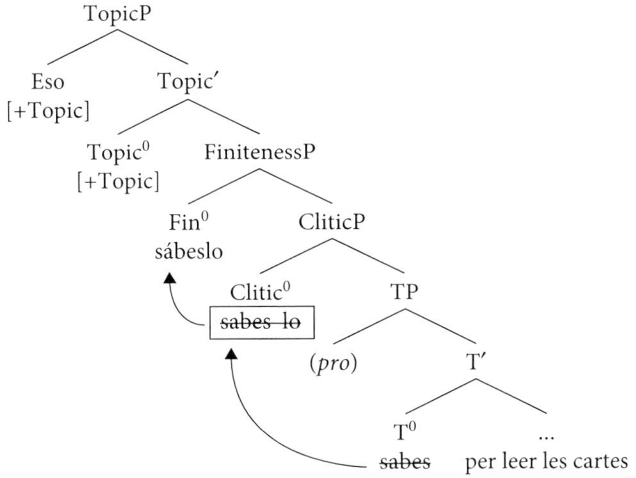

---

b. *El xenru, nun sé ónde se mató*
the son-in-law, not know$_{1SG}$ where rfl$_{CL}$ killed$_{3SG}$
'His son-in-law, I don't know where he got killed'

An anonymous reviewer points out that assuming topics are base generated is controversial, as they may show diagnostics of movement such as reconstruction effects. However, those reconstruction effects are not detected in Western Iberian (see Barbosa 1995 and Raposo 2000 for European Portuguese):

(i) a. *Toa madre$_i$ quier al su$_{i/j}$ fíu*
all mother love$_{3SG}$ to-the her son
"Every mother loves her son"

b. *Al su$_{*i/j}$ fíu, toa madre$_i$ lu quier*
to-the her son all mother him$_{CL}$ love$_{3SG}$
"Her son, every mother love him"

As the indices indicate, the possessive *su* "her" may be identified by the c-commanding antecedent *toa madre* "every mother" as in (ia), but not so in (ib), where the bound construal with *toa madre* "every mother" fails. If Topics were A′-moved elements and they reconstructed, we would expect the possessive to be optionally identified by "toa madre," which is not the case.

4.2 Proclisis and the edge-condition of Fin^0

Proclisis, on the other hand, is predicted to arise under the presence of A′-movement or a closer head to Fin^0 than T^0, as these elements would satisfy the edge condition of Fin^0 proposed in (26). Consider first the effect of a preverbal Focus in (6)/(33).

(33) *YO MESMA* ***me*** ***la*** *repito* *un*
I $self_{[FOC]}$ me_{CL} it_{CL} $repeat_{1SG}$ one
cientu *vegaes* [*repíto**mela**] Ast
hundred times
'I myself repeat it to myself one hundred times' [de Pablo, *Memoria*]

Being an instance of A′-movement, the focalized element in (33) must move to the left-periphery in order to check its criterial [+Focus] features (cf. Rizzi 2004), satisfying the edge condition of Fin^0 on its way to a criterial Focus position. The analysis proposed is shown below.[17]

(34)

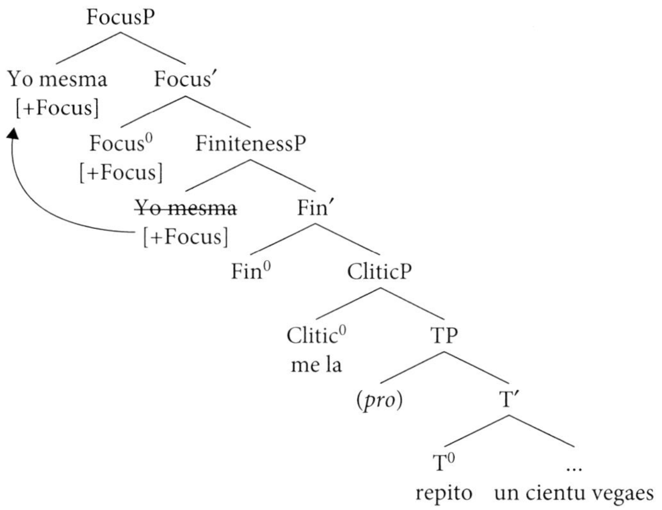

17. Whether each clitic projects its own CliticP, as in Sportiche (1996), or all the clitics in the structure are mapped onto the same CliticP projection has no bearing on the discussion and I will not delve into it. Regarding *yo mesma* "I myself," I assume it first merges in [Spec, *v**P] and raises to [Spec, FocusP] to license its [+Focus] criterial features, passing through the intermediate [Spec, FinP]. I take the *wh*-extraction test below to show that the *yo mesma* "I myself" instantiates A′-movement:

Similarly to Focus constituents, and under the assumption that both Focus and *wh*-constituents target [Spec, FocusP] as argued in Rizzi (1997, 2004), the proclisis we find in cases such as those in (5)/(35) can be explained similarly to those in (33)–(34): The preverbal *wh*-element moves to [Spec, FocusP], passing through [Spec, FinP], which licenses Fin^0's edge-condition and accounts for the proclisis that is observed.

(35) *Cómo* ***t'atreves?*** [*atréveste] Ast
how rfl$_{CL}$-dare$_{2SG}$
'How dare you?' [Rodríguez Medina, *Gaviotes*]

In turn, the proclisis we find after the negative marker in Western Iberian is also predicted by my analysis. Following Zanuttini's 1997 proposal for different Romance languages, I assume that the negative marker in Western Iberian is licensed in a NegP projection that takes T^0 as its complement. As it is closer to Fin^0 than T^0, it is the negative head sitting in Neg^0 that moves to Fin^0, licensing the proposed edge-condition of this phase head.[18] Thus, the proclisis we find in cases such as those in (2)/(36) is analyzed as shown in (37).

(36) *Nun* ***me*** *mancó* [*mancó-**me**] Ast
not me$_{CL}$ hurt$_{3SG}$
'S/he didn't hurt me' [Orton, *Mayordomu*]

(37)

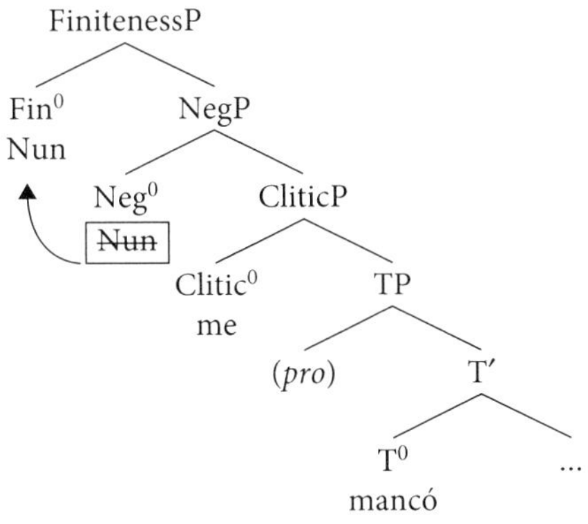

(i) **YO MESMA sabes qué me pregunto ~~YO MESMA~~ (, non Mon)*
I self$_{[FOCUS]}$ know$_{2SG}$ what rfl$_{CL}$ ask$_{1SG}$ not Mon
'I myself you know what I to myself ask (, not Mon)'

18. Any version of Minimality (cf. Chomsky 2000, 2001) or Attract Closest (cf. Chomsky 1995) would explain why Neg^0, and not T^0, must raise to Fin^0.

4.3 The edge-condition of Fin^0 and enclisis/proclisis alternations: A summary

Assuming Rizzi's (1997) Finiteness^0 is a phase-head (cf. Chomsky 2008) with an edge condition as proposed in (26), enclisis and proclisis alternations in matrix environments in Western Iberian can be explained as follows: In the absence of A′-movement or a closer head, T^0 moves to Fin^0 as a last resort, picking up the clitics on its way up and triggering enclisis. On the other hand, a closer head to Fin^0 than T^0 (as I argue to be the case with the negative marker) or an element undergoing A′-movement to the left-periphery of the clause licenses the edge condition of Fin^0 in (26) and explains the proclisis we find in these instances.

In what follows, I show how the analysis proposed to account for enclisis/proclisis alternations can also be extended to account for the different clitic patterns we find in the finite embedded context in Asturian, and the microparametric variation we find in Western Iberian in this context.

5. The edge-condition of Fin^0, the complementizer system and clitic placement alternations (or lack thereof) in the finite embedded context in Western Iberian

As already noted, Asturian differs from the other Western Iberian Romance languages in that enclisis is also attested in finite embedded contexts. The Topic/Focus articulation of the left-periphery in embedded contexts such as (7)/(38) triggers similar effects to those found in matrix environments: The Topic in (38a) gives rise to enclisis, whereas the Focus in (38b) gives rise to proclisis.

(38) a. *Repítote* [*que yo dexé**lo*** *aquel diecisiete*
repeat$_{1SG}$-you$_{CL}$ that I left$_{1SG\text{-}IND}$-it$_{CL}$ that seventeenth
de mayu] [***lo** dexé]
of May
'I repeat to you that I left it that May seventeenth' [de Pablo, *Memoria*]

b. *Repítote* [*que YO **lo** dexé aquel diecisiete*
repeat$_{1SG}$-you that I$_{[FOC]}$ it$_{CL}$ left$_{1SG\text{-}IND}$ that seventeenth
de mayu] (, non él) [*dexé**lo**]
of May
'I repeat to you that I (, and not him) left it that May seventeenth'

Further, in the absence of left-peripheral material, an embedded clause as in (8)/(39) shows that both enclisis and proclisis are grammatical.

(39) a. *Digo* [*qu'ayúdame*]
say$_{1SG}$ that-help$_{3SG\text{-}IND}$-me$_{CL}$
b. *Digo* [*que* ***me*** *ayuda*]
say$_{1SG}$ that me$_{CL}$ help$_{3SG\text{-}IND}$
'I say that s/he helps me out'

In this section, I first lay out the analysis of the complementizer system in Spanish proposed in Demonte and Fernández Soriano (2009), and I show how the analysis I propose can be extended to account for the clitic alternations we find in the finite embedded context in Asturian. Briefly put, I will show how Demonte and Fernández Soriano's (2009) proposal that the complementizer *que* "that" may be realized in Force^0 or in Finiteness^0 in the left-periphery of the clause can easily explain the Asturian data. Finally, I will show that the analysis laid out here may be also extended to account for the unavailability of enclisis in finite embedded contexts in Galician and European Portuguese, which I ultimately relate to the coexistence of a complementizer in Fin^0 even when there is one in Force^0.

5.1 Demonte and Fernández Soriano (2009): The *que1* "that1" and the *que2* "that2"

Demonte and Fernández Soriano (2009) argue that the complementizer *que* "that" can appear in different heads in the left-periphery in Spanish (Sp). Using evidence from what are standardly called recomplementation patterns, an example of which is shown in (40), these authors claim that in examples like (40) there is a *que1* "that1" in Force^0 and a *que2* "that2" in Fin^0. Thus, the embedded clause in (40) receives the analysis in (41).

(40) *Dijo* ***que*** *a ese empleado* ***que*** *no sabía cuánto*
said$_{3SG}$ that to that employee that not know$_{3SG}$ how-much
le pagaban Sp
him$_{CL}$ paid$_{3PL}$
'S/he said that s/he didn't know how much they paid that employee'

(41) [$_{ForceP}$ [*que1* Force^0 [$_{TopicP}$ a ese empleado$_{[+Topic]}$ [$_{Topic^0\,[+Topic]}$ [$_{FinP}$ [*que2* Fin^0 …]]]]]]

I extend Demonte and Fernández Soriano's (2009) analysis of Spanish to Asturian and I argue that this language also exhibits a *que1* in Force^0 and a *que2* in Fin^0, as in (42).

(42)

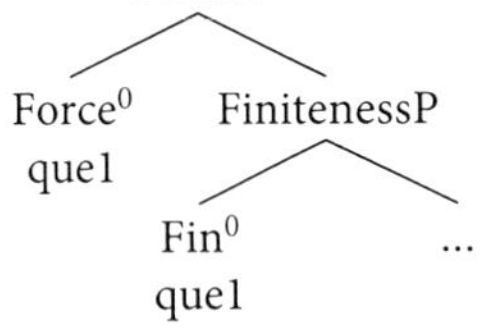

As I will show next, the position that the complementizer occupies and the edge-condition of Finiteness^0 explain the enclisis and proclisis alternations we find in the finite embedded context in Asturian.

5.2 Assertive predicates, selection, complementizers and enclisis/proclisis alternations in Asturian

In order to account for the enclisis/proclisis alternations that finite embedded contexts exhibit in Asturian, I claim that assertive predicates (cf. Hooper & Thompson 1973; Bosque 1990) may select one of two types of CP-complements, one headed by Force^0 or one headed by Finiteness^0. Consider now the data in (43).

(43) a. *Repítote* [*que yo* ***dexélo*** *aquel diecisiete*
repeat$_{1SG}$-you$_{CL}$ that I left$_{1SG\text{-}IND}$-it$_{CL}$ that seventeenth
de mayu] [***lo** dexé]
of May
'I repeat to you that I left it that May seventeenth' [de Pablo, *Memoria*]

b. *Repítote* [*que YO* ***lo*** *dexé aquel diecisiete*
repeat$_{1SG}$-you that I$_{[FOC]}$ it$_{CL}$ left$_{1SG\text{-}IND}$ that seventeenth
de mayu] (, non él) [*dexé**lo**]
of May
'I repeat to you that I (, and not him) left it that May seventeenth'

Repito "I repeat," an assertive predicate, may select a CP-complement headed by Force^0 or by Finiteness^0. For (43), I argue that Force^0, mapped as a *que1* "that1" complementizer, is selected in both cases, a selection which in turn is compatible with left-peripheral material, as hinted by the presence of a Topic and an element bearing Focus in the embedded clauses in (43a) and (43b) respectively. Assuming Topics are base-generated elements whereas Focus constituents are A′-moved, the proposed edge-condition of Fin^0 in (26) accounts for the observed clitic patterns in a similar way to those in matrix environments: Whereas T^0-to-Fin^0 movement is triggered in (43a) to license the proposed edge-condition as in (44a) and akin to the derivation for (30) and (31) in (32) above, Fin^0's edge-condition is licensed by the A′-moved Focus constituent in (43b), passing through [Spec, FinP] similarly to the derivation for (33) in (34) above, as in (44b).

(44) a. repítote +
repeat$_{1SG}$-you$_{CL}$

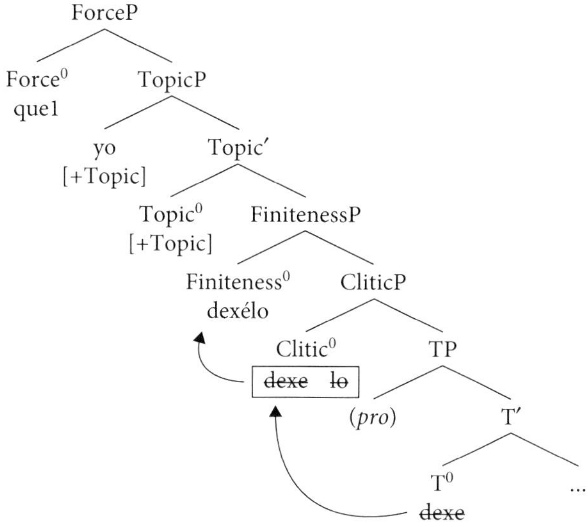

b. repítote +
repeat$_{1SG}$-you$_{CL}$

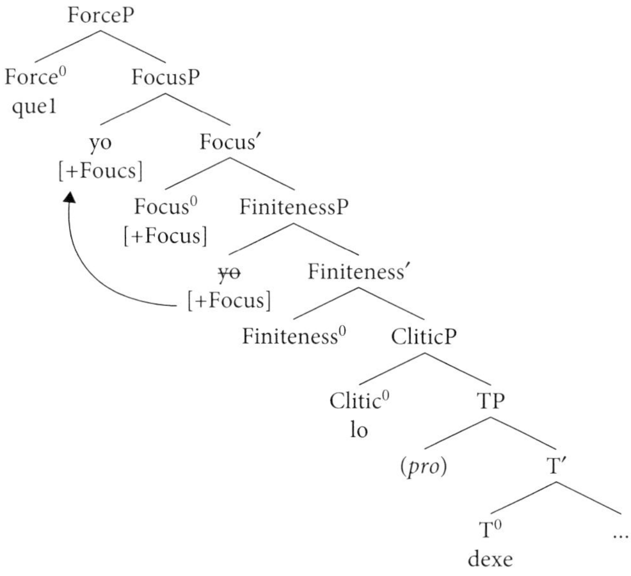

Turning now to embedded contexts with no overt left-peripheral material, as in (39)/(45), both enclisis and proclisis are grammatical in Asturian. The availability of both clitic patterns can also be explained by the analysis I entertain: *Digo* "I say" is an assertive predicate which may select two different types of CP-complements, either one headed by Force^0 or one headed by Finiteness^0. I argue that each clitic pattern correlates with a different selection pattern, with enclisis as in (45a) instantiating selection of Force^0 and *que1* "that1," and proclisis as in (45b) instantiating selection of Finiteness^0 and *que2* "that2." As shown in their respective derivations in (46), enclisis arises as a result of last-resort T^0-to-Fin^0 movement, whereas proclisis obtains by merger of the complementizer *que2* "that2" in Fin^0, licensing Fin^0's edge-condition.[19]

(45) a. *Digo* [*qu'ayúda**me***]
say$_{1SG}$ that-help$_{3SG\text{-}IND}$-me$_{CL}$
b. *Digo* [*que* ***me*** *ayuda*]
say$_{1SG}$ that me$_{CL}$ help$_{3SG\text{-}IND}$
'I say that s/he helps me out'

(46) a. digo +
say$_{1SG}$

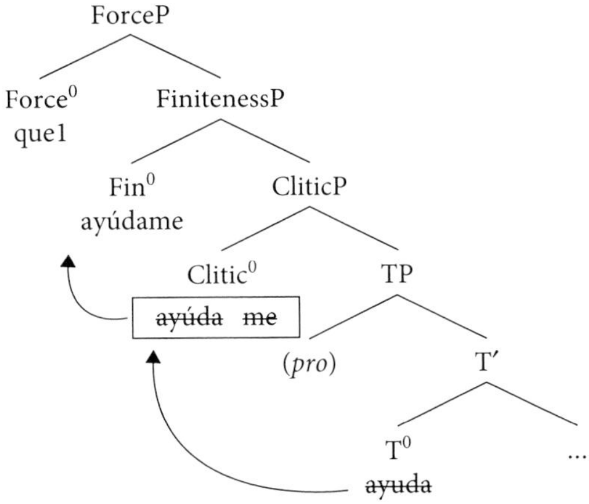

19. The data from Tarifit reported in Shlonsky (2005: 344, (35) and (36)) and attributed to Ouhalla (1989) may also be amenable to the same analysis I propose for Asturian:

(i) a. **Tnna* *qa-t* *yarzm* *sg* *tynjayt*
said$_{3SG}$ that it$_{CL}$ opened$_{3SG}$ with spoon
b. *Tnna* *qa* *yarzm* *-t* *sg* *tynjayt*
said$_{3SG}$ that opened$_{3SG}$ it$_{CL}$ with spoon
'She said that he opened it with a spoon'

b. digo +
say$_{1SG}$

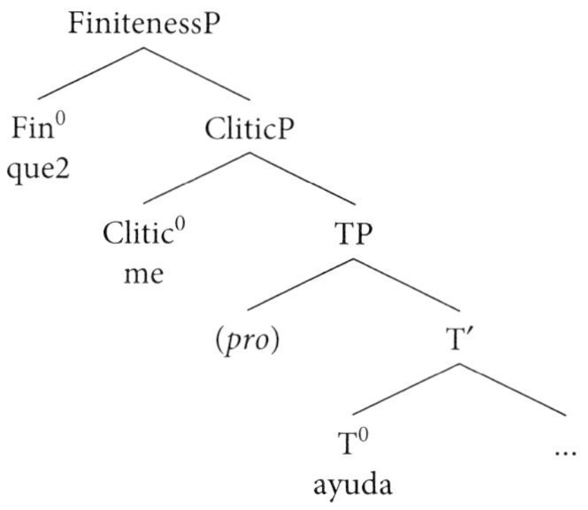

As I will show next, the microparametric variation that Western Iberian exhibits in the finite embedded context may also receive a uniform explanation under the analysis proposed here.

5.3 Microparametric variation in Western Iberian: The complementizer system of Galician and European Portuguese

Galician and European Portuguese differ from Asturian in that enclisis in the finite embedded context is either considered marginal or unacceptable, as shown in (9)/(47). As shown in (48), in the absence of left-peripheral material in the embedded clause, judgments are stronger and speakers of Galician and European Portuguese report the enclitic pattern to be unacceptable.

(47) a. *Xulia dixo [que Mon* ***o*** *dixera]* [??? dixera**o**] Gal
Xulia said$_{3SG}$ that Mon it$_{CL}$ had-said$_{3SG\text{-}IND}$
'Xulia said that Mon had said it'

b. *O Pedro disso [que o Paulo*
the Pedro said$_{3SG}$ that the Paulo
o *dissera]* [???/*dissera-**o**] EP
it$_{CL}$ had-said$_{3SG\text{-}IND}$
'Pedro said that Paulo had said it'

If *tnna* "said" selects *qa* "that," which sits in Force^0, and enclisis is triggered by an empty Fin^0, T^0-to-Fin^0 picking the clitics on its way up explains the clitic pattern in (ib). However, a full comparison between these languages falls beyond the scope of the present paper.

(48) a. *Xulia dixo [que o dixera]* [*/??? dixera**o**] Gal
Xulia said$_{3SG}$ that it$_{CL}$ had-said$_{3SG\text{-}IND}$
'Xulia said that s/he had said it'

b. *O Pedro disso [que o dissera]* [*/??? dissera-**o**] EP
the Pedro said$_{3SG}$ that it$_{CL}$ had-said$_{3SG\text{-}IND}$
'Pedro said that s/he had said it'

In order to account for the ungrammaticality of enclisis in the finite embedded context in Galician and European Portuguese, I would like to propose that the complementizer system in these two languages differs from that of Asturian as follows: Galician and European Portuguese license a complementizer in Fin^0, which may be null or overt, even when Force^0 is selected.[20] I contend that the presence of this (null or overt) complementizer in Fin^0 licenses the edge-condition I propose, blocks verb-movement and accounts for the exclusive proclisis that speakers of Galician and European Portuguese report. (47a) would then be analyzed as in (49).

(49)
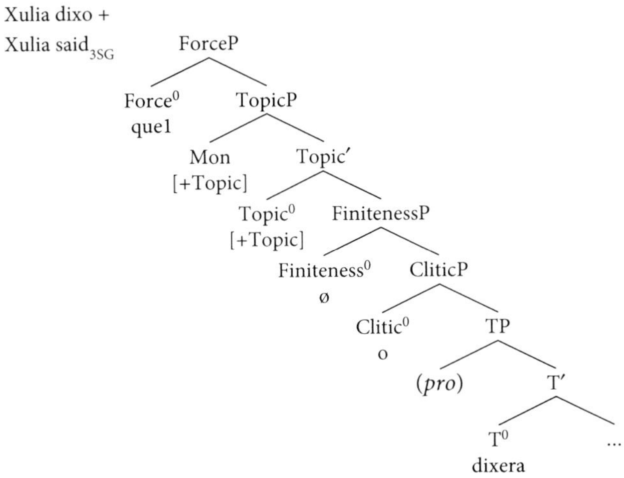

Further predictions and evidence for the analysis I propose are discussed next: The interpretation of enclisis/proclisis alternations in the finite embedded context in Asturian, and the effect of *wh*-extraction.

20. This analysis makes two correct predictions: First, Galician and European Portuguese would license recomplementation patterns (as in (40)), which the following datum from Barbosa (2000) confirms:

6. Further predictions and evidence

6.1 Force, Finiteness and [±conviction] pragmatic reading of the embedded clause

Enclisis/proclisis alternations in finite embedded contexts such as those in (45) above correlate with different interpretations (cf. Viejo 2008 and Fernández Rubiera 2009). Enclisis is reported to give rise to an interpretation that marks the content of the embedded clause as part of the belief state of the matrix predicate's subject or the speaker, what I call a [+conviction] pragmatic interpretation – see (50a). In turn, when the embedded clause shows proclisis, the fragment in brackets is not perceived as pragmatically odd, which I analyze as [-conviction] – see (50b).

(50) a. *Digo qu'ayúdame* [*#pero nun toi seguru*] Ast
say$_{1SG}$ that-help$_{3SG\text{-}IND}$-me$_{CL}$ but not am sure
'I say that s/he helps me, #but I am not sure (that s/he does help me)'

b. *Digo que me ayuda* [*pero nun toi seguru*]
say$_{1SG}$ that me$_{CL}$ help$_{3SG\text{-}IND}$ but not am sure
'I say that s/he helps me, but I am not sure (that s/he does help me)'

These interpretation differences follow naturally from the analysis I propose: selection of Force^0 yields a pragmatic [+conviction] reading, in turn associated with evidentiality as argued in Cinque (1999), whereas selection of a truncated structure (i.e. Fin^0) gives rise to a non-evidential [-conviction] interpretation.[21] In turn, both sentences in (43) are predicted to give rise to a [+conviction] reading of the embedded clause, which the infelicity of the fragment *pero nun toi seguru* "but I am not sure" following either of the sentences in (43) confirms.

(i) *Acho que$_1$ amanhã que$_2$ vai haver reunião*
think$_{1SG}$ that tomorrow that go$_{3SG}$ have$_{INF}$ meeting
"I think that tomorrow (that) there will be a meeting"

Second, Asturian would not license recomplementation, which the speakers I consulted confirm.

21. For the idea that a truncated structure of the left-periphery correlates with lack of evidentiality, see Speas (2008), among others.

6.2 Wh-extraction effects on clitic placement alternations

For a sentence like (51), speakers report that the embedded clause has a [+conviction] evidential reading. Further, they also report that the *wh*-element *ónde "where"* can only have a matrix construal (i.e. *where it was that Xulia said it*) and not an embedded one (i.e. **where it was that she had bought it*).

(51) *Ónde dixo Xulia que*
where said$_{3SG}$ Xulia that
compráralo? [*matrix* = ✓/*embedded* = *]
had-bought$_{3SG\text{-}IND}$-it$_{CL}$
'Where did Xulia say that she had bought it?'

On the analysis I propose, *dixo* selects Force^0 mapped to *que1* in this case, which accounts for the [+conviction] evidential interpretation. The enclitic pattern arises as a result of Fin^0's edge condition triggering last-resort T^0-to-Fin^0 movement in the absence of A′-movement passing through the embedded [Spec, FinP] or a closer head to Fin^0 than T^0. (51) is analyzed in (52).

(52)

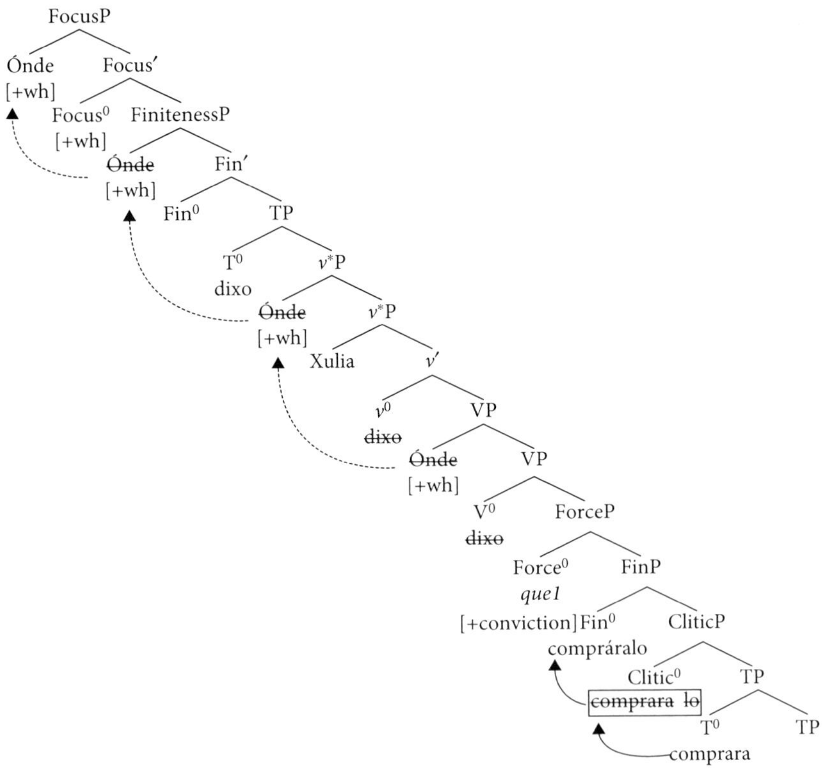

Consider now (53) and assume for the purposes of this discussion that *ónde* "where" launches from the embedded clause. Speakers report that the embedded clause is ambiguous: it may be interpreted as [+conviction] evidential or as [-conviction] non-evidential.

(53) *Ónde dixo Xulia que lo comprara?*
where $said_{3SG}$ Xulia that it_{CL} $had\text{-}bought_{3SG\text{-}IND}$
'Where did Xulia say that she had bought it?'

I argue that the *wh*-word *ónde* "where" passes through the intermediate [Spec, FinP] on its way to the left-periphery of the matrix clause, and that this step licenses (26) and explains why we find exclusively proclisis in (53). In turn, the ambiguity can be easily accounted for: the matrix predicate *dixo* "she said" may select $Force^0$ as in (54), giving rise to a [+conviction] evidential interpretation, or Fin^0 as in (55), predicting the non-evidential [-conviction].

(54)

(55)

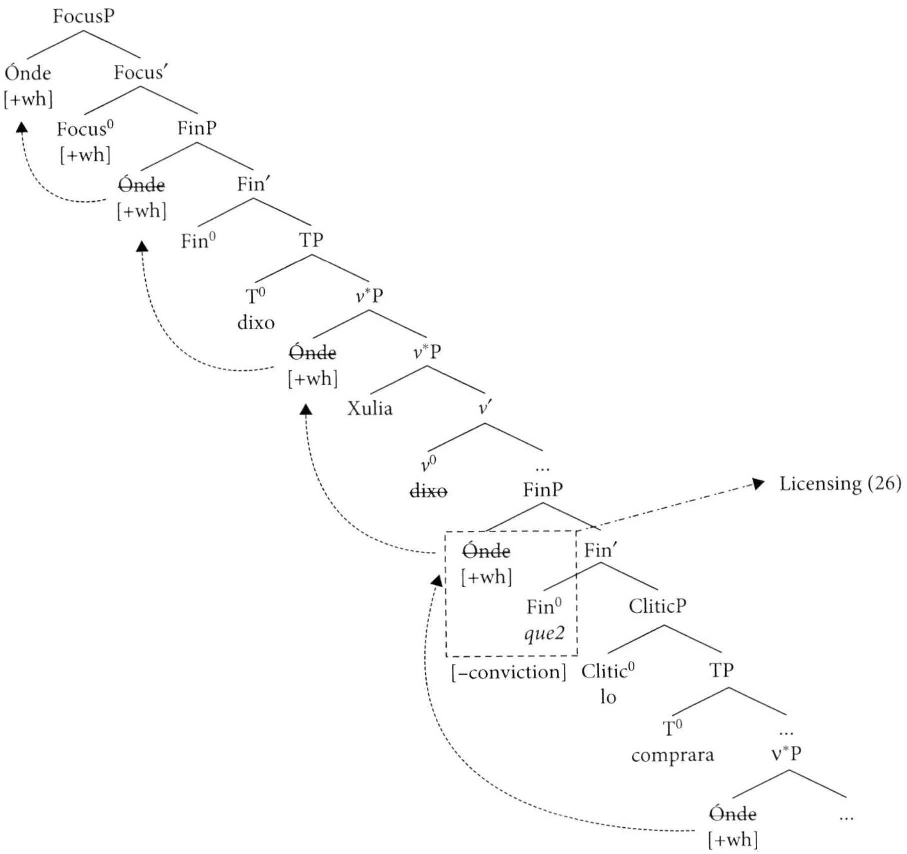

7. Summary and conclusions

In this article, I have argued for an analysis of enclisis/proclisis alternations in terms of Rizzi's Finiteness^0 being a phase-head with an edge condition. The different ways in which it may be licensed explain the different clitic patterns we find in Western Iberian Romance languages as follows. Enclisis obtains in the absence of A′-movement or a closer head to Fin^0 than T^0, which moves to Fin^0 picking up the clitics on its way up. An A′-moved element or a closer head to Fin^0 than T^0, as I claim to be the case of the negative marker, triggers exclusively proclisis.

This analysis has also been shown to account for the enclisis/proclisis alternations found in the finite embedded context in Asturian, as well as for the exclusively proclitic pattern that speakers of Galician and European Portuguese report: Differences in the complementizer system may be adduced to account for this microparametric variation. The analysis proposed also makes two right predictions: the different interpretations that enclisis and proclisis give rise to in the finite embedded context, and the effect of *wh*-extraction on clitic placement alternations.

Asturian corpus bibliography

Álvarez, Xurde. 2005. *Les llames del to llar antiguu*. Uviéu: Academia de la llingua asturiana.
González Álvarez, Arsenio. 1997. *Tres comedies*. Uviéu: Academia de la llingua asturiana.
Orton, Joe. 1995. *Lo que vio'l mayordomu*. Uviéu: Academia de la llingua asturiana (Translation by Lluis Aique Iglesias).
de Pablo, Eladio. 1996. *Memoria del llaberintu*. Uviéu: Academia de la llingua asturiana (Translated by Ramón d'Andrés Díaz).
Rodríguez Medina, Pablo. 2006. *Cantu de gaviotes*. Uviéu: Academia de la llingua asturiana.

References

Alexiadou, Artemis & Anagnostopoulou, Elena. 1998. Parametrizing Agr: Word order, V-movement and EPP-checking. *Natural Language and Linguistic Theory* 16(3): 491–539.
Álvarez, Rosario, Regueira, Xose Luis & Monteagudo, Henrique. 1986. *Gramática galega: Biblioteca básica da cultura galega*. Vigo: Galaxia.
Barbosa, Pilar. 1995. Null Subjects. Ph.D. dissertation, MIT.
Barbosa, Pilar. 2000. Clitics: A window into the null subject property. In *Portuguese Syntax: New Comparative Studies*, João Costa (ed.), 31–93. Oxford: OUP.
Bosque, Ignacio. 1990. Las bases gramaticales de la alternancia modal. Repaso y balance. In *Indicativo y subjuntivo*, Ignacio Bosque (ed.), 13–65. Madrid: Taurus.
Campos, Hector. 1989. Clitic position in modern Gallegan. *Lingua* 77: 13–36.
Chomsky, Noam. 1995. *The Minimalist Program*. Cambridge MA: The MIT Press.
Chomsky, Noam. 2000. Minimalist inquiries: The framework. In *Step by Step: Essays on Minimalist Syntax in Honor of Howard Lasnik*, Roger Martin, David Michaels & Juan Uriagereka (eds), 89–155. Cambridge MA: The MIT Press.
Chomsky, Noam. 2001. Derivation by phase. In *Ken Hale: A Life in Language*, M. Kenstowicz (ed.), 1–52. Cambridge MA: The MIT Press.
Chomsky, Noam. 2008. On phases. In *Foundational Issues in Linguistic Theory: Essays in Honor of Jean-Roger Vergnaud*, Robert Freidin, Carlos P. Otero & Maria L. Zubizarreta (eds), 133–167. Cambridge MA: The MIT Press.
Cinque, Giuglielmo. 1999. *Adverbs and Functional Heads: A Crosslinguistic Perspective*. Oxford: OUP.
Contreras, Heles. 1978. *El orden de las palabras en español*. Madrid: Ediciones Cátedra.
Contreras, Heles. 1991. On the position of subjects. In *Perspectives on Phrase Structure: Heads and Licensing*, Susan Rothstein (ed.), 63–79. New York NY: Academic Press.
Demonte, Violeta & Fernández Soriano, Olga. 2009. Force and finiteness in the Spanish complementizer system. *Probus* 21(1): 23–49.

Fernández Rubiera, Francisco J. 2009. Clitics at the Edge: Clitic Placement in Western Iberian Romance Languages. Ph.D. dissertation, Georgetown University.

Fernández Soriano, Olga (ed.). 1993. *Los pronombres átonos*. Madrid: Taurus.

Franco, Jon. 1994. On Object Agreement in Spanish. Ph.D. dissertation, University of Southern California.

Franco, Jon. 2000. Agreement as a continuum. In *Clitic Phenomena in European Languages*, Frits Beukema & Marcel den Dikken (eds), 147–189. Amsterdam: John Benjamins.

Hooper, Joan B. & Thompson, Sandra A. 1973. On the applicability of root transformations. *Linguistic Inquiry* 4: 465–497.

Martins, Ana M. 1994. Clíticos na História do Português. Ph.D. dissertation, Universidade de Lisboa.

Murphy-Armstrong, Kimberly. 1989. The Syntax of Spanish Clitics. Ph.D. dissertation, Georgetown University.

Olarrea, Antxón. 1997. Pre and Postverbal Subject Positions in Spanish: A Minimalist Account. Ph.D. dissertation, University of Washington.

Ordóñez, Francisco. 1998. Word Order and Clause Structure in Spanish and Other Romance Languages. Ph.D. Dissertation, City University of New York (CUNY). Published as Ordóñez (2000).

Ordóñez, Francisco. 2000. *The Clausal Structure of Spanish: A Comparative Study*. New York NY: Garland.

Ouhalla, Jamal. 1989. Clitic Movement and the ECP: Evidence from Berber and Romance Languages. *Lingua* 79: 165–215.

Raposo, Eduardo P. 2000. Clitic Positions and Verb Movement. In *Portuguese Syntax: New Comparative Studies*, João Costa (ed.), 266–298. Oxford: OUP.

Raposo, Eduardo P. & Uriagereka, Juan. 2005. Clitic Placement in Western Iberian: A Minimalist View. In *The Oxford Handbook of Comparative Syntax*, Guglielmo Cinque & Richard S. Kayne (eds), 639–697. Oxford: OUP.

Rivero, Maria L. 1986. Parameters in the typology of clitics in Romance and Old Spanish. *Language* 62(4): 774–807.

Rizzi, Luigi. 1997. The fine structure of the left periphery. In *Elements of Grammar: Handbook in Generative Syntax*, Liliane Haegeman (ed.), 281–337. Dordrecht: Kluwer.

Rizzi, Luigi. 2001. On the position "int(errogative)" in the left-periphery of the clause. In *Current Studies in Italian Syntax: Essays offered to Lorenzo Renzi*, Guglielmo Cinque & Giampaolo Salvi (eds), 287–296. Amsterdam: Elsevier.

Rizzi, Luigi. 2004. Locality and left periphery. In *Structures and Beyond: The Cartography of Syntactic Structures*, Adriana Beletti (ed.), 223–251. Oxford: OUP.

Rizzi, Luigi. 2006. On the form of chains: Criterial positions and ECP effects. In *Wh-movement: Moving on*, Lisa Lai-Shen Cheng & Norbert Corver (eds), 97–134. Cambridge MA: The MIT Press.

Rizzi, Luigi. 2007. On some properties of criterial freezing. In *CISCL Working Papers on Language and Cognition*, Vincenzo Moscati (ed.), Vol. 1, 145–158. Siena: Interdepartmental Centre for Cognitive Studies of Language.

Rizzi, Luigi & Shlonsky, Ur. 2005. Strategies of subject extraction. Ms. ⟨http://www.ciscl.unisi.it/doc/doc_pub/rizzi_shlonsky2005.pdf⟩

Shlonsky, Ur. 2004. Enclisis and proclisis. In *The Structure of CP and IP*, Luigi Rizzi (ed.), 329–353. Oxford: OUP.

Shlonsky, Ur. 2011. Feature incorporation and criterial freezing: Subject clitics in Northern Italian dialects and *wh* in situ in French. Keynote paper delivered at the Challenging Clitics workshop, University of Oslo.

Speas, Peggy. 2008. On the syntax and semantics of evidentials. *Language and Linguistics Compass* 2(5): 940–965.

Sportiche, Dominique. 1996. Clitic constructions. In *Phrase Structure and the Lexicon*, Johan Rooryck & Laurie Zaring (eds), 213–276. Dordrecht: Kluwer.

Uriagereka, Juan. 1995a. An F position in Western Romance. In *Discourse Configurational Languages*, Katalin É. Kiss (ed.), 153–176. Oxford: OUP.

Uriagereka, Juan. 1995b. Aspects of the syntax of clitic placement in Western Romance. *Linguistic Inquiry* 26(1): 79–123.

Viejo Fernández, Xulio. 2008. *Pensar asturiano. Ensayos programáticos de sintaxis asturiana.* Uviéu: Trabe.

Vulchanova, Mila. 2011. The evolution of the article in Old Bulgarian. Keynote paper delivered at the Challenging Clitics workshop, University of Oslo.

Zanuttini, Raffaella. 1997. *Negation and Clausal Structure: A Comparative Study of Romance Languages*. Oxford: OUP.

Handling Wolof clitics in LFG

Cheikh M. Bamba Dione
University of Bergen

Clitics often involve intricate interaction between different grammar components, including morphophonology, syntax and information structure. This phenomenon is challenging from a general theoretical perspective. In Wolof, clitization has been investigated using a transformational approach. In contrast, this paper proposes a formal analysis of Wolof clitics using a non-transformational model based on the Lexical Functional Grammar (LFG) theory. This approach needs no special rule for verb movements at all and preserves the *lexical integrity* of words. For sake of concreteness, the theoretical purpose is combined with an implementation that illustrates how the LFG formalism is well suited to a precise treatment of clitics.

1. Introduction[1]

Wolof clitics have previously been the topic of studies in the transformational-generative framework. There is much controversy in the theoretical linguistics literature as to whether clitichood and clitic placement are purely prosodic, are purely syntactic (Dunigan 1994) or result from interaction with the phenomenon of focus (Russell 2006). For Wolof, the most striking property of clitics is their typology and related special position, which raises empirical issues surrounding the clause structure of this language (see Section 4.3). In recent work, new proposals have been made to separate the syntactic and morphophonological properties of clitics. Among these new approaches, the most radically innovative is Zribi-Hertz and Diagne's (2002) work which proposes an analysis involving the syntax-phonology interface, while discarding an all-syntax analysis. The aforementioned transformational approaches to Wolof clitics, however, are limited in scope, since they supply analysis in terms of phrase structure configurations and movements, violating the Lexical Integrity Principle (Bresnan 2001). Furthermore, there has

1. I thank Koenraad De Smedt, Paul Meurer, Victoria Rosén and Helge Dyvik for valuable comments on different versions of this paper. Also, I thank the anonymous reviewers of the paper abstract for their constructive criticism.

been little attempt to integrate phonological information into syntactic analyses, although the interaction between phonology and syntax has clearly been attested in the analysis of clitic placement and most syntactically oriented frameworks acknowledge the importance of phonological information.

This paper outlines an analysis of Wolof clitics based on the LFG formalism (Kaplan & Bresnan 1982). This analysis incorporates recent findings on cliticization in Wolof and makes the right predictions about the distribution and placement of clitics in this language. Unlike almost all other accounts, the LFG-based analysis does not rely on the assumption of configurationality or movement. Furthermore, it preserves the Lexical Integrity Principle. It adopts an approach crucially separating functional representations from phrase structure configurations. More precisely, the interaction between phonology and other aspects of the grammar, including morphosyntax, information structure, and semantics is modeled using parallel but separate levels of linguistic representation. By separating structure from function and through the positing of productive processes in the lexicon, the LFG account is better able than structurally-based approaches to reflect the clitic patterns found in Wolof. In this paper, I argue that LFG's projection architecture provides an ideal platform for integrating phonological information into theoretical analyses, and present a concrete proposal[2] for such an integration, concentrating on Wolof. For the sake of concreteness, the syntactic aspects of this proposal have already been implemented by means of the notations and formal mechanisms that exist in the Xerox Linguistic Environment (XLE) tool (Crouch et al. 2012). A treebank-based LFG grammar (i.e. a parsed corpus) for Wolof has been created through a cooperation with the INESS project.[3] The treebank has been constructed using the LFG Parsebanker tool (Rosén et al. 2009) and is currently used for processing real corpus data.

The paper is structured as follows. Section 2 surveys those properties of Wolof clitics that are a challenge to grammatical analysis. Section 3 briefly introduces the LFG formalism on which the current proposal is based. The analysis of Wolof

2. However, it is necessary to mention that, in the current approach, prosodic information is mapped directly from syntax, and prosodic units are therefore assumed to be naturally aligned with syntactic constituents. This experimental work integrates phonological information with syntactic analysis of Wolof clitics and does not account for cases where syntax and prosody are misaligned, leaving this issue open for future research. It follows the standard architecture of LFG, which projects other levels of representation from the phrase structure. Under this view, syntax is primary and the phrase structure and functional structure are central to analyses in other projections.

3. http://iness.uib.no.

data and its implications for the proposed architecture for LFG are presented in Section 4. I conclude the discussion in Section 5.

2. Wolof personal and locative clitics

A defining characteristic of clitics is their prosodic deficiency in the sense that they often depend phonologically on an adjacent word, known as their host. A host may be located to their left (for enclitics) or to their right (for proclitics). In particular, a clitic should never be modified, stressed, or separated from its host, and clitic clusters should always have a fixed word order (Kayne 1975).

Clitic phenomena in Wolof, as in many other languages, crucially involve more than one type of linguistic information, as illustrated by the Wolof data in (1–2).[4]

(1) Wolof personal and locative clitics

a. Lexical simple clitics

nu lekk jën wi. — narrative clause

1PL eat fish DFSG.

'So, we ate the fish.'

b. Functional simple clitics

nu=a lekk jën wi. — [*nu=a>noo*]

1PL=COP.FOC.S eat fish DFSG.

'We ate the fish.'

c. Special clitics (phrasal affixes)

du =nu =fa fekk.

IPF.NEG.3SG =1PL =LOC join.

'He will not find us there.'

(2) Person-inflection markers (word-level affixes)

lekk na=nu jën wi.

eat +F=1PL fish DFSG.

'We have eaten the fish.'

4. In compliance with the Leipzig conventions for interlinear morpheme-by-morpheme glosses (http://www.eva.mpg.de/lingua/resources/glossing-rules.php), clitic boundaries, with exception of clitics located at the sentence beginning, are marked by an equals sign, both in Wolof and in the glosses. The following abbreviations will be used in the glosses: COP = copula; DF = definite; F = finite; FOC = focus; IPF = imperfective; LOC = locative; NEG = negation; NS = non-subject; PRES = present; PST = past tense; pl = plural; S = subj; sg = singular; STR = strong; V = verb; VF = verb form; WK = weak; 1, 2, 3 = first, second, third person.

The Wolof data in (1–2) involve interaction between different linguistic components, including most obviously syntax and prosody,[5] but also morphology and information structure. In (1a) the functional monosyllable *nu* is a clitic pronoun. It surfaces as a weakly stressed monosyllable,[6] although, according to Kayne's (1975) tests of clitichood, clitics can never be assigned independent stress. In fact, as Franks and King (2000, p. 6) pointed out, "a clitic can in principle bear stress if it happens to fall in an appropriate position in the stress domain to which it belongs". This is the case of the Wolof subject clitic which, like all functional monosyllables in this language, is inherently unstressed and usually encliticizes to the preceding full form in order to enter a phonologically well-formed word (Zribi-Hertz & Diagne 2002). However, if the clitic appears in domain-initial position, as in (1a), it will receive default stress due to Wolof's property as a straightforwardly initial-stress language (Ka 1988, 1994). Likewise, the same clitic form *nu* in (1b) has default initial stress. However, in contrast to (1a), it undergoes phonological coalescence with its rightward context (the focus-marking copula *a*), forming a subject agreement marker which bears a different function. In fact, the bi-morphemic word *nu-a*[7] bears a subject function and, additionally, expresses focus information. In (1c), the object and locative clitics *nu* and *fa* surface as phrasal affixes. These clitics form a cluster with a particular linearization which follows specific patterns partially imposed by the morphophonology.

Example (2) contrasts with the other examples in (1) in that *nu* has the properties of a word-level, inflectional affix (Zribi-Hertz & Diagne 2002) rather than a (morpho)syntactically independent clitic. It is bound to the functional morpheme *na*[8] and becomes morphologically part of the subject marker *na-nu*,

5. For a detailed discussion about the interaction between phonology and other aspects of the grammar, including syntax, information structure, and semantics, see e.g. Butt and King (1998).

6. The functional nominals of Wolof are typically classified into phonological paradigms: strong-stress and weak-stress forms (Zribi-Hertz & Diagne 2002). This study will only focus on weak-stress forms. The strong forms (i.e. Wolof independent pronouns) are not clitics in that they never behave as leaners. Instead, they are full-fledged or complete prosodic words which bear inherent, lexical stress. Furthermore, strong pronouns in Wolof, like those in French, are banned from structural-case positions. Hence, they do not occur as direct objects or complements of a verb inside of a verbal phrase (VP). They rather occur in positions otherwise open to a lexical determiner phrase (DP); e.g. object focus and P-governed positions, canonical oblique or topic positions in left-dislocated structures, etc.

7. Note that *nu-a* is not a proclitic (see Section 2.2).

8. Similar to Zribi-Hertz and Diagne (2002), I gloss the morpheme *na*, which typically occurs in independent affirmative or so-called neutral clauses, by '+finite'. Following Ka (1994), I

specifying its person and number features. This attachment is triggered by incorporation, a purely morphological operation (Zribi-Hertz & Diagne 2002) that highlights the existence of the widespread typological phenomenon called *pronoun incorporation* in Wolof. Bresnan (2001, p. 144) suggests that "*pronoun incorporation* or *pronominal inflection* can be analyzed in this way: an incorporated pronoun or pronominal inflection is a bound morpheme that specifies a complete pronominal f-structure. The functional specification of a pronoun is incorporated with the functional specifications of the stem to which the morpheme is bound". Such a morphological property of clitics is known across a wide range of languages. O'Connor (2002) analyses interesting behaviors of Serbian auxiliary and pronominal clitics, adopting Nordlinger's (1998) constructive morphology. The apparently complex distribution of Wolof data obviously presents a particular challenge for a general theory of pronominal clitics. The next sections survey the Wolof functional nominals relevant for this study (see Table 1), focusing on their phonological and syntactic idiosyncrasy.

Table 1. Wolof person and locative markers

	SUBJ pronouns	OBJ pronouns & locatives
1SG	ma	ma
2SG	nga	la
3SG	mu	ko
1PL	nu	nu
2PL	ngeen	leen
3PL	ñu	leen
LOC prep – prox/dist	–	ci/ca
LOC distance – prox/dist	–	fi/fa

2.1 Lexical simple clitics

The items in Table 1 are subject and object pronouns. Object pronouns are discussed in Section 2.3. Subject pronouns, e.g. *ñu* in (3b), have a syntactic distribution similar to their non-clitic counterparts, e.g. *xale yi* 'the children' in (3a).

---

also identify this affix as a neutral focus ('no-focus') marker. Additionally, it is assumed to introduce the perfective aspect, if and only if it does not attach to the auxiliary/imperfective marker *di* and to a stative main verb.

(3) a. *xale yi lekk jën wi.*
Child DF3PL eat fish DFSG.
'So, the children ate the fish.'

b. *ñu lekk jën wi.*
3PL eat fish DFSG.
'So, they ate the fish.'

Syntactically, Wolof subject pronouns exhibit a predictable distribution as they are specified for nominative case. Phonologically, they occur in sentence-initial position, bear default initial stress and remain unattached, as illustrated in (3b). Thus, subject pronouns, just like the proclitics in the languages with proclitic prepositions (King 2005), behave as simple clitics in the sense of Zwicky (1977).

2.2 Functional simple clitics

Subject agreement in Wolof varies according to different variables, including the clause type,[9] focus information and type of the focused constituent (Torrence 2003). Wolof morpho-syntactically distinguishes three kinds of focus (Robert 1991; Torrence 2005): subject focus, non-subject focus and verb/predicate focus, respectively exemplified by (4a), (4b) and (4c). Example (4d), in contrast, illustrates a neutral (i.e. non-focused) imperfective clause.

(4) Simple clitic (functional: INFL)
a. *ñu=a (> ñoo) lekk jën wi.* Subject focus
3PL=COP.FOC.S eat fish DFSG.
'THEY ate the fish.'

b. *Jën wi la=ñu lekk.* Non-subject focus
fish DFSG COP.FOC.NS=3PL eat.
'They ate the FISH.'

c. *da=ñu lekk jën wi.* Verb focus
COP.FOC.V=3PL eat fish DFSG.
'They ATE the fish.'

d. *di=na=ñu lekk jën wi.* Imperfective clause
IPF=+F=3PL eat fish DFSG.
'They will eat the fish.'

As shown in Examples (4a–4c), each focus clause is marked by means of a distinct copular morpheme. In the subject, object and verb focus constructions, the subject marker *ñu* morphologically attaches to the focus-marking copula *a*,

9. See Zribi-Hertz and Diagne (2002); Torrence (2005); Russell (2006) for more details about Wolof clauses.

la or *da*, respectively. Hence, it undergoes morphological attachment to its left or to its right, depending on the clause. However, according to Zribi-Hertz and Diagne (2002), right-attached subject markers (i.e. *ñu-a*) are not proclitics (Wolof is an initial-stress, all-enclitic language). In sentence-initial position, they bear default initial stress, and undergo phonological coalescence with their rightward context. This phonological operation does not specifically concern weak pronouns; it applies to lexical DPs as well. In contrast, left-attached subject markers (e.g. *la-ñu*) are unstressed. The subject markers in (4) express the person and number features required for subject-verb agreement.[10] These pronominal morphemes are amalgamated with a tense-aspect-mood or focus or polarity marker. All paradigms distinguish first, second, and third person plural and singular.

The clauses listed in (4) have the same person and number features (e.g. third person plural). In addition, in (4a) FOCUS is identified with the argument function SUBJ, while in (4b) and (4c) FOCUS is identified with OBJ and VERB, respectively. Neither the person/number nor the focus features come from the verb, rather from the words *ñu-a*, *la-ñu* and *da-ñu*. I assume that, like the finite auxiliary *di-na-ñu* in (4d), these Wolof simple clitics are functional and belong to the category usually called *I* (originally for *INFL*) which acts in the clause like a head. Whereas the functional position *I* proposed by Falk (1984) is filled by a finite main or auxiliary verb in different languages like English, German, Warlpiri, and Tagalog (Dalrymple 2001), each language defines the lexical categories which can fill this position. I argue that, in Wolof, the subject agreement markers appear in *I* in the same way the tensed auxiliary *di-na-ñu* in (4d) does.

2.3 Special clitics

Wolof object and locative clitics (OLCs)[11] show a very intricate distribution, with divergent requirements depending on the inflectional status of their host and on the clause type, as can be seen from (5).

(5) a. *xale yi lekk na=ñu* **=*ko*.** neutral clause
child the eat +F=3PL 3SG.
'The children ate it.'

b. *na* **=*ko*** *xale yi lekk !* optative clause
+F =3SG child DFPL eat
'(It is my wish that) the children eat it!'

10. Verbal agreement is for person and number of the subject.

11. The term OLCs is borrowed from Zribi-Hertz and Diagne (2002).

c. *xale yi lekk* =***ko***. narrative clause
child the eat =3SG.
'So, the children ate it.'

d. *ñu=a* =***ko*** *lekk (-oon).* subject focus clause
3PL=COP.FOC.S =3SG eat (-PST).
'THEY ate it.'

Example (5) illustrates the complex attachment of OLCs in different clauses. On the one hand, OLCs seem to be attracted by finiteness in neutral (5a) and in optative clauses (5b). This assumption, however, runs into empirical problems due to the contrast between (5c) and (5a). In the narrative construction in (5c), OLCs seem just as attracted by the noninflected verb as they are by the finite one in (5a). On the other hand, OLCs do not seem to be attracted by the inflected verb. As Example (5d) shows, they surface in special positions in (non-finite)[12] focused clauses like (5d), where they seem to be attracted by focus rather than by tense.

Furthermore, OLCs have a linear order which differs from the order of the phrases that realize the same grammatical functions. In imperfective or focused clauses, full noun phrase objects appear after the verb, while clitic object pronouns appear preverbally. In (4d) the nonpronominal object occurs after the finite auxiliary *dinañu* and the main verb *lekk* 'eat'. However, if the object is pronominalized, as in (6), then it occurs before the verb. Similar to Italian or French, in Wolof a few modal (e.g. *bëgg* 'want') and movement verbs behave like auxiliaries with respect to OLC placement.

(6) *xale yi di=na=ñu* =***ko*** *lekk.*
child the IPF=+F=3PL =3SG eat.
'The children will eat it.'

Wolof pronoun clitics behave in a similar manner to the Romance special clitics which exhibit the same subjacency effects, as illustrated by the following French examples from Butt et al. (1999, p. 81).

(7) a. *Il a vu la boîte.*
he has saw.Part.M the box.F
'He saw the box' (French)

12. Even though that might sound paradoxical, the presence of the past tense marker does not necessarily suggest that the verb is finite. The definition of finiteness may differ according to the clause type. The verb in subject and object focus clauses is considered to be poorly inflected or even "non-finite". This is because, unlike the verb in neutral VPs headed by *na*, V in focused VPs is only specified for aspect (±perfective), tense (±past) and polarity (±negation), but not person. For more detailed discussion of the verb-finiteness marking in Wolof see Zribi-Hertz and Diagne (2003).

b. *Il l' a vue.*
he it.Clitic has saw.Part.F
'He saw it.' (French)

This has been analyzed in other theories as an instance of apparent movement (Kayne 1975). Similarly, the special position of the accusative pronoun in (4d), contrasting with the accusative DP in (6), is what led Dunigan (1994) to propose the syntactic rule of Clitic Movement in Wolof. In fact, though, no special analysis is required for Wolof, and no "movement" need be assumed (see Section 4).

In addition to their special verb adjacent position, OLCs have a set order amongst themselves. That is, they may appear in clusters of multiple clitics with different functions, which must appear in a particular order, as illustrated in (8).

(8) a. *xale yi lekk na=ñu* ***=ko =fa****.*
child the eat +F=3PL 3SG =LOC.
'The children ate it there.'

b. *xale yi di=na=ñu* ***=ko =fa*** *lekk.*
child the IPF=+F=3PL =3SG =LOC eat.
'The children will eat it there.'

c. *xale yi *di=na=ñu* ***=fa =ko*** *lekk.*
d. *xale yi *di=na=ñu lekk* ***=ko =fa****.*

Example (8b) gives evidence for the clitic climbing phenomenon attested in Wolof (Ngom 2003; Voisin-Nouguier 2006). In fact, the clitics *ko* and *fa* appear preverbally, in the domain of the auxiliary, even though they are actually arguments of the verb *lekk* 'eat'. This contrasts with the post-verbal position these clitics typically occupy in the usual verb-complement construction shown in (5a). Clitic climbing is not possible in the standard verb-object construction, and, as such, a special morphosyntactic analysis must be posited.

OLCs also have special prosodic properties. As shown in (9), their linearization within the clusters follows specific patterns based on person and vowel length (Zribi-Hertz & Diagne 2002, p. 873).

(9) Linear ordering within Wolof OLC clusters
a. 1st person > 2nd person > 3rd person > Locative
b. long vowel > short vowel

The restriction (9a) is exemplified by (8) and (10a) from Zribi-Hertz and Diagne (2002, p. 873), while the restriction (9b) is depicted in (10b) and (10c).

(10) a. *xale yi wan =na =ñu [=ma =la]/ *[=la =ma].*
child DFPL show +F 3PL =1SG =2SG =2SG =1SG.
lit. The children have shown me you.
= (i) have shown me to you, or
= (ii) have shown you to me

b. *xale yi di=na=ñu [=*ko* =*leen*] wan.

c. *xale yi di=na=ñu [=leen =ko] wan.*
child DFPL IPF=+F=3PL =3PL =3SG show.
lit. The children will show them {him/her/it}.
= (i) will show them to {him/her}, or
= (ii) will show {her/him/it} to them.

In a Wolof double-object-construction, the object argument linked to the semantic role goal/recipient/beneficiary always precedes the second object linked to the theme (Becher 2005). Given that fact, the conclusion from (10a) is that this restriction does not hold in clitic clusters. The second person *la* must be linearized after the first person *ma*, regardless of the semantic role borne by each clitic. In contrast, the (un)grammaticality of (10b) and (10c) which contain both a third person object, results from the restriction in (9b). The prosodic domain is also relevant for the linearization of OLCs. In (11) and (12), the position of the clitics depends on whether the clause has a nominal or a pronominal as subject.

(11) a. *Bi* ***=ko =fa xale yi*** *lekk-ee.*
When =3SG =LOC child the eat-+F.
'When the children ate it there.'

b. *Bi *xale yi -ko fa lekk-ee.*

(12) a. *Bi* ***=ñu =ko =fa*** *lekk-ee.*
When =3PL =3SG =LOC eat-+F.
'When they ate it there.'

b. *Bi *-ko -fa =ñu lekk-ee.*

Finally, a particular challenge to the analysis of Wolof OLCs is the specific property of their syntactic target. Unlike the object clitics of French analyzed by Miller and Sag (1997), "Wolof OLCs do not necessarily spell out a syntactic feature of their syntactic target" (Zribi-Hertz & Diagne 2002). Thus, the OLCs of (11a) do not spell out features of *bi*; their syntactic target is left unrestricted as to both category (it is functional in, e.g. (8b): *di-na-ñu+ko*, and lexical in (5c): *lekk+ko*) and syntactic position (it may fill V, I, I_{foc}, or C).

Following Zribi-Hertz and Diagne's (2002) assumption, I identify OLCs as *special clitics* (Zwicky 1977). Their restricted behavior is captured via LFG's multiple projection architecture, including a syntax-phonology interface. Before going into details of the architecture and actual implementation, let us briefly introduce the LFG formalism on which the current proposal is based.

3. LFG theoretical assumption

Dalrymple (2001, p. 1) provided a general definition of LFG, as given in (13):

(13) Lexical Functional Grammar (LFG) is a nontransformational theory of linguistic structure which assumes that language is best described and modeled by parallel structures representing different facets of linguistic organization and information, related to one another by means of functional constraints.

As its name implies, LFG differs from the transformational approach in two important dimensions. First, LFG is a *lexical* theory and not transformational, meaning that words and the lexicon play a major role. One example that illustrates that words are an important focus of LFG is that the theory does not allow syntax to manipulate or to have access to the internal structure of words (i.e. syntax cannot see this internal structure). A manipulation in this context refers to a set of several operations, including movement, deletion or addition of word-internal material. The application of one of these operations is considered to be a violation of word integrity. In order to prevent such a violation, the LFG theory adopts the *Lexical Integrity Principle* (Bresnan 2001, p. 92) of words, as stated in (14).

(14) Lexical Integrity:
Morphologically complete words are leaves of the c-structure tree and each leaf corresponds to one and only one c-structure node.

The *Lexical Integrity Principle* constitutes the substance of the concept that word structure is different from phrase and sentence structure (Bresnan & Mchombo 1995). This concept is assumed to be universal in the sense that all languages distinguish between words and phrases. Another example illustrating the relevance of the lexicon is that LFG encodes the different relationships between the action (or state) that the verb expresses and the participants identified by its arguments (e.g. SUBJ and OBJ) in the lexicon rather than by means of syntactic transformations.

The LFG and transformational approaches differ in a second dimension. LFG supplies analysis in *functional* terms (Dalrymple 2001; Bresnan 2001) rather than in terms of phrase structure configurations and movements. What this suggests is best illustrated using an example. In (2) the word *na-nu* carries more than one feature: it is both a finiteness/perfective and a subject person marker. Such a phenomenon may be difficult to account for in a transformational model, where a one-to-one relation between form and content is preferred. In contrast, LFG's approach to morphology does not assume a one-to-one relation between form and function. In this model, the structure of syntactic constituents called constituent structure (c-structure) is separate from the functional information referred to as functional structure (f-structure). Accordingly, in the LFG syntactic tree, a word is always represented as one node, and the constituent morphemes of a word directly contribute to the representation of the meaning of the sentence without having to be assigned unmotivated syntactic structure. Thus, LFG deals with words like *na-nu* by having two functional features in the f-structure displayed by one morpheme in the c-structure. The mapping between the f- and the c- structures allows this.

The LFG formalism is well suited to analyze clitic phenomena in Wolof for several reasons. First, LFG provides a projection architecture that assumes parallel structures of the grammar. It views language as being made up of multiple dimensions of structure, as shown in Figure 1. Each of these dimensions is represented as a distinct structure with its own rules, concepts and form.

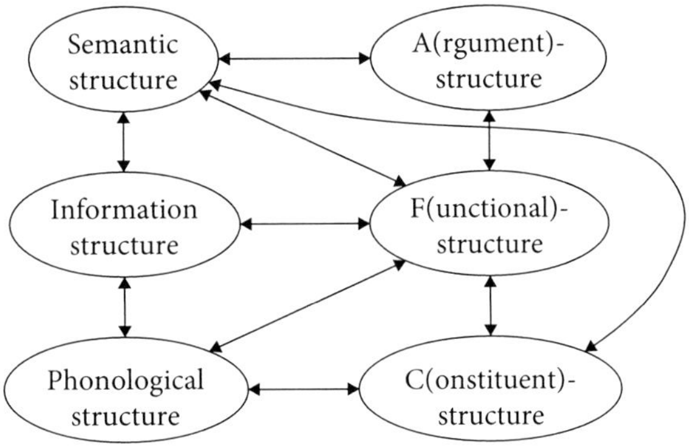

Figure 1. LFG projection architecture (Falk 2001, p. 25)

LFG's projection architecture includes all the components that are needed to account for clitic treatment. It gives access to each type of the information carried by clitics, including access from each type to the others. In addition, the interactions between the different architecture components are formally so well defined, that it is possible to predict the clitic phenomena in this language concretely. Another relevant aspect of the LFG formalism is that these components are independently proposed. Hence, as will be shown in the next section, the analysis of clitics may also reveal the nature of the interactions between the different projections.

4. An LFG approach to Wolof clitics

This section proposes a formal LFG model to analyze the Wolof data. First, Section 4.1 introduces the architecture of grammar relevant for this paper. Then, Section 4.2 illustrates how the Wolof clitics are annotated in the lexicon using the LFG notations and formal mechanisms. Next, Section 4.3 presents the c-structure proposed for Wolof and its interaction with the other linguistic projections. Finally, Section 4.4 discusses the linearization and placement of the special clitics.

4.1 Architecture

The architecture proposed in this work models the interaction between morphosyntax, prosody and information structure. In order to integrate the morphophonological representations into LFG, two structures are used in addition to the traditional c- and f-structure.

First, a p(honological)-structure is proposed to account for a prosodic analysis of the Wolof clitics. The p-structure builds on Butt and King (1998), who implemented the interaction between Bengali clitics and prosody as analyzed via a p(rosodic)-projection. This p-projection follows the standard LFG architecture in that it is projected from the c-structure in parallel to the f-structure. The prosodic analysis encodes the relevant phonological representations organized as a *Prosodic Hierarchy* (Selkirk 1984). Selkirk's hierarchy contains the types of prosodic units into which an utterance is divided, including intonational phrase (*INTONATIONAL-PHRASE*), phonological phrase (*P-PHRASE*), prosodic word (*P-WORD*), foot, syllable and mora. However, following Butt and King (1998), the prosodic hierarchy proposed for this work only includes intonational phrases, phonological phrases and prosodic words, since these interact most clearly with the syntax. The p-structure consists of DOMAINs which correspond to the prosodic hierarchy. It assumes that: (i) clauses form intonational-phrases, (ii) noun phrases form their own phonological-phrase, (iii) and main verbs always phrase separately (i.e. they do not form a phonological phrase with the object or subject).

Second, a m(orphosyntactic)-structure is proposed. The m-structure is a hierarchical projection from the c-structure (Butt et al. 1999). It is used to encode morphosyntactic wellformedness conditions, such as the inflectional features that the special clitics may require on their host. Hence, the m-structure is proposed to separate the projections of the auxiliary and the main verb. As Butt et al. (1999) pointed out, under the flat-structure approach, there is no place in the f-structure in which to state the hierarchically organized wellformedness restrictions. This is because all of the information contributed by the auxiliary is mapped to the same level of the f-structure, i.e. to the f-structure of the main verb. In order to solve this problem, each of the constituents (the auxiliary and the main verb) is assigned its own m-structure. The inflectional features of the m-structure primarily involve finiteness, verb form and, if required, aspect.

Formally, the proposed projections work similarly to the usual projection from c-structure to f-structure. They are realized in terms of annotations on c-structure rules, and as information in lexical entries. Using the regular notation by which ↓ is the node in question and ↑ its mother, and "x" indicates the name of the projection, the linguistic information provided by each projection can be expressed as usual. So the notation $\downarrow_p$ refers to the p-structure of the current node. This is similar to the functional notation of ↓ which is an abbreviation for $\downarrow_f$. The notation $\uparrow_p$ refers to the mother node, again in parallel to the functional notation ↑. Unless otherwise specified, the f- and p-structures corresponding to a node are assumed by default to be the same as the structures corresponding to its mother.

Much of the recent work on discourse functions within LFG has proposed an independent component for representing the information structure of a sentence instead of analyzing it within the f-structure (Butt & King 1996). In this paper, however, I follow the standard assumption of LFG in which syntacticized discourses roles like TOPIC and FOCUS, the so-called grammaticalised discourse functions (Bresnan & Mchombo 1987), are placed in the f-structure alongside grammatical functions such as subject and object. Accordingly, the information-structural functions[13] are represented by associating the value of FOCUS with different syntactic functions and in compliance with the *extended coherence condition* (Bresnan & Mchombo 1987, p. 746), as stated in (15).

(15) Extended Coherence Condition:
FOCUS and TOPIC must be linked to the semantic predicate argument structure of the sentence in which they occur, either by functionally or by anaphorically binding an argument.

The proposed architecture is a mutually constraining model, which is in accordance with both the general principles of LFG and the view of the syntax-phonology interface. That is, there are principles governing not only the wellformedness of the morphosyntax and phonology structure, but also of the possible mappings between them. As such, a p-structure, f-structure, c-structure and m-structure may all be well-formed independently but not be a possible representation of any given sentence. The next sections show the LFG-based analysis of Wolof clitics using these different projections.

4.2 Lexicon

The Wolof data presented so far have been analyzed in four different ways, as described in the following sections.

13. For an alternative approach to Wolof representing the discourse functions in information structure, see Dione (2012).

4.2.1 *Annotation of the simple clitics as pronouns*

Weak-stressed subject pronouns are treated as standard pronouns with nominative case specification and restricted to the [spec, IP] position. Hence, subject pronouns are lexically assigned the category *PRON* and associated with the information exemplified by (16).

(16) *ñu* PRON * (↑PRED)='pro' (↑CASE)=nom
(↑ NUM)=PL (↑ PERS)=3
(↑ PRON-TYPE)=pers (↑ NTYPE NSYN)= pronoun.

The lexical entry in (16) provides information about the f-structure corresponding to standard pronouns. It asserts that the f-structure ↑ corresponding to the PRON node immediately dominating *ñu* has an attribute PRED whose value is the semantic form 'pro'. Likewise, the f-structure has an attribute CASE whose value is nominative. Furthermore, the annotation in (16) specifies the type of nouns, which is also valid for pronouns.[14] The phonological features related to the subject pronouns are not directly encoded in the lexical entry since this association can only be done once the prosodic phrasing (and therefore also the syntactic analysis) has taken place. Thus, the entry is left without default phonological information which varies depending on the c-structure position of the pronoun.

4.2.2 *Subject agreement markers*

Subject agreement markers are treated as a functional category INFL or I (Falk 1984) which is the head of a finite clause. These functional clitics are assumed to contribute to the agreement and focus features of the subject, as shown in (17).

(17) Subject agreement markers with focus
ñu-a I * {(↑ SUBJ PRED)='pro'} (↑ SUBJ NUM)=PL
(↑ SUBJ PERS)=3 (↑ FOCUS)=(↑ SUBJ)
(↑ FOCUS-TYPE)=contrastive ($\uparrow_p$ P-FORM)=ñoo
($\uparrow_p$ DOM)=P-WORD ($\uparrow_p$ LEX-STRESS) = WK.

Example (17) illustrates the f-description of the lexical entries *ñu-a* which marks subject focus. The focus marker carries the information indicating its mother (i.e. *I*). It optionally contributes an f-description constraining the value of the PRED

14. In compliance with the Parallel Grammar (ParGram) convention (Butt et al., 1999), the Wolof subject pronouns are lexically specified with both attributes: an NTYPE and a PRON-TYPE. In this convention, the NTYPE can be syntactic (NSYN) or semantic (NSEM). Hence, the entry in (16) identifies the basic syntactic type of the noun as pronoun, specifically as a personal pronoun.

attribute of the subject.[15] Similar to the verbs in Chicheŵa (Bresnan & Mchombo 1987) which optionally carry information about their subject, Wolof functional clitics provide f-structure information. The equation {(↑ SUBJ PRED)='pro'} in (17) indicates that a Wolof functional clitic may, but need not, contribute to the minimal solution to the f-description for the sentence. If an overt subject noun phrase does not contribute its own PRED value, the f-structure for this sentence is incomplete unless this equation is satisfied. If an overt subject noun phrase appears, the equation may not be satisfied, since the PRED value of the overt subject would produce a clash; instead, the PRED value for the SUBJ is the one specified by the subject noun phrase. In addition, each functional clitic provides information about the person and number of the mother's subject.

Furthermore, the entry (17) contains focus information, encoded as *FOCUS-TYPE*, which has been lexically contributed by the focus clitic *a*. This specification is consonant with the *extended coherence condition*: the focus clitic *ñu-a* simultaneously bears the grammatical functions FOCUS and SUBJ. At the p-structure, the right-attached subject agreement marker is assumed to occur domain-initially, and therefore receives default stress as encoded in the entry.

4.2.3 *Special clitics*

Wolof OLCs have been assigned the lexical category clitic (*Cl*).

(18) Object and locative clitics ($Cl_{obj/loc}$)

ko	Cl_{obj}	*	{(↑ PRED)='moom'}	(↑ CASE)=acc
			(↑ NUM)=SG	(↑ PERS)=3
			(↑ NTYPE NSYN)=pronoun	(↑ PRON-TYPE)=pers
			($\uparrow_p$ CL-FORM)=ko	($\uparrow_p$ VL) = SV
			((CL $\uparrow_p$) DOM)=c P-WORD.	
fa	Cl_{loc}	*	(↑ PRED)='fa'	(↑ CASE)=LOC
			(↑ DEIXIS)=distal	(↑ PRON-TYPE)=locative
			((CL $\uparrow_p$) DOM)=c P-WORD	($\uparrow_p$ CL-FORM)=fa.

The clitics are encoded as either argument (e.g. object) or non-argument (adjunct) of the verb. Like standard subject pronouns, the object clitic *ko* provides information about person and number as well as about noun and pronoun type (i.e. NTYPE

15. Note that unlike subject agreement markers and other clitics, this optional equation does not hold for subject pronouns. A subject pronoun and a full noun phrase subject exclude each other.

and PRON-TYPE).[16] Note that, unlike subject pronouns, the PRED provided by object clitics is optional because the language uses the same form for resumption. Furthermore, object pronouns like *ko* are assumed to have PRED semantic forms different from those introduced by pro-drop constraints such as (↑PRED)='PRO'. In the XLE definition, the latter forms will not have a head. Accordingly, *ko* is assumed to have the same PRED as the corresponding independent pronoun (e.g. *moom* 'he'). This semantic form is particularly relevant for the linearization of OLCs (see Section 4.4), which involves head precedence relations.

Crucial to this analysis, special clitics are not encoded as independent p-words in the p-structure. They are instead taken to attach to a p-word and to be integrated into that p-word, as illustrated by the equation $((CL\ \uparrow_p)\ DOM)=c\ P\text{-}WORD$. Formally, the prosodic domain in which a clitic must find its host can be defined by means of expressions involving inside-out functional uncertainty[17] (Falk 2001; Dalrymple 2001). This equation allows reference to enclosing structures, i.e. those in which a particular functional structure (e.g. a p-structure) is contained. In the case at hand, inside-out functional uncertainty is used to define the prosodic domain relative to a clitic, the p-structure domain within which the clitic is required to find its host. Each special clitic is assumed to project its own prosodic sub-structure (denoted as *CL*) that is contained in the p-structure of its host. Since more than one clitic can be attached to a word, these embedded structures are provided with an index (e.g. *CL1* and *CL2*) that refers to the linear ordering of the clitics at the c-structure. Such information is particularly relevant for modeling the f- and p-structure correspondences. For instance, in double-object constructions, *CL1* and *CL2* will be assumed to map into the direct object (OBJ) or thematically unrestricted objects (i.e. secondary objects OBJ2, here referred to as OBJ-TH, which is more generic and more LFG compliant).

In addition, the prosodic structure projected by the special clitics bears two kinds of information: (i) the CL(itic)-FORM in which the clitic appears and (ii) the vowel length (VL) borne by this clitic. The latter attribute can have two possible values: *SV* for short vowels and *LV* for long vowels. Locative clitics do not provide information about the vowel length since this is not relevant for their linearization.

16. The lexical information also specifies the grammatical case for both clitic types. Note that the deixis value is lexically encoded in the locative clitics; this is a property of Wolof that distinguishes between proximal and distal reference.

17. Here a special clitic may refer to the *CL1* structure; in other examples, it might refer to the *CL2* structure. This functional uncertainty about the prosodic structure the clitic is referring to can be defined as a special abbreviatory symbol *CL* representing a disjunction of these potential prosodic structures, i.e. {CL1|CL2}.

4.2.4 *Person inflection markers*

Finally, person inflection markers are treated as inflectional affixes whose attachment is triggered by incorporation. So the inflectional person marker *ñu* is analyzed as a morphological affix which is functionally encoded within the functional specification of the perfective neutral and finiteness marker *na* to which it is bound. Note that this approach is equally applicable to the treatment of inflectional morphology in standard LFG (Bresnan 2001, p. 57), as exemplified by (19).

(19) Subject agreement as word-level affixes

na	Affix	*	~(↑ FOCUS)
			(↑ TNS-ASP ASP)=perf
			($\uparrow_m$ FIN)=+.
-ñu	INFL$_V$	*	(↑ SUBJ)=↓
			(↑ PERS)=3
			(↑ NUM)=PL.

The lexical specification (19) indicates that the person inflection marker *-ñu* carries the information about the person and number values of the mother's subject. The morpheme *na*, on the other hand, contributes to different features related to different projections: (i) at information structure level, it carries the information specifying that its mother's f-description is neutral, thus disallowing the focus on constituents (subject, object, etc.); (ii) at the functional level, *na* overtly expresses the perfective aspect of the main clause (e.g. this ensures that a unification with the imperfective aspect features borne by the auxiliary would fail); (iii) at the morphological level, it specifies a positive value of finiteness. The morpheme *na-* and its inflectional part together are treated as a subject clitic Cl_{subj}. These clitic types are the subject markers only found in neutral clauses like (5a). As illustrated in (20), the word *na-ñu* forms a unit (composed of different affixes) at the c-structure level, but introduces a complex functional structure that in other languages might be associated with a phrase rather than a single word.

(20)

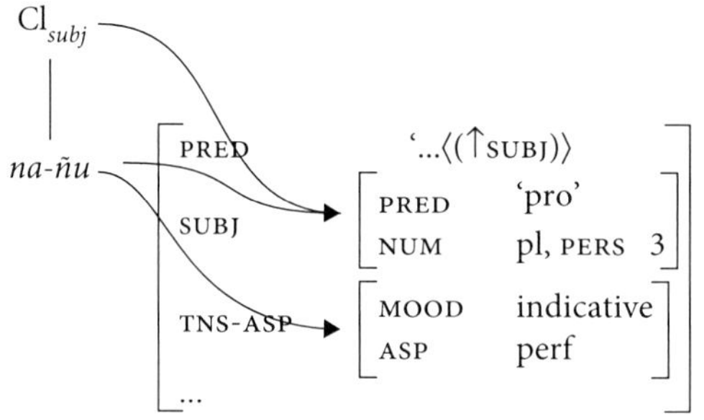

4.3 Wolof constituent structure within the LFG framework

An empirical issue related to the controversial distribution and placement of Wolof clitics is the clausal organization. This has been investigated in the transformational-generative framework (Dunigan 1994; Torrence 2003; Russell 2006). Dunigan (1994) postulates the existence of a sigma projection ΣP where focus markers (but also conditional, imperative and negative markers) may be generated. She suggests that all of these elements constitute a single syntactic category called *sigma* Σ with a maximal projection ΣP distinct from CP and TP. She assumes this distinction is obligatory since overt complementizers may take embedded *sigma phrase* complements. In such a case the ΣP is sandwiched between CP and TP.

For Torrence (2003), Wolof clauses are organized along imperfective-perfective asymmetries. These asymmetries involve subject agreement, negation and tense, which are generated in Agr^0, Neg^0, and T^0 respectively. Perfective and imperfective clauses structures should be derived from two different kinds of movement: head movement and *VP remnant* movement. Hence, the ordering of these elements in imperfective clauses is due to a head movement of V^0, while this ordering in perfective clauses gives rise to *VP remnant* movement.[18] Furthermore, Torrence (2003) assumes that the object clitic is a syntactic head of a clitic phrase *CliticP* located higher than the agreement phrase AgrP. He argues that this clitic always occupies the same position in some constructions, e.g. in neutral clauses.

Following Rizzi (1997) and the assumption that topics and foci are distinct in Wolof, Russell (2006, p. 126) postulates a CP layer with the following structure: topics occupy TopicP, with TopicP preceding FocusP. She argues that there are two domains at work in the positioning of the lexical subject: the CP and TP domain. Accordingly, all lexical subjects that appear at the left edge of the clause are topicalized elements and are generated in [spec, TopicP]. Focus markers appear in $Focus^0$, and focused XPs in [spec, FocusP]. On the other hand, lexical subjects which do not appear at the left edge of the clause occupy the [spec, TP] position.

This section presents the proposed LFG-based analysis of the Wolof constituent structure in a non-transformational model that needs no special rule for verb movements. It includes a typical analysis of 'head movement' phenomena within a framework that does not involve movement at all, but rather lexical specification of a functional category such as I^0 for a verb. This approach, additionally, preserves the word structure.

18. Torrence defines a *VP remnant* as a VP that contains the verb and the trace of the subject and dependents of V.

As pointed out in Bresnan (2001), the c-structure categories of languages may have an endocentric or exocentric organization. Endocentric organization is found in languages with highly hierarchical c-structures where the grammatical functions are encoded by syntactic means, e.g. word order. In contrast, in exocentric organization the grammatical functions cannot be retrieved through the hierarchy but rather are given by morphological means. The first organization gives rise to configurational languages like English, the second to non-configurational ones, including Warlpiri, Jiwarli, Hungarian, and Wambaya (Bresnan 2001).

I argue that Wolof exhibits a mixture of both types of structure. On the one hand, a Wolof sentence itself can be identified with IP, possibly dominated by CP (for a sentence with a complementizer or a displaced phrase in sentence-initial position). I argue that this (non)focused sentence IP(foc) is the projection of I^0 capturing the generalization that the Wolof finite auxiliary or inflectional markers occupy a unique position in the sentence.

On the other hand, Wolof has a c-structure organization in which grammatical functions are related with features borne by words. This is evidenced, for instance, by the typology of non-subject focused clauses (see 4b). Unlike the canonical clause types, in non-subject focus clauses information about grammatical functions must be localized by means of agreement morphology. I assume for Wolof a nonprojective exocentric category S (Bresnan 2001) which lacks a categorial head and has an f-structure head of a different category (here I assume VP). S may be dominated by I′ or I'_{foc}, depending on whether the clause contains a focused constituent or not.

The two basic Wolof c-structures IP and IP_{foc}[19] can be represented in abstract form as trees given in (21a) and (21b).

(21)

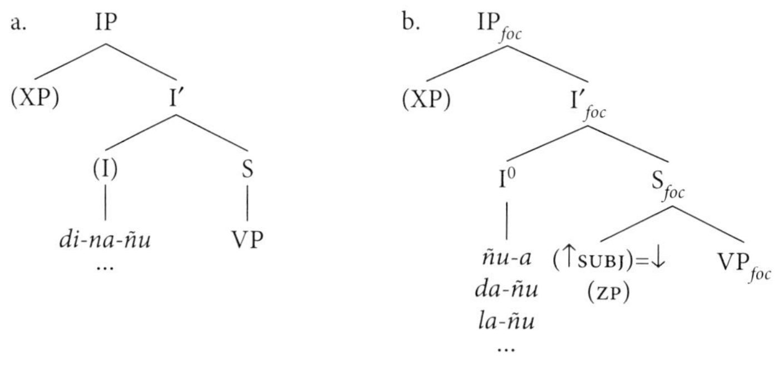

19. Note that IP_{foc} is singled out as a formal category for purely parsing efficiency reasons. From a theoretical point of view, focus (*foc*) is a functional feature and could equally well have been handled in the f-structure.

The Wolof I′ or I'_{foc} consists of an I, in which a subject agreement marker or the finite auxiliary appears, and an S(foc) complement. A phrasal constituent of any category (XP) appears as the specifier of IP and IP_{foc}. The specifier of IP in (21a) is optional. It may but need not be filled by a subject phrase.[20] Wolof subject pronouns are analyzed as occupying this position, as shown in (22).[21]

(22) *ñu lekk.*
3PL eat
'So they ate.'

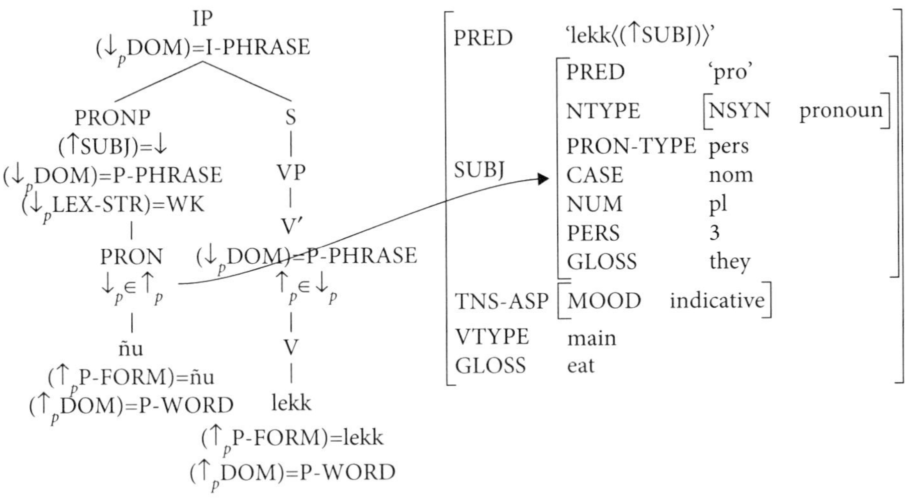

Example (23) shows the prosodic analysis proposed for the sentence in (22). Following Butt and King (1998), the prosodic phrasing is represented as an attribute-value matrix (AVM). The AVM primarily contains attributes such as P(honological)-FORM and DOMAIN (prosodic) which relate to prosodic

20. The categorial head of IP is not realized when the verb embedded under S functions as an f-structure head like in neutral, negative, narrative clauses etc. In such cases, the *I′* projection is also no longer required and should be omitted following the principle of *economy of expression* (Bresnan, 2001, p. 90). However, some representations shown in this paper may depart from the theoretical point of view of LFG in the sense that they are motivated by the XLE platform which does not implement this principle.

21. Unless otherwise specified and as is conventional for LFG, the f-structures corresponding to a daughter node are assumed by default to be the same as the structures corresponding to its mother. Due to the lack of space, only some prosodic information relevant for the analysis of the clitics is represented on the tree.

structure. It additionally includes, where required, other information such as predictable word stress or embedded prosodic structures contributed by the clitics. Phonological information irrelevant for Wolof (e.g. TONE) or unrelated to other parts of the grammar is not included. So, the AVM in (23) encodes information known about the phonology of the sentence in (22) which is projected from the related tree structure in (22). The p-structure is particularly characterized by a weak lexical stress on the first p-word, i.e. the simple clitic *ñu*, which bears an independent prosodic domain.

(23) P-structure associated with Example (22)

```
[DOM  INTENTIONAL-PHRASE
      { [DOM  P-PHRASE
             {[DOM  P-WORD, P-FORM  ñu, LEX-STR  WK]} ]
        [DOM  P-PHRASE
             {[DOM  P-WORD, P-FORM  lekk]} ] } ]
```

Now let us consider the clausal organization of focused clauses, as in (24).

(24) *xale* *yi* *ñu=a* *lekk.*
child the 3PL=COP.FOC.S eat
'The CHILDREN ate.'

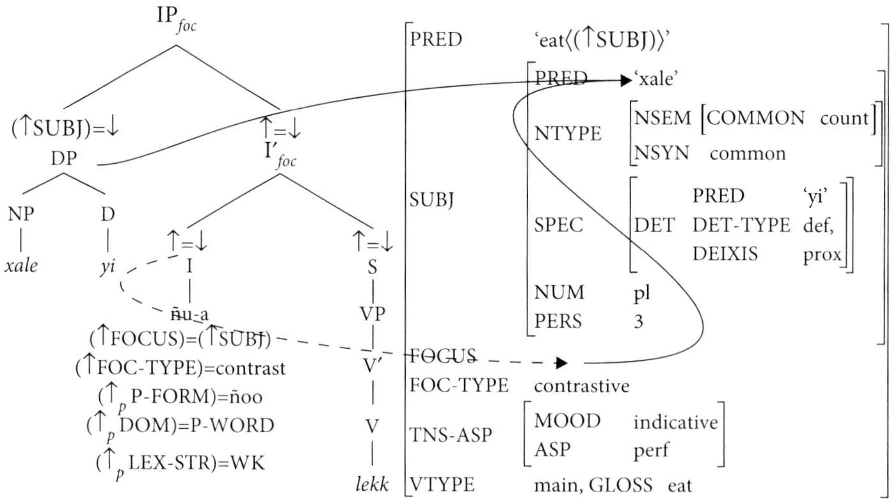

Similar to IP, the specifier of IP_{foc} is optional. However, the structure of the focused phrase IP_{foc} in (21b) differs from IP on two major points. First, the specifier of IP_{foc} is not necessarily a subject position. It may be filled by phrases mapped to other grammatical functions, depending on the structure of the clause. Second, the head of IP_{foc} needs to be realized. I assume that Wolof focus clitics function as the categorial head of the clause and appear in this position, with the verb in the V position under VP. As the c-structure/f-structure correspondence in (24) shows, the f-structure of the subject marker *ñoo* is unified with the f-structure of the DP (i.e. the lexical subject "*xale yi*"). This unification illustrates that this analysis is consonant with the *extended coherence condition*: the marker simultaneously fills the subject and focus function.[22] The p-structure associated with Example (24) is given in (25). It shows that simple weak pronouns and functional heads are analyzed in a very similar way.

(25) P-structure associated with Example (24)

$$\left[\begin{array}{ll} \text{DOM} & \text{INTENTIONAL-PHRASE} \\ & \left\{\begin{array}{l} \left[\begin{array}{ll} \text{DOM} & \text{P-PHRASE} \\ & \left\{\left[\text{DOM P-WORD, P-FORM xale}\right]\right\} \end{array}\right] \\ \left\{\begin{array}{l} \left[\begin{array}{ll} \text{DOM} & \text{P-PHRASE} \\ & \left\{\left[\text{DOM P-WORD, P-FORM ñoo, LEX-STR WK}\right]\right\} \end{array}\right] \\ \left[\begin{array}{ll} \text{DOM} & \text{P-PHRASE} \\ & \left\{\left[\text{DOM P-WORD, P-FORM lekk}\right]\right\} \end{array}\right] \end{array}\right\} \end{array}\right\} \end{array}\right]$$

4.4 Linearization and placement of the special clitics

As mentioned in Section 2.3, the placement of special clitics is a particularly challenging problem for designing the Wolof c-structure. First, let us consider the perfective neutral clauses as in (26).

(26) *lekk na=ñu =ko =fa.*
eat +F=3PL =3SG =LOC.
'They ate it there.'

22. The discourse information contributed by the functional element *ñoo* is indicated by dashed lines.

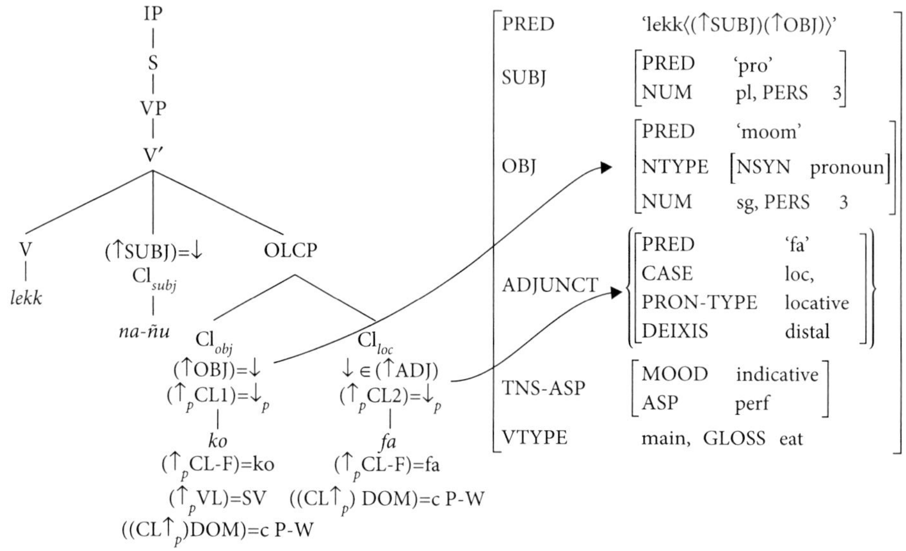

As can be seen, the lexical verb targeted by OLCs is inflected for finiteness and person. The subject marker *na-ñu* found in neutral clauses and the special clitics are structurally represented as a word group. This group is headed by the lexical verb V which projects its properties to the constituent V′. In turn, V′ immediately dominates the subject marker (here treated as clitic subject Cl_{subj}) and the cluster formed by the special clitics identified as an object and locative clitic phrase (OLCP). Example (26) shows how the clusters formed by the subject, object and locative clitics and the linearization of these elements within the clusters are captured at the constituent structure level.[23]

The linearization of OLCs within the cluster is handled at the phonology-syntax interface. It is syntactically captured in terms of linear precedence and head precedence, as defined in XLE (Crouch et al. 2012). First, the linear precedence principle is used to enforce the order in which the object pronouns and locatives appear. Formally, the constraint $Cl_{obj} < Cl_{loc}$ imposes a linear order on the

23. Note that the tree structure given in (26) does not constitute a violation of the X-bar syntax in LFG, since "LFG's theory of c-structure does not posit any principle that dictates that multiply branching structures are disallowed" (Asudeh and Toivonen, 2009, p. 434). Thus, all relevant clitics (clusters) are allowed to be sisters of the lexical verb. Note also that in the proposed analysis, a lexical DP within the VP does not function as the complement of V′, but rather as its sister. In addition, this tree illustrates the optionality of the specifier and the categorial head of IP.

locative clitics that must follow the object pronouns. This constraint is satisfied by any string in which there is no substring satisfying Cl_{obj} in front of a substring satisfying Cl_{loc}. Then, the ordering of the object pronouns in double-object-constructions has been defined in terms of constraints on the person features contributed by each clitic. For this, the notion of head precedence was used. This models the scoping order of the object clitics which map into OBJ and OBJ-TH. By specifying the person constraints on the object functions as e.g. "(↑OBJ PERS)$=_c$ 2 (↑OBJ-TH PERS)$=_c$ 3", precedence relations on the object f-structures are added (in XLE notation: "(↑OBJ) <h (↑OBJ-TH)"), which follow the surface (head-precedence) order.

However, if both object arguments are third person, then the phonological constraints apply. The latter have also been defined in terms of head precedence. This precedence relation, however, refers to the p-structure projected by the clitics, e.g. ($\uparrow_p$ CL1). Using the mathematical symbol ↦ 'maps into', the relation between the object functions and the corresponding p-structures projected by the clitics can be characterized via the following mapping: OBJ ↦ CL1; OBJ-TH ↦ CL2. Accordingly, the head precedence between the object pronouns is checked against the vowel length borne by each clitic at the p-structure. For instance, the following constraining equation *($\uparrow_p$ CL1 VL)$=_c$ LV* checks if the argument linked to OBJ (and, therefore, to CL1) has the vowel length feature required to fill the first position in the cluster. In this case, it will be linearized before the argument linked to CL2 that has a shorter vowel length.[24]

(27) a. P-structure of Example (26)

$$\begin{bmatrix} \text{DOM} & \text{INTENTIONAL-PHRASE} \\ & \left\{ \begin{bmatrix} \text{DOM} & \text{P-PHRASE} \\ & \left\{ \begin{bmatrix} \text{DOM} & \text{P-WORD} \\ \text{P-FORM} & \text{lekk-na-ñu} \\ \text{CL1} & \begin{bmatrix} \text{CL-FORM} & \text{ko} \\ \text{VL} & \text{SV} \end{bmatrix} \\ \text{CL2} & \begin{bmatrix} \text{CL-FORM} & \text{fa} \end{bmatrix} \end{bmatrix} \right\} \end{bmatrix} \right\} \end{bmatrix}$$

24. Note that grammatical function assignment depending on the person and vowel length features leads to structurally ambiguous constructions, as illustrated by the English translations in (10).

b. m-structure of Example (26)

$$\begin{bmatrix} \text{DEP} & \begin{bmatrix} \text{FIN} & +\text{, VFORM} \quad \text{base} \\ \text{ASP} & \text{perf} \end{bmatrix} \\ \text{DOM} & \text{INFL} \end{bmatrix}$$

The f-structure in (26) illustrates the contribution of the special clitics at the functional level, while Examples (27a) and (27b) show the p-structure and m-structure associated with *V*. At the p-structure level, the finiteness marker *na* encliticizes to the adjacent inflected verb, and incorporates the person feature contributed by *ñu*, resulting in the prosodic word *lekk-na-ñu*. The subject marker followed by OLCs attach to the inflected verb, whose relevant inflectional features are shown in (27b). Crucially, the object and locative clitics are not encoded as independent prosodic words in the p-structure. Relying on the fact that the special clitics must have a host, a restriction is imposed on the verb via the constraint ((CL $\uparrow_p$) DOM)=c P-WORD. The constraint registers the presence of the clitic so that the host is tested for that feature and, in the event of a successful test, assigns the prosodic structure provided by the clitics.

Next consider the imperfective neutral clause in (10c) represented in (28a). Compared to (26), the special clitics have a different position which results from their attachment to the auxiliary as a functional category. This contrasts with the attachment to the lexical category, i.e. the main verb, given in (26).

(28) a.

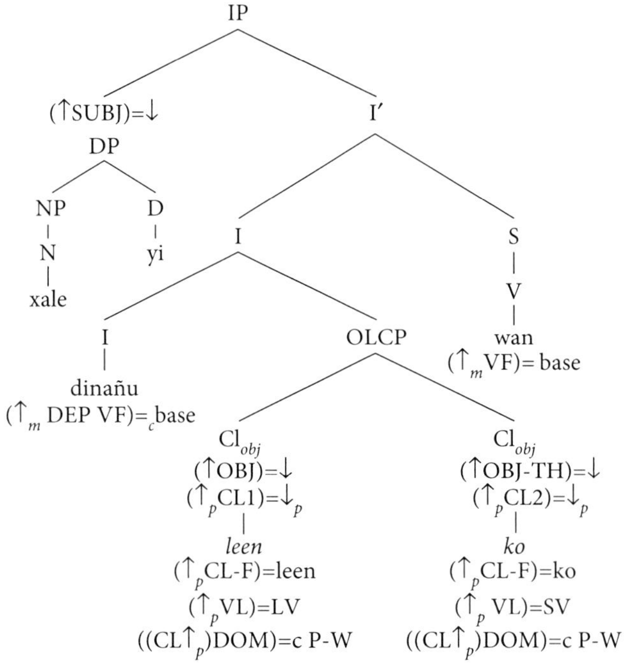

b. m-structure associated with (28a)

$$\begin{bmatrix} \text{DEP} & \begin{bmatrix}\text{VFORM} & \text{base}\end{bmatrix} \\ \text{FIN} & + \\ \text{ASP} & \text{ipf} \\ \text{DOM} & \text{INFL} \end{bmatrix}$$

The m-structure assigned to the auxiliary in (28a) is given in (28b). It allows for the specification of constraints on the relationship between the auxiliary and its dependent (DEP), i.e. the main verb. For instance, the auxiliary always requires DEP to have the feature base verbal form (i.e. it requires a non-inflected verb). Recall from Example (5c) that special clitics may have a post-verbal position, even if the verb is not inflected. Hence, in order to rule out Example (8d), the following morpho-syntactic constraint is needed: the clitics cannot appear in a post-verbal position if the mother structure containing DEP has been inflected for aspect. In neutral constructions, it is not possible for the clause to fill aspect features from the clitic subject *na-ñu* and the auxiliary: this would cause the head function to be associated with an f-structure with two different aspect values. However, by stating that "in a given f-structure a particular attribute may have at most one value" (Kaplan & Bresnan 1982, p. 9), *LFG's Uniqueness Principle* (Kaplan & Bresnan 1982) would rule out this ill-formed possibility.

Example (10c) will have the p-structure in (29). As can be seen, the main predicate of the clause and the auxiliary phrase separately. In addition, the prosodic phrase of the auxiliary contains the forms associated with the object and locative clitics, specifying the fact that these clitics are hosted by AUX rather than by V.

(29) P-structure of Example (10c)

$$\begin{bmatrix} \text{DOM} & \text{INTENTIONAL-PHRASE} \\ & \left\{ \begin{bmatrix} \text{DOM} & \text{P-PHRASE} \\ & \left\{ \begin{bmatrix} \text{DOM} & \text{P-WORD, P-FORM} & \text{xale} \end{bmatrix} \right\} \end{bmatrix} \right\} \\ & \left\{ \begin{bmatrix} \text{DOM} & \text{P-PHRASE} \\ & \left\{ \begin{bmatrix} \text{DOM} & \text{P-WORD, P-FORM} & \text{dinañu} \\ \text{CL1} & \begin{bmatrix} \text{CL-FORM} & \text{leen} \\ \text{VL} & \text{LV} \end{bmatrix} \\ \text{CL2} & \begin{bmatrix} \text{CL-FORM} & \text{ko} \\ \text{VL} & \text{SV} \end{bmatrix} \end{bmatrix} \right\} \end{bmatrix} \\ \begin{bmatrix} \text{DOM} & \text{P-PHRASE} \\ & \left\{ \begin{bmatrix} \text{DOM} & \text{P-WORD, P-FORM} & \text{wan} \end{bmatrix} \right\} \end{bmatrix} \right\} \end{bmatrix}$$

The tree in (30) represents the c-structure proposed for Example (12a). It shows the crucial fact that OLCs may attach to constituents higher than VP, S and IP. The additional structures for Example (12a) are not presented due to lack of space.

(30)

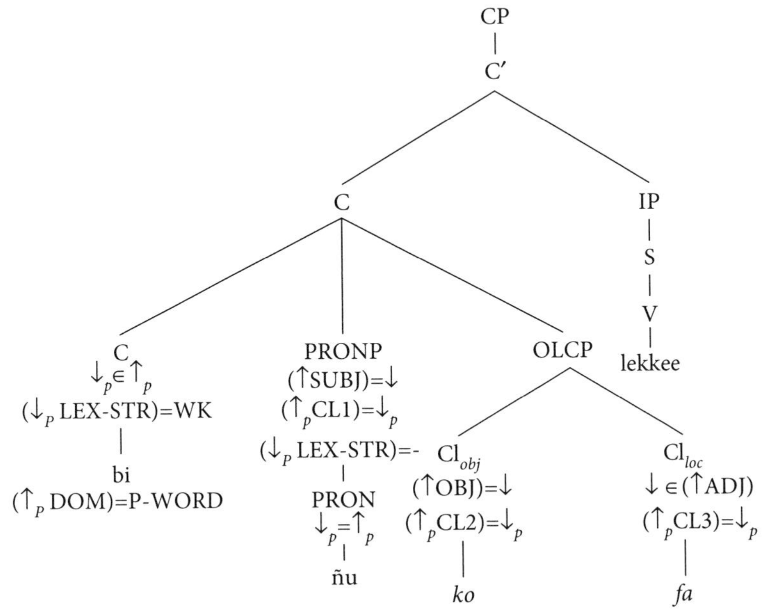

Finally, note that clitic climbing in fact is not a local phenomenon, but is possible over much greater distances. As illustrated in (31), the object and locative clitics are quite distant from the verb *lekk* that selects for them.

(31) Clitic climbing over long distances
*bëgg na =**ko** =**fa** jéem a jëkk a **lekk**.*
want +F =3SG =LOC try Part do.first Part eat
'He wants to try to eat it there first.'

In LFG, such distances are captured via equations that establish the syntactic relation between the clitic phrase and its within-clause grammatical function. A possible clitic phrase rule for object and locative clitics (OLCP) is given in (32). A path can be defined as a regular expression {COMP | XCOMP}* which denotes paths containing any number of open or closed complements, i.e. XCOMPs or COMPs (Butt et al. 1999), in any order.

(32) OLCP → Cl_{obj}: (↑ PATH OBJ)=↓;
(Cl_{loc}: ↓ $ (↑ PATH ADJUNCT)).

5. Conclusion

This paper addresses the treatment of clitics in Wolof. The Wolof data presented in this work confirm the extent to which clitics interact with different grammar components. Whereas previous approaches have tried to account for this phenomenon using transformational derivations, this paper has presented a non-transformational model which does not rely on configurations or movements to explain the derivation of the structure. The positions of the different clitics are not explained by deriving them from an underlying structure. Instead, the syntactic realization of the phrase and its parallel mapping are described on the surface level, taking into account the fundamental principle of word integrity. Constituent morphemes of words are thus described as directly contributing to the representation of the meaning of the sentence without having to be assigned unmotivated syntactic structure.

The current proposal has shown that LFG is an ideal theory in which to investigate clitics because its projection architecture provides a clear division between grammar components and a concrete notation with which to frame analyses within each component. This flexible modular architecture has allowed encoding of the information carried by clitics at independent levels. This information is made accessible to the separate components of grammar such as c-structure, f-structure, p-structure and m-structure, via mappings between structures defined in terms of functions and relations. This proposal explicitly accounts for the special properties of clitics at the morphology-syntax-phonology interface. It has presented a different way of dealing separately with the phonological and morphosyntactic properties of clitics that is still compatible with the overall framework of LFG. The prosodic information is made accessible to syntax, so that it is possible to condition syntactic rules and preferences on prosodic domains.

There are some theoretical issues that need to be addressed, however. The present approach builds on Butt and King's (1998) co-description architecture, which does not easily allow for prosodic units that are misaligned with syntactic constituents. Hence, this model does not explicitly account for misalignment. Integration of an architecture that allows such mismatches (Bögel et al. 2009) into the present proposal requires further investigation.

Acknowledgements

This research received support from the EC under FP7, Marie Curie Actions SP3-People-ITN 238405 (CLARA).

References

Asudeh, Ash & Toivonen, Ida. 2009. Lexical-Functional Grammar. In *The Oxford Handbook of Linguistic Analysis*, Bernd Heine & Heiko Narrog (eds), 425–458. Oxford: OUP.

Becher, Jutta. 2005. Ditransitive Verben und ihre Objekte im Wolof: Positionsregeln und Kombinierbarkeit. *Hamburger Afrikanistische Arbeitspapiere (HAAP)* 3: 13–27.

Bögel, Tina, Butt, Miriam, Kaplan, Ronald M., Holloway King, Tracy & Maxwell III, John. 2009. Prosodic phonology in LFG: A new proposal. In *The Proceedings of the LFG '09 Conference*, Miriam Butt & Tracy Holloway King (eds), 146–166. Trinity College, Cambridge.

Bresnan, Joan. 2001. *Lexical-Functional Syntax*. Oxford: Blackwell.

Bresnan, Joan & Mchombo, Sam A. 1987. Topic, pronoun, and agreement in Chicheŵa. *Language* 63: 741–782. Reprinted in *Working Papers in Grammatical Theory and Discourse Structure: Interactions of Morphology, Syntax, and Discourse*, Masayo Iida, Steven Wechsler & Draga Zec (eds), 1–59. Stanford CA: CSLI.

Bresnan, Joan & Mchombo, Sam A. 1995. The lexical integrity principle: Evidence from Bantu. *Natural Language and Linguistic Theory* 13: 181–254.

Butt, Miriam & Holloway King, Tracy. 1996. Structural topic and focus without movement. In *The Proceedings of the LFG '96 Conference*, Miriam Butt & Tracy Holloway King (eds), Grenoble: Rank Xerox.

Butt, Miriam & Holloway King, Tracy. 1998. Interfacing phonology with LFG. In *The Proceedings of the LFG '98 Conference*, Miriam Butt & Tracy Holloway King (eds), Brisbane: University of Queensland

Butt, Miriam, Holloway King, Tracy, Niño, María-Eugenia & Segond, Frédérique. 1999. *A Grammar Writer's Cookbook*. Stanford CA: CSLI.

Crouch, Dick, Dalrymple, Mary, Kaplan, Ron, King, Tracy, Maxwell, John & Newman, Paula. 2012. *XLE Documentation*. On-line documentation, Palo Alto Research Center (PARC).

Dalrymple, Mary. 2001. *Lexical-Functional Grammar* [Syntax and Semantics, Vol. 34: Syntax and Semantics]. San Diego CA: Academic Press.

Dione, Cheikh Mouhamadou Bamba. 2012. An LFG approach to Wolof cleft constructions. In *The Proceedings of the LFG '12 Conference*, Miriam Butt & Tracy Holloway King (eds). Stanford CA: CSLI.

Dunigan, Melynda B. 1994. On the Clausal Structure of Wolof. Ph.D. dissertation, The University of North Carolina at Chapel Hill.

Falk, Yehuda. 2001. *Lexical Functional Grammar: An Introduction to Parallel Constraint-Based Syntax*. Stanford CA: CSLI.

Falk, Yehuda N. 1984. The English auxiliary system: A lexical-functional analysis. *Language* 60: 483–509.

Franks, Steven & Holloway King, Tracy. 2000. *A Handbook of Slavic Clitics*. Oxford: OUP.

Ka, Omar. 1988. Wolof Phonology and Morphology: A Non-linear Approach. Ph.D. dissertation, University of Illinois at Urbana-Champaign.

Ka, Omar. 1994. *Wolof Phonology and Morphology*. Lanham MD: University Press of America.

Kaplan, Ronald M. & Bresnan, Joan. 1982. Lexical-functional grammar: A formal system for grammatical representation. In *The Mental Representation of Grammatical Relations*, Joan Bresnan (ed.), 173–281. Cambridge MA: The MIT Press.

Kayne, Richard. 1975. *French Syntax*. Cambridge MA: The MIT Press.

King, Tracy Holloway. 2005. Cliticizing LFG. In *The Proceedings of the LFG '05 Conference*, Miriam Butt & Tracy Holloway King (eds), Norway: University of Bergen.

Miller, Philip H. & Sag, Ivan A. 1997. French clitic movement without clitics or movement. *Natural Language & Linguistic Theory* 15: 573–639.
Ngom, Fallou. 2003. *Wolof.* Munich: Lincom.
Nordlinger, Rachel. 1998. *Constructive Case: Evidence From Australian Languages.* Stanford CA: CSLI.
O'Connor, Rob. 2002. Clitics and phrasal affixation in constructive morphology. In *The Proceedings of the LFG '02 Conference*, Miriam Butt & Tracy Holloway King (eds), National Technical University of Athens.
Rizzi, Luigi. 1997. The fine structure of the left periphery. In *Elements of Grammar*, Liliane Haegeman (ed.), 281–337. Dortrecht: Kluwer.
Robert, Stéphane. 1991. Approche énonciative du système verbal: Le cas du wolof. Paris: CNRS.
Rosén, Victoria, Meurer, Paul & De Smedt, Koenraad. 2009. LFG parsebanker: A toolkit for building and searching a treebank as a parsed corpus. In *Proceedings of the 7th International Workshop on Treebanks and Linguistic Theories (TLT7)*, Frank Van Eynde, Anette Frank, Gertjan van Noord & Koenraad De Smedt (eds), 127–133. Utrecht: LOT.
Russell, Margaret A. 2006. The Syntax and Placement of Wolof Clitics. Ph.D. dissertation, University of Illinois at Urbana-Champaign.
Selkirk, Elisabeth. 1984. *Phonology and Syntax: The Relation between Sound and Structure.* Cambridge MA: The MIT Press.
Torrence, Harold. 2003. Verb movement in Wolof. *UCLA Working Papers in Linguistics,* 1–31.
Torrence, William Harold. 2005. On the Distribution of Complementizers inWolof. Ph.D. dissertation, University of California Los Angeles.
Voisin-Nouguier, Sylvie. 2006. L'infinitif en wolof. In *Les formes non finies du verbe*, Odile Blanvillain & Claude Guilmier (eds), 61–83. Rennes: Presses Universitaires de Rennes.
Zribi-Hertz, Anne & Diagne, Lamine. 2002. Clitic placement after syntax: Evidence from Wolof person and locative markers. *Natural Language and Linguistic Theory* 20(4): 823–884.
Zribi-Hertz, Anne & Diagne, Lamine. 2003. Déficience flexionnelle et temps topical en wolof. In *Typologie des langues d'Afrique et universaux de la grammaire, Vol. 2: Benue-kwa, wolof,* Patrick Sauzet & Anne Zribi Hertz (eds), 205–231. Paris: L'Harmattan.
Zwicky, Arnold. 1977. *On Clitics.* Bloomington IN: Indiana University Linguistics Club.

Clitic placement and grammaticalization in Portuguese

Filomena Sandalo & Charlotte Galves
Departamento de Linguística, IEL / Unicamp, Campinas-SP 13083-970, Brazil

In this paper, we argue that the architecture of grammar proposed in Distributed Morphology can shed light on the diachronic shift that has occurred in Portuguese enclisis. Employing such a view of the architecture of grammar allows us to interpret this shift as a case of grammaticalization, thus broadening the treatment of this concept in the framework of generative grammar. In Modern European Portuguese, enclitic pronouns are more affix-like than proclitic pronouns, both syntactically and phonologically. We argue that enclisis in Modern Portuguese is due to Lowering, a post-syntactic incorporation process, whereas clitics in Classical Portuguese must be displaced from the beginning of an Intonational Phrase, and as such, enclisis in this language period is a result of Prosodic Inversion.

1. Introduction[1]

European Portuguese exhibits a complementary distribution between pronominal enclisis and proclisis that cannot be attributed to finitness distinctions as in other Romance languages. In Portuguese, clitic placement is sensitive to the presence of certain triggers such as negation:

(1) a. *Eu vi-o*
I saw-CL1ACC
'I have seen him.'

b. *Eu não o vi*
I NEG CL1ACC saw
'I have not seen him.'

---

1. For valuable comments, we are grateful to audiences at the Challenging Clitics Conference in Oslo, 2011, and to Andrew Nevins and Morris Halle. Moreover, the authors would like to thank the anonymous reviewer for comments that helped improve the manuscript.

This article deals with clitic placement in Portuguese from a diachronic point of view, and argues that enclitics have undergone a grammaticalization process from clitic to affix from Classical European Portuguese (ClP) to Modern European Portuguese (EP). The discussion is couched within the framework of Distributed Morphology.

Distributed Morphology (DM) is a theory of the architecture of grammar in which there is no Lexicon in the sense of generative grammar from the 1970s and 1980s. The different degrees of dependence between morphemes are captured by the different *loci* of the processes distributed in different levels of the grammatical architecture. Within this perspective, Embick and Noyer (2001) develop a derivational theory of movement operations that occur after syntactic derivation. Embick and Noyer's architecture in (1) can predict both cliticization showing dependencies that are purely prosodic (a clitic simply leans on its host), and post-syntactic affixation in which a unit becomes merged to its host. Such *Merger* processes create units that are more closely attached to each other than they are to their prosodic hosts, since Merger is a morphological incorporation process. In their proposal, there are two kinds of Merger: Lowering and Prosodic Inversion.

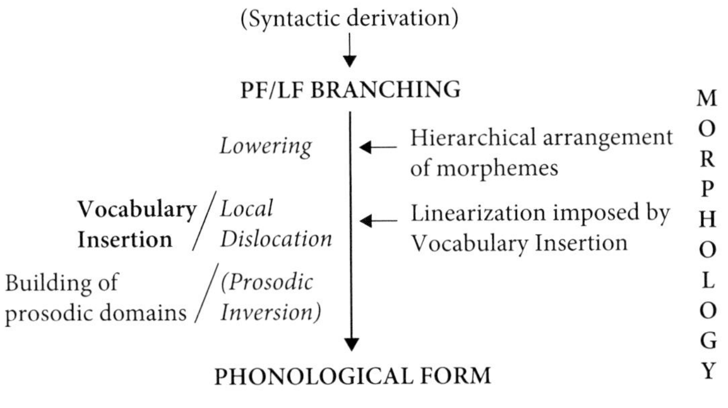

Figure 1. The PF branch of the grammar, from Embick and Noyer (2001: 566)

In the schema in (1), Lowering is a right dislocation operation of Merger, in which a head lowers to another head. The two heads need not be linearly adjacent since this is head-to-head movement in Morphology. Therefore, Lowering is potentially non-local. It is only necessary for it to occur before linearization so that syntactic structure is visible and intervening XPs can be skipped. Local Dislocation occurs after linearization, and, in this case, the relevant relation is not hierarchical structure but rather linear precedence and adjacency. Prosodic Inversion, defined by Halpern (1995) as operating in terms of prosodic subcategorization, only applies to sentence-peripheral elements. That is, if a clitic has a dependency that is purely prosodic, it would, all other things being equal, simply lean on a host rather than undergoing incorporation.

In the history of European Portuguese, from the 16th to the 19th century, clitic placement underwent significant changes. We attempt to show that enclisis is generated by Merger, specifically Lowering (Section 2), in Modern European Portuguese, whereas clitic placement was a result of Prosodic Inversion in Classical European Portuguese (Section 3). Finally, in Section 4, we show that our analysis sheds light on the nature of the historical shift in Portuguese and broadens the treatment of grammaticalization in generative linguistics.

2. Clitic placement in Modern European Portuguese

There is an interesting asymmetry between proclisis and enclisis in EP that was first noticed by Rouveret (1999), indicating that enclitics (as opposed to proclitics) behave as affix-like elements. Note the contrast between the following sentences. The sentences in (2a–b) differ in that in (2a) the third-person pronoun is proclitic, while it is enclitic in (2b). In (2b), coordination is unavailable and the sentence is ungrammatical:

(2) a. *Todos o aplaudiram e festejaram*
all CL3ACC applauded and celebrated
'They all applauded and celebrated it.'

b. **João aplaudiu-o e festejou*
John applauded-CL3ACC and celebrated
'John applauded and celebrated it.'

Rouveret (1999: 648) claims that 'the relation between proclitics and their host is less tight than the relation between enclitics and their host' since whereas proclitics function as independent items visible for coordination, enclitics do not. The claim that pronominal clitics in Portuguese display affix-like behavior is not new in the linguistic literature (e.g. Klavans 1985; Zwicky 1977; Spencer 1991; Halpern 1995; Duarte & Mattos 1995, 2000). Among the properties that pronominal clitics share with lexical affixes are the following: *(i)* high selectivity with respect to the category of the host/base they attach to; *(ii)* special phonology triggered by the clitic-verb sequences; and in some cases, *(iii)* the ordering of clitics with respect to inflection: enclitics can occur closer to the root than certain inflectional affixes (e.g. *falar-lhe-ia* speak-3CL-tense). More recently, Bermudez-Otero and Luís (2009) note an asymmetry between proclisis and enclisis in Portuguese that further indicates that enclitics are affix-like elements. Whereas a proclitic clitic can be separated from its host, an enclitic cannot. In (3), a proclitic, *lho*, is separated from the verb, *disse*, by an adverb and by the negative morpheme.[2]

(3) *Acho que ela lho ainda não disse*
I think that she CL3DAT+3ACC still NEG told
'I think that she has not told it to him/her yet'
(Cf. *Ela disse-lho* 'she has told it to him', where the verb and the clitic must be closely attached and nothing can intervene between them.)

Bermudez-Otero and Luís (2009) also provide morphophonological evidence for a greater dependency of the enclitic in relation to its host. They note that in verb + clitic clusters, the clitic shows arbitrary allomorphy (cf. Procuramo-**lo** 'we look for him') that does not show up in sequences cl + verb (cf. 'Não **o** procuramos 'we do not look for him').

Phonological evidence for the claim that enclitics have properties of affixes is given in Vigário (2003):

(4)
a. pel*e* alva 0/#[j] 'pale skin'
b. beb*e* agora 0/#[j] '(he) drinks now'
c. ped*e*-o já *0/[j] '(he) already asks it'
d. med*e*-a depois *0/[j] '(he) measures it later'
e. peço-t*e* agora 0/#[j] '(he) asks you now'
f. disse-me ontem 0/#[j] '(he) said it to me yesterday'

The data in (4a) and (b) show that the final unstressed *e* of a word is deleted when followed by another vowel, whereas (c) and (d) show that such a deletion does not occur when the *e* is followed by an enclitic pronoun. This reveals that when the verb is followed by a pronominal clitic, the verb's final vowel no longer behaves as if it were at the word boundary. However, as shown by (e) and (f), the *e* of enclitic pronoun does behave like the final vowel of a verb, since it is deleted when followed by a vowel. The data in (c–f) therefore provide evidence that the word boundary is not located between the verb and the clitic, but after the clitic.

Vigário (1999), however, argues that clitics are not **exactly** like affixes. Vigário shows that the operation that attaches pronominal enclitics to their hosts is different from regular affixation. The author's arguments include the fact that, unlike inflectional affixes, clitics are invisible to stress. Another important piece of evidence is that the insertion of clitics does not block the process of word final nasal gliding. In Portuguese, a nasal consonant in coda position is realized

2. Clitics can be combined in Romance languages. In Portuguese, certain combinations of clitics are fused into just one morpheme. The clitic *lho* is a combination of a third-person dative pronoun and a third-person accusative pronoun. It was, thus, glossed CL3DAT + Cl3ACC.

as a nasal glide palatal glide, [j̃], when it is at the word boundary. As noted by Vigário, EP only presents nasal gliding in word final position, never *inside* a word (regardless of its internal structure). According to her, the existence of nasal gliding before clitics (cf. *batem-te* (*bate[j̃]-te*) 'they hit you') indicates that the clitic is not fused with the verb like an actual affix would be.

In order to solve this puzzle, Vigário (2003), working within the framework of Lexical Phonology, was the first to propose that the operation that attaches clitics to their host is post-syntactic affixation. We reformulate Vigário's insight that enclisis is a post-syntactic operation within Distributed Morphology in order to account for the distribution of clitic placement in Portuguese that includes affix-like properties but still differs from canonical affixes. Moreover, within this framework, as will be seen, the historical changes in Portuguese can be straightforwardly captured.

Barbosa (2008) claims that at the syntactic level of the derivation, a proclitic is attached to a projection of T. That is, proclitics are adjoined to T-bar or to TP. In other words, what is crucial here is that proclitics are attached to a phrase, not a head.

We maintain Barbosa's syntactic analysis of proclitic clitic placement; however, unlike Barbosa, we argue that enclisis is generated via Lowering at the morphological level. An analysis along these lines can predict the affixal properties of clitics since they undergo Merger (i.e. a kind of incorporation). This is different, however, from a true affix that is derived via syntactic Merger (cf. Embick 2010, and Costa 1998 for the derivation of tense affixes in Portuguese via syntactic movement).

The distribution of enclisis and proclisis in EP (shown in 5–14 below) provides evidence for the sensitivity of clitic placement to hierarchical structure. The evidence in fact suggests that we are dealing with Lowering. Note in the data in (5–14) that a clitic lowers to V (i.e. is an enclitic) when it is not c-commanded by another functional head. In effect, although referential subjects linearly precede the verb, they do not count for clitic placement (cf. 7 below).

(5) a. *Encontrei-o ontem.*
I-met-CL3ACC yesterday.

b. **O encontrei ontem*
CL3ACC I-met yesterday
'I met him yesterday'

(6) a. *Ontem, encontrei-o*
yesterday, I-met-CL3ACC

b. **Ontem, o encontrei.*
Yesterday, CL3ACC I-met.
'Yesterday, I met him.'

(7) a. *O Paulo falou-me.*
Det.3SG Paul he-spoke-CL1DAT

b. **O Paulo me falou.*
Det.3SG Paulo CL1DAT he-spoke
'Paulo has spoken to me.'

Proclisis occurs in the following cases, namely, when there is a c-commanding functional head:

a. in negative clauses

(8) a. *O Paulo não me fala.*
Det.3SG Paul NEG CL1DAT he-spoke

b. **O Paulo não fala-me*
Det3SG Paul NEG he-spoke-CL1DAT
'Paulo has not spoken to me.'

b. in subordinate clauses

(9) a. *Todo mundo sabe que a viste.*
Everybody knows COMP CL3ACC you-saw

b. **Todo mundo sabe que viste-a*
Everybody knows comp you-saw-CL3ACC
'Everybody knows that you have seen her.'

(10) a. *Se tu me tivesses dito…*
If you CL1DAT had said

b. **Se tu tivesses-me dito*
If you had-CL1DAT said
'If you had said to me…'

c. in clauses in which the preverbal phrase is a quantifier (11), a WH operator (12), a focalized phrase (13), or an adverb of a certain class (14):

(11) a. *Alguém me chamou*
Somebody CL1DAT-called

b. **Alguém chamou-me*
Somebody called-CL1DAT
'Somebody has called me'

(12) a. *Quem me chamou?*
Who CL1ACC called

b. **Quem chamou-me?*
Who called-CL1ACC
'Who called me?'

(13) a. *Só ele a entende*
Only 3PRO CL3ACC understands

b. **Só ele entende-a*
Only 3PRO understands-CL3ACC
'Only he understands her.'

(14) a. *Eu (sempre, ainda, já) a encontrei*
1PRO (always, still, already) CL3ACC I-met

no mercado
at-Det.3SG market

b. **Eu (sempre, ainda, já) encontrei-a no mercado*
1PRO (always, still, already) I-met-CL3ACC at-Det.3SG market
'I (always, still, already) met her at the market.'

We will now review the cases in which proclisis is obligatory in order to show that in all of them, the clitic is c-commanded by some functional head. In embedded contexts, the clitic is c-commanded by C. As for quantified phrases, we will assume that they occupy the specifier of FocP, even when they are subjects. In this case, a head higher than T and distinct from it is activated, so that the clitic does not occupy the highest head of the clause in the sense defined above. The effect of negation is straightforwardly derived from the projection of a Neg head that c-commands the clitic. The only remaining case is that of the class of adverbs that force proclisis. These are aspectual adverbs generally analyzed as being adjoined to T. It is interesting to note that they behave like heads: in particular, in contrast with other adverbs, they do not accept modifiers (although they can be modifiers of other adverbs). We conclude from this special behavior that they are both heads and maximal projections. They therefore adjoin to the projection of TP as a head. As such, they prevent the clitic from occupying the first position in CP. By contrast, the other adverbs adjoin to the clause as a maximal projection and do not interfere with clitic placement.

Note that EP is not an isolated case of a language that displays proclisis/enclisis alternation in tensed clauses (cf. Shlonsky 2004; Ouhalla 2005; Mavrogiorgos this volume). Ouhalla (2005) describes a very similar pattern in some dialects of Berber, the main difference being that the class of clitics is broader in Berber than in EP. He argues that the correct formulation of the constraint that prevents the placement of clitics in the first position of a domain is (15) (op. cit., p. 619):[3]

(15) 'CL cannot be the first head constituent in the minimal domain (CP, DP, or PP) that includes it.'

---

3. It is important to note that our transposition of Ouhalla's constraint into the Distributed Morphology framework allows us to maintain the claim that first position restrictions are post-syntactic. What is syntactic in the constraint is only the definition of the domain. This is not a contradiction in the theoretical framework we adopt since, before linearization and

We propose to re-formulate it in terms of c-command:

(16) 'CL cannot be the first head of a minimal domain that is not c-commanded by any other head in the same minimal domain' (Galves & Sandalo 2012)

In our proposal, if the clitic is c-commanded, it remains in situ. But if a clitic is not c-commanded by another head, it undergoes Merger. Constraints that ban certain configurations (or filters) are common after syntax, in phonological form, and (16) is an instance of such a constraint (cf. also Arregi & Nevins 2012 for post-syntactic constraints).

Merger processes create units that are more closely attached to each other than those resulting from prosodic attachments, since Merger is an incorporation process. Now, if a clitic undergoes Merger, it follows that it turns out to be an affix-like element. It is worth noting an important feature of the analysis proposed here, which constitutes one of the main advantages it has over purely syntactic analyses. Duarte and Matos (1995) emphatically claim that "EP clitics are one step further in the Jespersenian cycle' than those of other Romance languages, 'that is, EP clitics are more affix-like than other Romance clitics.'[4] Deferring until the last section of this paper the question of the change from clitic to affix, what we want to emphasize now is that, using the Distributed Morphology model, we straightforwardly derive the affix-like nature of enclitics, without having to claim that clitic pronouns are affixes in all their occurrences in EP. Lowering derives an element that is closer to the verb than a free functional head, such as a proclitic, but less close to the verb than an inflectional affix. This is exactly what the phonological evidence shows.[5]

Barbosa (2008) also assumes that enclisis is the result of Merger. However, she argues that the rule responsible for enclisis is Local Dislocation. She claims that the ban on first position clitics is derived from a restriction that prevents

vocabulary insertion, the morphological component of the grammar (more precisely, the rule of Lowering) has access to the syntactic structure.

4. Note however that Ordoñez and Repetti (2012) have worked on Argentinian (and Sardinian) enclitics which attract/count for stress, and hence would also be Romance languages relatively far along on this continuum.

5. Magro (2008) also uses a Distributed Morphology analysis of enclisis in EP. It must be noted, however, that the main issue she raises concerns not the movement of the clitic itself but the movement of an empty syntactic category Σ. This analysis encounters a theoretical problem. Local Dislocation is a phenomenon that occurs after vocabulary insertion and linearization. That is, it is a phenomenon that occurs in the phonology itself. It is therefore problematic to derive clitic dislocation from the need of an element (Σ) that is not visible for phonology. It is commonly accepted that, although overt syntactic categories may lead to the

the clitic from remaining in this position when there is no linguistic material on its left. According to her, Local Dislocation is applied only when the clitic is the first phonologically visible element in CP. The obligatory enclisis when the verb is preceded by a referential subject shows that no preceding material provides an adequate host for the clitic. This in fact is a problem for a proposal based on Local Dislocation. In order to account for this problem, Barbosa argues that the subject is outside of the CP phase, against much empirical evidence in the Portuguese literature (cf. Costa 1998; Galves & Sandalo 2012, among others). Second, this analysis needs two principles of explanation. The first is the linear restriction on clitics being first in the CP phase, which forces Local Dislocation to apply. The second is a prosodic filter that forces the affixation of the clitic onto the right of the verb. This means that Local Dislocation must look at the prosodic phrasing to work. Nevertheless, if one assumes Embick and Noyer's grammar architecture, Prosody follows Local Dislocation in the derivation. Therefore, Prosody is not accessible when Local Dislocation applies.

Finally, the main argument provided by Barbosa in support of Local Dislocation is that the allomorphic forms of enclitic pronouns are sensitive to the verbal endings, as pointed out by Bermudez-Otero and Luís (*-o* when the verb ends in vowel, *-lo* when it ends in *-r* or *-s* and *-no* when it ends in a nasal consonant), which would indicate that the process applies after vocabulary insertion. But this cannot be taken as evidence that the rule responsible for lowering the clitic applies after vocabulary insertion, since these alternations can be considered to be instances of allomorphic variation (cf. Vigário 1999). This means that what applies after vocabulary insertion are the phonological rules responsible for allomorphic variation, not necessarily the rule that lowers the clitic.[6]

Lowering faces none of these problems. The subject does not intervene because the process applies when the clitic is in the first head of CP, independently of whether a subject is present or not.[7] We are therefore not obliged to assume the ad-hoc claim that the subject is outside CP. Moreover, our proposal straightforwardly accounts for the fact that the clitic appears on the right side of the verb. This is a consequence of Lowering, since head-to-head structures in Morphology are a mirror image of head-to-head structures in syntax.

---

construction of prosodic constituents that can be detected by phonological rules, phonological operations systematically ignore empty syntactic elements (cf. Truckenbrodt 1995).

6. See also Lowenstamm (2010) for a view of morphophonological alternations within Distributed Morphology.

7. See Galves and Sandalo (2012) for a discussion of Portuguese external arguments.

Moreover, our proposal can capture the fact that enclisis does not affect stress. Lowering creates a post-syntactic incorporated element. Tense morphology shows other kind of phonological rules, such as gliding and stress sensitivity, since its incorporation has applied at another level of the derivation. In DM, roots have phonological features in the syntax, as opposed to functional morphemes. Main stress is phonological information of the root in Portuguese (cf. Sandalo et al. 2009). At the level at which enclitics are merged, primary stress is not active.

Proclitics do not undergo Merger. They remain in their final syntactic position. At the prosodic level, their attachment is prosodic – i.e. they are phrasally dependent elements. Our analysis is in accordance with Bermudez-Otero and Luís (2009), although we employ different frameworks. Whereas enclitics are attached as word-level elements (i.e. merged elements in our view), proclitics are phonologically adjoined to a phrase.

3. Classical Portuguese

We label the language written in Portugal between the fifteenth and the eighteenth centuries as ClP (Classical Portuguese). The ClP data for this work comes from the Tycho Brahe Corpus. The Tycho Brahe Corpus contains 52 texts (2,407,422 words) of parsed prose text samples that are useful for historical syntax research. Figure 2 shows the evolution in time of the rate of enclitic constructions in contexts in which we observe enclisis/proclisis variation[8] (cf. Galves et al. 2005).

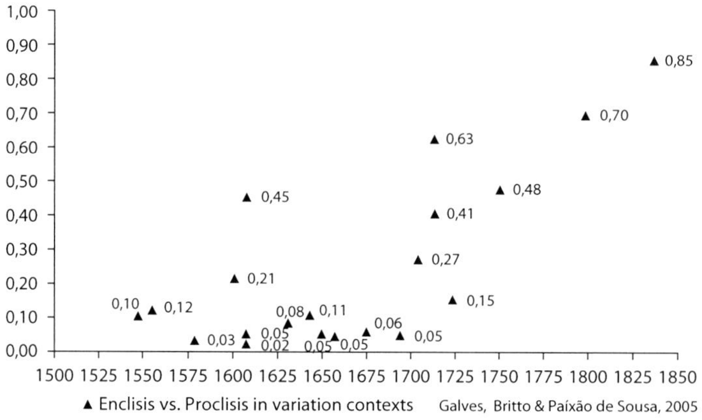

Figure 2. Enclisis/proclisis alternation in variation contexts

8. For more details on the syntax of clitic-placement in Classical Portuguese, we refer the interested reader to Galves and Sandalo (2012).

We see that the authors born up to 1700 do not use more than 20% enclisis. The only exceptions are Padre Vieira's sermons, which use enclisis in abundance. However, Galves (2002) shows that in *all* the cases of enclisis in these sermons, the pre-verbal phrase is clearly a contrastive topic, presented in opposition to another term.

(17) *Elles conheciam-se, como homens, Christo conhecia-os, como Deus.*
They knew-CLREFL, as men, Christ knew-CL3ACC, as God
'They knew themselves, as men, Christ knew them, as God.'

(18) *As outras prophecias cumprem-se a seu tempo, esta do dia*
The other prophecies achieve-CLREFL at their time, this one of
do Juiso tem o seu cumprimento antes de tempo;
the Final Judgment has its achievement before its time
'The other prophecies are achieved at their time; this one of the Final Judgment has its achievement before its time.'

The sensitiveness to contrastive topics favors the hypothesis that we are indeed dealing with a prosodic phenomenon in ClP. Selkirk (2005) points out that the Intonational Phrase organization of a sentence is subject to certain variation. It sometimes shows a correlation with the semantic properties of the sentence, and it sometimes appears to be correlated with the length of the constituents of a sentence. In fact we find both effects in ClP, which favors our prosodic analysis of clitics in this variety. As seen above, clitics are sensitive to contrastive topics and they are sensitive to length as shown below. Galves et al. (2005) measured the length of pre-verbal clauses in terms of the number of words. One would expect longer pre-verbal clauses to be more likely to correspond to autonomous Intonational Phrases, in which case the verb would be the first element of the intonational contour of the main clause, and this is the case as shown in Table 1 below. Table 1 shows that the frequency of enclisis increases when the pre-verbal clause is long (more than nine words), pointing to a correlation between the length of the pre-verbal clause and the position of the clitic.

Table 1. The effect of the length of pre-verbal dependent clauses on clitic-placement in authors born in the 16th–19th centuries

	16th			17th			18th			19th		
Size of fronted embedded clause (in phonological words)	P	E	%E	P	E	%E	P	E	%E	P	E	%E
1–4words	68	29	0,30	38	35	0,48	12	35	0,74	0	10	1,00
5–8words	33	18	0,35	27	28	0,51	16	31	0,66	0	4	1,00
9+words	8	9	0,53	10	25	0,71	15	15	0,50	0	0	–
	109	56		75	88		43	81		0	14	

Selkirk (1986) investigated the mapping from syntax to prosody and explored the possibility that prosodic structure can be derived from surface syntactic structure by a unified set of constraints and parameters. Following such work, we assume a grammatical principle demanding the alignment of the edge of a syntactic constituent to a prosodic constituent (right alignment for Portuguese). Given the clitics' sensitivity to the edge of a root sentence, we assume that clitics are prevented from occurring at the beginning of an Intonational Phrase, as proposed by Barbosa (1995). More specifically, a clitic will be displaced if it is at the beginning of an Intonational Phrase. The interesting thing is that this correlation ceases to exist from the 18th century onwards, indicating a linguistic change.

Although the extent to which Local Dislocation and Prosodic Inversion are distinct devices in the mapping to PF remains a controversial question, we follow Embick and Noyer (2001) in assuming that Prosodic Inversion differs from Local Dislocation in that the elements that it affects are prosodic categories rather than morphological ones. Thus, we assume given the prosodic clues presented above that in ClP, clitics are attached via Prosodic Inversion to a prosodic constituent that contains the verb, whereas in modern Portuguese they are attached via Merger, more specifically via Lowering. This means that we claim that in modern Portuguese (EP) clitics are insensitive to prosodic factors. This analysis goes against Vigário and Frota (1998). Vigário and Frota claim that enclisis is possible in subordinate clauses when the functional category that yields proclisis is separated from the verb by an Intonational Phrase boundary. According to them, this would be a case of a 'weight effect' on syntactic structures. However, it must be noted that this phenomenon is restricted to the complement of epistemic verbs, and only occurs with verbs in the indicative mood. This is very much reminiscent of the cases of CP-recursion which license V2 in embedded clauses in some Germanic languages. If it is indeed a case of CP recursion, our analysis of Merger straightforwardly applies to this case, since the proclitic pronoun would stand in the first head of (the second) CP.

Our analysis predicts that in ClP, clitics are not affix-like elements in the sense of EP, since they lean on a host. This is obviously almost impossible to confirm empirically, since we do not have access to the phonetic implementation of the written texts of this period. However, such a situation is shown by Brazilian Portuguese, in which there is no phonological process that differentiates the boundary between a prosodic word and a clitic from the boundary between two prosodic words, as is the case in the EP data in (4). Moreover, Simioni (2008) argues that, in Brazilian Portuguese, clitics behave neither as pre-tonic syllables in the case of proclisis nor as post-tonic syllables in the case of enclisis, and she concludes that in this language, there is no distinction between proclisis and enclisis in terms of prosodic structure. This is, therefore, a case of a variety of Portuguese in which clitics never undergo Merger, and we believe that in ClP the facts were similar.

Selkirk (1986, 1995), among many others, has shown that phonological rules often target prosodic domains, such as the prosodic word or phonological phrase, and therefore proposed a separate post-syntactic level of prosody. Since it is usually assumed that adjunction to a prosodic category incorporates the moved element into that prosodic domain, Prosodic Inversion is an answer to prosodic deficiency; that is, it is a way for the prosody to satisfy the Prosodic Licensing Condition, which states that all phonological elements must be assigned to a prosodic category. However, this is still an adjunction or phrasal phenomenon, as opposed to Lowering, which is post-syntactic affixation to a word.

Thus, we maintain that enclisis in ClP is phrasal and the clitic incorporates to a prosodic domain. In EP, however, there is post-syntactic incorporation to a word, specifically Lowering in Embick & Noyer's terminology.

4. Grammaticalization

According to our analysis, Portuguese shifted from Prosodic Inversion in ClP to Lowering in EP. That is, the language went from having a clitic that leans on its host to a morphologically incorporated element. We understand this shift as a case of the second cline of grammaticalization.

Grammaticalization is a term introduced by Meillet (1912), which refers to a historical process in which a lexical category becomes a grammatical category (the first cline of grammaticalization), which can be further grammaticalized into an affix (the second cline of grammaticalization).

As mentioned above, the traditional schema of grammaticalization includes two different moments. The first one has to do with the change in categorization accompanied by semantic bleaching. The second one consists of further steps of phonological dependency and reduction. Roberts and Roussou (2003) propose a generative account of the first moment in terms of the emergence of new functional words out of lexical words. In their approach, grammaticalization is associated with structural simplification, which they argue is a natural mechanism of change.

According to Campbell (2001), 'grammaticalization is derivative, that is, it has no independent status of its own, but rather relies on other processes and mechanisms of linguistic change which are independent of grammaticalization but which provide the explanations for the phenomena involved in grammaticalization'. In accordance with Campbell's view, Lash (2012) argues that the two clines of grammaticalization must be independently captured by mechanisms of the grammar.

Lash (2012) approaches the Modern Irish particle *ná* 'than' and shows that *ná* is a phonologically reduced and syntactically reanalyzed form of the Old Irish sequence *ol daäs* 'beyond how is.' Lash argues that the history of this particle is particularly instructive as a case study in grammaticalization. He shows that there are two steps or clines in the change of *ná*. First, there is a shift from V (in T) to C due to a shift in the parameter setting of C (Roberts & Roussou 2003). In a second step, as a C element, the particle was unstressed and could cliticize to the preposition before it at PF. This led to the possibility of analyzing the original verb as prepositional agreement, whence a C to P shift. This second step cannot be seen as a case of grammaticalization in the sense of Roberts and Roussou (2003) as it does not appear to conform to the idea of grammaticalization as a phenomenon associated with upward reanalysis due to parameter change. This is, however, an instance of grammaticalization from the perspective of Givón (1979), since it is an example of the development of 'today's morphology [from] yesterday's syntax.' That is, it instantiates the development of a morphologically dependent unit from a syntactically free one. Lash thus urges for broadening the notion of grammaticalization. Although Roberts and Roussou (2003) can capture the first cline of grammaticalization within the principles of generative linguistics, the second cline cannot be captured within that view.

We have dealt here with morphologization (in Lash's terminology) and phonological dependency, and we also claim that the understanding of grammaticalization in generative linguistics must be broadened. We adopt a derivational model (Distributed Morphology) to deal with the second cline. Note that the idea of using a derivational model of the interface between phonology and morphology to account for historical change is not new in historical linguistics. This is what we have attempted here in the specific case of enclisis in varieties of Portuguese.

We see in the history of this language a case of a change towards greater phonological dependency of a clitic. In such a process, a clitic shifted into an affix-like element. Distributed Morphology and its grammatical architecture can elegantly capture the second cline of grammaticalization and the shift that Portuguese has undergone.

References

Arregi, Karlos & Nevins, Andrew. 2012. *Morphotactics: Basque Auxiliaries and the Structure of Spellout*. Dordrecht: Springer.

Barbosa, Pilar. 2008. Deslocação local, cliticização e Spell Out cíclico. *Diacrítica* 22(1): 131–156.

Bermudez-Otero, Ricardo & Luís, Ana. 2009. Cyclic domains and prosodic spans in the phonology of European Portuguese functional morphs. Handout 'Old World Conference in Phonology 6', Edinburgh, 24 January 2009.

Campbell, Lyle (ed.). 2001. *Grammaticalization: A Critical Assessment*. Special issue of *Language Sciences* 23(2–3).
Costa, João. 1998. *Word Order Variation: A Constraint-based Approach*. Leiden: HIL/Leiden University.
Duarte, Inês & Matos, Gabriela 1995. Romance clitics and the minimalist program. Paper presented at the V Colloquium on Generative Grammar, La Coruña.
Duarte, Inês & Matos, Gabriela. 2000. Romance clitics and the minimalist program. In *Portuguese Syntax*, João Costa (ed.), 116–142. Oxford: OUP.
Embick, David & Noyer, Rolf. 2001. Movement operations after syntax, *Linguistic Inquiry* 32(4): 555–596.
Embick, David & Noyer, Rolf. 2006. Distributed morphology and the syntax-morphology interface. In *The Oxford Handbook of Linguistic Interfaces,* Gillian Ramchand & Charles Reiss (eds), 289–324. Oxford: OUP.
Galves, Charlotte. 2002. Syntax and style: Clitic-placement in Padre Antonio Vieira. *Santa Barbara Portuguese Studies* 6: 387–403.
Galves, Charlotte, Britto, Helena & Paixão de Sousa, Maria Clara. 2005. The change in clitic placement from Classical to Modern European Portuguese: Results from the Tycho Brahe Corpus. *Journal of Portuguese Linguistics* 4(1): 39–68.
Galves, Charlotte & Sandalo, Filomena. 2012. From phonological phrase to syntactic phase: The grammaticalization of enclisis in the history of Portuguese. *Lingua* 122(8): 952–974.
Givón, T. 1979. *On Understanding Grammar*. New York NY: Academic Press.
Halpern, Aaron. 1995. *On the Placement and Morphology of Clitics*. Stanford CA: CSLI.
Klavans, Judith. 1982. *Some Problems in the Theory of Clitics*. Bloomington IN: Indiana University Linguistics Club.
Lowenstamm, Jean. 2010. Derivational affixes as roots (Phasal spellout meets English stress shift). Ms, University of Paris 7.
Lash, Elliott. 2012. The diachronic development of the Irish comparative particle. In *Parameter Theory and Linguistic Change* Charlotte Galves, Sonia Cyrino, Ruth Vasconcelos, Filomena Sandalo & Juanito Avelar (eds). Oxford: OUP.
Magro, Catarina. 2008. Clíticos: Variação sobre o tema. Ph.D. dissertation, Universidade de Lisboa.
Meillet, Antoine. 1912. L'évolution des formes grammaticales. In *Antoine Meillet: Linguistique Historique et Linguistique Générale,* 131–148. Paris: Champion.
Ouhalla, Jamal. 2005. Clitic placement, grammaticalization, and reanalysis in Berber. In *The Oxford Handbook of Comparative Syntax,* Guillelmo Cinque & Richard Kayne (eds), 607–638. Oxford: OUP.
Ordoñez, Francisco & Repetti, Lori. 2012. On the morphological restriction of hosting clitics in Italian Dialects and Sardinian. Ms, Stony Brook University.
Roberts, Ian & Roussou, Anna. 1999. A formal approach to 'grammaticalization'. *Linguistics* 37: 1011–1041.
Roberts, Ian & Roussou, Anna. 2003. *Syntactic Change, A Minimalist Approach to Grammaticalization* [Cambridge Studies in Linguistics 100]. Cambridge: CUP.
Rouveret, Alain. 1999. Clitics, subjects and tense in European Portuguese. In *Clitics in the Languages of Europe*, Henk van Riemdsijk (ed.), 1–30. Berlin: Mouton de Gruyter.
Selkirk, Elisabeth. 1986. On derived domains in sentence phonology. *Phonology* 3: 371–405.
Selkirk, Elisabeth. 1995. Sentence prosody: Intonation, stress and phrasing. In *The Handbook of Phonological Theory*, John Goldsmith (ed.). London: Blackwell.

Selkirk, Elizabeth. 2005. Comments on intonational phrasing in English. In *Prosodies*, Sónia Frota, Marina Vigário & Maria João Freitas (eds). Berlin: Mouton de Gruyter.

Sandalo, Filomena, Abaurre, Maria Bernadete, Mandel, Arnaldo & Galves, Charlotte. 2006. Secondary stress in two varieties of Portuguese. *Probus* 18(1): 97–125.

Shlonsky, Ur. 2004. Enclisis and proclisis in the structure of CP and IP. In *The Structure of CP and IP*, Vol. 2, Luigi Rizzi (ed.), 239–253. Oxford: OUP.

Simioni, Taíse. 2008. O clítico e seu lugar na estrutura prosódica em português brasileiro. *Alpha-Revista de Linguística*, UNESP, 52(2): 431–446.

Spencer, Andrew. 1991. *Morphological Theory. An Introduction to Word Structure in Generative Grammar.* Oxford: Blackwell.

Truckenbrodt, Hubert. 1995. Phonological Phrases: Their Relation to Syntax, Focus, and Prominence. Ph.D. dissertation, MIT.

Vigário, Marina. 1999. Pronominal cliticization in European Portuguese: A postlexical operation. *Catalan Working Papers in Linguistics*, 219–237.

Vigário, Marina. 2003. *The Prosodic Word in European Portuguese*. Berlin: Mouton de Gruyter.

Vigário, Marina & Frota, Sónia. 1998. Between syntax and phonology on phrasal weight effects in European Portuguese, 8th colloquium on Generative Grammar, Palmela, Portugal.

Zwicky, Arnold. 1977. *On Clitics*. Bloomington IN: IULC.

Diachronic source of two cliticization patterns in Slavic

Krzysztof Migdalski
University of Wrocław

This paper presents an analysis of a diachronic modification in the position of pronominal clitics in Slavic. The modification involved a switch from verb-adjacent clitics to second position clitics, but it occurred only in those languages that also lost tense morphology. The paper interprets the change as a loss of the TP projection, as a result of which clitics may not adjoin to a suitable syntactic head. The change has repercussions for the syntactic process of cliticization: second position clitics no longer have a designated position in the clause structure, but instead they land in specifiers of different functional heads above VP.

1. Introduction[1]

Clitics challenge a number of assumptions made about the architecture of grammar in the linguistic literature. They seem to crosscut traditional boundaries between the domains of morphology, phonology, and syntax. They are not affixes, but they are not entirely independent lexical items either, as they often need to adjoin to an element belonging to a specific grammatical category. In most cases they do not bear stress lexically, but they may form an accentual unit with the word that follows or precedes them. Their syntactic status is also ambiguous. According to Chomsky (1995: 249), clitics share properties of heads and phrases. Their ambiguous status allows them to move from phrasal argument positions within the VP, climb up the structure as XP elements and finally adjoin as heads to the inflectional head T^0.

---

1. I would like to thank Željko Bošković, Roumyana Pancheva, Julio Villa-García, and the audience present at the *Challenging Clitics* workshop for their invaluable comments. Special thanks are due to the two anonymous reviewers of the paper for their insightful and detailed feedback. This research was initially funded by the Netherlands Organization for Scientific Research (NWO) under the *Rubicon* grant 446-05-008 completed at the University of Connecticut, and currently under the *Focus* grant from the Foundation for Polish Science.

In part due to their ambiguous nature, clitics have attracted considerable attention in the literature. Until recently, however, a large part of this work concentrated on Romance languages, which have verb-adjacent clitics. Accordingly, most of the assumptions about the nature of cliticization have been derived on the basis of verb-adjacent clitics. In the early 1990's, second position cliticization in Slavic came into focus. This type of cliticization is found less often in well-studied contemporary languages, although it has been attested in many historical languages such as Ancient Greek and Sanskrit, most notably discussed by Wackernagel (1892), who claimed that this phenomenon was the main principle of 'syntax' in Proto-Indo-European (PIE). Supposedly, word order in PIE was free, but unstressed elements such as personal pronouns and certain particles had to occur after the initial element in a clause.

In contemporary Slavic languages both second-position and verb-adjacent patterns of cliticization are to be found. The latter type is currently restricted to Bulgarian and Macedonian, although it was more common historically, in the earlier stages of Slavic languages. A study of diachronic data indicates that pronominal clitics in some Slavic languages switched from verb-adjacent to second position cliticization. The aim of this paper is to establish the trigger for the shift of pronominal clitics to second position as well as to determine what property conditions the existence of the two types of cliticization. The paper will show that the relevant condition is morphological tense marking.

This paper has the following organization. Following the introduction in Section 1, Section 2 presents general properties of clitics in Slavic. Section 3 discusses syntactic contrasts that coincide with the two types of cliticization in Slavic. Section 4 outlines a diachronic change in the position of pronominal clitics in Slavic, which involves a shift of verb-adjacent clitics to second position. Section 5 demonstrates that the change described in Section 4 largely overlaps with a decline of tense marking in Slavic over centuries. Section 6 presents an analysis that shows how these two changes can be captured in syntactic terms.

2. Clitics in Slavic

Slavic languages display a relatively large inventory of clitic forms. They include not only pronominal elements, but also the auxiliary 'be' that is used in periphrastic tenses, copula and passive constructions; modal clitics used in future tenses, and so-called 'operator clitics,' which are complementizers and focus markers that express the illocutionary force of a clause.

Only two Slavic languages, Bulgarian and Macedonian, have verb-adjacent clitics. The remaining ones that do have the full range of clitics (that is, Czech,

Serbo-Croatian, Slovak, and Slovene) place them in second position. These two groups coincide with a number of other properties that exist in Slavic. For instance, only Bulgarian and Macedonian have articles and a rich system of tense distinctions. On the other hand, they do not have infinitives and they show morphological case marking only on pronouns.

East and West Slavic languages (except Czech and Slovak) in general have a poorer clitic inventory. Polish has weak pronouns instead of pronominal clitics, whereas its auxiliary clitics are in the process of being reduced into verbal affixes. Russian and Ukrainian exhibit only operator clitics; they do not have pronominal or auxiliary clitics.

The internal order of clitics is fairly constant across Slavic and is the same in main and embedded clauses. It is given in the template in (1) and is exemplified for Macedonian, a language with verb-adjacent clitics, in (2) and for Serbo-Croatian, a language with second position clitics, in (3).

(1) OPERATOR – MOOD/AUX (except 3rd SG) –DAT – ACC – GEN – REFL – 3rd SG AUX
(see, e.g., Tomić 1996; Franks & King 2000:45)

(2) a. *Po Marija li ḱe ti go prati?*
by Maria Q will you.DAT it.ACC send.3SG
'Is it with Maria that (s)he will send it/ to you?'
(Mac, Tomić 1996:826)

b. *Da li mi ih je danas kupio?*
that Q me.DAT them.ACC is.AUX today bought
'Did he buy me them today?' (SC, Franks 1998:5)

The sequence in (1) opens with operator clitics, which include the interrogative complementizer *li* and the focus particle że/že. Next comes a sequence of (modal and temporal) auxiliary verbs and pronominal clitics. The ordering in (1) holds both for languages with verb-adjacent clitics and for those with second position clitics. It is subject to some variation across Slavic. For instance, the reflexive clitic precedes the accusative and genitive clitics in Czech (see Franks & King 2000: 105). The clitic forms of the auxiliary verb 'be' display an interesting split between the third person singular forms and the remaining ones, with only the former occurring at the end of the clitic cluster. See Tomić (1996), Boskovic (2001), and Migdalski (2006:220–221) for different accounts of this phenomenon.

As a rule, clitics must stay adjacent and may not be separated from each other (see a discussion in Section 3, though). Operator clitics, which occur at the beginning of the clitic cluster, are in many ways exceptional. They are the only clitics that do not have non-clitic (tonic) counterparts. They always occur in second position, whether there are other second position clitics in a language or not. In Bulgarian, they are the only clitics that need not be verb-adjacent or that can be separated from the remaining clitics, as shown in (3) for the focus operator enclitic *li*.

(3) *Včera* ***li*** *Penka* ***ja*** *e* *dala*
yesterday Q Penka her.ACC is.AUX give.PART.F.SG
knigata na Petko?
book-the to Petko
'Was it yesterday$_{\text{FOC}}$ that Penka$_{\text{TOP}}$ gave the book to Petko?'
(Bg, Tomić 1996: 833)

Furthermore, in other languages they often impose special restrictions with respect to the syntactic or categorial status of their host. For instance, in Serbo-Croatian the operator clitic *li* may only be preceded by single words (heads), such as the adjective *skupe* in (4a). By contrast, auxiliary clitics (see 4b) and pronominal clitics (see (8) below) may be preceded by heads and phrases alike. In Section 4 I show that the special behavior of operator clitics in Slavic is also reflected in historical data.

(4) a. *Skupe* (***li***) *knjige* (****li***) *Ana čita?*
expensive Q books Q Ana reads
'Does Ana read expensive books?'

b. *Skupe* (***je***) *knjige* (***je***) *Ana čitala.*
expensive is.AUX books is.AUX Ana read.PART.F.SG
'Ana read expensive books.' (SC, cf. Bošković 2001: 27)

As far as the placement of clitics within the clause structure is concerned, verb-adjacent clitics in Bulgarian and Macedonian resemble Romance languages in this regard. Bulgarian and Macedonian differ with respect to the direction of cliticization. In Macedonian, clitics are proclitic on the verb (see 5a), while in Bulgarian they are proclitic and obligatorily require an overt element, such as *Vera* in (5b), to their left. In both languages clitics may not be separated from the verb (see 5c).

(5) a. (*Vera*) ***mi*** *go* *dade* *včera.*
Vera me.DAT it.ACC gave.3.SG yesterday
'Vera gave it to me yesterday.' (Mac)

b. *(Vera) *mi go* dade včera. (Bg)

c. *Vera *mi go* včera dade. (Bg/Mac, Franks & King 2000: 63)

Moreover, on a par with many Romance languages, Macedonian clitics must encliticize on imperatives (cf. 6) and gerunds (cf. 7).

(6) a. *Penkaloto kupuvaj* ***mi*** ***go!***
Pen-the buy.IMP.2SG me.DAT it.ACC
'Buy me the pen!'

b. *Penkaloto *mi go* kupuvaj! (Mac, Franks 1998)

(7) a. *Nemarno pišuvajḱi* ***go*** *pismoto,...*
carelessly writing.GER it.ACC letter-the
'Carelessly writing the letter, ...'

b. *Nemarno *go* pišuvajḱi pismoto (Mac, Franks & King 2000: 84)

The exact position of second position clitics in the clause structure is more difficult to determine. First of all, in general they can be preceded by any element, a head or a phrase of virtually any grammatical category except prepositions and conjunctions. For example, Tomić (1996: 817) shows that that the first element that precedes the clitics may be the first constituent of the clause (cf. 8a), the first phrase of the first clausal constituent (cf. 8b), or the first phonological word (cf. 8c).

(8) a. *Veoma lepu haljinu* ***si*** ***mi*** *kupio.*
very beautiful dress are.AUX me.DAT bought

b. Veoma lepu *si mi* haljinu kupio.

c. Veoma *si mi* lepu haljinu kupio.
'You bought me a very beautiful dress.' (SC, Tomić 1996: 817)

Moreover, Browne (1975) reports that Serbo-Croatian clitics may even intervene between the first name and the family name.

(9) *Lav* ***je*** *Tolstoj veliki ruski pisac.*
Leo is.AUX Tolstoi great Russian writer
'Leo Tolstoi is a great Russian writer.'

Such data may at first sight give the impression that second position cliticization disregards syntactic constituency and perhaps is driven by prosodic requirements. However, Franks (1997) points out that non-clitic finite verbs may occur between the first name and the family name, too, so this property is not specific to clitics.

(10) a. *Lava* ***sam*** *Tolstoja čitala.*
Leo.ACC am.AUX Tolstoi.ACC read.PART.F.SG
'Leo Tolstoi, I have read.'

b. *Lava čitam Tolstoja.*
Leo.ACC read.PRES.1SG Tolstoi.ACC
'Leo Tolstoi, I read.' (SC, Bošković 2001: 16)

Furthermore, Franks (1997) observes that the data in (10) are subject to a morphological restriction. Namely, in the case of some first + last name complexes in Serbo-Croatian it is possible to inflect one of the names for a different structural case than the other, as shown in (11).

(11) a. *Lava* *Tolstoja* *čitam.*
Leo.ACC Tolstoi.ACC read.1SG
'Leo Tolstoi, I read.'

b. *?Lava* *Tolstoj* *čitam.*
Leo.ACC Tolstoi.NOM read.1SG

c. *Lav* *Tolstoja* *čitam.*
Leo.NOM Tolstoi.ACC read.1SG (SC, Bošković 2001: 16)

Interestingly, the splitting is possible only if both parts of the name are declined, whether the proper name is split by a clitic or a tonic verb (see (12)). This suggests that the restriction related to the splitting is driven by the same syntactic principle in both cases, so it cannot be motivated by prosody.

(12) a. *Lava* ***sam*** *Tolstoja* *čitala.*
Leo.ACC am.AUX Tolstoi.ACC read.PART.F.SG
'I read Leo Tolstoi.'

b. **Lava* ***sam*** *Tolstoj* *čitala.*
Leo.ACC am.AUX Tolstoi.NOM read

(SC, Bošković 2001: 16)

(13) a. *Lava* *čitam* *Tolstoja.*
Leo.ACC read.1SG Tolstoi.ACC
'I am reading Leo Tolstoi.'

b. **Lava* *čitam* *Tolstoj.*
Leo.ACC read.1SG Tolstoi.NOM

(SC, Bošković 2001: 16)

Examples such as the one in (14) due to Tomić 1996 (see also Progovac (1996)) are even more conclusive. Here, the group of pronominal clitics should in principle be able to encliticize to and form a morphological word with the first member of a conjoined structure. This sentence is, however, unacceptable, as it violates the syntactic principle of the coordinate structure constraint, and the clitics may only follow the second conjunct.

(14) a. **Mira* ***su*** ***ti*** ***ga*** *i* *Jasna* *dale.*
Mira are.AUX you.DAT it.ACC and Jasna gave

b. Mira i Jasna *su ti ga* dale.
'It was Mira and Jasna who gave it to you.' (SC, Tomić 1996: 820)

In all the Serbo-Croatian examples discussed so far, the clitics occur in a cluster. This may give an impression that pronominal and auxiliary clitics uniformly target a designated head together and adjoin to it as a unit. While such a proposal may be plausible for Bulgarian and Macedonian, it does not seem to be correct for Serbo-Croatian and other languages with second position clitics. This will be shown in the next section, where the two types of cliticization are contrasted.

3. Second position and verb-adjacent cliticization

Although both second-position and verb adjacent clitic languages display the same clitic inventory in roughly the same order, there are a number of crucial differences regarding their syntax. First, Ćavar (1999) observes that Serbo-Croatian allows VP fronting in which a clause-mate pronominal clitic is separated from the auxiliary clitic outside the fronted VP (see (15a)). This suggests that clitics do not adjoin to a single syntactic head. Bošković (2001: 189) shows that this type of separation is not possible in Bulgarian (see (15b)).

(15) a. [*Dali* ***ga*** *Mariji*] ***su*** *Ivan i Stipe.*
gave it.ACC Marija.DAT are.AUX Ivan and Stipe
'Give it to Marija, Ivan and Stipe did.' (SC)

b. *[*Celunala* ***go***] *Maria* ***e.***
kissed him.ACC Maria is.AUX
'Kissed him, Maria has.' (Bg)

Correspondingly, Bošković (2001: 50) observes that Serbo-Croatian clause-mate clitics may also be split from each other by a parenthetical (see (16a)). However, the material that occurs between the clitics must be a full intonational phrase so that each clitic is the second element in its own intonational phrase. By contrast, the splitting is not possible in Bulgarian, as observed by Bošković (2001: 189) and indicated in (16b).

(16) a. *Ti* ***si*** ***me,*** *kao što* ***sam*** *već.*
you are.AUX me.DAT as am.AUX already
rekla, lišio ***ih*** *juče.*
said deprived them yesterday
'?You, as I already said, deprived me of them.' (SC, Bošković 2012)

b. **Te sa, kakto ti kazah, predstavili*
they are.AUX, as you.DAT told introduced
gi na Petŭr.
them.ACC to Peter
'They have, as I told you, introduced them to Peter.'
(Bg, Bošković (2001: 189)

More evidence against the idea that Serbo-Croatian pronominal clitics cluster in the same head position comes from ellipsis data (see Stjepanović (1998: 532)). Stjepanović discusses examples of the type given in (17), which contain two conjoined clauses. In both of them the subject is followed by the auxiliary clitic, which in turn is followed by two pronominal clitics: the indirect object *mu* and the direct object *ga*. She shows that that the accusative (lower) clitic in the second conjunct may be deleted under identity in VP ellipsis while only the dative (higher) pronominal clitic is pronounced. It is also possible to delete both pronominal clitics and pronounce only the auxiliary. Bošković (2002: 331) points out that the deletion of this type is not possible in Bulgarian.

(17) a. *Mi smo mu ga dali, a i*
we are.AUX him.DAT it.ACC gave and also
vi ste mu ~~ga~~ ~~dali~~.
you are.AUX him.DAT it.ACC gave
'We gave it to him, and you did, too.' (SC)

b. **Nie sme mu go dali, i vie*
we are.AUX him.DAT itACC gave and you
ste ~~mu~~ ~~go~~ ~~dali~~ (sŭšto).
are.AUX him.DAT it.ACC gave too
'We gave it to him, and you did too.' (Bg)

Given the standard assumption that only constituents can be deleted, Stjepanović concludes that rather than being clustered and forming a uniform syntactic constituent, pronominal clitics must be placed hierarchically with respect to each other, with each pronominal clitic occupying a separate specifier as an XP-element in the extended VP projection.

More support for the idea that pronominal clitics in Serbo-Croatian target phrasal positions comes from their movement possibilities. Progovac (1993) observes that in a specific syntactic context pronominal clitics may move from an embedded clause to the matrix clause. The movement is possible if the main clause contains a verb that selects a subjunctive complement, and it is excluded if the main verb selects an indicative complement (note that the distinction is based on semantics; the subjunctive mood is not morphologically marked on the verb here).

(18) a. *Milan kaže da* ***ga*** *vidi.*
Milan says that him.ACC sees
'Milan says that he can see him.'

b. *Milan *ga* kaže da vidi.

(19) a. *Milan želi da* ***ga*** *vidi.*
Milan wishes that him.ACC sees
'Milan wishes to see him.'

b. ?Milan *ga* želi da vidi. (SC, Progovac 1993)

Building on Progovac's data, Stjepanović (1999) and Bošković (2012) demonstrate that in the context presented in (19), pronominal clitics display flexibility of movement typical of XP elements, yet they are also subject to locality restrictions. They observe that it is also possible to front both pronominal clitics out of a subjunctive clause (see (20a)). If only one of them is preposed, it must be the higher one (see (20b)). Movement of the lower (accusative) clitic across the dative is precluded by minimality (see Stjepanović (1999)).

(20) a. *?Marija* ***mu*** ***ga*** *želi da predstavi.*
Marija him.DAT him.ACC wishes that introduces

b. ?Marija *mu* želi da *ga* predstavi.

c. *Marija *ga* želi da *mu* predstavi. (S-C, Bošković (2012)

The data in (18) through (20) are contrasted with Bulgarian facts in Migdalski (2006: 217), who observes that clitic climbing is never an option in Bulgarian.

(21) a. *Manol iska da* ***go*** *vidi.*
Manol wishes that him.ACC sees
'Manol wishes to see him.'

b. *Manol *go* iska da vidi. (Bg)

Furthermore, the two groups of languages differ with respect to the way clitics pattern with negation. Across Slavic the negative marker *n(i)e* incorporates into other elements. For instance, in Polish it incorporates into verbs, which is evidenced by the contrast in (22), in which the negation immediately precedes the verb and the insertion of any intervening material is not tolerated.

(22) a. *Jan nie czyta gazet.*
Jan NEG read.3SG newspapers.GEN
'Jan doesn't read newspapers.'

b. *Jan nie gazet czyta. (Pl, cf. Willim 1990: 212)

Correspondingly, Rivero (1991: 338) shows that in Serbo-Croatian verbs incorporate into negation as well. Her argument is based on the position occupied by second position pronominal clitics. In (23), the negative marker must have incorporated into the verb, because it is followed by the pronominal clitic *ga*. Otherwise, if the sequence 'neg + verb' were analyzed as two words, the clitic *ga* would occur in a non-second position, which is excluded in all other contexts in Serbo-Croatian.

(23) *Ne* (**ga*) *vidim* *ga.*
NEG him.ACC see.PRES.1SG him.ACC
'I don't see him.' (SC, Rivero 1991: 338)

Serbo-Croatian differs from verb-adjacent clitic languages with respect to the categories that negation can incorporate into. As shown in (25), in Bulgarian negation incorporates into pronominal clitics, which is not possible in Serbo-Croatian (see (24)).

(24) a. *Ne cini* ***mi*** *se da...*
NEG seems me.DAT REFL that
'It doesn't seem to me that...'

b. *Ne *mi se* cini da... (SC, Migdalski 2006: 218)

(25) a. *Ne* ***mi*** *se struva, če...*
NEG me.DAT REFL seems that
'It doesn't seem to me that...'

b. *Ne struva *mi se*, če... (Bg, Migdalski 2006: 218)

Migdalski (2006: 218) explains the contrast between (24) and (25) by appealing to the Chain Uniformity Condition, which states that incorporation may only take place between elements of an equal syntactic status (that is, only between heads, but not between a phrase and a head). Given that pronominal clitics are phrasal elements in Serbo-Croatian, they may not incorporate into the negative head.

Finally, the two types of languages differ with respect to the availability of the Person Case Constraint (PCC). The PCC is a constraint restricting the combination of pronominal clitics. In a nutshell, in languages in which it is operative it requires that the accusative clitic that appears with a dative clitic be specified for the 3rd person (see 26c) or else a full (non-clitic) form of the accusative must be used (see 26b). The PCC is operative in Bulgarian and Macedonian, in which it leads to severe ungrammaticality. However, second position clitic languages such as Serbo-Croatian (see (27)) and Slovene in general do not show PCC effects. Although an anonymous reviewer points out that some speakers of Serbo-Croatian do not accept the clitic combination given in (27), there is a clear contrast between languages with second position and verb-adjacent clitics with respect to the PCC effects.

(26) a. **Az* ***im*** ***te*** *preporŭčvam.*
I them.DAT you.ACC recommend.1.SG

b. *Az* ***im*** *preporŭčvam na tjax.*
I them.DAT recommend.1.SG to them.DAT
'I am recommending you to them.'

c. *Az* ***im*** ***ja*** *preporŭčvam.*
I them.DAT her.ACC recommend.1.SG
'I am recommending her to them.' (Bg, cf. Hauge 1999)

(27) *Ja* ***im*** ***te*** *preporučujem.*
I them.DAT you.ACC recommend
'I recommend you to them.' (SC, Migdalski 2006: 198)

To account for the distribution of the PCC effects, Migdalski (2006: 198) adopts Anagnostopoulou's (2003) analysis of the PCC. In her analysis, she assumes that the PCC results from the incompatibility of person and number feature checking. It takes place when a dative clitic is adjoined to a single head (such as T) to check a person feature and then subsequently an accusative clitic adjoins to the same head. Given that the person feature of T has already been checked, the accusative may only check the remaining number feature of T. As a result, the derivation converges only if the accusative pronoun carries just a number feature, and on the assumption that the 3rd person is a null person, the accusative clitic may only be marked for the 3rd person.

Anagnostopoulou's (2003) account implies that the PCC is at work only when pronominal clitics adjoin to the same head. The fact that it is not operative in Serbo-Croatian or Slovene suggests that pronominal clitics do not cluster in these languages.

In sum, the data discussed in this section indicate that the two groups of languages differ not only with respect to the linear position of their clitics. The two cliticization types represent different syntactic operations. Whereas Bulgarian and Macedonian pronominal clitics adjoin to a single syntactic head such as T, second position pronominal clitics target specifiers and do not form a syntactic constituent.

4. The diachronic distribution of clitics in Slavic

This section of the paper examines diachronic changes in the position of clitics in Slavic, with an aim to determine the reason for the existence of the two patterns of cliticization in Modern Slavic. It shows that in Old Slavic the cliticization pattern initially resembled the one currently found in languages with verb-adjacent clitics. In languages other that Bulgarian and Macedonian,[2] pronominal clitics later moved to second position. In Section 5, I demonstrate that the switch was contemporaneous with the loss of morphological tense.[3]

For the purpose of this study I use Old Church Slavonic and Old Serbian data collected and investigated by Radanović-Kocić (1988). I also make use of the *University of Southern California Parsed Corpus of Old South Slavic* compiled by Roumyana Pancheva and her colleagues, mainly *Codex Zographensis* and *Codex Marianus*. Both *Codex Zographensis* and *Codex Marianus* are Gospel Books dating back from the late 10th/early 11th century. The former represents the dialects spoken in western Bulgarian while the latter exhibits Macedonian and Serbian features (Gardiner 1984).

All the Old Church Slavonic data sources are religious texts. A potential objection for using only religious manuscripts for the investigation of a grammatical system of a language might be the possibility that they do not reflect the spoken language of the area and perhaps may copy certain grammatical structures from the language of the source text. However, it is known that Old Church Slavonic translators paid attention to reflect semantic differences between the languages by using different tense forms in their translations. They would, for example, replace an aorist form in a Greek text with a present perfect construction in the Slavic translation (see Słoński (1926: 8); Hewson & Bubenik 1997: 91). It is therefore very likely that the clitic placement in their translations mirrored the standard patterns found in Old Slavic as well. By and large, the position of clitics is very strict crosslinguistically, even in languages with 'free' word order. Whereas tense modifications in translations may only change the semantics of the text, any alteration to the clitic positions makes sentences unpronounceable. Thus, it seems that the diachronic data we have access to faithfully represents the patterns of cliticization in Old Church Slavonic.

2. This does not imply that the position of clitics in Bulgarian and Macedonian remained the same over centuries. In particular, see Pancheva (2005), who shows that Bulgarian had second position clitics between the 9th and the 14–15th centuries.

3. The investigation here focuses on operator and pronominal clitics. I do not examine the position occupied by auxiliary clitics because there are relatively few examples of the present perfect tense forms (in which the auxiliary clitics are used) in Old Church Slavonic relics. According to Dostál's (1954: 599ff.) calculations, present perfect constitutes only around 5% of all tense uses in Old Church Slavonic texts. An anonymous reviewer draws my attention to the fact that there are more examples of the conditional, which is composed of the auxiliary *bimь/ byxъ* and the *l*-participle. Both auxiliaries tend to be verb-adjacent and show a semi-clitic behavior.

The basic pattern of Old Church Slavonic cliticization is presented in examples (28) and (29). The sentences in (28) contain operator clitics: *bo* 'for', 'because'; the interrogative focus particle *li*; and the focus marker (translated also as the conjunction 'and') že. According to Radanović-Kocić (1988: 151), they all occur in second position without exception.

(28) a. *Približi* **bo** *sę* *crstvie* *nbskoe.*
approach.AOR.3SG because REFL kingdom heaven
'For the kingdom of heaven is at hand.'
(OCS, *Matthew* 3:2, Radanović-Kocić 1988: 152)

b. *Ašte* **li** **že** *ni* *i* *novõjõ* *razderetъ.*
if Q FOC not also new tear.FUT
'Or he will tear the new one.'
(OCS, *Luke* 5: 36, Pancheva et al. 2007a)

As far as the position of pronominal clitics is concerned, in most cases they are verb-adjacent. This is particularly true of accusative clitics, which were always next to a verb in the material Radanović-Kocić (1988) investigated.

(29) a. *Oca* *moego* *vъ* *těxъ* *dostoitъ* **mi** *byti.*
father.GEN my.GEN in these be-appropriate.INF me.DAT be
'I had to be in my Father's house?'
(OCS, *Luke* 2:49, Pancheva et al. 2007a)

b. *Ašte* *desnaě* *tvoě* *rõka* **sъblažněetъ** **tę.**
if right your hand sinPRES.3SG you.ACC
'If your right hand causes you to sin.'
(OCS, *Matthew* 5:30, Radanović-Kocić 1988: 154)

Pronominal clitics can also be separated from operator clitics, as in (30). The same pattern holds for embedded clauses, as indicated in (31), in which the operator clitic *že* is in the second position in the embedded clause, following the initial element after the complementizer, whereas the pronominal clitic *ě* is right adjacent to the participle *sъtvorilъ*.

(30) *Elisaveti* *že* *isplъni* *sę* *vrěmę*
Elizabeth CONJ fulfilled REFL time
roditi **ei.** *I* *rodi* *snъ.*
give-birth.INF her.DAT and give-birth.PAST son.ACC
'And it was time for Elizabeth to have her baby, and she gave birth to a son.'
(OCS, *Luke* 1: 57, Pancheva et al. 2007a)

(31) *G[lago]ljǫ vamъ ěko nikotory že pror[o]kъ*
say.1SG you.DAT that no FOC prophet
prijętenъ estъ vъ otečъstvii svoemъ.
accept.PASS.N.SG be.3.SG in homeland his
'I say to you that no prophet is accepted in his homeland.'
(OCS, *Luke* 4: 24, Willis 2000: 326)

The position of dative clitics was somewhat less regular. Radanović-Kocić (1988) claims they could appear in second position when they were accompanied by operator clitics and she provides the data in (32). Note though that in all of these examples the dative clitic is also adjacent to a verb. Furthermore, in (32c), the dative could be analyzed as a non-argumental, ethical dative clitic (Željko Bošković, p.c.). Such clitics are also operator clitics. In contemporary Serbo-Croatian they are located higher in the structure than argumental dative clitics, as they may cross sentential adverbs, whereas regular pronominal clitics may not (see Bošković (2001: 60)). Thus, if the dative element in (32c) is non-argumental, it is not surprising that it reaches the same position as other operator clitics.

(32) a. *Ne běhъ* ***li ti*** *reklъ.*
NEG was.IMPR.1SG Q you.DAT tell.PART.M.SG
'Did not I tell you?' (OCS, Radanović-Kocić 1988: 153)

b. *Sǫdii* ***tę*** *prědastъ sloudzě.*
judge you.DAT hand-over.PRES.3SG guardDAT
'The judge hands you over to the guard.'
(OCS, *Matthew* 5: 21, Radanović-Kocić 1988: 156)

c. *Dobrěe* ***bo ti*** *estъ.*
better as you.DAT is
'It is better for you.' (OCS, *Matthew* 5: 30, Radanović-Kocić 1988: 153)

In other cases, dative clitics did not need to appear in second position, but they were verb-adjacent.

(33) a. *Vъ těxъ dostoitъ* ***mi*** *byti.*
in these be-appropriate me.DAT be
'In them it is suitable for me to be?'
(OCS, *Luke* 2: 49 Pancheva et al. 2007a)

b. *Ăko podobaetъ* ***ti*** *vsě slava.*
since fit.PRES.3SG you.DAT all glory
'Since you deserve all the glory.'

c. *Idi jako věrova da bǫdetъ* ***ti.***
go as believe that be.PRES.3SG you.DAT
'Go be it done for you as you have believed.'
(OCS, *Matthew* 8: 13, Radanović-Kocić 1988: 154)

Moving from Old Church Slavonic to Old Serbian, Radanović-Kocić (1988) points out that the oldest Serbian texts (12th–15th c.) exhibit the same distribution as Old Church Slavonic. Operator clitics always occur in Wackernagel position. Pronominal clitics are either verb-adjacent (see (34a and b) or appear in second position (see (34c)), obligatorily so if they co-occur with operator clitics (see (34d)).

(34) a. *Ězъ veli župan klъnu* ***se.***
I great prince swear.PRES.1SG REFL.ACC
'I, great prince, swear...'

b. *I sie učiniv* ***imъ.***
and this do them.DAT
'And having done that to them.'
(OS, Radanović-Kocić 1988: 160)

c. *Takoge* ***ti se*** *i mi klъnemo.*
also you.DAT REFL and we.NOM swear.PRES.1PL
'We also swear to you.' (OS, Radanović-Kocić 1988: 159)

d. *Kto* ***li ga*** *ime taiti.*
who Q him.ACC has hide.INF
'Who will be hiding him? (OS, Radanović-Kocić 1988: 158)

However, sometimes it is difficult to determine the exact cliticization type. For instance, Radanović-Kocić describes certain occurrences of pronominal clitics as of the Wackernagel type, yet at the same time these clitics are verb-adjacent. (In (35b) negation incorporates into the following verb, so the two elements form a single word).

(35) a. *Ašte* ***li se*** *obrěte edno selo.*
if Q REFL find.PRES.3SG one village
'If a village is found...' (OS, Radanović-Kocić 1988: 157)

b. *Dokle* ***mu se*** *ne ispravi.*
until him.DAT REFL NEG corrects
'Until it is corrected (for him).' (OS, Radanović-Kocić 1988: 158)

What is evident, though, is that all pronominal clitics gradually gravitate towards second position. From the 16th century onwards, if operator clitics occur in a clause, pronominal clitics must be adjacent to them and follow the first constituent, even if this means that they are separated from the verb by some non-clitic lexical material.

(36) *On* ***li se je*** *na ńe povratila.*
Or Q REFL.ACC is.AUX to it return.PART.F.SG
'Or she returned to it.' (Bosnia, 17th c., Radanović-Kocić 1988: 163)

In the absence of operator clitics, pronominal clitics show remarkable variation, as they may target second position or they may remain verb-adjacent. In addition, pronominal clitics do not need to be adjacent to an auxiliary clitic, unlike in contemporary Serbo-Croatian.

(37) a. *Verom* ***ti*** ***se*** *mojom obetuju.*
faith.INSTR you.DAT REFL my swear.PRES.1SG
'I swear to you by my faith.'
(Croatia, 16th c., Radanović-Kocić 1988: 165)

b. *Ona starež ktio* ***mi*** ***je*** *učinit.*
that old man want me.DAT is.3SG do.INF
'That old man wanted to do me...'
(Croatia, 16th c., Radanović-Kocić 1988: 166)

c. *Ako iguman sakrivi* ***mi.***
if prior does-wrong me.DAT
'If the prior does me wrong.'
(Montenegro, 18/19th c., Radanović-Kocić 1988: 166)

Interestingly, some of the texts in which pronominal clitics were still verb-adjacent in the 19th century come from Montenegro (see (37c)). I take this fact to be significant, because the dialects of this area preserved tense distinctions the longest, which suggests a correspondence between the availability of verb-adjacent pronominal cliticization and the presence of morphological tense. The way tense marking in Slavic has changed over time is presented in the next section.

5. Diachrony of tense marking in Slavic

It is not necessary to mark temporal distinctions in a language via tense morphology. Some languages dispense with tense morphology completely and use aspect or modal forms instead. It is commonly assumed in diachronic studies (see, for example, Lehmann 1974) that in Early Proto-Indo-European (PIE) verbs were only specified for aspect and that tense did not exist as a separate category. Thus, initially a distinction was made only between perfective and imperfective variants. A similar distinction is made in contemporary Slavic languages, in which almost all verbs occur in aspectual pairs, exemplified in (38) for contemporary Polish. In Slavic the (im)perfective contrast is marked via regular affixation; this was not the case in PIE, as pointed out by an anonymous reviewer.

(38) *czytać* */przeczytać.*
read.IMPF.INF read.PERF.INF

In later stages of PIE, aspect morphology was simplified, and the temporal and aspectual relations started to be expressed through newly formed simple past tenses, the aorist and imperfect, which also rendered aspectual distinctions. Old Slavic, however, retained the rich aspectual morphology, which meant that it expressed aspect twice on a single verb form: through aspect marking and the aspectual tenses. This is illustrated in chart (39), which presents forms of the tenses used in Old Church Slavonic for the verb *nesti* 'to carry.' The chart also shows that Old Church Slavonic had three regular compound tenses: future II, present perfect and pluperfect. All of them used different aspectual variants of the verb 'be' as the auxiliary, which was accompanied by the main verb in the form of the so-called *l*-participle. The main verb could be in the perfective or imperfective variant. It should be noted though that, as remarked by an anonymous reviewer, not all OCS verbs are attested in all the aspectual forms listed in this chart. In particular, non-motion verbs are not found in all these variants.

(39) Tense and aspect forms in OCS

TENSE/ASPECT	IMPERFECTIVE	PERFECTIVE
3SG PRESENT	nesetъ	ponesetъ
3SG AORIST	nese	ponese
3SG IMPERFECT	nesěaše	ponesěaše
3SG FUTURE II	bǫ̃detъ neslъ	bǫ̃detъ poneslъ
3SG PERFECT	neslъ jestъ	poneslъ jestъ
3SG PLUPERFECT	bě neslъ	bě poneslъ

(OCS, partly based onVan Schooneveld 1951: 97)

With the exception of Bulgarian and Macedonian, the aspectual tenses were lost in the Slavic languages that subsequently evolved. It seems that the timing of the decline coincides with the switch of pronominal clitics from verb-adjacency to second-position placement. For instance, in Old Slovene pronominal clitics must have shifted to second position very early, as they are found already in *The Freising Manuscripts*, the oldest Slovene manuscript from the 10th–11th century. Correspondingly, Vaillant (1966: 60) points out that the aspectual tenses were lost early in Old Slovene, as in the earliest texts aorist is limited to certain verb forms. According to Stieber (1973: 53), both aorist and imperfect were lost in Czech in the 14th century. The loss may have correlated with the switch of pronominal clitics to Wackernagel position. However, the data are not entirely conclusive; although pronominal forms were verb-adjacent in Old Czech, it is not clear whether they were clitic or tonic elements (Pavel Kosek, p.c.). The changes in the patterns of cliticization in Serbian/Croatian were discussed in Section 4, where it was shown that pronominal clitics were verb-adjacent in Montenegro as late as in the 19th century. It is also the area where aorist is still actively used by a number of contemporary fiction writers as a narrative tense (Lindstedt 1994: 39). Still, the change was not completely uniform. An anonymous reviewer informs me that that the Montenegrin national epic *Gorski vijenac* by Petar II Petrović-Njegoš (published in 1847) contains aorist and imperfect tenses, but its clitic placement is second position. Noting that texts of this type are often archaic in nature, I suggest that this might be a case of grammar competition in the sense of Kroch (1989): there exist two competing analyses of the same linguistic phenomenon in the native speakers' individual grammars during a language change.

Bulgarian, a language with verb-adjacent pronominal clitics in all contexts, has retained the tense system of Old Church Slavonic to the highest degree of all Slavic languages. It still uses the aspectual tenses aorist and imperfect, which can be combined with both perfective and imperfective aspect forms (see Lindstedt 1985). In Macedonian, the aorist is the default past tense for perfective verbs, whereas the imperfect is the default past tense for imperfective verbs, though an anonymous reviewer informs me that in Macedonian imperfects are formed from perfective verbs when the future particle *ḱe* is used with them. Although until as recently as the middle of the 20th century Macedonian allowed aorist variants of verbs to be marked for imperfective aspect, this is no longer the case (Friedman 2002: 267). The gradual reduction of the tense system in Macedonian seems to go hand in hand with the modification of its cliticization patterns. Bošković (2001: 254–264) claims that Macedonian is in an intermediate stage between a language with verb-adjacent and Wackernagel clitics. Like Bulgarian, it has verb-adjacent clitics, but in the context of non-verbal predicates it requires that they be in second position. For instance, as shown in (40), in the presence of predicative nominals, clitics must occur in second position and may not appear clause-initially.

(40) a. **Petko tatko mi e.*
Petko father me.DAT is

b. **Mi e tatko.*
me.DAT is father

c. *Petko mi e tatko.*
Petko me.DAT is father
'Petko is my father.'

d. *Tatko mi e.*
father me.DAT is

(Mac, Tomić 2000: 295; Bošković (2001: 255)

The same constraint holds for clitics that occur with adjectives and passive participles. However, there is dialectal variation concerning the acceptability of these constructions. Namely, whereas all native speakers disallow clause-initial clitics in the presence of nouns, clitics may both precede and follow adjectives and passive participles in the Western dialects of Macedonian. In the Eastern dialects there is a preference for a postpositional placement of clitics in these contexts (see Migdalski 2006: 186).

(41) a. *?**Mu** e rečeno da bide točen poveḱe pati.*
him.DAT is tell.PASS to be.SUBJ punctual more times
'He was told to be punctual more than once.'

b. Rečeno *mu e* da bide točen poveḱe pati. (Mac, Tomić 2000: 296)

It is clear that we are witnessing a diachronic change whose progress varies across dialects. In specific contexts, pronominal clitics require second position placement. At the same time, tense distinctions are becoming simplified. Thus, it seems that Macedonian might be undergoing the change that occurred centuries ago in the other Slavic languages except Bulgarian. It would be useful to determine whether the dialectal variation concerning the position of clitics is matched by the tense simplification.

The remaining Slavic languages have lost the aorist and imperfect entirely, so they do not have any morphological exponents of tense distinctions any more. For instance, Serbo-Croatian, like all the Slavic languages without verb-adjacent clitics, adopted the compound tense constructed with the *l*-participle used as the main verb and the imperfective form of 'be' that functions as the auxiliary verb. The *l*-participle may occur in the perfective or imperfective aspect, but it is not specified for any tense; it carries adjectival morphology, and it agrees with the subject in gender and number. The auxiliary does not have a past interpretation, either. It is morphologically the same as the copular verb in the present tense.

(42) a. *Ja **sam** čitao knjigu.*
I am.AUX read.PART.M.SG book
'I have read the book.' (SC)

As far as the expression of future events is concerned, South Slavic languages use a modal verb as a future marker. North Slavic languages exploit two options. First, they may use a complex tense construction with the perfective form of the auxiliary 'be' that is accompanied by the infinitive (in Polish and Slovene the auxiliary may also be accompanied by the *l*-participle, cf. (43a)). Second, they may use a perfective form of the verb in the present tense (cf. 43b).

(43) a. *Będę czytać/czytał książkę.*
Am.PFV read.IPFV.INF/PART.M.SG book
'I will be reading a book.'

b. *Przeczytam książkę.*
read.PFV book
'I will read a book.' (Polish)

6. Towards an analysis

The data discussed in this paper indicate that there is a close relation between the presence of morphological tense distinctions and the possibility of clitic adjunction to verbs. I would like to capture these two properties by suggesting that in languages without morphological tense the TP layer is absent. As a result, pronominal clitics do not have suitable host (the T-head) that they can adjoin to.

This suggestion is in line with a common assumption made in the literature on Romance languages that clitics adjoin to (the verb in) T^0 (see, e.g. Kayne (1991), Sportiche (1999); see also Matushansky (2006) for a proposal that the clitics move to Spec, TP and undergo morphological merger with the verb in T^0). Let us see how this idea is substantiated in the literature. According to some proposals, clitics must cliticize onto the verb in T^0 due to PF requirements. For instance, Belletti (1999: 550) assumes that before raising to T^0, pronominal clitics reside in agreement projections. Since agreement projections are not strong heads, they may not contain any material that needs a PF interpretation. Therefore, they must be emptied before Spell-Out.

Two recent proposals made by Bošković (2012) motivate clitic adjunction to T^0 by alluding to PF requirements as well. In the first proposal he assumes that clitics are D-heads. A general property of functional heads is that they cannot be stranded. Hence, they require a specifier or a complement, or they need to assume a head-adjunction configuration. One way in which clitics may circumvent being stranded is to incorporate into the V/T complex. In this way they are also able to check case through incorporation.

Bošković's (2012) second proposal rests on the assumption that verb-adjacent clitics are D+*pro* complexes (as in Jaeggli 1986; Sportiche 1996; Franco 2000). *Pro* needs to be licenced; this can be done through verbal morphology, similarly to the way subject *pro* is licensed in null-subject languages like Spanish. Hence, the D-clitics in the form of the D+*pro* complex must move to V+T.

Without appealing to PF-requirements, Nash and Rouveret (2002: 177) postulate that the cliticization on T occurs because clitics must adjoin to a 'substantive' (lexical) category endowed with active φ-features. This is an interesting proposal in the sense that by referring to φ-features it makes a correlation with the empirical facts discussed in this paper concerning the PCC effect. I adopt this postulate and, assuming Anagnostopoulou's (2003) account of the PCC, I propose that cliticization proceeds in the following way in a a TP-language such as Bulgarian. The auxiliary forms are merged in T. The pronominal clitics originate within the VP, from which they climb up the structure. The dative clitic moves out first; subsequently it lands in T by adjoining to the auxiliary or the finite verb if they are present there and checks the person feature of T. Next, the accusative clitic climbs up and checks the remaining number feature on T, tucking in beneath the dative clitic. The derivation may converge only if the accusative clitic carries just a number feature, and not a person feature, because the latter has already been checked by the dative. Assuming, as is standard, that the 3rd person pronouns contain only a number feature, they are the only eligible candidates for the operation. If a non-3rd person pronominal clitic raises, the derivation will crash, as the person feature on the accusative will remain unchecked.

(44) $[_{TP} [_{T} \langle cl_{DAT} \rangle_i + \langle cl_{ACC} \rangle_j + T] \ldots [_{Aux} (e) [_{VP} V\ t_i\ t_j]]]$

This derivation will not be possible in a TP-less language, because there is no suitable head for the clitics to adjoin to. Instead, each pronominal clitic will raise to the specifier of a different functional head in the extended VP projections.

A question that might be asked is why second position cliticization is the 'second best' option and why pronominal clitics do not target second position when T is present. I suggest that this can be explained by a principle that favours structures in which a syntactic constituent corresponds to a prosodic word. This principle is observed in the case of verb-adjacent cliticization, in which pronominal clitics form a prosodic word and are adjoined to a single head as a constituent, but not in Wackernagel cliticization, in which elements creating a prosodic word end up in specifiers of different projections.

The idea developed in this paper implies that there is a parametric variation between languages with respect to the presence or absence of the TP projection. In this way this paper relates to Bošković's (2010) recent proposal that that the TP layer is not universally available, but rather it is projected only in those languages that also have the DP layer. Bošković bases the TP/DP parallelism on Chomsky's (1986) idea that Spec, DP is the landing site of the counterpart of movement to Spec, TP in nominalizations such as *John's destruction of the city*. This assumption allows him to straightforwardly account for many properties that DP/TP-less languages have in common, such as the lack of expletives, certain subject-object asymmetries, the fact that nominative is the default case in these languages rather than accusative (as in English), and the unavailability of the sequence of tenses.

Admittedly, TP is a core syntactic projection, but several linguists have argued that it need not be a universal one. For example, it is a matter of debate whether the syntax of Chinese can be accounted for in a more explanatory way by assuming that it does not project TP (see Sybesma (2007) for a TP-account of Chinese and Lin (2010) for arguments against it). Likewise, a number of diachronic studies propose that TP may emerge in some languages as a result of a diachronic change. For instance, Van Gelderen (1993) proposes that the category T evolves at the end of the Middle English period (ca. 1380) and coincides with the rise of *do*-support. Kiparsky (1996) suggests that the rise of T (his I) is responsible for the OV to

VO shift in Germanic. Interestingly, Kiparsky and Condoravdi (2002) argue that the emergence of TP (their IP) triggered a switch in the cliticization pattern in Ancient Greek. Namely, Homeric Greek was an article-less and a TP-less language, in which pronominal clitics adjoined to CP via prosodic inversion and occurred in second position. In later classical Greek TP emerges, pronominal clitics adjoin to it, whereas finite verbs may move to C. The current study indicates that the reversal of this process is also possible and that the TP layer may be lost as well.

7. Conclusion

This paper has addressed a diachronic modification in the position of pronominal clitics in Slavic. The modification involved a switch from verb-adjacent to second position clitics, but it occurred only in those languages that simultaneously lost the morphological marking of tense. The change is argued to have been triggered by the loss of T^0 to which clitics adjoin in verb-adjacent clitic languages. As a further consequence of the loss of T^0 clitics may not adjoin to a single head, but rather land in separate specifiers, which has repercussions for their movement and ellipsis possibilities as well as for the presence of the PCC. If this analysis is correct, it provides more support for the idea that DP and TP are not universal projections and that they can be lost or emerge in language history.

References

Anagnostopoulou, Elena. 2003. *The Syntax of Ditransitives: Evidence from Clitics*. Berlin: Mouton de Gruyter.

Belletti, Adriana. 1999. Italian/Romance clitics: Structure and derivation. In *Clitics in the Languages of Europe*, Henk van Riemsdijk (ed.), 543–580. Berlin: Mouton de Gruyter.

Bošković, Željko. 1997. *The Syntax of Nonfinite Complementation: An Economy Approach*. Cambridge MA: The MIT Press.

Bošković, Željko. 2001. *On the Nature of the Syntax–Phonology Interface. Cliticization and Related Phenomena*. Amsterdam: Elsevier.

Bošković, Željko. 2002. Clitics as non-branching elements and the linear correspondence axiom. *Linguistic Inquiry* 33: 329–340.

Bošković, Željko. 2010. On NPs and clauses. Ms, University of Connecticut.

Bošković, Željko. 2012. On clitic doubling and second position cliticization: How much does D matter? Paper presented at Clitics and Beyond, 3–5 May 2012, University of Göttingen.

Browne, Wayles. 1975. Serbo-Croatian enclitics for English-speaking learners. In *Contrastive Analysis of English and Serbo-Croatian* Vol. 1, Rudolf Filipović (ed.), 105–134. Zagreb: University of Zagreb.

Ćavar, Damir. 1999. Aspects of the Syntax–phonology Interface. Ph.D. dissertation, University of Potsdam.

Chomsky, Noam. 1986. *Knowledge of Language: Its Nature, Origin, and Use*. New York NY: Praeger.
Chomsky, Noam. 1995. *The Minimalist Program*. Cambridge MA: The MIT Press.
Dostál, Antonín. 1954. *Studie o vidovém systému v staroslověnštině*. Prague: Státní pedagogické nakladatelství.
Franco, Jon. 2000. Agreement as continuum: The case of Spanish pronominal clitics, In *Clitic Phenomena in European Languages* [Linguistik Aktuell/Linguistics Today 30], Frits Beukema & Marcel den Dikken (eds), 147–190. Amsterdam: John Benjamins.
Franks, Steven. 1997. South Slavic clitic placement is *still* syntactic. *Penn Working Papers in Linguistics* 4: 111–126.
Franks, Steven. 1998. Clitics in Slavic. Paper presented at Comparative Slavic Morphosyntax Workshop, Bloomington IN.
Franks, Steven & Holloway King, Tracy. 2000. *A Handbook of Slavic Clitics*. Oxford: OUP.
Friedman, Victor, A. 1977. *The Grammatical Categories of the Macedonian Indicative*. Columbus: Slavica.
Gardiner, Sunray Cythna. 1984. *Old Church Slavonic: an Elementary Grammar*. London: Cambridge University Press.
Hauge, Kjetil Rå. 1999. The word order of predicate clitics in Bulgarian. *Journal of Slavic Linguistics* 7: 91–139.
Hewson, John & Bubenik, Vit. 1997. *Tense and Aspect in Indo-European Languages: Theory, Typology, Diachrony* [Current Issues in Linguistic Theory 145]. Amsterdam: John Benjamins.
Jaeggli, Osvaldo. 1986. Three issues in the theory of clitics: Case, doubled NPs, and extraction. In *Syntax and Semantics 19, The Syntax of Pronominal Clitics*, Hagit Borer (ed.), 15–42. Orlando FL: Academic Press.
Kayne, Richard. 1991. Romance clitics, verb movement and PRO. *Linguistic Inquiry* 22: 647–686.
Kiparsky, Paul. 1996. The shift to head-initial VP in Germanic. In *Comparative Germanic Syntax*, Höskuldur Thráinsson, Samuel David Epstein & Steve Peter (eds), 140–79. Dordrecht: Kluwer.
Kiparsky, Paul & Condoravdi, Cleo. 2002. Clitics and clause structure. *Journal of Greek Linguistics* 2: 1–39.
Kroch, Anthony S. 1989. Function and grammar in the history of English periphrastic do. In *Language Change and Variation* [Current Issues in Linguistic Theory 52], Ralph Fasold & Deborah Shiffrin (eds), 133–172. Amsterdam: John Benjamins.
Lehmann, Winfred P. 1974. *Proto-Indo-European Syntax*. Austin: University of Texas Press.
Lin, Jo-wang. 2010. A tenseless analysis of Mandarin Chinese revisited: A response to Sybesma 2007. *Linguistic Inquiry* 41: 305–329.
Lindstedt, Jouko. 1985. On the Semantics of Tense and Aspect in Bulgarian. Ph.D. dissertation, University of Helsinki.
Lindstedt, Jouko. 1994. On the development of the South Slavonic perfect. *Three Papers on the perfect. EUROTYP Working Papers*, Series VI, July 1994. 5: 32–53.
Matushansky, Ora. 2006. Head movement in linguistic theory. *Linguistic Inquiry* 37: 69–109.
Migdalski, Krzysztof. 2006. The Syntax of Compound Tenses in Slavic. Ph.D. dissertation, Tilburg University.
Nash, Léa & Rouveret, Alain. 2002. Cliticisation as unselective attract. *Catalan Journal of Linguistics* 1: 157–199.
Pancheva, Roumyana. 2005. The rise and fall of second-position clitics. *Natural Language and Linguistic Theory* 23: 103–167.

Pancheva Roumyana, Łazorczyk, Agnieszka, Krivokapić, Jelena & Minkova, Yulia. 2007a. Codex marianus. In *USC Parsed Corpus of Old South Slavic*.

Pancheva Roumyana, Kagle, Janine & Łazorczyk, Agnieszka. 2007b. Codex Zographensis. In *USC Parsed Corpus of Old South Slavic*.

Progovac, Ljiljana. 1993. Locality and subjunctive-like complements in Serbo-Croatian. *Journal of Slavic Linguistics* 1: 116–144.

Progovac, Ljiljana. 1996. Clitics in Serbian/Croatian: Comp as the second position. In *Approaching Second: Second Position Clitics and Related Phenomena*, Aaron Halpern & Arnold Zwicky (eds), 411–428. Stanford CA: CSLI.

Radanović-Kocić, Vesna. 1988. The Grammar of Serbo-Croatian Clitics: A Synchronic and Diachronic Perspective. Ph.D. dissertation. University of Illinois, Urbana-Champaign.

Rivero, María-Luisa. 1991. Long head movement and negation: Serbo-Croatian vs. Slovak and Czech. *The Linguistic Review* 8: 319–351.

van Schooneveld, Cornelis H. 1951. The aspectual system of the Old Church Slavonic and Old Russian verbum finitum *byti*. *Word* 7: 93–103.

Słoński, Stanisław. 1926. Tak zwane perfectum w językach słowiańskich. *Prace Filologiczne* 10.

Sportiche, Dominique. 1996. Clitic constructions. In *Phrase Structure and the Lexicon*, Johan Rooryck & Laurie Zaring (eds), 213–276. Dordrecht: Kluwer.

Sportiche, Dominique. 1999. Subject clitics in French and Romance, complex inversion and clitic doubling. In *Beyond Principles and Parameters: Essays in Memory of Osvaldo Jaeggli*, Kyle Johnson & Ian Roberts (eds), 189–222. Dordrecht: Kluwer.

Stieber, Zdzisław. 1973. *Zarys gramatyki porównawczej języków słowiańskich. Fleksja werbalna*. Warszawa: PWN.

Stjepanović, Sandra. 1998. On the placement of Serbo-Croatian clitics: Evidence from VP ellipsis. *Linguistic Inquiry* 29: 527–537.

Stjepanović, Sandra. 1999. What do Second Position Cliticisation, Scrambling, and Multiple wh-fronting have in Common? Ph.D. dissertation, University of Connecticut.

Sybesma, Rint. 2007. Whether we tense-agree overtly or not. *Linguistic Inquiry* 38: 580–587.

Tomić, Olga. 1996. The Balkan Slavic clausal clitics. *Natural Language and Linguistic Theory* 14: 811–872.

Tomić, Olga. 2000. On clitic sites. In *Clitic Phenomena in European Languages* [Linguistik Aktuell/Linguistics Today 30], Frits Beukema & Marcel den Dikken (eds), 293–316. Amsterdam: John Benjamins.

Vaillant, André. 1966. *Grammaire comparée des langues slaves*, Tome III: *Le verbe*. Paris: Éditions Klincksieck.

van Gelderen, Elly. 1993. *The Rise of Functional Categories* [Linguistik Aktuell/Linguistics Today 9]. Amsterdam: John Benjamins.

van Schooneveld, Cornelis H. 1951. The Aspectual System of the Old Church Slavonic and Old Russian verbum finitum *byti*. *Word* 7: 93–103.

Wackernagel, Jacob. 1892. Über ein Gesetz der Indogermanischen Wortstellung. *Indogermanische Forschungen* 1: 333–436.

Willim, Ewa. 1990. On case marking in Polish. *Papers and Studies in Contrastive Linguistics* 25: 204–220.

Willis, David. 2000. Verb movement in Slavonic conditionals. In *Diachronic Syntax: Models and mechanisms*, Anthony Warner (ed.), 322–348. Oxford: OUP.

The Freezing Principle in Hungarian polarity, non-polarity and multiple *wh*-questions

Gréte Dalmi
Eszterházy College

This paper[1] explores how weak erotetic[2] *vajon* 'whether, if…at all' interacts with the interrogative clitic *-e* 'QCL' in polarity questions and with *wh*-words in non-polarity and multiple *wh*-questions in Hungarian. *Vajon* 'if…at all', sitting in ForceP, forms an expletive–associate chain with FINP, which hosts the polarity interrogative clitic *-e* 'QCL'. Whenever the INT operator forms an OP-variable chain with the interrogative clitic *-e* 'QCL', this chain blocks Long *wh*-movement out of subordinate clauses. Weak erotetic *vajon* 'if…at all' signals such OP-variable chains. The same holds for subordinate multiple *wh*-questions, where the INT….*wh*-word chain blocks the extraction of another *wh*-word.

1. Some cross-linguistic background[3]

It has been noted in the syntactic and semantic literature (Adger & Quer 2001; Eckardt 2007) that the interrogative complementiser *whether* in English subordinate polarity questions has a number of properties that distinguish it

---

1. I express my gratitude to Huba Bartos, Ágnes Bende-Farkas, Anna Bondaruk, Edith Moravcsik, Halldór Sigurðsson and Gabriella Tóth for their helpful comments and criticism. I am also grateful to the anonymous reviewers and the editors of this volume for their useful comments, which helped me make my claims clearer.

2. The weak erotetic 'if…at all' reading of *whether* usually emerges in non-veridical contexts (see Eckardt 2007; Schwabe 2004, 2007). *Wh*-questions used with *whether* in certain *MWF*-languages (see Boeckx & Grohmann 2003) automatically create such contexts, whereby the weak erotetic 'if…at all' reading of *whether* emerges.

3. *Abbreviations:* ACC = accusative case; ASSERT = assertoric operator; COM = comitative case; COND = conditional mood; CP = complementiser phrase; DAT = dative case; DEF = definiteness feature; ELAT = elative case; EXPL = expletive; FinP = finiteness phrase; ForceP* = iterable force phrase targeted by remnant movement; INESS = inessive case; INT = interrogative operator; MWF = multiple *wh*- fronting; PRTC = participle; PFX = prefix; QCL = interrogative clitic *-e;* SBL = sublative case; SPR = superessive case; [+/–q] = interrogative feature.

from *if*. Syntactically, *whether* occurs both in finite and infinitival clauses, whilst *if* is restricted to finite clauses. Semantically, while *if*-clauses are biased towards a positive answer, *whether*-clauses are not committed in this respect. As a consequence of this, *if*-clauses function as true polarity questions but *whether*-clauses can also be used as alternative questions (Eckardt 2007):

(1) Elsie can tell us *if* there will be a party (*or not).

(2) Elsie can tell us *whether* there will be a party (or not).

In the first sentence the speaker expects a positive answer, while the second is unbiased, i.e. either a positive or a negative answer is acceptable.

Eckardt (2007) also notes that the acceptability of *whether*-clauses increases in non-veridical contexts, compared to *if*-clauses (on the veridical vs. non-veridical distinction see Giannakidou 1998 and 2000):

VERIDICAL
(3) The queen told Edward *whether* her hair was dyed.

NON-VERIDICAL
(4) The queen didn't tell Edward *whether* her hair was dyed.

This may be related to the fact that in non-veridical contexts either the weak erotetic 'if…at all' reading or the alternative 'whether…or not' reading of *whether* emerges, whereas *if* is positively biased and has neither of these interpretations.

Interrogative complementisers are banned in *wh*-interrogative clauses in English and German:

(5) a. *Peter didn't know [$_{CP}$ *whether who* had arrived].
b **Peter wusste nicht* [$_{CP}$ *ob wer angekommen war*].
Peter knew not whether who arrived was
'Peter didn't know who had arrived.'

In the South Slavic languages, however, this ban seems to be lifted. One crucial difference between English *whether* or German *ob* vs. South Slavic *li* is that the latter may also appear in *wh*-interrogative clauses (see Rudin 1988; Rivero 1993; Bošković 1997, 2001, 2002, 2003; Krapova 2002 and Schwabe 2004 for details):

(6) *Kakvo li nameri?*
what whether find.PAST3SG
'What (if anything at all) did she find?' (Bulgarian)

(7) *Sta li si mi to kupio?*
what whether AUX2SG I.DAT PRT buy-PRTC
'What (if anything at all) did you buy for me?' (Serbo-Croatian)
(examples from Schwabe 2004 and Bošković 2001)

That the South Slavic languages allow Multiple *Wh*-Fronting (MWF) in the sense of Boeckx and Grohmann (2003) and also accommodate the interrogative complementiser *li* in matrix and subordinate *wh*-interrogative clauses (see Rudin 1988; Rivero 1993; Bošković 1997, 2001, 2002, 2003; Krapova 2002 and Schwabe 2004) is not a coincidence: the *INT(errogative)* operator produces a special freezing effect in both environments (Bošković 1997, 2002, 2003). This relates Hungarian *vajon*-clauses to South Slavic *li*-clauses.

Hungarian is a Multiple *wh*-fronting (MWF) language (Surányi 2002, 2004) that allows for the weak erotetic 'if ...at all' reading of *vajon* 'whether' in main and subordinate polarity, non-polarity and multiple *wh*-questions (see Gyuris & Gärtner 2008 for a pragmatic account of *vajon* 'whether').

Despite its similar distribution, the syntactic properties of Hungarian *vajon* 'whether, if...at all' are substantially different from those of Slavic *li* 'whether' (see Dalmi 2011). Its optional occurrence and flexible syntactic positioning, its co-occurence with the interrogative clitic *-e* 'QCL' or with *wh*-words, as well as its successive cyclic insertion along with the complementiser *hogy* 'that' point in the direction that, unlike its Germanic or Slavic cousins, Hungarian *vajon* 'whether, if...at all' is not a complementiser. Its seemingly low position calls for a complex syntactic operation, which is nonetheless flexible enough to account for all pre-, and post-*vajon* occurences of the interrogative clitic *-e* 'QCL'.

This paper addresses the following questions: (i) What is the syntactic role of *vajon* 'whether' in polarity interrogative clauses with the interrogative clitic *-e* 'QCL' in Hungarian? (ii) How does weak erotetic *vajon* 'if...at all' interact with Long *wh*-movement in subordinate non-polarity and multiple *wh*-interrogative clauses?

The answers to be offered to these questions are the following. Hungarian *vajon* 'whether, if...at all' signals operator-variable chain (OP-variable chain). This becomes apparent in subordinate interrogative clauses from which Long *wh*-movement has taken place. It will be shown that the *Freezing Principle* (Bošković 1997, 1998, 2001, 2003), operative in Multiple *wh*-fronting (MWF) languages, is also at work in certain cases of Long *wh*-movement in this language.

Veridical doxastic epistemic predicates select a [-q] subordinate clause; however, they allow Operator Raising, i.e. the extension of the scope of *INT* to the whole sentence. This makes Long *wh*-movement possible (see É.Kiss 1987, 1994, 1998, 2002 and the references therein). When weak erotetic *vajon* 'if...at all' is added to the subordinate clause, Long *wh*-movement is suddenly blocked. This is due to the fact that the *INT* operator forms an OP-variable chain with the interrogative clitic *-e* 'QCL' and freezes there, blocking Long *wh*-movement altogether. *Vajon* 'if...at all' signals OP-variable chain formation in such sentences.

Non-veridical doxastic epistemic predicates optionally select a [+q] subordinate clause. Long *wh*-movement options improve in these clauses when weak erotetic *vajon* 'if…at all' is added, i.e. no freezing effect is observed there. The reason for the absence of the freezing effect is that these predicates allow a second *INT* operator in the subordinate clause after Operator Raising has taken place. This neutralises the freezing effect of the original *INT.....QCL* chain. The freezing effect is also found in subordinate Multiple *wh*-questions used with weak erotetic *vajon* 'if…at all'. Here the *INT……wh*-word chain blocks the extraction of another *wh*-word.

2. The syntactic positioning of Slavic *li* and Hungarian *vajon* in polarity questions

Interrogative clauses contain an *INT* operator, responsible for their interrogative force (Krifka 2001). Schwabe (2004, 2007) associates the interrogative vs. assertoric illocutionary force of clauses with the ForceP functional projection of the cartographic model (Rizzi 1997, 2004, 2006). She assumes an *INT* operator in all clauses with interrogative illocutionary force and an *ASSERT* operator in all clauses with assertoric illocutionary force:

(8) $[_{\text{ForceP}}$*INT/ASSERT…* $[_{\text{TOPP*}}$…$[_{\text{FocP}}$…$[_{\text{TOPP*}}$…$[_{\text{FINP}}$…]]]]]……

In her theory, both *ASSERT* and *INT* are pragmatic operators, hence they do not have any direct influence on the semantic interpretation of ordinary clauses. While the *ASSERT* operator binds a proposition variable, the *INT* operator binds ⟨q,a⟩ pairs of variables, where *q* and *a* represent questions and answers, respectively.

Polarity questions, just like non-polarity and multiple *wh*-questions, have an *INT* operator in their C-domain (Dayal 1994, 2000, 2002) (examples modelled on Schwabe 2007: 6):

(9) $[_{\text{ForceP}}$ *INT* $[_{\text{FinP.}}$ Komm-t-0 Hans]]?
come-PRES-3SG Hans
'Is Hans coming?'

(10) *Er frag-te* $[_{\textit{ForceP}}$ *ob/wie INT* $[_{\textit{FinP}}$ *Hans komm-en wird*]]].
he ask-PAST3SG whether/how Hans come-INF will
'He asked whether/how Hans would come.' (German)

In the South Slavic languages the *INT* operator is taken to be distinct from the interrogative clitic *li* 'QCL' (Bošković 1997, 2000, 2001, 2003). *INT* has scope over the interrogative clause. *Li* 'QCL' attaches to the verbal head and moves together with it along the C-domain. If there is a focussed XP in the clause, it must precede *li* 'QCL'. The *INT* operator forms an OP-variable chain with *li* 'QCL' and this chain blocks *wh*-movement from the clause. The blocking effect of OP-variable chains on *wh*-extraction is called the *Freezing Principle* by Bošković (1997, 2000, 2001, 2003). It is operative also in multiple *wh*-questions (see Boeckx & Grohmann 2003), as a subcase of the general ban on QR (Lasnik & Uriagereka 1989).

2.1 Slavic *li*

The Slavic interrogative complementiser *li* 'whether' appears under the Force^0 head in polarity interrogative clauses (Schwabe 2004).[4] In the (a) sentences of (11)–(14), V_0-*li* sequences are produced by V_0-movement, whereby the verb left-adjoins the interrogative clitic *-li* in Force^0 and thus linearly precedes it. XP-*li* sequences, on the other hand, come about only when the XP has a [+focus] feature. In such cases the XP first targets [Spec, FocP], to check its [+focus] feature. The focussed XP then moves to [Spec, ForceP] by Wackernagel's Law (Wackernagel 1892) (examples from Schwabe 2004; Bošković 2001, and Lazarova-Nikovska 2002, respectively, with focussed XPs capitalized):

(11) a. $[_{ForceP}$ $[_{Force0}$ *Čitaet* *li* *Petr* *interesn-uju* *knig-u*]]?
read-PRES3SG whether Peter interesting-ACC book-ACC
'Is Peter reading and interesting book?'

b. $[_{ForceP}$ *KNIG-U* $[_{Force0}$ *li* $[_{FocP}$ ~~*KNIG-U*~~ *Petr* *čitaet*]]]?
book-ACC whether book-ACC Peter read-PRES3SG
'Is it a BOOK that Peter is reading?' (Russian)

(12) a. $[_{ForceP}$ $[_{Force0}$ *Čita* *li* *Ana* *skupje* *knjige*]]?
read-PRES3SG whether Anna expensive books
'Is Anna reading expensive books?'

b. $[_{ForceP}$ *KNJIGE* $[_{Force0}$ *li* $[_{FocP}$ ~~*KNJIGE*~~ *Ana* *čita*]]]?
books whether books Anna read-PRES3SG
'Is Anna reading a BOOK?' (Serbo-Croatian)

(13) a. $[_{ForceP}$ $[_{Force0}$ *Čet-e* *li* *Petr* *stara* *kniga*]]?
read-PRES3SG whether Peter old book
'Is Peter reading an old book?'

4. I will remain agnostic as to where exactly the Slavic interrogative clitic *li* 'whether' originates, given that it has no direct consequence for the relative syntactic positioning of *vajon* 'whether, if...at all' and *-e* 'QCL' in Hungarian (but see Bošković 2001 for a discussion of this problem in South Slavic).

b. [$_{ForceP}$ *RIZA* [$_{Force0}$ *li* [$_{FocP}$ *nova-ta zelena* ~~*RIZA*~~ *ti*
shirt whether new-the green shirt you.DAT
podari Krasi]]]?
give.PAST3SG Krasi
'Is it the new green shirt that Krasi has given to you?' (Bulgarian)

(14) a. [$_{ForceP}$ [$_{Force0}$ *Vozi li majka ti avtomobil*]]
drive whether mother CL2SG.GEN car
'Does your mother drive a car?'

b. [$_{ForceP}$ [$_{Force0}$ *KOSARKA li* [$_{FocP}$ ~~*KOSARKA*~~ *trenira Goce*]]]?
basketball whether basketball practise for Goce
'Is it BASKETBALL that Goce is practising for?' (Macedonian)

As will be shown in 2.2, Hungarian *vajon* 'whether, if…at all' has a more flexible syntactic positioning than its Slavic counterpart: it may appear clause-initially, clause-internally and even clause-finally. This makes its complementiser status questionable.

2.2 The interaction of *vajon* 'whether, if…at all' with the interrogative clitic *-e* 'QCL'

The Hungarian interrogative clitic *-e* 'QCL' always attaches to the V_0 head of finite polarity interrogative clauses (Kenesei 1992a,b, 1994; Craenenbroeck & Lipták 2008). In a cartographic account, it is, therefore, merged under the Fin^0 head (Dalmi 2011).[5] Whenever the verb raises higher than FinP, it left-adjoins the interrogative clitic *-e* 'QCL', which moves together with it (/ and \ indicate falling and rising intonation contour):

(15) [$_{ForceP}$ *INT*[$_{TOPP}$*Péter/* [$_{FocP}$*\EL-men-t-e* [$_{FinP}$ *t a party-ra*]]]]?
Peter PFX-go-PAST3SG-QCL the party-SBL
'Did Peter attend the party?'

(16) [$_{ForceP}$ *INT* [$_{TOPP}$ [$_{FocP}$*\EL-men-t-e$_i$* [$_{FinP}$ *t_i Péter a party-ra*]]]]?
PFX-go-PAST3SG-QCL Peter the party-SBL
'Did Peter attend the party?'

5. In standard Hungarian the interrogative clitic *-e* primarily occurs in subordinate polarity and alternative questions. In addition, it may also appear in matrix rhetorical questions (see Kassai 1995 on the sociolinguistic aspects, and Kenesei 1992a,b and 1994 for a syntactic analysis). In most Hungarian dialects main and subordinate interrogative clauses show no asymmetry in the use of the interrogative clitic *-e*.

Vajon 'whether, if…at all' seemingly has a flexible distribution in main and subordinate interrogative clauses; it can be found clause-intitially, clause-internally and clause-finally.[6] In the present account, *vajon* 'whether, if…at all' has a fixed syntactic position. It appears in the specifier position of ForceP*, below the canonical finite subordinate *hogy* 'that' under C_0:

(17) [$_{CP}$ *(hogy)* [$_{ForceP*}$*(vajon) INT* [$_{TOPP}$ *Péter* [$_{FocP}$ *EL-men-t-e*
that (whether) Peter PFX-go-PAST3SG-QCL

[$_{FinP}$ *t a party-ra*]]]]].
the party-SBL

'….whether Peter attended the party at all.'

(18) [$_{CP}$ *(hogy)* [$_{ForceP}$*Péter* [$_{ForceP}$*(vajon) INT* [$_{FocP}$ *EL-men-t-e*
that Peter (whether) PFX-go-PAST3SG-QCL

[$_{FinP}$ *t a party-ra*]]]]]
the party-SBL

'….whether Peter attended the party at all.'

(19) [$_{CP}$ *(hogy)* [$_{ForceP}$ *EL-men-t-e* [$_{ForceP}$ *vajon) INT*
that PFX-go-PAST3SG-QCL (whether)

[$_{FinP}$ *t a party-ra* [$_{VP}$ *Péter t*]]]]].
the party-SBL Peter

'whether Peter attended the party at all.'

(20) [$_{CP}$ *(hogy)* [$_{ForceP}$ *PÉTER men-t-e* [$_{ForceP}$ *(vajon) INT*
that Peter go-PAST3SG-QCL (whether)

[$_{FinP}$ *t el a party-ra*]]]]].
PFX the party-SBL

'whether PETER attended the party (if anybody did at all).' (Hungarian)

Krapova (2002) proposes a stylistic rule moving the interrogative complementiser *dali* 'whether' along the C-domain of Bulgarian interrogative clauses:

COMPLEMENTISER MOVEMENT IN BULGARIAN (Krapova 2002: 124)

(21) [$_{CP}$…[$_{ForceP}$……[$_{TOPP}$ ….[$_{TOPP}$ ….[$_{FocP}$ … *dali* [$_{FINP}$……..]]]]]]

6. The complementiser *hogy* 'that' always precedes *vajon* 'whether, if …at all'. CP-recursion has proved problematic in the Germanic languages (see Branigan 1996). Therefore Dalmi (2010, 2011) proposes a more articulated C-domain with a distinct CP and an iterable ForceP*position for Hungarian. Independent motivation for a more articulated C-domain comes, among others, from Icelandic Stylistic Fronting (see Sigurðsson 2010), from various types of topicalisation in Italian and German (see Frascarelli & Hinterhölzl 2007) and from the numerous subject positions proposed by Cardinaletti (2004).

This rule correctly accounts for the clause-initial, clause-final and interspersed positions of *dali* 'whether' in Bulgarian matrix and subordinate clauses. The reason why it cannot be adopted in the present proposal is that it would leave no room for the pre-*vajon* occurrences of the interrogative clitic *-e* 'QCL' in (19)–(20).

As was already mentioned in the first paragraph of 2.2, the interrogative clitic *-e* 'QCL', attached to the finite verb in FinP, may be accompanied by *vajon* 'whether, if…at all' in main and subordinate interrogative clauses. Thus, (18) and (19) are simply stylistic variants of (17), with no semantic difference introduced by *vajon* 'whether, if…at all' in them. The semantic difference in (20) emerges due to the focussed XP.

The syntactic rule that can produce the flexible syntactic positioning of *vajon* 'whether, if…at all' in Hungarian is reminiscent of Slavic *Prosodic Inversion*, moving focussed XPs to the left of the interrogative clitic *-li*. The reasons why Slavic *Prosodic Inversion* could not produce (17)–(20) are listed in (22):

(22) i. The syntactic position of *vajon* 'whether, if…at all' is not conditional on focussing, a factor that motivates Slavic *Prosodic Inversion* with clause-initial XPs preceding *li* 'whether' (see Bošković 2001).
ii. The high syntactic positioning of the interrogative clitic *-e* 'QCL', resulting from V_0-movement combined with optional XP-movement, cannot be produced by Slavic *Prosodic Inversion*.
iii. *Prosodic Inversion* would not explain why optional *vajon* 'whether, if… at all' appears in polarity questions at all, once the interrogative clitic *-e* 'QCL' takes care of the interrogative force of the clause.

These facts necessitate a more complex syntactic mechanism in Hungarian, consisting of two steps: (i) remnant VP-movement (see Hinterhölzl 2000, 2002) targets ForceP* and takes the finite verb to the left of *vajon* 'whether,' as in (18)–(19); (ii) XPs already in their designated discourse-semantic positions within the C-domain move further up to ForceP* by a PF-triggered Stylistic Fronting rule (see Holmberg 2000), as in (20). This rule is similar to *Prosodic Inversion* in the Slavic languages but is not conditional on focussed XPs.

In subordinate polarity and non-polarity interrogative clauses the complementiser *hogy* 'that' always precedes *vajon* 'whether', see (25a–b). Within the cartographic model (Rizzi 1997, 2004, 2006), the ForceP projection hosts operators responsible for the illocutionary force of the clause. Since Rizzi (1997) it has been proposed in the literature that the C-domain should be further split (i) to allow Stylistic Fronting in Icelandic subordinate clauses (Sigurðsson 2010); (ii) to accommodate the various kinds of topic in Italian and German (Frascarelli & Hinterhölzl 2007) and (iii) to host the numerous subject positions in

Italian (Cardinaletti 1997, 2004). The co-occurrence of the true finite subordinate complementiser *hogy* 'that' and the interrogative item *vajon* 'whether, if…at all' in Hungarian calls for a distinct CP projection and an iterable ForceP*position within the C-domain (see Braningan 1996 on some problems of CP-recursion in the Germanic languages):[7]

(23)

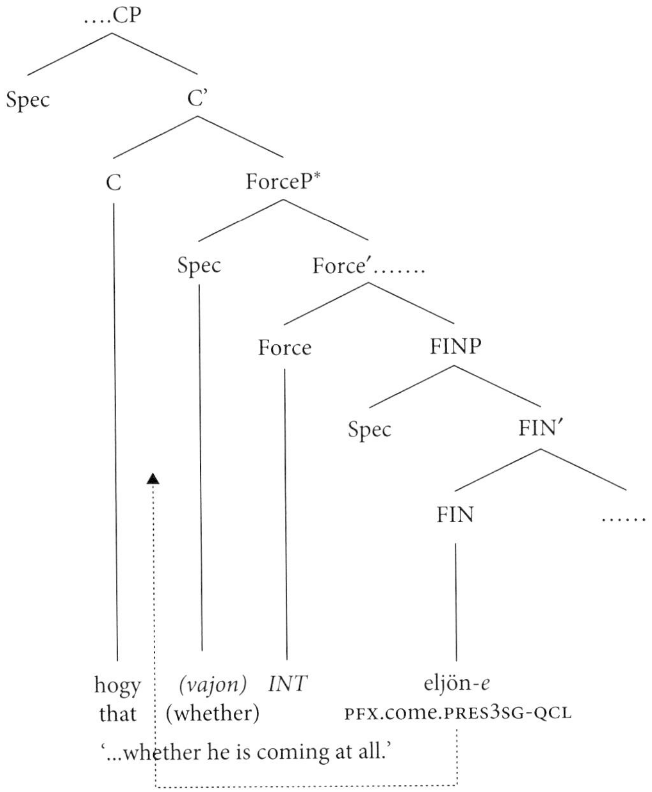

Vajon 'whether' appears in [Spec, ForceP] and forms an expletive–associate chain with FinP in the modified cartographic model of Hungarian (Dalmi (2010, 2011).

7. The cartographic model of Hungarian clauses assumed here includes a QP interspersed between TOPP* and FocP* in the sense of É Kiss (1998, 2002):

i. $[_{CP}$ *hogy* $[_{ForceP^*}$ *vajon* $[_{TOPP^*}$ *Péter* $[_{QP}$ *mindig*
that whether Peter always

$[_{FocP^*}$ *MARI-VAL* $[_{FinP}$ *jön-e* [*VP*….]]]]]]
Mary-COM come-PRES3SG-QCL

'whether Peter always comes with MARY.'

The *vajon*–FinP chain ensures LF-reconstruction in sentences like (19)–(20), where the interrogative clitic *-e* 'QCL' precedes *vajon* 'whether, if…at all'.

The pre-*vajon* occurrences of *-e* 'QCL' are derived by remnant VP-movement targeting ForceP* in overt syntax (see Hinterhölzl 2000, 2002). XPs are evacuated to the designated discourse-semantic positions of the C-domain, as usual (see É. Kiss 1994, 2002). Stylistic Fronting ensures the pre-*vajon* ordering of XPs already moved to the C-domain.

Horvath (1995, 1997, 1998, 2000) assumes an iterative CP-Pied Piping rule at LF, adjoining the embedded CP to the matrix FocP after Partial *wh*-movement has taken place. An LF-rule of this kind, however, would not produce the pre-*vajon* occurrences of the interrogative clitic *-e* 'QCL' and is therefore empirically less lucrative than the mechanism proposed here (but see Stechow 2000 for the benefits of an iterative CP-Pied Piping rule at LF in calculating *wh*-scope). Remnant VP-movement combined with a PF-triggered Stylistic Fronting rule can produce the required order without resorting to iterative CP-Pied Piping at LF.

A central claim made by Dalmi (2011) is that while South Slavic *li* is commonly analysed as an interrogative complementiser (see Rudin 1988; Rivero 1993; Krapova 2002, and Bošković 2001, 2002, 2003 for details), Hungarian *vajon* 'whether, if….at all' does not display the properties of ordinary complementisers; it simply signals OP-variable chains. This claim is based on the following facts:

(24) The syntactic properties of Hungarian *vajon* 'whether' (Dalmi 2011)
  (i) unlike Slavic *-li*, Hungarian *vajon* is optional;
  (ii) it occurs only in finite interrogative clauses;[8]
  (iii) it can co-occur with the interrogative clitic *-e*;[9]
  (iv) when it appears in subordinate interrogative clauses, it cannot precede the subordinate complementiser *hogy* 'that', (25b);
  (v) it can be introduced successive cyclically, along with the subordinate complementiser *hogy* 'that' in the sentence, (25a).

8. As Hungarian has no real interrogative infinitival clauses, neither *vajon* 'whether, if…at all' nor the interrogative clitic *-e* 'QCL' can appear in infinitival clauses:

(i) **Nem tud (vajon) MI-T tenni-e?*
not know-PRES3SG[-DEF] whether what-ACC to do-QCL
'Doesn't he know (whether) WHAT to do?'

9. When *vajon* 'whether' is present in the clause, the interrogative clitic *-e* may be absent; the interrogative illocutionary force of the sentence is obtained via the /\ intonation contour. This option is available only in matrix polarity questions.

(25) a. *Meg-kérdez-te, hogy (vajon) nem tud-om-e, hogy*
PFX-ask-PAST3SG that (whether) not know-PRES1SG-QCL that
(vajon) Péter el-jön-Ø-e.
(whether) Peter PFX-come-PRES3SG-QCL
'He asked whether I knew if Peter would come at all.'

b. **Meg-kérdez-te, vajon hogy nem tud-om-e, vajon*
PFX-ask-PAST3SG whether that not know-PRES1SG-QCL whether
hogy Péter el-jön-Ø-e.
that Peter PFX-come-PRES3SG-QCL
'He asked whether I knew if Peter would come at all.' (Hungarian)

The facts listed in (24)(i)–(iv) and illustrated in (25a–b) exclude Hungarian *vajon* 'whether, if…at all' from the set of potential complementisers for the following reasons:

i. The ordering of *vajon* 'whether, if…at all' and the subordinate complementiser *hogy* 'that' necessitates a position lower than the canonical C_0, which is reserved for true complementisers.
ii. Flexible syntactic positioning (ranging from clause-initial to clause-internal and clause-final position) is not characteristic of complementisers; this calls for a syntactic mechanism that can predict the distribution of *vajon* 'whether, if…at all' in Hungarian main and subordinate interrogative clauses.
iii. The fact that *vajon* 'whether, if…at all' optionally co-occurs with other interrogative elements (interrogative clitic, *wh*-words) excludes the logical possibility that it is the lexical realization of the *INT* operator. *Vajon* 'whether, if…at all' occupies [Spec, ForceP] and can be dropped, while *INT* occupies $Force^0$ and cannot be dropped (see also Adger & Quer 2001 on the specifier status of *whether* in English).

3. Hungarian non-polarity questions with weak erotetic *vajon* 'if….at all'

In addition to polarity questions, *vajon* 'whether, if…at all' may also appear in non-polarity questions, i.e. *wh*-interrogative clauses (see Gyuris & Gärtner 2008 for details). In such contexts the existential presupposition induced by the *wh*-word is suppressed and the weak erotetic 'if…at all' reading of *vajon* emerges. This is illustrated in (26):

(26) *Vajon KI jön-Ø el a party-ra?*
whether who come-PRES3SG PFX the party-SBL
'Who is coming to the party (if anybody is coming to the party at all)?'

Weak erotetic *vajon* 'if...at all' can also be found in subordinate clauses from which Long *wh*-movement has taken place. This makes *vajon* an ideal candidate to test the interrogative force of subordinate clauses out of which Operator Raising[10] has taken place (see É. Kiss 1987, 1994, 1998, 2002 and Gervain 2002 for details).

3.1 Partial vs. Long *wh*-movement in Hungarian

In languages that allow Partial *wh*-movement at all (see McDaniel 1989 for German and Romani; Dayal 1994, 2002 for Hindi; Horvath 1995, 1997, 1998 for Hungarian; Sabel 2000, 2003 for Malagasy), it usually appears as an alternative syntactic operation to, and co-exisiting with, Long *wh*-movement.

It is argued by Horvath (1995, 1997, 1998, 2000) that in the case of Hungarian Partial *wh*-movement the true *wh*-word performs movement to the subordinate C-domain, while another *wh*-word, called the *wh*-scope marker, is merged in the matrix [Spec,FocP]. The scope of *INT* is extended to the whole sentence by Operator Raising. In (27), the *wh*-scope marker *mi-t$_i$* 'what-ACC' forms an expletive–associate chain with the subordinate CP, in which the true *wh*-word is located. The expletive-associate chain is marked by coindexation:

PARTIAL *WH*-MOVEMENT

(27) [$_{ForceP.}$*INT* [$_{FocP}$ *MI-T$_i$* *mond-tál* [$_{DP}$ [$_{CPi}$ *hogy* [$_{ForceP}$ ~~*INT*~~
what-ACC say-PAST2SG EXPL that
[$_{FocP}$ *MELYIK* *fiú-t$_j$* *hív-od* *meg* *a party-ra t$_j$*]]]]]?
which boy-ACC invite-PRES2SG[+DEF] PFX the party-SBL
'What did you say: which boy will you invite to the party?'

When Long *wh*-movement takes place, the true *wh*-word moves via the expletive DP and targets the matrix [Spec,FocP] position (see É. Kiss 1994, 1998; Kenesei 1992b, 1994; Horvath 1995, 1997, 1998):[11]

10. Operator Raising is an overt syntactic operation that serves to extend operator scope. NEG Raising in English is an example of this:

i. *Mary thinks that John will *not* leave.
ii. Mary does *not* think that John will leave.

In the case of Hungarian Partial and Long *wh*-movement, the *INT* operator raises to the matrix clause and extends its scope to the whole sentence (see É.Kiss 1998, 2002; Gervain 2000; Horvath 1995, 1997, 1998, 2000 and the references cited therein).

11. Only *bridge verbs*, including verbs of diction, perception verbs, epistemic verbs, modal verbs and interrogative verbs allow Long *wh*-movement from their subordinate CP (see É. Kiss 1987, 1994, 1998 and the references cited therein). With verbs selecting a [+q] subordinate CP

LONG *WH*-MOVEMENT

(28) $[_{ForceP}$ *INT* $[_{FocP}$ *MELYIK* *fiú-t$_j$* *mond-tad,* $[_{DPi}$ $t_j]$
which boy-ACC say-PAST2SG[+DEF] EXPL

$[_{CPi}$ *hogy* $[_{ForceP}$..... $[_{FinP}$ *meg-hív-od* t_j *a* *party-ra*]]]]]?
that PFX-invite-PRES2SG[+DEF] the party-SBL

'Which boy did you say you would invite to the party?'

When weak erotetic *vajon* 'if ...at all' is added to such subordinate clauses, an interesting asymmetry arises between Partial vs. Long *wh*-movement:

PARTIAL *WH*-MOVEMENT

(29) $[_{ForceP}$ *INT* $[_{FocP}$ *MI-T* *gondol-sz,* $[_{CP}$ *hogy* $[_{ForceP}$ (*vajon*).....
what-ACC think-PRES2SG[−DEF] that (whether)

$[_{FocP}$ *KI* *men-ne* *el* *a* *party-ra*]]]]?
who go-COND3SG PFX the party-SBL

'What do you think: who would attend the party (if anybody would attend it at all)?'

LONG *WH*-MOVEMENT

(30) *$[_{ForceP}$ $[_{FocP}$ *KI-T$_i$* *gondol-sz* $[_{CP}$*hogy* $[_{ForceP}$ (*vajon*)
who-ACC think-PRES2SG that (whether)

$[_{FocP}$ *el-men-ne-e* t_i *a* *party-ra*]]]]]?
PFX-go-COND3SG-QCL the party-SBL

'Who do you think would attend the party (if anybody would attend it at all)?'

While Partial *wh*-movement, illustrated in (29), is always possible from subordinate interrogative clauses containing weak erotetic *vajon* 'if....at all,' Long *wh*-movement, shown in (30), is blocked in the same environment, even though it is unproblematic out of subordinate clauses without *vajon*'if...at all,' as in (28). As a matter of fact, Long *wh*-movement in (30) is not blocked by *vajon* 'if...at all' but by the OP-variable chain, established between the *INT* operator and the interrogative clitic *-e* 'QCL'. *Vajon* 'if...at all' simply signals this chain. When standard Long *wh*-movement takes place, the *INT* operator raises to the matrix clause, as in (28). There is no OP-variable chain that would block Long *wh*-movement out of the subordinate clause, hence the sentence is grammatical.

(*kérdez* 'ask', *érdekődik* 'enquire'), the interrogative clitic *-e* 'QCL' is compulsory whenever Long *wh*-movement takes place from the subordinate clause (see Horvath 1995, 1997, 1998, 2000).

3.2 OP-variable chains in Long *wh*-movement contexts

Horvath (1995, 1997, 1998) argues that Partial *wh*-movement in Hungarian requires an expletive–associate relationship to hold between the *wh*-scope-marker, sitting in the matrix [Spec, FocP], and the subordinate CP:

PARTIAL *WH*-MOVEMENT

(31) [$_{ForceP}$ *INT* [$_{FocP}$ *MI-T*$_i$ *mond-tál* t_i [$_{CPi}$ …*hogy* [$_{FocP}$*MIKOR*$_j$
what-ACC say-PAST2SG that when

jön-Ø *a vonat* t_j]]?
come-PRES3SG the train

'What did you say: when is the train coming?'

Horvath (1995) convincingly shows that the upstairs *wh*-word cannot form an expletive–associate chain with the downstairs *wh*-word (contrary to MacDaniel 1989 and Dayal 1994, 2002) as it does not originate in the subordinate clause at all. One crucial argument in support of this claim comes from object agreement.

Hungarian verbs show obligatory definiteness agreement with their object (see Bartos 1997 for details). In the affirmative sentence in (32) the matrix verb *hitted* 'believe.PAST2SG[+DEF]' shows definiteness agreement with the expletive pronoun *az-t* 'it-ACC'. No definiteness agreement is found on the matrix verb, however, when Partial *wh*-movement takes place, as in (33). This would be unexpected under the assumption that the two *wh*-words form a chain:

(32) [$_{ForceP}$ *ASSERT*…. [$_{FocP}$ *Az-t*$_k$ *hitted,* [$_{DPi}$ t_k [$_{CPi}$*hogy*
it-ACC believe.PAST2SG[+DEF] that

[$_{FocP}$ *EZ-T* *a* *fiú-t* *hív-om* *meg*]]].
this-ACC the boy-ACC invite-PRES1SG PFX

'You believe (it) that I would invite this boy.'

PARTIAL *WH*-MOVEMENT

(33) [$_{ForceP}$*INT* … [$_{FocP}$ *MI-T*$_i$ *hittél,* [$_{DPi}$ *Ø* [$_{CP}$*hogy*
what-ACC believe.PAST2SG[−DEF] that

[$_{ForceP}$ (*vajon*) …. [$_{FocP}$*MELYIK* *fiú-t*$_j$
(whether) which boy-ACC

hív-om *meg* t_j]]]]]]?
invite-PPRES1SG[+DEF] PFX

'What did you believe: which boy would I invite (if any boy at all)?'

The inherently indefinite interrogative pronoun *mi-t* 'what-ACC[-DEF]' in (33), functioning as the expletive *wh*-scope-marker, could not have moved across the expletive DP position, as no definiteness agreement is shown on the matrix verb (see Kenesei 1992b, 1994; Horvath 1995, 1997, 1998, 2000 for details). This argues against the *wh*-chain analysis (Dayal 1994, 2000) and supports the *wh*-expletive–CP-associate chain account, proposed by Horvath (1995, 1997, 1998, 2000).

Long *wh*-movement, on the other hand, moves the *wh*-word through the expletive DP position to the matrix clause, where it can check/probe its features in passing. This triggers definiteness agreement on the matrix verb, (34):

LONG *WH*-MOVEMENT

(34) [$_{ForceP}$ *INT*... [$_{FocP}$ *MELYIK* *fiú-t*$_k$ *hi-tted,* [$_{DPi}$ t_k
which boy-ACC believe-PAST2SG[+DEF]

[$_{CPi}$ *hogy* [$_{ForceP}$ ....[$_{FinP}$ *meg-hív-om* t_k]]]]]]?
that PFX-come-PRES1SG

'Which boy did you believe that I would invite?'

I adopt the analysis proposed by Horvath (1995, 1997, 1998, 2000), in which Long *wh*-movement always takes place *via* the expletive DP position in standard non-polarity questions, as shown in (34). Compare now (34) with (35):

(35) *[$_{ForceP}$ *INT* ...[$_{FocP}$ *MELYIK* *fiú-t*$_k$ *hi-tt-ed,* [$_{DPi}$ t_k
which boy-ACC believe-PAST2SG[+DEF]

[$_{CPi}$ *hogy* [$_{ForceP}$ (*vajon*) *INT* [$_{FinP}$ *meg-hív-om-e*]]]]]]?
that (whether) PFX-come-PRES1SG-QCL

'Which boy (if any boy at all) did you believe whether I would invite?'

(34) differs from the ungrammatical (35) in that the subordinate clause in the latter is a polarity question. This is shown by the interrogative clitic *-e* '*QCL*,' whose presence is obligatory in subordinate polarity interrogative clauses. Unfortunately, under the Operator Raising account, ungrammatical sentences like (35) cannot be excluded.

3.2.1 *Operator Raising and Long* wh-*movement*

The general assumption about Hungarian bridge verbs selecting a [−q] CP (*gondol* 'think', *hisz* 'believe', *mond* 'say') is that they force movement of the downstairs *wh*-element via an expletive DP argument position to the matrix clause because there is no potential functional head downstairs that would check/probe the *wh*-feature locally (see É. Kiss 1994, 1998, 2002 and the references cited therein).

Indeed, the CP-associate[12] in (34)–(35) cannot have a [+wh] feature of its own, as the verb *hisz* 'believe' takes only [−q] CPs. The expletive DP argument, subcategorized by the matrix verb, however, may have one (see É.Kiss 1987, 1998, 2002).[13] This enables the downstairs *wh*-word to move *via* the expletive DP argument position, checking its [+wh] and [+acc] features in passing, as in (34). This operation, in turn, is only possible if the *INT* operator raises to the matrix clause and extends its scope to the whole sentence (see Gervain 2000). Once Operator Raising has taken place, nothing can prevent the introduction of a second *INT* operator in the subordinate clause (see Horvath 1997 on Partial vs. Long *wh*-movement out of subordinate multiple *wh*-questions), which leads to ungrammaticality in (35). For this reason, some further restrictions need to be made.

It is proposed here that Long *wh*-movement from the subordinate non-polarity interrogative clause with weak erotetic *vajon* 'if....at all' is blocked in sentences like (35) due to a special freezing effect, familiar from Multiple *wh*-fronting (MWF) languages: if an operator enters into an OP-variable chain, it is frozen there. This is called the *Freezing Principle* by Bošković (1997, 2003):

Freezing Principle (Bošković 1997, 2003)
(36) OP in OP-variable chain cannot undergo movement.

Given that the *INT* operator in Force^0 forms an OP-variable chain with the interrogative clitic *-e* 'QCL', the operator freezes there. The frozen *INT* operator cannot raise, thus Long *wh*-extraction out of the subordinate clause is blocked in (35). In (34) Operator Raising takes place but no OP-variable chain is formed in the subordinate clause, hence no freezing effect is observed.

In the light of this observation, the data in 3.2.2. seem surprising, as they reveal some unexpected properties of doxastic epistemic predicates allowing Long *wh*-movement out of subordinate clauses, even when weak erotetic *vajon* 'if...at all' is added. Under the assumption that *vajon* 'if...at all' faithfully signals OP-variable chains in subordinate clauses, such sentences can remain grammatical only if a second *INT* operator is introduced, after Operator Raising has taken place. This will be demonstrated in the case of Long *wh*-movement and Multiple *wh*-fronting with such predicates.

12. Hungarian finite subordinate clauses usually appear as CP-associates of an expletive DP directly subcategorised by the verb. This DP may be filled by a fully referential, case-marked nominal, by a pronoun (which may or may not have a [+*wh*] feature), or even by a null expletive.

13. This view is shared by É. Kiss (1994, 1998), Horvath (1995, 1997, 1998, 2000), and Kenesei (1992b, 1994).

3.2.2 *The Freezing Principle in Long* wh-*movement contexts with weak erotetic* vajon *'if…at all'*

Predicates expressing doxastic epistemic modality in the sense of Kratzer (1991) can be either veridical or non-veridical in Hungarian. Veridical ones select a [-q] subordinate clause (e.g. *gondol* 'think of,' *hisz* 'believe,' *gyanakszik* 'suspect') and are therefore incompatible with either reading of *vajon*. Non-veridical doxastic epistemic predicates select either a [−q] or a [+q] subordinate interrogative clause (e.g. *tűnődik* 'wonder, speculate,' *nem tud* 'not know,' *gondolkodik* 'think about,' *kétségesnek tart* 'consider doubtful.DAT') (see Stechow 2000: 453 for a similar selectional classification of predicates in German). The members of this latter group are compatible with weak erotetic *vajon* 'if…at all' both in the case of Partial *wh*-movement and in the case of Long *wh*-movement.[14,15]

DOXASTIC EPISTEMIC PREDICATES OPTIONALLY TAKING A [+Q] CP, USED WITH WEAK EROTETIC *VAJON* 'IF…AT ALL'

(37) [$_{FocP}$*MI-N* *tűnőd-sz,* [$_{CP}$*hogy* [$_{ForceP}$*(vajon)…..* [$_{FocP}$ *KI*
what-SPR wonder-PRES2SG that whether who
jön-Ø *el* *a* *party-ra*]]]]?
come-PRES3SG PFX the party-SBL
'Who do you wonder will come to the party (if anybody will come at all)?'

(38) [$_{FocP}$*KI-N* *tűnőd-sz,* [$_{CP}$*hogy* [$_{ForceP}$ *(vajon)…*
who-SPR wonder-PRES2SG that (whether)
el-jön-Ø-e *a* *party-ra*]]]]?
PFX-come-PRES3SG-QCL the party-SBL
'Who do you wonder will come to the party (if anybody will come at all)?'

---

14. These verbs sound equally good with an assertive or an interrogative subordinate CP. This clearly distinguishes them from interrogative verbs always selecting a [+q] CP:

i. Mari az-on tűnőd-ött, hogy jó lenne haza-men-ni.
Mary it-SBL speculate-PAST3SG that good COP.COND3SG home-go-to
'Mary was speculating that it would be good to go home.'

ii. Spock nem tud-ta, hogy a Mars régen
Spock not know-PAST3SG that the Mars a long time ago
lakatlan volt.
uninhabited was
'Spock didn't know that the Mars used to be uninhabited.'

15. The intonation contour of both clauses must be falling after the *wh*-word: ______. This clearly distinguishes Partial *wh*-movement from *wh*-echo-questions, which have a rise-fall intonation contour at the end of both clauses: /\\.

(39) [$_{FocP}$*MI-T* *nem* *tud-sz,* [$_{CP}$*hogy* [$_{ForceP}$*(vajon)....* [$_{FocP}$*KI*
what-ACC not know-PRES2SG that whether who
jön-Ø *el* *a* *party-ra*]]]]?
come-PRES3SG PFX the party-SBL
'Who don't you know will come (if anybody will come at all)?'

(40) [$_{FocP}$*KI-T* *nem* *tud-sz,* [$_{CP}$*hogy* [$_{ForceP}$*(vajon)....*
who-ACC not know-PRES2SG that whether
[*el-jön-Ø-e* *a party-ra*]]]]?
PFX-come-PRES3SG-QCL
'Who don't you know will come (if anybody will come at all)?'

Under the Operator Raising account, Long *wh*-movement in (38) and (40) should be ungrammatical for the same reason as with matrix verbs like *hisz* 'believe' in (35). Operator Raising ought to be blocked here by the Freezing Principle, contrary to the evidence.

The freezing effect is absent for the following reason. Unlike veridical doxastic epistemic verbs (*hisz* 'believe' and *gondol* 'think of'), the non-veridical subclass of doxastic epistemic predicates, optionally selecting a [+q] CP, allows the introduction of a second *INT* operator in the subordinate clause, after Operator Raising has taken place. This property places these predicates between veridical doxastic epistemic predicates selecting a [−q] CP and inherently interrogative verbs selecting a [+q] CP.

Inherently interrogative verbs selecting a *wh*-interrogative clause (*megkérdez* 'ask' and *érdeklődik* 'enquire') are incompatible with weak erotetic *vajon* 'if... at all' in the subordinate *wh*-interrogative clause merely for pragmatic reasons. Removing *vajon* 'if...at all' makes these sentences fully acceptable:

(41) #[*Péter* *meg-kérdez-te,* [*hogy* [*vajon* [*KI-T*
Peter PFX-ask-PAST3SG that whether who-ACC
hív-tam *meg* *a* *party-ra*]]]].
invite-PAST1SG PFX the party-SBL
'Peter asked who I had invited to the party (if anybody at all).'

(42) [*Péter* *érdeklőd-ött,* [*hogy* [*KI-T* *hív-tam* *meg*
Peter enquire-PAST3SG that who-ACC invite-PAST1SG PFX
a *party-ra*]]].
the party-SBL
'Peter enquired who I had invited to the party.'

With such verbs, the speaker is committed to the factuality of the event expressed by the complement clause. Weak erotetic *vajon* 'if......at all' undermines this commitment. Here it is not the existence of the potential participants that is called into question but the whole event. Both Partial and Long wh-movement lead to a pragmatic contradiction in the presence of weak *vajon* 'if…at all':

(43) #[*MI-T kérdez-ett Péter,* [*hogy* [*vajon* [*MELYIK FIÚ-T*
what ask-PAST3SG Peter that whether which boy-ACC
hív-tad meg a party-ra]]]]?
invite-PAST2SG[+DEF] PFX the party-SBL
'What did Peter ask: which boy did you invite to the party (if any boy at all)?'

(44) #[*MELYIK FIÚ-T*$_i$ *kérdez-te Péter,* [*hogy* [*vajon*
which boy-ACC ask-PAST3SG Peter that (whether)
meg-hív-tad-e a party-ra]]]?
PFX-invite-PAST2SG[+DEF]-QCL the party-SBL
'Which boy did Peter ask whether you had invited to the party (if any boy at all)?'

Cognitive factive verbs,[16] not selecting an interrogative subordinate clause, give bad results both in the case of Partial *wh*-movement and Long *wh*-movement:

(45) *[*MI-T sajnál-sz,* [*hogy* [(*vajon*)
what-ACC regret-PRES2SG that (whether)
[*HOGYAN viselked-tek a gyerekek a mozi-ban*]]]]?
how behave-PAST3PL the children the movie-INESS
'What do you regret: how did the children behave in the movie (if anyhow at all?'

(46) *[*HOGYAN sajnál-od,* [*hogy* [(*vajon*) *viselked-tek-e*
how regret-PRES2SG that (whether) behave-PAST3PL-QCL
a gyerekek a mozi-ban]]]?
the children the movie-INESS
'How do you regret the children behaved in the movie (if anyhow at all)?'

The semantic incompatibility of factive verbs with subordinate interrogative clauses, in general, stems from the requirement that factive verbs must presuppose the truth of their complement clause. As interrogative clauses are neither true nor

16. Cognitive factive verbs in Hungarian include *tud* 'know,' *emlékszik* 'remember,' *elfelejt* 'forget,' *eltitkol* 'conceal,' *tagad* 'deny,' *cáfol* 'refute, deny,' and *rájön* 'realize' (see Kiefer 1978 for a list of factive verbs in Hungarian).

false, their truth cannot be presupposed. The subordinate interrogative clause in (47) violates the lexical semantic properties of factive verbs even if the matrix clause is uttered with interrogative intonation and with *vajon*'if…at all' added to both clauses):

(47) *[$_{ForceP}$ … *INT Péter (vajon) be-vall-otta* [$_{CP}$*hogy*…. [$_{ForceP}$ *Mari*
Peter whether admit-PAST3SG that Mary
[$_{ForceP}$*(vajon) INT el-jön-Ø-e a party-ra*]]]?
whether PFX-come-PRES3SG-QCL the party-SBL
'Did Peter admit whether Mary would come to the party?'

The options of Long *wh*-movement from subordinate non-polarity interrogative clauses with erotetic *vajon* 'whether' are summarized below. The bullets indicate the illocutionary force value of the CP selected by the matrix verb. The tick and the cross indicate Long *wh*-movement options from CPs with weak erotetic *vajon* 'if…at all':

Table 1. Long *wh*-movement from subordinate non-polarity interrogative clauses with weak erotetic *vajon* 'if…at all'

Matrix verb	Obligatory [+q] CP	Optional [+q] CP	Obligatory [−q] CP
Epistemic$_{dox}$ *1*		• ✓	
Epistemic$_{dox}$ 2			• ×
Interrogative	• ×		
Factive			• ×

The *INT-QCL* chain produces a special freezing effect that blocks Operator Raising. As a consequence of this, Long *wh*-movement is also blocked out of subordinate clauses with weak erotetic *vajon* (even if such movement is possible with doxastic epistemic verbs selecting a [−q] CP).

This freezing effect is absent in the case of doxastic epistemic verbs optionally taking a [+q] CP. Here the *INT* operator raises from the subordinate clause, extending its scope to the whole sentence, as usual. The only reason *vajon* 'if… at all' can survive in the subordinate clause is that a second *INT* operator was introduced there after Long *wh*-movement had taken place.

In the case of interrogative matrix verbs selecting a [+q] CP (*kérdezni* 'ask;' *érdeklődni* 'enquire'), the speaker's commitment to the factuality of the complement clause cannot be called into question. These verbs do not tolerate weakly erotetic *vajon* 'if….at all' as this would lead to a pragmatic contradiction; therefore they do not show the asymmetry observed with doxastic epistemic predicates optionally taking a [+q] CP. Finally, factive verbs not selecting interrogative clauses give bad results both in Partial and in Long *wh*-movement from subordinate interrogative clauses with erotetic *vajon* 'if….at all.'

3.2.3 *The Freezing Principle in multiple* wh-*questions with weak erotetic* vajon *'if…at all'*

Independent evidence for OP-variable chain formation in Hungarian subordinate polarity and non-polarity interrogative clauses comes from subordinate multiple *wh*-questions. Horvath (1998) points out that multiple *wh*-words in Hungarian subordinate *wh*-interrogative clauses may also undergo Partial *wh*-movement. The *wh*-scope marker in such cases is inserted in the matrix FocP projection, just as in standard Partial *wh*-movement cases discussed in 2.1. Long *wh*-movement from subordinate multiple *wh*-questions, by contrast, gives grammatical results only if all the *wh*-words move together as a single unit[17] (see Boeckx & Grohmann 2003):

PARTIAL *WH*-MOVEMENT FROM SUBORDINATE MULTIPLE *WH*-QUESTIONS

(48) [*Mi-t* *hi-ttél,* [*hogy* [*ki-t*
what-ACC believe-PAST2SG that who-ACC
ki-nek *mutat-nak* *be*]]]?
who-DAT introduce-PRES3PL PFX
'What did you believe: who would they introduce to whom (if anybody would be intrdocued to anybody at all?'

LONG *WH*-MOVEMENT FROM SUBORDINATE MULTIPLE *WH*-QUESTIONS

(49) *[*Ki-t* *hi-ttél,* [$_{CP}$*hogy* [*ki-nek*
who-ACC believe-PAST2SG that who-DAT
mutat-nak *be*]]]?
introduce-PRES3PL PFX
'Who did you believe they would introduce to whom?'

17. Multiple *wh*-questions in the Slavic languages come in two types. In the Bulgarian type only the first *wh*-word has the [+q] feature and targets [Spec,CP]; the others merely have a [+focus] feature and land in FocP. In Serbo-Croatian, on the other hand, where the ordering of the fronted *wh*-words is free, they form a single cluster and occupy [Spec,CP] together (see Bošković 1997, 1998, 2001, 2002, 2003). Superiority effects are found in Bulgarian, where multiple *wh*-words may target both [Spec,CP] and [Spec,Foc], while no Superiority effects are observed in Serbo-Croatian, where *wh*-words move to [Spec,CP] as a cluster together.

MULTIPLE *WH*-FRONTING FROM SUBORDINATE MULTIPLE *WH*-QUESTIONS

(50) [*Ki-t* *ki-nek* *hi-tted,*
who-ACC who-DAT believe-PAST2SG[DEF]
[$_{CP}$*hogy* *be-mutat-nak*]]?
that PFX-introduce-PRES3PL
'Who did you believe they would introduce to whom?'

The same scenario is found when weak erotetic *vajon* 'if…at all' is added in the subordinate clause. In the cartographic model of Hungarian polarity and non-polarity interrogative clauses proposed in this paper, the special freezing effect found in the case of subordinate polarity, non-polarity and multiple *wh*-questions can be given a unified account. Remember that weak erotetic *vajon* 'if…at all' signals the presence of an OP-variable chain. In the case of Partial *wh*-movement, the scope of the operator is extended to the whole sentence, which is signalled by the overt *wh*-scope marker to the matrix clause:

PARTIAL *WH*-MOVEMENT FROM SUBORDINATE MULTIPLE *WH*-QUESTIONS WITH WEAK EROTETIC *VAJON* 'IF…AT ALL'

(51) [$_{ForceP}$*INT* [$_{FocP}$*MI-T* *hi-ttél,* [$_{CP}$*hogy* [$_{ForceP}$*vajon* ~~*INT*~~
what-ACC believe-PAST2SG that whether
[$_{FocP}$*KI-T* *KI-NEK* *mutat-nak* *be*]]]]]?
who-ACC who-DAT introduce-PRES3PL PFX
'What did you believe: who would they introduce to whom (if anybody would be introduced to anybody at all)?'

In (51) the upstairs and the downstairs *wh*-words are both in the scope of the raised *INT* operator and the sentence is well-formed. In (52), however, the *INT* operator, introduced in the subordinate clause, forms an OP-variable chain with the downstairs *wh*-word and gets frozen there. This blocks Long *wh*-movement altogether:

LONG *WH*-MOVEMENT FROM SUBORDINATE MULTIPLE *WH*-QUESTIONS USED WITH WEAK EROTETIC *VAJON* 'IF….AT ALL'

(52) *[$_{ForceP}$ *INT* [$_{FocP}$*KI-T* *hi-ttél,* [$_{CP}$*hogy* [$_{ForceP}$ (*vajon*) *INT*
who-ACC believe-PAST2SG that whether
[$_{FocP}$*KI-NEK* *mutat-nak* *be*]]]]?
who-DAT introduce-PRES3PL PFX
'Who did you believe they would introduce to whom (if any introduction would take place at all?)'

Remember that doxastic epistemic predicates normally force Operator Raising. The reason why Operator Raising is impossible in (52) is the presence of the OP-variable chain formed between the INT operator and the *wh*-word in the subordinate clause. After OP-variable chain formation has taken place, the *INT* operator cannot raise any longer and therefore Long *wh*-movement is blocked. The same freezing effect is found in the case of multiple *wh*-fronting from subordinate clauses used with weakly erotetic *vajon* 'if …at all':

MULTIPLE *WH*-FRONTING FROM SUBORDINATE CLAUSE USED WITH WEAK EROTETIC *VAJON* 'IF…AT ALL'

(53) *[$_{FocP}$*KI-T KI-NEK hi-tted,* [$_{CP}$*hogy*
who-ACC who-DAT believe-PAST2SG[DEF] that
[$_{ForceP}$ *(vajon) INT….* [$_{FinP}$*be-mutat-nak-e*]]]]?
whether PFX- introduce-PRES3PL-QCL
'Who (if anybody at all) did you believe would be introduced to whom?'

On the basis of what has been said so far, the absence of such freezing effects in the case of Long *wh*-movement and Multiple *wh*-fronting is predictable in non-veridical contexts (i.e. when a doxastic epistemic predicate optionally takes a [+q] CP). This prediction is borne out, as (54)–(56) demonstrate:

PARTIAL *WH*-MOVEMENT IN MULTIPLE *WH*-QUESTIONS WITH WEAK EROTETIC *VAJON* 'IF….AT ALL'

(54) [$_{FocP}$*MI-T nem tudott Elvira,* [$_{CP}$*hogy*
what-ACC not know-PAST3SG Elvira that
[$_{ForceP}$ *vajon* [$_{FocP}$*KI-RŐL MI-T állít-ottak*]]?
whether who-ELAT what-ACC claim-PAST3PL
'What didn't Elvira know: what did they claim about whom (if any claim about anybody was made at all)?'

LONG *WH*-MOVEMENT IN MULTIPLE *WH*-CLAUSES WITH WEAK EROTETIC *VAJON* 'IF…AT ALL'

(55) [$_{FocP}$*KI-RŐL nem tud-ta Elvira,* [$_{CP}$*hogy* [$_{ForceP}$*vajon* ……
who-ELAT not know-PAST-3SG Elvira that whether
[$_{FocP}$*MI-T állít-ottak*]]]]?
what-ACC claim-PAST3PL
'What didn't Elvira know (whether) they claimed about whom? (if any claim about anybody was made at all)'

MULTIPLE *WH*-FRONTING FROM MULTIPLE *WH*-CLAUSES WITH WEAK EROTETIC *VAJON* 'IF…AT ALL'

(56) [$_{FocP}$*KI-RŐL MI-T nem tud-ott Elvira,* [$_{CP}$*hogy*
who-SBL what-ACC not know-PAST3SG Elvira that
[$_{ForceP}$ *(vajon)… állít-ottak-e*]]]?
whether claim-PAST3PL-QCL
'What didn't Elvira know that they claimed about whom?'

The fact that the Freezing Principle is operative in polarity, non-polarity and multiple *wh*-questions selected by veridical doxastic epistemic predicates corroborates the view advocated by Bošković (2003) that this principle is a subcase of the ban on QR (Lasnik & Uriagereka 1988). The reason why the Freezing Principle is neutralised in certain non-veridical contexts, where a doxastic epistemic predicate optionally takes a [+q] subordinate clause, lies in the presence of a second *INT* operator introduced in the subordinate clause after Operator Raising has taken place. The second *INT* operator can be attested in the course of Long *wh*-movement out of subordinate multiple *wh*-questions and of Mutiple wh-movement out of multiple wh-interrogative clauses, shown in (55) and (56), respectively.

4. Conclusion

This paper discusses some unexpected syntactic properties of Hungarian *vajon* 'whether, if…at all.' Its optionality, flexible syntactic positioning and co-occurrence with the interrogative clitic *-e* undermine its complementiser status. It is claimed that, unlike Germanic *whether/ob* and Slavic *li* 'whether,' Hungarian *vajon* 'whether, if… at all' is not a complementiser but a context-sensitive interrogative item signalling OP-variable chains. Syntactically, it occupies [Spec,ForceP] and forms an expletive-associate chain with FINP. Its seemingly low position is derived by a two-step mechanism consisting of remnant VP-movement targeting ForceP*and Stylistic Fronting.

In the case of non-veridical doxastic epistemic predicates optionally taking a [+q] CP, both Partial and Long *wh*-movement yield grammatically correct sentences with weak erotetic *vajon* 'if…at all.' This is unexpected in view of the fact that in veridical contexts (i.e. in the case of doxastic epistemic predicates selecting a [-q] CP) the *INT-QCL* chain blocks Long *wh*-movement from subordinate clauses with weak erotetic *vajon* 'if…at all.' With doxastic epistemic predicates optionally taking a [+q] CP, a second *INT* operator is introduced in the clause. This explains the absence of the freezing effect. This option is not available in the case of veridical doxastic epistemic predicates selecting a [−q] subordinate clause. Long *wh*-movement from such subordinate clauses is blocked by the *INT-QCL* chain, in accordance with the Freezing Principle (Bošković 1997, 1998, 2001, 2002, 2003). Chain formation is signalled by weak erotetic *vajon* 'if…at all.'

References

Adger, David & Quer, Josep. 2001. The syntax and semantics of unselected embedded questions. *Language* 77: 107–133.

Bartos, Huba. 1997. On subjective and objective agreement in Hungarian. *Acta Linguistica* 44: 363–384.

Boeckx, Cedric & Grohmann, Kleanthes (eds). 2003. *Multiple Wh-fronting* [Linguistik Aktuell/ Linguistics Today 64. Amsterdam: John Benjamins.

Bošković, Željko. 1997. Superiority effects with multiple *wh*-fronting in Serbo-Croatian. *Lingua* 102: 1–20.

Bošković, Željko. 1998. On the interpretation of multiple *wh*-questions. In *A Celebration: Essays for Noam Chomsky's* 70th *Birthday*, Janet Fodor, Jay Keyser & Amy Brand (eds). Cambridge MA: The MIT Press.

Bošković, Željko. 2001. *On the Nature of the Syntax-phonology Interface*. Amsterdam: Elsevier.

Bošković, Željko. 2002. On multiple *wh*-fronting. *Linguistic Inquiry* 33: 351–383.

Bošković, Željko. 2003. On *wh*-islands and obligatory *wh*-movement contexts in South Slavic. In Boeckx & Grohmann (eds), 27–51.

Branigan, Philip. 1996. Verb second and the A-bar syntax of subjects. *Studia Linguistica* 50(1): 50–79.

Cardinaletti, Anna 1997. Subjects and clause structure. In *The New Comparative Syntax*, Liliane Haegemann (ed.), 33–63. London: Longman.

Cardinaletti, Anna. 2004. Toward a cartography of subject positions. In *The Structure of CP and IP. The Cartography of Syntactic Structures*, Luigi Rizzi (ed.),115–166. Oxford: OUP.

Craenenbroeck, van, Jeroen & Lipták, Anikó. 2008. On the interaction between verb movement and ellipsis: New evidence from Hungarian. In *Proceedings of the* 26th *West Coast Conference on Formal Linguistics*, Charles B. Chang & Hannah J. Haynie (eds), 138–146. Somerville MA: Cascadilla Proceedings Project.

Dalmi, Gréte. 2010. *Copular Sentences, Predication and Cyclic Agree*. Saarbrücken: Lambert (VDM).

Dalmi, Gréte. 2011. Hungarian *vajon*: Whether a complementiser or a scope-marker? In *SLAM4: Modules and Interfaces*, Anna Boch-Rozmej & Maria Bloch-Trojnar (eds), 113–139. Lublin: John Paul II Catholic University.

Dayal, Veneeta. 1994. Scope-marking as indirect *wh*-dependency. *Natural Language Semantics* 2: 137–170.

Dayal, Veneeta. 2000. Scope-marking: Cross-linguistic variation in indirect dependency. In Uli Lutz, Gereon Müller & Arnim von Stechow (eds), 157–195.

Dayal, Veneeta. 2002. Single pair vs. multiple pair answers: *Wh*-in-situ and scope. *Linguistic Inquiry* 33: 512–520.

Eckardt, Regine. 2007. The syntax and semantics of embedded *yes/no* questions. In Schwabe & (eds), 447–466.

É. Kiss, Katalin. 1987. *Configurationality in Hungarian*. Budapest: Akadémiai Kiadó.

É. Kiss, Katalin. 1994. Sentence structure and word order. In *The Syntactic Structure of Hungarian* [Syntax and Semantics 27], Ferenc Kiefer & Katalin É. Kiss (eds), 1–84. New York: Academic Press.

É. Kiss, Katalin. 1998. Mondattan. In *Új magyar nyelvtan* (New Hungarian Grammar), Katalin É. Kiss, Ferenc Kiefer & Péter Siptár (co-authors), 17–186. Budapest: Osiris.

É. Kiss, Katalin. 2002. *Hungarian syntax*. Cambridge: CUP.

Frascarelli, Mara & Hinterölzl, Roland. 2007. Types of topics in German and Italian. In Kerstin Schwabe & Susan Winkler (eds), 87–116.

Gyuris, Beáta & Gärtner, Hans-Martin. 2008. Interpreting *vajon*. Talk given at ICSH-8, New York CUNY.

Gervain, Judit. 2002. Linguistic Methodology and Micro-variation in Language: The Case of Operator Raising in Hungarian. MA thesis, Szeged University.

Giannakidou, Anastasia. 1998. *Polarity Sensitivity as (non)Veridical Dependency* [Linguistik Aktuell/Linguistics Today 23]. Amsterdam: John Benjamins.

Giannakidou, Anastasia. 2000. Negative.....concord? *Natural Language and Linguistic Theory* 18: 457–523.

Hinterhölzl, Roland. 2000. Licensing movement and stranding in the West Germanic OV-languages. In *The Derivation of VO and OV* [Linguistik Aktuell/Linguistics Today 31], Peter Svenonius (ed.), 293–326. Amsterdam: John Benjamins.

Hinterhölzl, Roland. 2002. Remnant movement and partial deletion. In *Dimensions of Movement: From Features to Remnants* [Linguistik Aktuell/Linguistics Today 48], Artemis Alexiadou, Elena Anagnostopoulou, Sjef Barbiers & Hans-Martin Gärtner (eds), 127–151. Amsterdam: John Benjamins.

Holmberg, Anders. 2000. Scandinavian stylistic fronting: How any category can become an expletive. *Linguistic Inquiry* 31: 445–485.

Horvath, Julia. 1995. Partial *wh*-movement and *wh*-scope-markers. In *Approaches to Hungarian* 5, István Kenesei (ed.), 89–125. Szeged: JATE Press.

Horvath, Julia. 1997. The status of *wh*-expletives and the partial *wh*-movement construction in Hungarian. *Natural Language and linguistic Theory* 15: 509–572.

Horvath, Julia. 1998. Multiple *wh*-questions and the *wh*-scope-marker strategy in Hungarian interrogatives. *Acta Linguistica Hungarica* 45: 31–60.

Horvath, Julia. 2000. On the syntax of "wh-scope marker" constructions: Some comparative evidence. In Uli Lutz, Gereon Müller & Arnim von Stechow (eds), 271–317.

Kassai, Ilona. 1995. Prescription and reality: The case of the interrogative particle in Hungarian. *International Journal of the Sociology of Language* 111: 21–30.

Kenesei, István. 1992a. Functional categories in Finno-Ugric. In *Complementation in the Languages of Europe,* Kersti Börjars & Nigel Vincent (eds). Dordrecht: Kluwer.

Kenesei, István. 1992b. Az alárendelt mondatok szerkezete (The structure of subordinate clauses). In *Strukturális magyar nyelvtan* (The structure of Hungarian), Ferenc Kiefer (ed.), 529–715. Budapest: Akadémiai Kiadó.

Kenesei, István. 1994. Subordinate clauses. In *The Syntactic Structure of Hungarian,* Katalin É.Kiss & Ferenc Kiefer (eds), 275–375. New York NY: Academic Press.

Kiefer, Ferenc. 1978. Factivity in Hungarian. *Studies in Language* 2(2): 165–197.

Krapova, Iliyana. 2002. On the left periphery of the Bulgarian sentence. *Working Papers in Linguistics* 12: 107–128. University of Venice.

Kratzer, Angelika. 1991. Modality. In *Semantics. An International Handbook of Contemporary Research,* Arnim von Stechow & Dietrich Wunderlich (eds), 639–650. Berlin: Gruyter.

Krifka, Manred. 2001. Quantifying into question acts. *Natural Language Semantics* 9: 1–40.

Lasnik, Howard & Uriagereka, Juan. 1988. *A Course in GB syntax. Lectures on Binding and Empty Categories.* Cambridge MA: The MIT Press.

Lazarova-Nikovska, Ana. 2003. On interrogative sentences in Macedonian: A generative perspective. *RCEAL Working Paper in English and Applied Linguistics* 9: 129–159.

Lutz, Uli, Müller, Gereon, & Arnim von Stechow (eds). 2000. *Wh-scope Marking* [Linguistik Aktuell/Linguistics Today 37. Amsterdam: John Benjamins.

McDaniel, Dana. 1989. Partial and multiple *wh*-movement. *Natural Language and Linguistic Theory* 7: 565–604.

Rizzi, Luigi. 1997. The fine structure of the left periphery. In *Elements of Grammar,* Liliane Haegeman (ed.), 281–337. Dordrecht: Kluwer.

Rizzi, Luigi. 2004. On the cartography of syntactic structures In *The Structure of CP and IP. The Cartography of Syntactic Structures,* Luigi Rizzi (ed.), 3–17. Oxford: OUP.

Rizzi, Luigi. 2006. On the form of chains. Criterial positions and chain effects. In *Wh-movement: Moving on,* Lisa Cheng & Nigel Corver (eds), 97–134. Cambridge MA: The MIT Press.
Rivero, Luisa-Maria. 1993. Bulgarian and Serbo-Croatian yes/no questions: V^0-raising to *-li* vs. *li*-hopping. *Linguistic Inquiry* 24: 567–575.
Rudin, Catherine. 1988. Multiple questions and multiple *wh*-fronting. *Natural Language and Linguistic Theory* 6: 445–501.
Sabel, Joachim. 2000. Partial *wh*-movement and the typology of *wh*-questions. In Lutz, Müller & von Stechow (eds), 409–446.
Sabel, Joachim. 2003. Malagasy as an optional multiple *wh*-fronting language. In Boeckx & Grohmann (eds), 229–255.
Schwabe, Kerstin. 2004. The particle *-li* and the left periphery of Slavic *Yes/No* interrogatives. In *The Syntax and Semantics of the Left periphery*, Horst Lohnstein & Susanne Trissler (eds), 385–430. Berlin: Mouton de Gruyter.
Schwabe, Kerstin & Winkler, Susanne (eds). 2007. *On Information Structure, Meaning and Form* [Linguistik Aktuell/Linguistics Today 100]. Amsterdam: John Benjamins.
Schwabe, Kerstin. 2007. Interrogative complement clauses. In Kerstin Schwabe & Susanne Winkler (eds), 425–446. Amsterdam: John Benjamins.
Sigurðsson, Halldór Ármann. 2010. On EPP-effects. *Studia Linguistica* 64(2): 159–189.
Stechow, von, Arnim. 2000. Partial wh-movement, scope-marking and transparent Logical Form. In Uli Lutz, Gereon Müller & Arnim von Stechow (eds), 447–479.
Surányi, Balázs. 2002. Multiple Operator Movements in Hungarian. PhD dissertation, University of Utrecht.
Surányi, Balázs. 2004. The left periphery and cyclic spell-out: The case of Hungarian. In *Peripheries: Syntactic Edges and their Effects,* David Adger, Cécile de Cat & George Tsoulas (eds), 49–73. Dordrecht: Kluwer.
Wackernagel, Jacob. 1892. Über ein Gesetz der Indogermanischen Wortstellung. *Indogermanische Forschungen* 1: 333–436.

Pronominal markers in Cajun French

Francine Alice Girard
University of Agder

This article examines subject and object pronominal markers in Cajun French, a mainly oral variety of French spoken in Southwestern Louisiana. The data show that although Cajun shares a certain amount of features with other colloquial and dialectal French varieties, it cannot be analyzed along quite the same lines. I will show that it has come further than these varieties in the grammaticalization process of its pronominal markers towards affixal agreement markers, and that they are even in the process of being reduced to nothing and replaced by strong forms.

1. Introduction[1]

In Girard (2010) I discuss how subject clitics[2] in Cajun[3] have to be treated differently from their Standard French counterparts and that their behaviour is closer to that of clitics in other colloquial French varieties.

In this article I will give a global description of both subject and object weak pronouns in Cajun, in order to discuss how the analysis of Cajun pronominal markers as a whole constitutes a challenge. The main issues to be raised here are both morphological and syntactical: are Cajun pronominal markers best analyzed as special clitics in the sense of Zwicky (1977) or as affixal elements bound to the verb? Should they be considered as arguments, i.e. elements bearing a theta-role

1. I would like to thank Hans Petter Helland, Christine Meklenborg Salvesen and two anonymous reviewers for their useful comments and suggestions.

2. In this description of Cajun French, I will use the term *clitic* for weak pronouns as it is the term generally used in the literature regarding those elements in French. The purpose of this article is to discuss to what extent this term is appropriate for Cajun pronominal markers.

3. Cajun is an oral variety of French spoken in Southwestern Louisiana, a region called Acadiana or the francophone triangle because of its shape. Louisiana is an interesting place to study variation as we find at least three varieties of French on a continuum from Standard French to Creole French, Cajun being situated between those two extremes.

and moved from the canonical subject and object positions to a position where they cliticize on the verb as sustained by Kayne (1975) and Rizzi (1986) among others, or should they be analyzed as agreement markers generated directly on the finite verb, as argued by Auger (1995) and (2003), Roberge (1990) and Zribi-Hertz (1994)?

I will start by providing data about subject and object pronouns in Cajun, then I will show that these data exhibit opposing tendencies: some criteria suggest that Cajun pronominal markers should be treated like affixal agreement markers while others, however, suggest they should be analysed as arguments in the syntactic sense. This leads us to hypothesize that Cajun pronominal markers are involved in a grammaticalization process propelling them towards the status of agreement marker affixes. This conclusion has already been reached for other varieties of colloquial and dialectal French, but I will show in this paper that Cajun French not only provides us with another illustration of the same phenomenon, but that the behaviour of its pronominal markers differs in several respects from what has been registered in other varieties of colloquial French, and that Cajun French has come further in this grammaticalization process.

2. Clitic pronouns in Cajun French

As is the case for other varieties of French, the study of Cajun data[4] shows a number of similarities between the behaviour of Cajun clitics and those of Standard French, and the classical tests of clitic-hood from the Kaynian tradition (Kayne 1975) apply to them. Unlike the unbound or strong forms, they lack stress, they cannot be coordinated, they cannot be modified, they cannot be used alone, and

4. There is a great deal of variation in Cajun French and therefore I have limited my study to one of the two French-speaking zones in Acadiana as they are defined in the works of Brasseaux (1992) and (1998) and Breton (1998). The data presented here come from the Lafayette area, a region corresponding to the first wave of Acadian immigration. The other zone, comprising the coastal marshes of Lafourche and Terrebonne, has already been described in detail by Rottet (2001). The examples are extracted from the LSU corpus collected under the direction of Professor Dubois. This is an oral corpus composed of three interviews per speaker: one interview conducted by a Cajun native speaker, one by a Standard French speaker, and a third interview in English. I have selected the Cajun French interviews of 24 speakers from St Landry and Vermillion parishes. Among these 24 speakers are twelve men and twelve women spread across three age groups: 20–30, 40–50, 60 and above. Cajun French is mainly an oral variety, but a literature has been developing since the seventies, and some examples come from *Cajun and Creole Folktales* collected by Ancelet (1994) and *Cadjins et créoles en Louisiane* (Griolet 1986).

they cannot be subject of participial sentences or of an exclamative infinitive as the following examples show:

(1) a. *Moi et toi*
me-1SG.STR[5] and you-2SG.STR
'Me and you'

b. **Je et tu*
I-1SG.CL and you-2SG.CL
'Me and you'

(2) a. *Pas moi*
not me-1SG.STR
'Not me!'

b. **Pas je*
not I-1SG.CL
'Not me!'

(3) a. *Moi!*
me-1SG.STR!
'Me!'

b. **Je!*
I-SG.CL!
'Me!'

(4) a. *Lui arrivé, ils ont dîné.*
he-3SG.M.STR arrived, they have dined.
'When he had arrived, they had dinner.'

b. **Il arrivé, ils ont diné.*
he-3SG.M.CL arrived, they have dined.
'When he had arrived, they had dinner.'

(5) a. *Lui mentir! Jamais!*
He-3SG.M.STR lie! Never!
'He lying! Never!'

b. **Il mentir! Jamais!*
he-3SG.M.CL lie! Never!
'He lying! Never!'

However, the Cajun pronoun system behaves quite differently from Standard French, and I will now introduce the characteristics of Cajun subject clitics before turning to objects. As Cajun is a variety of colloquial French, it will not be

5. The abreviations STR and CL are used respectively for the pronominal strong forms (non-clitic) and for the clitic (weak) forms.

surprising that it shares some of the features described here with other colloquial or dialectal varieties of French. However, what makes Cajun a novel and interesting object of study for the investigation of French clitics is the fact that it groups together a series of features that do not form a conglomerate in the same way in any of those other varieties.

2.1 Subject clitics

Cajun subject clitics differ in several ways from their Standard French counterparts. Some data presented in this Section (2.1.1 to 2.1.3) show that the clitic subject paradigm is receding and that one can even speak of clitic loss: Cajun prefers to use a strong pronoun or *ça* 'that' rather than a clitic, and when a clitic does occur, it is often phonologically reduced. The last feature that points in this direction is the existence of null subject sentences in Cajun in impersonal as well as personal constructions. But certain other characteristics of Cajun show another tendency: subject clitics are always repeated in coordinated structures and subject doubling is frequent with all kinds of NPs. A final characteristic to be mentioned is a lack of mobility, demonstrated by the absence of enclisis of subject clitics in Cajun.

2.1.1 *Regress of the subject paradigm*

As I mentioned above, Cajun makes extensive use of strong personal pronouns and of the pronoun *ça* 'that' instead of the clitic. This regress goes together with a significant simplification of verb morphology where the verb paradigm is reduced to mainly one phonic form as shown in (6b–e).

- Use of strong forms

This phenomenon concerns nearly all persons as shown in (6):

(6) a. *Quand toi es venu*
when you-2SG.STR is come
'When you came'

b. *Lui travaille asteur*
he-3SG.M.STR works now
'He's working now'

c. *Nous-autres parle pas comme ça*
we-1PL.STR speak NEG like that
'We don't speak like that'

d. *Vous-autres va pas à des bals?*
You-2PL.STR go NEG to the dances?
'You don't go dancing?

e. *Eux-autres aiment ça, danser*
They-3PL.STR like that, dance-INF
'They like dancing'

This use of strong pronominal forms instead of the clitic is more generalized for the plural first, second and third persons and less frequent for the singular second and third persons. The forms *je* 'I' (always reduced to [ʒ]) and *elle* 'she' (reduced to [a] before a consonant and often to [l] in front of a vowel) are the only subject forms to resist in this variety:

(7) a. *J' i dis ça*
I-1SG.CL him-3SG.M.DAT.CL tell that
'I tell him so'

b. *L' avait sept ans plus vieux que moi*
she-SG.F.CL had seven years more old than me
'She's seven years older than me'

– Expansion of the use of the pronoun *ça 'that'*

The examples (8) to (10) show that the use of the pronoun *ça* is expanding to a considerable extent and is taking over several domains in which clitics appear in Standard French, where *ça* 'that' is currently described as a pronoun without specific reference and considered almost exclusively as a stylistic variant of the full form *cela* 'that'.

In (8) *ça* 'that' functions like the impersonal *il* 'it' from standard French, appearing here as the subject of verbs indicating the weather:

(8) a. *Ça mouille*
That rains
'It rains'

b. *Ça neigeait*
That snowed
'It snowed'

In (9) *ça* 'that' refers to a third person singular in (a) and plural in (b). *Ça* 'that' has in both cases an indefinite and exclusive meaning and functions as a generic pronoun:

(9) a. *Un Cadien, ça travaillait pas, ça buvait, ça buvait*
a Cajun, that worked NEG, that drank, that drank
tout le temps
all the time
'A Cajun didn't work and drank all the time'

b. *Les Cadiens ça fait la boucherie*
the Cajuns, that makes the butchering
'Cajuns make butchering'

In (10) *ça* 'that' replaces both singular and plural third person clitics as well as the second person plural, even though it refers to definite animate beings in all of these cases:

(10) a. *Mais elle jouait l' guitare …ça jouait le guitare*
but she-3SG.F.CL played the guitar …that played the guitar
'She played the guitar… she played the guitar'

b. *Ça fait, ça [=mes petits-enfants] parle pas français*
that does that [=my grand-children] speak NEG French
'So they don't speak French'

c. *Vous-autres, ça va à des bals?*
You-2PL.STR that goes to DET dances?
'Do you go dancing?'

The occurrences of *ça* 'that' presented in the examples (8) to (10) are not subject to stylistic constraints. This confirms Brown's observation (1988: 124): 'Based on empirical evidence gathered in the field, there is no reason to believe at this point that it (*ça*) carries a stylistic marking for any particular speech style.'

Some of the uses of *ça* 'that,' such as those in (8) and (9) with expletive and generic reading, are well known from other colloquial varieties of French. However, the sentences in (10) where *ça* 'that' has a specific reference show that its expansion is more extensive in Cajun as it also pervades the personal pronoun domain more generally.

2.1.2 *Phonic reduction of subject clitics*

The phonic reduction of subject clitics is systematic in Cajun. It affects the whole paradigm, and the corpus also witnesses the frequent reduction of *on* 'one' to [n] as in (11c) and of *ça* 'that' to [s] as in (11d). This phonic reduction is independent from the categorical nature of the following segment, which may be a verb as in the examples in (11) or another clitic as in (12):

(11) a. *J' va pas aux bals*
I-1SG.CL go NEG to-the dances
'I don't go dancing'

b. *Mom l' a jeté ses pills*
mom she-3SG.F.CL has thrown-away her pills
'Mom has thrown her pills away'

c. *N' a passé beaucoup d' bon temps sur la galerie*
one-3SG.CL has spent much of good time on the porch
'We had a lot of fun on the porch'

d. *Ç' appelle ça une frotteuse*
that-3SG.CL calls that a washboard
'They call that a washboard'

(12) *J' i ai dit ça*
I-1SG.NOM.CL him-3SG.M.DAT.CL have said that
'I told him that'

2.1.3 *Omission of subject clitics (null subject sentences)*

Null subject sentences are found in Cajun. Subject deletion follows specific constraints when occuring in sentences other than nearly lexicalised expressions, as in (13) where *y a* 'there is' (lit. 'there has') is used instead of *il y a* (lit. 'it there has'), and *faut* 'must' and *fallait* 'must' are used instead of *il faut* 'it must' and *il fallait* 'it must':

(13) a. *_ Y a du monde, ils vont pas aller si ils vont pas boire*
_ there has of-the world, they will NEG go if they will NEG drink
'There are people who won't go if they don't drink'

b. *_ Y en a des tout gris*
_ there of-them has of-them all grey
'There are some that are totally grey'

c. *Pour aller à l'école, _ fallait je marche*
for go to the school, _ had-to I walk
'To go to school, I had to walk'

In other cases of subject omission, the deleted clitics must be recoverable in the context. This accounts for the omission in (14) where the reflexive pronoun carries the number and person features, and to a certain extent for the frequent omission of the clitic *je* 'I' where the clitic is recoverable from the situational context, as exemplified in (15):

(14) *_ Me rappelle bien*
_ myself-1SG.REF.NOM remember well
'I remember well'

(15) a. *Oh, _ l' aime l' ouvrage!*
oh, _ it-3SG.ACC love the work!
'Oh, I love the work!'

b. *Euh, je crois. _L'entends parler des fois*
eh, I think. _Him hear talk DET times
'Eh, I think so. I hear him talk sometimes'

c. *Si la musique est pas en français, _vas aller le mettre*
if the music is NEG in French, _goes go-INF it put

euh sur la musique en français.
on the music in French

'If the music is not in French, I will tune it to French music'

d. *Euh, mais _ jongle, _ jongle de euh aller danser*
eh, but _ think, _ think of eh go-INF dance-INF
'Eh, but I think, I think about eh I will go dancing'

Here again I want to mention that Cajun behaves differently from other colloquial varieties of French. Dropping of the impersonal clitics as we have seen in (13) no doubt occurs in other varieties of French, but dropping of the clitic in personal constructions as in (14) and (15) is not found to the same extent in other varieties.

2.1.4 *Repetition of subject clitics in coordinated structures*

Subject clitics are not deleted in coordinated structures, as shown in (16):

(16) a. *Ils chassaient et ils trouvaient pas grand chose à tirer*
they hunted and they found NEG big thing to shoot
'They went hunting and they did not find much to shoot'

b. *Je travaillais en l' été avec mon beau-père et je*
I worked in the summer with my father-in-law and I

mettais les briques
put the bricks

'I worked in the summertime with my father-in-law and I laid bricks'

2.1.5 *Subject doubling*

I have noted numerous cases of subject doubling in Cajun, specifically involving a proclitic co-occuring with a full NP or a strong pronoun. The absence of a pause and the fact that all kinds of NPs can be doubled indicate that these sentences are not cases of left-dislocation. This clitic doubling in Cajun has been observed earlier by Dubois (2001) and Rottet (2001) for the first person singular:

(17) *Moi j' ai mangé.* (Dubois 2001)
me-1SG.NOM.STR I-1SG.NOM.CL have eaten.
'I have eaten'

The data show that this is a widespread phenomenon, and I have also found numerous examples of subject doubling with second and third person pronouns, as in (18), as well as with all types of NP subjects as exemplified in (19–21). The examples in (21), where clitic doubling of quantified NPs occurs, are of particular interest as this type of clitic doubling plays a central role in the analysis of clitics (cf. Section 3).

(18) a.

toi	*tu*	*vas*	*jouer*	*encore*
you-2SG.NOM.STR	you-2SG.NOM.CL	go	play-INF	again

'you're going to play again'

b.

Mon	*mari*	*parle*	*pas*	*le*	*français,*	*mais*	*lui*
my	husband	speak	NEG	the	French,	but	he-3SG.NOM.STR

il	*aime*	*la*	*musique*	*français*
he-3SG.NOM.CL	loves	the	music	French

'My husband does not speak French, but he loves French music'

c.

Nous-autres	*n'*	*a*	*dansé*	*sur*	*la*	*galerie*
we-1PL.NOM.STR	one-3SG.N.NOM.CL	has	danced	on	the	porch

'We danced on the porch'

d.

Vous-autres	*ça*	*va*	*à*	*l'*	*école*
You-2PL.NOM.STR	that-3SG.N.NOM.CL	goes	to	the	school

'You go to school'

e.

Et	*eusse*	*ça*	*venait*	*back*	*à*
And	them-3PL.NOM.STR	that-3SG.N.NOM.CL	came	back	to

la	*maison*
the	house

'And they came back home'

(19) a.

Pop	*il*	*veut*	*pas*	*aller*	*au*	*bal*
pop	he-3SG.M.NOM.CL	wants	NEG	go-INF	to-the	dance

'Pop doesn't want to go dancing'

b.

Mom	*l'*	*a*	*jeté*	*ses*	*pills*
mom	she-3SG.F.NOM.CL	has	thrown-away	her	pills

'Mom has thrown her pills away'

c.

Lui	*et*	*Jebby*	*ils*	*jouaient*	*tout*	*le*	*temps*
he	and	Jebby	they-3PL.M.NOM.CL	played	all	the	time

'He and Jebby played all the time'

d.

Ce	*monde*	*ça*	*dépense*	*pas*	*d'argent*
this	world	that-SG.N.NOM.CL	spends	NEG	any money

'Those people don't spend any money'

(20) a.

Un	*Cadien*	*ça*	*travaillait*	*pas*
a	Cajun	that-3SG.N.NOM.CL	worked	NEG

'A Cajun didn't work'

b.

Les	*Cadiens*	*ça*	*fait*	*la*	*boucherie*
the	Cajuns	that-3SG.N.NOM.CL	makes	the	butchering

'Cajuns make butchering'

(21) a.

Personne	*il*	*a*	*rien*	*dit*
nobody	he-3SG.M.NOM.CL	has	nothing	said

'Nobody said anything'

b. *Tout quelqu'un ils faisaient ça*
all somebody they-3PL.M.NOM.CL did that
'Everybody did that'

2.1.6 *No enclisis*

Cajun French does not have subject enclitics, and subject inversion is absent from the corpus in questions and in reporting clauses. As is the case in Quebec and European colloquial French varieties, there is neither simple nor complex inversion in Cajun, and the sentences in (22) show the same subject-verb word order in questions as is found in declarative sentences:

(22) a. *Mais quoi il faisait?*
but what he did?
'But what did he do?'

b. *Mais quoi ça fait?*
but what that makes?
'But does it matter?'

There is no inversion of the subject clitics in reporting clauses either, irrespective of their place in the structure, within or after the direct speech:

(23) a. "*Mom, si je retourne pas back", il dit, "lâche*
"Mom if I return NEG back" he says "unleash
mes chiens." (from Ancelet 1994)
my dogs."
"Mom, if I do not come back", he said, "send my dogs."

b. "*Ah, j' peux mourir en paix", il dit.* (from Griolet 1986)
"Ah I can die in peace", he said
'"Ah, I can die in peace", he said.'

2.2 Object clitics

If we now turn to object clitics, we notice, as was the case for subject clitics, a reduction of the paradigms materialized by the regress of the neuter *le* 'it,' the expansion of *ça* 'that' and the syncretism of the third persons. Moreover, the number of clitics that can appear in front of the verb is highly limited. Here we might have an example of a change in progress leading to a reduction of the violations of the canonical word order SVO.

2.2.1 *Regress of the use of the neuter pronoun* le *'it'*

The use of the neuter pronoun *le* 'it' is clearly receding. It can be either omitted as in (24) or replaced by *ça* 'that' as in (25). The Cajun use of object *ça* 'that' as compared to neuter *le* 'it' does not entail a semantic distinction where *ça 'that'* would connote emphasis, as is the case in metropolitan French (Brown 1988).

– *Omission of the neuter* le

(24) *Je voyais la domestique faire*
I saw the servant do
'I saw the servant do that'

– *Use of* ça *instead of* le

(25) *Moi je pense j' ai fait ça plus parce que j' ai*
Me I think I have done that more because that I have
voyagé avec lui [ça = manger au restaurant]
travelled with him [that = eat at restaurants]
'I think I did that more often because I travelled with him'

2.2.2 *Expansion of* ça *'that'*

The use of *ça* 'that' is not only taking over for the neuter *le* 'it,' it can also replace all the forms of the third person when the referent is not a human, as shown in (26):

(26) a. *Et il a vendu cette pouliche, [...] il a vendu ça pour*
and he has sold this filly, [...] he has sold that for
250 piastres
250 dollars
'and he sold this filly, [...] he sold it for 250 dollars'

b. *J' les ai donné ça (ça = les tartes)*
I them-3PL.OBJ.CL have given that (that = the pies)
'I gave them that'

2.2.3 *Syncretism of the third persons*

The selected corpus shows a widespread syncretism of the direct object pronouns *le* 'him' and *la* 'her' as well as the indirect object pronoun *lui* 'him/her'; they are used interchangeably by Cajun speakers. The sentences in (27) illustrate this phenomenon. In (27a-b) the dative form *lui* 'him/her' fills the function of a direct object, and in (27c-h), the accusative forms of the pronouns are indirect objects. This syncretism is most advanced for the third person plural, where the accusative form *les* 'them' has taken over for the dative form *leur* 'them,' as exemplified in (27e–h), to such an extent that the indirect pronoun *leur* 'them' is absent from the corpus.

(27) a. *Elle voulait que Jane lui aide à élever*
she wanted that Jane her-3SG.F.DAT.CL help to bring-up
ses enfants
her children
'She wanted Jane to help her bring up her children'

b. *Et j' lui ai mordu sur le pouce*
and I him-3SG.M.DAT.CL have bitten on the thumb
'And I bit his thumb'

c. *J' la parlais anglais*
I her-3SG.F.ACC.CL spoke Englih
'I spoke to her in English'

d. *Il l' a fait peur*
he her-3SG.F.ACC.CL has made frightened
'He frightened her'

e. *Moi j' les dis ça*
me I them-3PL.ACC.CL tell that
'I tell them so'

f. *J' les ai donné ça (ça = les tartes)*
I them-3PL.ACC.CL have given that (that = the pies)
'I gave them that'

g. *Nous les pardonnons*
we them-3PL.ACC.CL forgive
'We forgive them'

h. *Tu les donnais quelque chose*
You them-3PL.ACC.CL gave some thing
'You gave them something'

This syncretism makes the object forms ambiguous. This may to a certain extent explain why Cajun avoids sequences of clitics in front of the verb and prefers instead to postpose one of the objects after the verb, as in (27f) for instance.

One could object that this might be evidence of a change in the construction of the verbs in those sentences. This is not the case, as is shown in (28), where the verbs from the examples in (27) are in construction with full NPs or PPs. The NPs *sa mère* 'his/her mother' and *le chat* 'the cat' in (28a–b) are direct objects of the verbs *aider* 'help' and *mordre* 'bite,' and in the sentences (28c–g) the PPs introduced by the preposition *à* 'on' are indirect objects.

(28) a. *Elle aide sa mère*
she helps her mother
'She helps her mother'

b. *Le chien voulait mordre le chat*
the dog wanted bite the cat
'The dog wanted to bite the cat'

c. *Je parlais à les petits*
I spoke to the small
'I spoke to the children'

d. *Il a fait peur à son chien*
he has made fear to his dog
'He frightened his dog'

e. *La maman dit à les petits ouaouarons.'*
the mother says to the small frogs
'The mother said to the small frogs'

f. *Ça donnait du lait à elle et à son petit*
that gave of-the milk to her and to her little
'It gave milk to her and to her little one'

g. *J' pardonne à cila* [*cila=celui-là*]
I forgive to that-one
'I forgive this one'

2.2.4 *Reduction in the number of clitics in front of the verb*

There is a clear limitation to the number of clitics in front of the verb, and if the verb takes two objects, only one of them will cliticize to its left, as in (29a). In many cases the strong pronominal form is prefered to the clitic even when the verb takes only one object, as in (29b–c).

(29) a. *Au junk park ça fait, il a arrangé un de les*
on-the junk park that makes he has arranged one of the
bicyclettes, he painted it, et puis il m' a donné
bikes he painted it and then he me-1SG.DAT.CL has given
ça (= la bicyclette)
that (= the bike)
'At the junk park, in fact, he fixed one of the bicycles, he painted it and then he gave it to me'

b. *Ils ont dit ça*
they have said that
'They said that'

c. *Ils ont envoyé un chèque à elle*
they have sent a check to her
'They send her check'

However, this limitation does not apply systematically when the dative clitic is first or second person, in which case we can find instances of the combinations *me le* 'me it' and *te le* 'you it' reduced to [mlø] and [tlø] in front of the verb:

(30) a. *Ma femme m' l' achète*
my wife me-1SG.DAT.CL it-3SG.M.ACC.CL buys
'My wife buys it for me'

b. *J' vas m' le sortir encore*
I go me-1SG.DAT.CL it-3SG.M.ACC.CL leave again
'I'm going to take it out once more'

c. *On va t' le donner*
one goes you-2SG.DAT.CL it-3SG.M.ACC.CL give
'We're going to give it to you'

2.2.5 *Object doubling*

Several examples of object doubling are found in the corpus, but this doubling is far from being as frequent as subject doubling in Cajun and is usually limited to the doubling of the strong pronominal forms. The sentences in (31) illustrate this phenomenon. They cannot be interpreted as instances of right dislocation as the objects in argument position do not carry emphasis or special prosody. Moreover, it is interesting to notice that these instances behave in a similar way to what Uriagereka (2000: 412) observed for Spanish clitic doubling, where 'all doubles stand in an inalienable possession relation with regards to the referent of the clitic they double.' The sentences in (31) are cases of such strict reference.

(31) a. *Et dans le matin, grand-père nous*
and in the morning, grand-father us-2PL.ACC.CL
réveillait nous-autres
woke-up us-2P.STR
'And in the morning, grand-father woke us up'

b. *Ah, j' veux tu m' dis à moi*
ah, I want you me-1SG.DAT.CL say to me-1SG.STR
'Ah, I want you to tell me'

c. *J' vas la dire à elle l' achète*
I go her-3SG.F.CL say to her-3SG.F.STR it buy-INF
'I'm going to tell her to buy it'

The only verb allowing doubling of NPs in the corpus is *aimer* '*love*':

(32) a. *J' l' aime du boudin*
I it-3SG.N.ACC.CL love the sausage
'I love sausages'

b. *Si tu l' aimes quelque chose assez...*
If you it-3SG.N.ACC.CL love some thing enough...
'If you love something enough...'

c. *L'monde l' aimait le country*
world it-3SG.N.ACC.CL loved the country-music
'People love country music'

d. *On l' aime marcher*
one it-3SG.N.ACC.CL loves walk-INF
'We love to walk'

The instances of doubling with the verb *aimer* 'love' are in fact so frequent that one might talk of lexicalisation in this particular case. It is worth noting that this agglutination of *le* 'it' and *aimer* 'love' is also frequent in Louisiana Creole (Klingler 2003; Neumann 1985) and in varieties of French spoken in Quebec and New Brunswick (Brasseur 2001).

3. The categorial status of Cajun pronominal markers

In this section I will show that the features of Cajun clitics presented in Section 2 indicate that the Cajun pronominal system cannot be analyzed along the lines of existing treatments of French clitics since it differs from both Standard French and from colloquial varieties like colloquial metropolitan French or Picard, Quebec colloquial French and pied-noir French, even though it shares several features with those colloquial varieties, as I have pointed out in the previous section.

3.1 Traditional analyses proposed for French clitics

Two main approaches have emerged during the last fifty years: one proposed for Standard French clitics, which is an analysis by movement; and the other, mainly for colloquial French, which treats the pronominal elements in these varieties as affixes generated directly in the position they occupy.

3.1.1 *Analysis of clitics in standard French*

Because Cajun does not have enclisis of subject pronominals, I will focus exclusively on proclitics. The traditional approaches of Standard French subject proclitics proposed by Kayne (1975, 1983), Rizzi (1986) or De Cat (2005) are to treat them as arguments. Their analyses are based mainly on the complementarity of full NPs and clitics since clitic doubling is not allowed in Standard French. Clitic placement to the left of the verb is accounted for by movement, with the cliticization being post-syntactic and phonological.

As far as object clitics in standard French are concerned, Kayne (1975) argues that they are generated in argument position at D-structure and then moved and attached to the verb at S-structure, while subject clitics wait until the phonological level to undergo this transformation. Object clitics are treated as arguments since they usually appear in complementary distribution with a full object. As they play the same semantic role, they cannot co-occur within the same sentence and there is no object doubling in Standard French.

3.2 Analysis of clitics in colloquial French

Roberge (1990), Zribi-Hertz (1994) and Auger (1995, 2003), among others, argue in favour of a non-argumental status for subject clitics in colloquial French varieties. Their analyses are based essentially on the following facts: the obligatoriness of the subject clitic in front of the verb and the existence of subject doubling. They argue that, since colloquial French subject clitics can co-occur with a full subject NP, they cannot have argumental status, but must be analysed as affixes that are agreement markers. Cliticization is not phonological, as Kayne (1975) suggested for Standard French proclitics, but rather morpho-syntactic with a representation similar to what is proposed for North Italian dialects where subject proclitics are base-generated under AGRs^0, as shown in the tree-structure in (33):

(33)

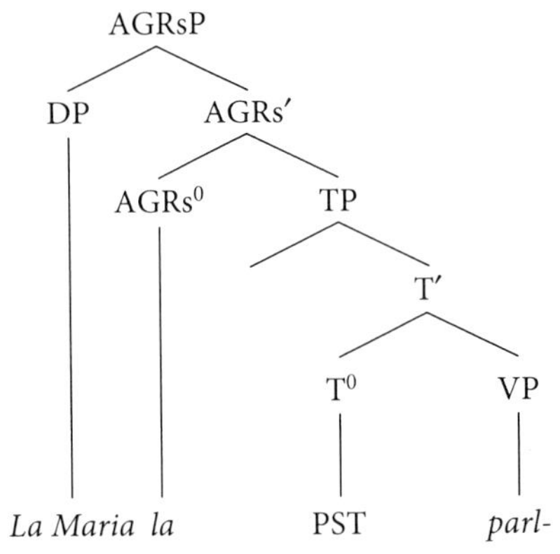

La Maria la parla
The Maria she speaks
'Maria is speaking'

More recent research by Culbertson and Legendre (2008) and Culbertson (2010) using a corpus of dialogues between adults and children in European colloquial French show the same tendencies. They observe the absence of enclisis, the repetition of the clitic in coordinated structures and the high frequency of subject doubling. These observations lead them to an analysis of subject clitics as inflectional affixes in colloquial French.

As far as object clitics in these colloquial varieties of French are concerned, they are more widely analysed as affixes. According to Roberge (1990), clitic doubling of the object in colloquial French shows that object clitics must be directly generated in their surface position. Moreover, Miller and Monachesi (2003) argue that, since there is no full object doubling by an object clitic in colloquial French, object clitics cannot have the status of agreement marker.

The morphological analysis of clitics in colloquial French has been heavily criticized. This is especially the case for the analysis of subject clitics as affixal agreement markers. Côté (2001) and De Cat (2005) contest the existence of subject doubling in colloquial French altogether. They refute the validity of the criteria used to distinguish between dislocation and subject doubling by Auger (1995) and Zribi-Hertz (1994), who argue that the fact that quantified NPs are doubled shows that those instances cannot be dislocation cases, as quantified NPs cannot be dislocated. Quantified subjects in French include indefinite subjects (NPs headed by *un* 'a,' *quelques* 'some,' *aucun* 'none'/'no-one,' *rien* 'nothing,' *personne* 'nobody' and numbers) and universal quantifiers (*tout/tous* 'all' and *chaque/chacun* 'every '/'everybody'`every'/'everyone'). Côté (2001) points out that only indefinite NPs with existential readings are excluded from dislocation, while indefinite NPs with generic readings can be freely dislocated. She argues that the examples of subject doubling used by Zribi-Hertz, among others, to ground the analysis of clitics as non-argumental are either indefinite NPs with generic readings or archaic sentences. She concludes that these varieties of French do not accept subject doubling.

De Cat (2005) argues that French subject clitics are not agreement markers and shows that the morphological analysis is based on false premises. She gives counterexamples taken from a Belgian and Canadian corpus of spontaneous speech. She shows that these colloquial varieties allow clitic inversion and the presence of the negative particle *ne* between the clitic and the verb, and, following Côté, she objects to the notion that there is subject doubling in French.

I will not dispute the validity of the above-mentioned criticism for these varieties of colloquial French here, but I will come back to it in the next section where I will discuss its validity in the case of Cajun.

3.3 The categorial status of Cajun clitics

3.3.1 *Cajun subject clitics*

If we now focus on the analysis of Cajun subject clitics, several features give support to an analysis of these elements as affixes: their repetition in coordinated structures, their phonic reduction, the lack of enclitics, the absence of the negative particle *ne* and finally the high frequency of subject doubling.

I showed in 3.2 that this last point, subject doubling, was a crucial argument for an affixal analysis, and that the existence of clitic doubling in French has been severely contested. The decisive argument in this criticism was whether or not subject doubling of quantified NPs occurred in French.

A look at the Cajun examples in (21), repeated here as (34), where we have instances of doubling of quantified NPs with non-generic readings, shows that Cajun is a variety of French which indeed allows subject doubling:

(34) a. *Personne il a rien dit*
nobody he-3SG.M.NOM.CL has nothing said
'Nobody said anything'

b. *Tout quelqu'un ils faisaient ça*
all somebody they-3PL.M.NOM.CL did that
'Everybody did that'

As Cajun subject clitics can co-occur with a full subject NP, they cannot have argumental status and must be analysed as agreement markers. This is what is proposed for other colloquial varieties of French, as commented on in Section 3.2, and this is what Auger (2003) suggests also for Picard. But Cajun differs from Picard, which allows subject doubling with WH-phrases, whereas Cajun does not.

In her work on colloquial French, Culbertson (2010) places colloquial French and Picard on the implicational hierarchy scale of doubled subject features established by Poletto (2006: 14) for her description of North Italian dialects (35).

(35) Strong pronouns > non-quantified NPs > quantified NPs > WH-variables

The Cajun data indicate, then, that Cajun should be placed at the same level as Trentino, between colloquial French and Picard, in this partial typology of doubled subjects adapted from Culbertson (2010: 121) (Table 1).

Table 1. Typology of doubled subjects

Language	Pronoun	Definite DP	QP	*WH*-Variable
Standard French	–	–	–	–
Central Veneto	+	–	–	–
Colloquial French	+	+	–	–
Trentino/cadien	+	+	+	–
Fiorentino/Picard	+	+	+	+

This hierarchy of subject doubling highlights important similarities and differences between Cajun and other varieties of French. Cajun, like colloquial French, allows doubling of pronouns and definite NPs, but Cajun differs from colloquial French, which does not allow doubling of quantified NPs. If we compare Cajun to Picard, Cajun is similar as far as doubling of pronouns and NPs is concerned, but differs from Picard in that the latter allows doubling also with WH-phrases.

However, in spite of all the arguments in favour of an affixal analysis, some features of Cajun subject clitics, such as the optionality of cliticization and of subject doubling visible in the data, remain unaccounted for by such an analysis. This shows that they have not yet reached a complete affixal status.

3.3.2 *Object clitics in Cajun*

As shown in Section 2, one of the characteristics of the Cajun object clitic system is the regress of the paradigms, with the strong form often being prefered to the clitic. I have mentioned the reduction of the two object paradigms towards a unique paradigm that assumes both direct and indirect object functions with the accusative *la* 'her' replacing dative *lui* 'her' and accusative *les* 'them' replacing dative *leur* 'them,' the latter being nearly absent from Cajun. The only 'pure dative' form left is *lui* 'him'/'her,' often pronounced [i]. I have commented on the reduction of the number of clitics in front of the verb, which reduces the violations of the canonical SVO word order in French: if a verb takes two objects, only one of them will be cliticized when both pronouns are third person. When the dative pronouns are first and second persons, we find some occurrences of two object clitics to the left of the verb, but these clitic sequences are subject to phonic reduction and pronounced as one syllable.

I have also recorded some occurrences of object doubling, as in (31) and (32). These examples cannot be analyzed as dislocations, as there is no special prosody or emphasis in these sentences. The unquestionable existence of object doubling in Cajun constitutes an argument in favour of an analysis of Cajun object clitics that regards them as moving towards a status of affixal agreement markers, but I must emphasize the scarcity of this phenomenon.

We can thus conclude, as far as object clitics are concerned, that we witness a reduction of the paradigms, and that the clitics remaining in what is left of the paradigms show a more affix-like behaviour, just as in other varieties of colloquial French. But, as was the case for subject clitics, the optionality of clititicization, the fact that the strong form is often preferred to the clitic, and the optionality of object doubling show that they cannot be considered as fully affixal.

4. Conclusion

According to Zwicky (1977: 1), clitics are by definition neither clearly words nor clearly affixes, and this is also the case for Cajun. Section 3 shows that the corpus gives ample support for a morphological approach to both subject and object clitics as they occupy a specific position in front of the verb: they cliticize onto an adjacent word and the domain of cliticization is lexical, with the verb acting as a host; furthermore, they are phonologically reduced. Moreover, some data show that subject clitics function as agreement markers since Cajun allows extensive use of a subject marker even when a lexical subject is employed (subject doubling).

However, consideration must be paid to the fact that some features of Cajun clitics constitute arguments against such an analysis. I pointed out that subject and object doubling are optional and that cliticization is not obligatory, while affixation is (at least in European languages). The optional character of cliticization is illustrated by the existence of null subject sentences and the frequent use of a strong pronominal form instead of a clitic.

Cajun pronominal markers therefore represent an analytical challenge because of these opposed tendencies. Their properties lead us to hypothesize that they are undergoing a process of grammaticalization from independent morphemes towards affixes, and from arguments to agreement markers. The fact that this process is in progress is what makes these pronominals so difficult to analyze in terms of their synchronic grammatical properties, as Spencer and Luis (2012: 319) point out for clitics in general. They are elements "in transition" which are best accounted for in a scalar fashion, and are most usefully considered as being closer to affixes than to function words.

In this way, Cajun is very similar to other varieties of colloquial French. However, what makes Cajun a different and interesting variety is the combination of the features it groups together. Some of these features are also found in colloquial Quebec French or metropolitan French, while others are shared with Picard or pied-noir French, but what makes Cajun an interesting contribution to the analysis of French clitics is its special bundle of characteristic features for the behaviour of its pronominal markers, in particular: its loss of clitics, which we observed through the frequent use of the strong pronominal subject form without doubling; the existence of null subject sentences even with personal constructions; the reduction of the object paradigms; and the limitation of clitic sequences to the left of the verb.

All these features show that Cajun is an original variety of colloquial French which has gone very far in the grammaticalization process of its clitics towards affixes, and that these clitics are situated more towards the affixal end of the continuum beween clitic and affix than the other varieties of colloquial French.

Cajun has come further than other colloquial varieties in its evolution towards becoming a null subject language, and the data indicate that its subject clitics can function as agreement marker prefixes. Moreover, if we consider the end point of the grammaticalization cline to be the zero form, one can say that Cajun is even in the process of having its clitics reduced to nothing and replaced by strong forms.

References

Ancelet, Barry. 1994. *Cajun and Creole Folktales*. New York NY: Garland.

Auger, Julie. 1995. Les clitiques pronominaux en français parlé informel: Une approche morphologique. *Revue Québécoise de Linguistique* 24(1): 21–60.

Auger, Julie. 2003. Les pronoms clitiques sujets en picard: Une analyse au confluent de la phonologie, de la morphologie et de la syntaxe. *French Language Studies* 13(1): 1–22.

Brandi, Luciana & Cordin, Patricia. 1989. Two Italian dialects and the null subject parameter. In *The Null Subject Parameter*, Oswald Jaeggli & Ken Safir (eds), 111–142. Dordrecht: Kluwer.

Brasseaux, Carl. 1992. *Acadian to Cajun: Transformation of a People, 1803–1877*. Jackson MS: University Press of Mississipi.

Brasseaux, Carl. 1998. Acadian settlement patterns, 1765–1900. In *Creoles and Cajuns: French Louisiana – La Louisiane Française*, Wolfgang Binder (ed.), 17–52. Frankfurt: Peter Lang.

Brasseur, Patrice. 2001. *Dictionnaire des régionalismes du français de Terre-neuve*. Tübingen: Max Niemeyer.

Breton, Roland J.L. 1998. Comment mesurer l'extension géographique de la francophonie en Louisiane? In *Creoles and Cajuns: French Louisiana – La Louisiane Française*, Wolfgang Binder (ed.), 33–51. Frankfurt: Peter Lang.

Brown, Rebecca. 1988. Pronominal Equivalence in a Variable Syntax. Ph.D. dissertation, University of Texas at Austin.

Conwell, Marilyn Jane & Juilland, Alphonse. 1963. *Louisiana French Grammar*. The Hague: Mouton.

Côté, Marie-Hélène. 2001. On the status of subject clitics in child French. In *Research on Child Language Acquisition*, Margareta Algren, Andoni Barreña, Maria-José Ezeizabarrena, Itziar Idiazabal & Brian MacWhinney (eds), 1314–1330. Sommerville MA: Cascadilla Press.

Culbertson, Jennifer & Legendre, Géraldine. 2008. Qu'en est-il des clitiques en français oral contemporain? In *Actes du premier Congrès Mondial de Linguistique Française*, Jacques Durand, Benoît Habert & Bernard Laks (eds), 2651–2662. Paris: EDP Sciences.

Culbertson, Jennifer. 2010. Convergent evidence for categorial change in French: From subject clitic to agreement marker. *Language* 86(1): 85–132.

De Cat, Cécile. 2005. French subject clitics are not agreement markers. *Lingua* 115: 1195–1219.

Dubois, Sylvie. 2001. Attrition linguistique ou convergence dialectale: JE, MOI/JE et MOI en français cadien. *Revue de Linguistique*18: 149–165.

Gadet, Françoise. 1995. *Le français en partage: L'intérêt de la francophonie pour l'étude du français*.LINX 33/2: 7–14.

Girard, Francine. 2010. Le statut des clitiques sujets cadiens. In *Actes du deuxième Congrès Mondial de Linguistique Française*, François Neveu, Valelia Muni Toke, Jacques Durand, Thomas Klingler, Lorenza Mondada & Sophie Prévost (eds), 2103–2112. Paris: EDP Sciences.

Griolet, Patrick. 1986. *Cadjins et créoles en Louisiane*. Paris: Payot.

Kayne, Richard. 1975. *French Syntax: The Transformational Cycle*. Cambridge MA: The MIT Press.

Kayne, Richard. 1983. Chaînes, catégories extérieures à S et inversion complexe en français. *Langue Française* 58: 36–65.

Klingler, Thomas A. 2003. *If I could turn my tongue like that. The Creole Language of Pointe Coupée Parish, Louisiana*. Baton Rouge LA: Louisiana State University Press.

Miller, Philip & Monachesi, Paola. 2003. Les pronoms clitiques dans les langues romanes. In *Les langues romanes, problèmes de la phrase simple*, Danièle Godard (ed.), 67–123. Paris: Editions du CNRS.

Neumann, Ingrid. 1985. *Le créole de Breaux-Bridge, Louisiane. Étude morphosyntaxique, texts, vocabulaire*. Hambourg: Helmut Buske.

Perlmutter, David. 1971. *Deep and Surface Structure Constraints in Syntax*. New York NY: Holt, Rinehart and Winston.

Poletto, Cecilia. 2006. Doubling as economy. *University of Venice Working Papers in Linguistics* 16: 211–235.

Rizzi, Luigi. 1986. On the status of subject clitics in Romance. In *Studies in Romance Linguistics*, Oswald Jaeggli & Carmen Silva Corvalàn (eds), 391–419, Dordrecht: Foris.

Roberge, Yves. 1990. *The Syntactic Recoverability of Null Arguments*. Kingston: McGill-Queen's University Press.

Rottet, Kevin J. 2001. *Language Shift in the Coastal Marshes of Louisiana*. Frankfurt: Peter Lang.

Spencer, Andrew & Luís, Ana R. 2012. *Clitics. An Introduction*. Cambridge: CUP.

Uriagereka, Juan. 2000. Doubling and possession. In *Clitics in Phonology, Morphology and Syntax* [Linguistik Aktuell/Linguistics Today 51], Birgit Gerlach & Janet Grijzenhout (eds), 405–431. Amsterdam: John Benjamins.

Zribi-Hertz, Anne. 1994. La syntaxe des clitiques nominatifs en français standard et avancé. *Travaux de Linguistique et de Philologie* 32: 131–147.

Zwicky, Arnold. 1977. *On Clitics*. Bloomington IN: Indiana University Linguistics Club.

The morphosyntax of *-nde* and post-verbal clitics in Cypriot Greek

Natalia Pavlou & Phoevos Panagiotidis
University of Chicago / University of Cyprus

This paper explores pronominal clitic placement in a mixed clitic placement variety, Cypriot Greek, and the restrictions on it in the presence of the dialectal element *-nde*. *-Nde* appears as a verb suffix, but imposes syntactic and morphological restrictions in the clause. We argue that *-nde* is a borrowed element from Turkish and it behaves as a *validational* marker (Weber 1986) in Cypriot Greek, expressing the truth validity of the speaker's judgment. Challenging the true nature of clitics and affixes, the discussion focuses on the possibility of clitic-like elements appearing as suffixes. The ungrammaticality yielded with both *-nde* and post-verbal object clitics leads to the observation that the two need to appear adjacent to the verb.

1. Introduction[1]

This article intends to present a first account of the morphosyntactic distribution of the marker *-nde* in Cypriot Greek (hence, CG) and the syntactic implications drawn from the constraints it imposes on post-verbal clitic placement. The main aim of this paper is to analyse the distribution of this marker, which appears as a verb suffix but affects the syntax of the clause by disallowing post-verbal clitic placement.

1. We would first like to thank the anonymous reviewers and editors of our paper for their insightful feedback and suggestions for improvement. We also thank the audience of the Challenging Clitics workshop (University of Oslo, 27th–28th October, 2011) for their valuable feedback. We especially thank Paco Fernandéz-Rubiera, Mohamed Jlasi and Alexandra Galani for their suggestions. Thanks also go to Evelina Leivada, Theoni Neocleous and Elena Papadopoulou for their judgments of the SMG and CG examples included in the text, as well as their detailed suggestions.

(1) a. *Ipcame-nde* *to* *krasin*
drank.nde-1PL the-ACC wine-ACC
'We drank the wine'

b.* *Ipcame-nde* *to*
drank.nde-1PL it-ACC
'We drank it' (CG)

CG is a mixed clitic placement variety, which has however only recently been extensively studied (Terzi 1999a, 1999b; Grohmann 2011; Grohmann et al. 2012) with regard to this topic. Consequently, this study is the first to refer to the constraints of *-nde* in post-verbal clitic placement and will be drawing data from a limited number of clitic studies in CG, which mainly refer to L1 acquisition, as well as presenting some new data related to this topic.

Clitic placement in Cypriot Greek is mixed; that is, it allows for both pre-verbal and post-verbal clitic positioning in specific syntactic environments (see Section 2 for further details). Most of the studies on clitics in CG have focused on the acquisition of the mixed system based on the complex sociolinguistic status of Cyprus (Rowe & Grohmann 2012; Grohmann & Leivada 2012) and the process under which children switch from post- to pre-verbal clitic placement due to the school factor (Grohmann 2011; Grohmann et al. 2012). Syntactic accounts of mixed clitic placement in CG have also been proposed (Terzi 1999a, 1999b; Agouraki 2001) and they will be discussed in more detail in Section 2.

Our interest in the dialectal element *-nde* stems from the fact that it seems to be one of the purely Cypriot-specific characteristics which is undergoing a process of 'death,' as it appears to be used less by the young population. In fact, Rowe and Grohmann (2012), following Auer (2005), predict that CG is undergoing 'dialect moribundity,' in the sense of 'dialect loss' associated with loss of specific features. In Section 3 below, we present the morphological and syntactic specifics of *-nde* in different environments.

The main conclusions of this paper in Section 4 are the revealing implications of the constraints that *-nde* imposes on post-verbal object clitic placement. In the presence of *-nde*, post-verbal object clitic placement is not allowed (see Section 3.2). Given the fact that *-nde* seems to behave as a suffix, the restriction in this environment emphasizes the subtle line between clitics and affixes, even if they are interpreted in fundamentally different ways. It also contributes to related work on other mixed clitic placement languages, suggesting that post-verbal clitic placement may be related to phrasal affixes (Galves, Ribeiro & Moraes 2005; Galves & Sândalo 2004), or affixes in general.

Finally, we conclude with some further questions on the issue that await future research and may be addressed with input from other languages showing the same phenomena.

2. Clitic placement in Cypriot Greek

The linguistic status of the Republic of Cyprus is traditionally described as diglossic, with a sociolinguistically 'low' variety of CG co-existing with the 'high' Standard Modern Greek (SMG), a variety spoken in Greece. Cyprus exhibits *de jure* bilingualism (Greek, Turkish; referring to the standard varieties in both cases) and *de facto* trilingualism in Greek, Turkish and English (Arvaniti 2002) or bilingualism in SMG and CG (Newton 1972; Vassiliou 1995) or bidialectism in SMG and CG (e.g. Pavlou & Christodoulou 2001; Yiakoumetti et al. 2005) or more generally a 'bi-*x*' context (Grohmann 2011; Grohmann & Leivada 2012; Grohmann et al. 2012) proposed to cover any possible mixing of languages/dialects. A more recent approach (Rowe & Grohmann 2012) suggests that the *co-overt prestige* of CG has prevented its death and that diglossia in Cyprus relates to a type B diglossia. Type B (medial) diglossia refers here to dialect moribundity with a high degree of entropy. In this sense, the individual speakers of this society are identified as (discrete) 'bilectal.'

The defined linguistic environment clarifies that we have at least two linguistic codes (whatever their status is), whose grammars, even if not clearly defined, can interfere with one another, as SMG input is copiously available through the medium of television programs, books, and education. The co-existence of two varieties results in a complex interplay between certain morphosyntactic properties of the two varieties. As Grohmann and Leivada (2012) point out, in contexts that involve the coexistence of a standard and a regional variety, syntactic differences fade away with the passing of time in favor of an intermediate (Cornips 2006) or 'diglossic' speech repertoire (Auer 2000, 2005), based on a more standard dialect continuum.

The two varieties show many differences in all aspects of grammar. One of the more studied ones is the syntax and L1 acquisition of pronominal clitics (Grohmann et al. 2010; Leivada et al. 2010, and Grohmann et al. 2012; Grohmann 2011). Clitic placement in CG is mixed; clitics can appear pre-verbally or post-verbally depending on the syntactic environment.

More particularly, post-verbal clitics cannot appear in *na*-clauses, negative environments or *wh*-questions (2–4), whereas post-verbal clitics can appear in simple declaratives (6) – cf. the situation in SMG in (5). Moreover, both placement options are possible with the complementizers *oti* 'that' and *jati* 'because' (7–8). Finally, in imperative sentences,[2] only post-verbal clitics are allowed (9).

(2) *Thelo na to pco (*to)* — CG *na*-clause
want-1SG to it-CLI.3SG drink-1SG
'I want to drink it'

(3) *En to pino (*to)* — CG negation
not-NEG it-CLI.3SG drink-1SG
'I am not drinking it'

(4) *Pcos/Pu/Pote/Jati to pini (*to)?* — CG *wh*-question
who/where/when/why it-CLI.3SG drink-3SG it-CLI.3SG
'Who is drinking it/Where/when/why is he drinking it?'

(5) *To ipje* — SMG declarative
it-CLI.3SG drank-3SG
'S/he drank it'

(6) *Ipcen ^{n}do* — CG declarative
drank-3SG it-CLI.3SG
'S/he drank it'

(7) *Kseri oti (to) ipces (to)* — CG *oti*-complementizer
knows-3SG that it-CLI.3SG drink-2SG it-CLI.3SG
'She knows that you drank it'

(8) *Kseri jati (to) ipces (to)* — CG *jati*-complementizer
knows-3SG because it-CLI.3SG drank-2SG it-CLI.3SG
'She knows because you drank it'

(9) *Fa' to* — CG imperative
eat-2SG it-CLI.3SG
'Eat it'

Syntactic analyses of mixed clitic placement in CG (Agouraki 2001; Terzi 1999a, 1999b) suggest that the verb in CG moves to a higher position and generates the verb-clitic order. Agouraki proposes that the verb moves to C^0 in order to satisfy the 'filled C′-criterion in CG. On a feature-based account, Terzi suggests that the verb needs to move to the Mood° to satisfy strong V features. In both cases, though, verb movement is assumed for the possibility of generating both positions.

2. Bošković (2006) argues for 'affix hoping + copy and delete' accounts for post-verbal clitics in imperatives, with special reference to the possible appearance of dative-accusative and accusative-dative clitic orders in Greek. Post-verbal clitic placement in imperatives is a matter of a switch forced by PF considerations, and not syntax.

(10)

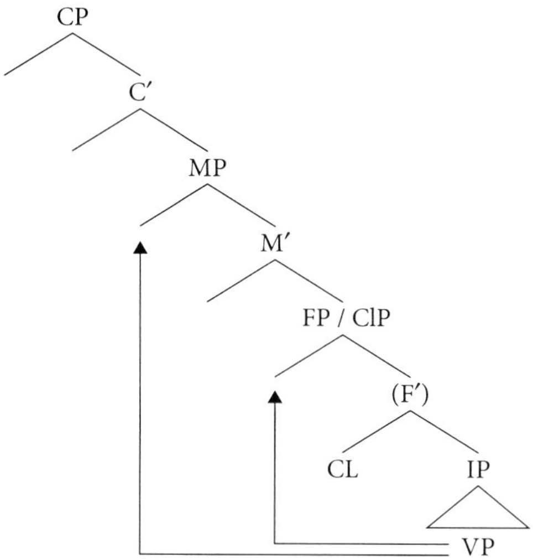

Picture 1 Terzi (1999a, 1999b) and Agouraki's (2001) accounts (Neocleous 2012)

Placement of clitics has been a central issue in the acquisition literature on Cypriot Greek. Acquisition findings (Grohmann 2011; Grohmann et al. 2012) led to the hypothesis of a socio-syntactic factor in diglossic environments such as the one in Cyprus. The possible diglossic context and the competence of bilectal speakers has become relevant in many studies following Grohmann et al. (2012). For the sake of providing a complete picture of clitic placement in CG, we will review some of the basic conclusions in a number of relevant studies.

A longitudinal study (Petinou & Terzi 2002) showed that children acquire CG clitic production at 32 to 36 months of age. Based on a picture-based task administered to Greek Cypriot children aged 2;0 and 6;11 years of age, Grohmann et al. (2012) investigate the acquisition of direct object clitics and suggest that acquisition of object clitics in indicative clauses is acquired by age 3;0. Replicating the same experiment, Leivada et al. (2010) collected data from (i) Hellenic Greek children (children from mainland Greece, who were born in Greece and at the time of the experiment, the majority schooled in Cyprus), (ii) Greek Cypriot children and (iii) binational children (born in either Greece or Cyprus, with one parent from each country, and schooled in Cyprus) This study presented two different versions of the same task to the three different populations. Greek Cypriot children were observed to increase their number of proclisis answers after their presence in school, where only the 'high' variety is used. Neocleous (2012) also concludes that in the first years, Greek Cypriot children misplace clitics. Last, an ongoing study (Papadopoulou, Leivada & Pavlou 2012) is testing the hypothesis that Greek Cypriot speakers base their decisions of whether to use pre-verbal or post-verbal placement in mixed environments on the syntactic and lexical input they get. The study so far has shown that Greek Cypriot adults identify the difference and switch from pre-verbal to post-verbal placement, or the opposite, on the basis of two different blocks in the experiment, one with CG lexical and syntactic input and the other one with SMG.

Based on the aforementioned studies, it appears that mixed clitic placement, especially in diglossic contexts, is a complex matter and different syntactic environments intervene with its syntax. One of these is the use of *-nde*, which, as explained below, is problematic in the presence of clitics. Let us now examine the morphosyntactic distribution and pragmatic functions of *-nde* in CG, as well as its relevance to the Turkish clitic *dA*.

3. *Validational* markers: A cross-linguistic overview

Classification of markers characterized by the way in which a speaker treats a statement tagged with a given marker was proposed very early on (Bally 1932/1965: 36) with the notion of *Dictum* and *Modus*. The dictum was thought of as the representation of the sentence itself, whereas the modus involved other operations carried by the utterer of the sentence.

Since then, a number of speech act markers in the form of affixes, particles and clitics have been identified and discussed in a number of languages. These range from the Turkish topic-introducing marker *ee* 'so,' focus marker *ya* 'well,' *iste* 'you know,' and clarification marker *yani* 'I mean' (Özbek 1995) to the Romanian pragmatic marker *hai* expressing a strong speaker-oriented interpretation (Hill 2009), the Hungarian formal/informal markers *nánk/-nénk* and *nók/-nók* (Kiefer 1998), the Penutian Wintu non-visual sensory evidence suffix *-nthEr* and the hearsay markers *-kee*, *-ree* and *-ʔel* (Willett 1988: 64–5), and many others.

For the purposes of this paper, we will retain the meaning of the *evidential*, or even better *validational* (Weber 1986) function of discourse markers. We follow Weber's definitions; an *evidential* marker indicates the source of the information (Anderson 1986), but a *validational* marker indicates the degree of certainty and the truth of the proposition that is uttered. The *validational* aspect has been argued to come from an extralinguistic axiom that defines one's own experience as reliable. In Karaja, spoken on and around the Bananal island in the Araguaia river in Brazil, the marker *-tyhy* is used as a verb form and is used to attest to the veracity of a statement. Similarly, in Cusco Quechua, the enclitic *-mi* (11) has been classified as *validational* (Nuckolls 1993) based on the criteria above and on the fact that *-mi* is used even if the speaker has not witnessed the action uttered (it could be that someone else, who is trustworthy, has witnessed it). Similarly, Nuckolls notes that utterances concerning future happenings which cannot be directly witnessed express the assertion of the *validational* markers, even if appearing as affirmative suffixes. *Affirmative suffixes* have been argued to be *evidential* (Muysken 1995; Weber 1986) or *validational* (Nuckolls 1993; Floyd 1997).

(11) *Pilar-mi llalli-rqa-n.*
pilar-mi win-PST.3
'Pilar won' (Quechua)

These morphological markers can show characteristics of grammaticalization ranging from free functional morphemes to bound forms appearing as inflectional paradigms. In other cases, grammaticalization occurs so a formerly bound form becomes a lexical unit. In Karaja, the bound form *-tyhy* can also appear as a noun form *inatyhy* 'truth' (Maia 2004). CG also shows lexicalised forms, such as *imishi* 'supposedly,' borrowed from the Turkish hearsay marker *miş*. In addition, the Turkish clitic *dA* has undergone grammaticalization (Schiering 2006) characterized by its insertion between the converb marker and the second verb stem (this is possible with *-A-dur-*, less acceptable with *-Abil-* and presumably ungrammatical with *-Iyor-*). As argued in the same study, grammaticalization in mora- and syllable-based languages keeps the phonological substance of cliticized elements, which leads to disyllabic clitics and affixes, whereas in stress-based languages it reduces the phonological substance of cliticized elements, resulting in '*subminimal clitics and affixes in the course of morphologization*' (Schiering 2006: 2).

The sharing of common properties between the markers mentioned above can help us identify the universal grammatical properties of these elements.

3.1 The marker -*nde* in Cypriot Greek

Greek discourse markers have not been extensively studied, with the exception of the distribution of *re* in SMG, which seems to be used in the contexts where a speaker wishes to bring the hearer into the conversation (Sifianou 1992; Archakis & Tzanne 2009).

SMG also uses *(n)de* as a prosodically prominent lexical item which plays an important role in the meaning of the sentence. Consider the following:

(12) a. *Kala*
fine-ADV
'Fine'

b. *Kala de!*
fine-ADV de
'Yeah, fine.'[3]

3. Even if the given translation in English may indicate the speaker's lack of trust towards the addressee, the targeted reading for (12b) is one where the speaker simply compromises to the addressee's requests.

(13) a. *Ela mou?*
come me-DAT.CLI
'Excuse me?'

b. *Ela mou de!*
come me-DAT.CLI de
'Fancy that!'

(14) a. *Siya*
slowly-ADV
'Slowly'

b. *Siya de*
slowly-ADV de
'Take it easy!' (SMG)

SMG *(n)de* could possibly be related to *lipon* (which has a direct translation 'so') (Leivada, pc), but *lipon* is uttered in contexts where it appears in the clause-final position and comes as an objection to the previously uttered statement. In SMG, *(n)de* is purely a discourse particle which possibly adds emphasis to the context in certain occasions. In all the examples above, it is used in the final position in the clause and does not appear to be affected by the preceding item. SMG *(n)de* can also be found in the initial position in the clause, as the following examples show:

(15) a. *De ke kala (na pame ekdromi)*
de and well-ADV (to go-1PL excursion-ACC)
'We should go to the excursion' [lit. whatever happens][4]

b. *De ke soni*
de and enough-adv
'whatever happens' (Leivada, pc)
(SMG)

It seems from the examples in (15) that *(n)de* imposes a certain meaning in initial positions in the clause, but due to the limited number of examples we could find, we will make no further claims. The similarity we can observe with the CG *-nde* lies in their shared ability to add or alter meaning of the sentence in which they occur.

In contrast, CG *-nde* behaves very differently. Agouraki (2010) lists *-nde* (mentioned as *-te*) as an optional marker of V-in-C checking Emphasis on C. First, it always appears as a bound form and can only take a verb as its host.

4. *De ke kala* and *de ke soni* ('no matter what') can translated as 'willy-nilly,' to express that an action will happen whether you desire it or not.

(16) Efame-nde
ate.nde-1PL
'We ate' (CG)

Grammatically, it can only attach to inflectional suffixes expressing 1st person plural, as in (17d):

(17) a. **Ipca-nde pollin.*
drank.nde-1SG much
'I drank too much'

b. **Ipces-nde pollin*
drank.nde-2SG much
'You drank too much'

c. **Ipce-nde pollin.*
drank.nde-3SG much
'S/he/it drank too much'

d. *Ipcame-nde pollin*
drank.nde-1PL much
'We drank too much'

e. **Ipcete-nde pollin*
drank.nde-2PL much
'You drank too much'

f. **Ipcasi-nde pollin*
drank.nde-3PL much
'They drank too much' (CG)

Additionally, it cannot be incorporated into a verb carrying the plural ending -*an*, which is the past tense suffix used for non-active voice in CG:

(18) a. **Emaxumasta-nde pollin ora*
were.kept.busy.nde-1PL much time-ACC
'We were kept busy for a long time'

b. **Esazumasta-nde ullon to apoyevma.*
get.ready.nde-1PL all the-ACC afternoon-ACC
'We were getting ready all afternoon' (CG)

The distribution of -*nde* with deponent verbs,[5] such as *peripiume* 'take care', shows that it is not the case that -*nde* cannot appear with non-active morphology, but

5. We would like to thank one of the anonymous reviewers for pointing out that this condition can be used as a diagnostic test to identify the syntactic/morphological compatibility of -*nde* with Voice.

with non-active syntax/semantics. Deponent verbs are transitive and active in meaning, but show non-active morphology, so we get the following:

(19) *Peripiumaste-nden ton kipo*
take-care.nde-1PL the-ACC garden-ACC
'We take care of the garden' (CG)

However, if we consider the past form of the same verb *peripiumastan/un-nde* 'take care,' judgments vary among the speakers, but the ungrammaticality is not as strong as the case in (18).

Based on what we have said above, *-nde* cannot be assumed to be an inflectional suffix, since the 1st person plural suffix *-me* already carries the inflection features. It should also be noted that *-nde* cannot appear before *-me* (e.g. **ipcandeme*), so it always needs to appear after inflection has taken place (regardless of whether inflection is a procedure in the lexicon or the syntax). Inflectional clitics are argued to be lexical clitics only if they can interact with canonically distributed inflectional affixes and appear inside of other inflections (Halpern 1995). In arguing that *-nde* is an inflectional affix, two problems occur. One problem is the redundancy of the assumption that there are two suffixes for 1st person plural suffixes in Cypriot Greek, with one of them appearing optionally or with both of them appearing at the same time. The other problem is that, if *-nde* is an inflectional affix and can affect the distribution of pronominal clitics, then this should be the case for other inflectional affixes as well.

The CG marker *-nde* does not show any restriction with respect to tense, as it can be used to refer to the past (20), the present (21) or the future (22).

(20) *Epiame-nde sto panairin.*
went.nde-1PL to-the-ACC feast-ACC
'We went to the feast'

(21) *Pame-nde sto panairin.*
go.nde-1PL to-the-ACC feast-ACC
'We are going to the feast'

(22) *Enna pame-nde sto panairin.*
will go.nde-1PL to-the-ACC feast-ACC
'We will go to the feast' (CG)

The grammatical properties of *-nde* can be revealing with regard to its semantic or pragmatic function. Given that an evidential marker designates a grammatical element that indicates the speaker's source of information (Anderson 1986) and it requires direct experience, *-nde* is not included in this classification based on its lack of tense restrictions. Consider the following, where a speaker who has not experienced an action can use *-nde* for a future event:

(23) *Enna pame-nde sto xorkon*
will go.nde-1PL to-the-ACC village-ACC
'We will go to the village' (CG)

Similarly, the Quechua suffix -*puni*, which has been classified as a pure *validational* discourse marker and has the meaning of 'definitely/certainly,' can be used with future actions:

(24) *Papa-ta-n/-s/-chá wayk'u-nqa-puni.*
potato-ACC-mi/-si/chá cook-3FUT-puni
'She will definitely cook potatoes' (Faller 2003) (Quechua)

In addition, the example in (25) is grammatical in a context where the speaker refers to the future by using the past form of the verb, as if the action has already been completed:

(25) *Ate efiame-nde!*
come.on left.nde-1PL.
'Let's go' [lit. 'We left'] (CG)

So, *validational* markers can be argued to share the property of 'unspecified' direct experience, meaning that direct experience comes from the speaker, but the actual time of the action is irrelevant for the truth value of the proposition. In other words, CG -*nde* assigns the speaker/speakers himself/themselves as a reliable source of information, gained in unspecified time, who believes in the proposition being expressed (p) (26).

(26) Direct Evidence (s,p) → Believe (s,p) (Faller 2003)

Further, the restriction that the *validational* -*nde* can only attach to 1st plural can be explained with the assumption that it requires the speaker to have direct experience with the uttered proposition. We could not find any further support to explain why -*nde* cannot occur with 1st person singular, but we expect to address this issue in future work.

It could be generalized, then, that -*nde* performs the following functions:

(27) a. Assigns a commitment to the truth value of the proposition.
b. The proposition is associated with personal (direct) experience.
c. The truth validity is not based only on (past) experience (but also maybe on the trustworthiness of the speaker).

Experience is hereby not related to the actual details of the happening of the action, since -*nde* can also appear with *wh*-questions. In these cases, the speaker asserts certainty that the action which -*nde* suffixes has happened, or will happen. CG *validational -nde* is optionally used and it mainly strengthens the certainty of a statement.

CG is a variety without a rich repertoire of modality markers. We argue that *-nde* has been borrowed from neighboring (Standard) Turkish, a variety which Cypriot Greek has had contact with since 1570. More specifically, we claim that *-nde* is a Turkish loan, from the Turkish clitic *dA/dE*. Standard Turkish here refers to the Turkish spoken in Turkey, whereas Cypriot Turkish refers to the variety spoken by Turkish Cypriot speakers on the north territory of Cyprus. We refer to Standard Turkish, as the data were drawn from Turkish grammar books, and not from personal communication with any speaker.

Turkish *dA* is a multi-function particle (Göksel & Özsoy 2002; Özbek 1995) which acts as a discourse connective through its additive, adversative, continuative and enumerating functions.[6] Göksel and Özsoy (2003) explain that the additive function is not given by *dA* alone, but by the presupposition of *dA* interpreted with the rest of the sentence. It shows vowel harmonization with the preceding syllable (Göksel & Kerslake 2005), as in (28):

(28) a. Annem de 'my mother too'
b. Yaparım da 'I will do [it], too' (Turkish)

Turkish *dA* is found at the right outermost boundary of a word; it follows other markers such as number, person and Case and it cliticizes onto any type of phrase. Most important, though, is the fact that when the host of *dA* is focused, *dA* can occur anywhere in the pre-verbal position, but not in the post-verbal position.

(29) a. *Ahmet bu arada SINAV-A da hazırlan-acak-tı.*
Ahmet in.the.meantime exam-DAT dA prepare-FUT-P
'In the meantime, Ahmet was supposed to get prepared for the exam.'
b. **Ahmet bu arada hazırlan-acak-tı SINAV-A da.*
Ahmet in.the.meantime prepare-FUT-p exam-DAT dA (Turkish)
(Göksel & Özsoy 2003)

When the host of Turkish *dA* is not focused, it can only occur in clause-initial position or post-verbal position. Both of these have been argued to be associated with background information or 'after-thought' (Erguvanlı 1984).

6. An example for its additive function is given in (i), even though we will not expand on this point.

(i) *seyretmedim de*
'and moreover I didn't watch (it)' (Göksel & Kerslake 2005)

Semantically, *dA* is argued to assert the truth in Turkish (Göksel & Özsoy 2003), in the presence of an existential operator, as opposed to analyses claiming that *dA* is a focus particle.

Given the above, Turkish *dA/dE* and CG -*nde* (but no form of *-*nda*) display similar semantic properties. The fact that two varieties have been in long and steady contact may have resulted in the borrowing of the Turkish 'multi-function' particle *dA*, which has only maintained the characteristics mentioned above for CG -*nde*. The CG marker -*nde* has been classified in this section as *validational* based on the truth value that it shows, associated with personal experience and the need for direct experience or trustworthiness of the speaker.

3.2 The validational -*nde* and clitic placement

We have presented in the previous section a well-rounded picture of the grammatical properties of -*nde* in order to provide the reader with better knowledge of the kind of restrictions it imposes.

While -*nde* seems to similar to other markers of its kind that are found cross-linguistically, it also happens to appear in a language that follows a mixed system of clitic placement (see Section 2). As also mentioned in (5–6), and repeated below in (30a & b), pronominal object clitics can be post-verbal in CG and pre-verbal in SMG:

(30) a. (*To*) *ipje* — SMG – simple clause
it-CLI. drank-3SG
'S/he drank it'

b. *Ipcen* ^{n}*do* — CG – simple clause
drank-3SG it-CLI
'S/he drank it'

Interestingly, -*nde* is not allowed in the presence of a post-verbal clitic, as follows:

(31) **Ipcame-nde* *to*
drank.nde-1PL. it-CLI.ACC
'We drank it' (CG)

In obligatory proclisis contexts, ungrammaticality as in (31) does not appear (Neocleous, pc):

(32) Speaker A: *Idete* *to* *ergo?*
saw-2PL the-ACC movie-ACC
'Have you seen the movie?'

Speaker B: *Theloume* *na* *to* *dume-nde.*
want-1PL to it-CLI.ACC see.nde-1PL
'We want to see it' (CG)

In other proclisis environments, like *wh*-questions, *-nde* can also be used:

(33) a. *Pcoi epiame-nde taksidi to perasmeno kalotzieri?*
who went.nde-1PL trip-ACC the-ACC last-ACC summer-ACC
'Who went on a trip last summer?'

b. *Pci embu epiame-nde taksidi to*
who embu went.nde-1PL trip-ACC the-ACC
perasmeno kalotzieri?
last-ACC summer-ACC
'Who went on a trip last summer?' (CG)

In the same context, *wh*-questions can appear with clitics and *-nde* can also be used:

(34) *Pci to idame-nde?*
who it-CLI.ACC saw.nde-1PL
'Who saw it?' (CG)

In negative environments, *-nde* can appear with a full DP (35).

(35) *En efame-nde to psomi*
not-NEG ate.nde-1PL the bread-ACC
'We did not eat bread' (CG)

With regard to clitic appearance and negation, there is variation among speakers (36).

(36) (?) *En to efame-nde*
not-NEG it-CLI.ACC ate.nde-1PL
'We did not eat it' (CG)

Some speakers claim that the example above can be grammatical, while others claim that in negative environments, they would omit *-nde*. In case that *-nde* in indicatives with negation is grammatical, then we assume that the analysis provided in this paper applies in this case as well. If it is ungrammatical, then it could relate to the semantics imposed by *-nde* and the negative value of the clause.

In this paper, we nevertheless focus mainly on the ungrammaticality of *-nde* with post-verbal clitics in simple indicative clauses and the syntactic restrictions appearing in that environment. In the following section, we will attempt to explain the ungrammaticality of *-nde* with post-verbal clitics by exploring the literature on languages with mixed clitic placement.

4. The boundaries between clitics and affixes

For a long time, discussions related to the nature of clitics and affixes have focused on the subtle line distinguishing them. According to Muysken (2008), clitics can vary between discourse connectives and many other functional categories with the common characteristics of being reduced phonological forms, allomorphs or bound forms. Even the common Latin inscription in (37) shows a form of affixation, showing that the range of possible affixes is very wide.

(37) *Senatus populus-que romanus*
senate people-and roman
'the Senate and the people of Rome' (common inscription)

One of the most cited works on this topic (Zwicky & Pullum 1983) provides some diagnostic conditions for the distribution of cliticized and inflected forms, but these do not necessarily exist in all languages. Based on these diagnostics, one can find support for the argument that -*nde* is an inflectional affix. The counter-evidence to that is the already-checked inflectional feature related to number and person on the verb in a feature-based model. In later work, Zwicky (1985) claims that words that are bound should be labelled as clitics and that the items labelled as particles are dependent. In fact, the Latin conjunctive particle -*que*, the Tagalog clitic particles and the English possessive '*s* have been classified as special clitics (Zwicky & Pullum 1983), because they do not correspond to a full form, nor do they have the same distribution as full forms.

As Hogeweg, de Hoop and Malchukov (2009) explain, it happens that certain suffixes appear as enclitics, which may or may not be restricted to verbs as their host and can often add to the discourse interpretation of the clause. They further argue that epistemic and evidential modality is expressed by means of enclitics, just as event modality is expressed by means of affixes.

CG object clitics may differ substantially from the kind of clitics that appear as affixes, which are briefly mentioned above. The example in (31), however, indicates that the *validational* marker -*nde*, which appears as a suffix on the verb, cannot occur with a post-verbal object clitic. In order to explain this phenomenon, we will focus on the possibility of the cliticization in some languages.

European Portuguese, which is also a mixed clitic placement language with certain restrictions on the syntactic environment (Lobo & Costa 2012), has pronominal object clitics as mentioned for CG, but can also have clitics attaching to auxiliary verbs in the following contexts:

(38) a. *tinha-me dado*
had-me-CLI given
'has given me'

b. *Vai-me dar*
go-me-CLI give-inf
'is going to give me'

c. *vai dar-me*
go give-me-CLI (European Portuguese)
(Lobo, pc)

Similarly, French clitics attach to auxiliaries:

(39) *Il me l' a dit*
he-nom me it-CLI has-aux say-3SG
'He told me' (anonymous reviewer)
(French)

These examples show how clitics can attach to their host in certain syntactic environments, but they are not given in this paper to provide any arguments for the syntactic position of European Portuguese clitics. Galves, Ribeiro and Moraes (2005) claim in fact that clitics in European Portuguese can be classified as Infl-clitics and have a morpho-phonological property, subject to word formation rules like any other affixes. In their paper, they also include the possibility of a clitic attaching to an auxiliary:

(40) *tinham-se entendido perfeitamente*
and had-CLI.3SG understood perfectly
'and they had understood each other perfectly' (European Portuguese)
(Galves, Ribeiro & Moraes 2005)

They also argue that enclitics can attach to auxiliaries in examples with a preposition appearing before the verb:

(41) *O senhor está-me a guiar em silêncio*
the sir is-CLI.1SG to lead in silence
'You are leading me in silence' (European Portuguese)
(Galves, Ribeiro & Moraes 2005)

Given the examples in (40–41), Galves, Ribeiro and Moraes (2005) claim that a late syntactic or post-syntactic process reorders the syntax so that the phonological or morphological criteria are satisfied and that a special feature is responsible for this. In their analysis, the position of clitics is defined by morphological rules, like the position of word affixes is.

Additionally, other forms that have been argued to be cliticized in the form of suffixes include the English and French pronouns. The English 3rd person singular and 3rd person plural pronouns have phonologically reduced clitic forms Déchaine and Wiltschko (2002) (42).

(42) I like [$_{\varphi}$ 'em] (Déchaine & Wiltschko 2002: 422)

The French *l*-clitics are also argued to function as bound variables:

(43) a. *[Chaque homme]$_i$ pense qu' [il]$_i$ est intelligent*
each man thinks that he is intelligent

b. *[Chaque homme]$_i$ pense que Marie [l]$_i$ 'a vu*
each man thinks that Marie him has seen
(French; Déchaine & Wiltschko 2002: 429)

It seems that based on the discussion, above pronominal clitics can be found in bound forms in some languages, just as discourse connectives can (Muysken 2008).

With regard to the case of -*nde* in CG, we already argued that this element is a borrowing of Turkish *dA*, which harmonizes its vowel according to the preceding word. *DA* in Turkish does not appear as a pronominal clitic, but as a multi-function particle with discourse properties. So, the restriction of the CG -*nde* with post-verbal pronominal clitics does not seem to originate from *dA*. It should be noted that vowel harmony, which appears in the Turkish *dA*, can also be found in the enclitics of an Italian variety. In other words, elements that attach to their host can show vowel harmony.

(44) *Metto-lo*
puts-it
Mettu-lu
puts-him (Italian; Vogel 1997)

This case also shows enclitics in a bound form, as previously presented for European Portuguese, English and French.

Assuming that -*nde* is a borrowing of *dA*, or the harmonized Turkish form *dE*, the ungrammaticality appearing with the non-active suffix -*an* in (17), repeated as (45), initially appeared as a possible result of this phonological process. However, CG does not show any other instances of *vowel harmony*, so we refrain from making strong claims about the phonological relations of -*nde* with other segments in its environment. As argued in Section 3.1, CG -*nde* is not allowed when there is non-active syntax, not simply non-active morphology (e.g. -*an*).

(45) a. **Emaxumasta-nde pollin ora*
were.kept.busy.nde-1PL much time-ACC
'We were kept busy for a long time' (CG)

It is clear at this stage that the originating positions of a post-verbal pronominal clitic and -*nde* are definitely different. We argue, however, that on the basis of the common property of enclitics to attach to their host as bound forms, pronominal enclitics in Cypriot Greek compete with the *validational* marker -*nde* for the same position that is immediately adjacent to their host.

To give a clearer picture of the position of -*nde*, we assume that it attaches to the verb before any movement, and not after movement to a higher position like C^0 (Agouraki 2010) or $Mood^0$ (Terzi 1999a, 1999b), since it can appear with pre-verbal object clitics. Generating the clitic–verb or verb–clitic structure has been argued to depend on the movement of the verb to higher projections, which is commonly assumed to be the case in feature-driven verb movements in null-subject languages. For the purposes of this paper, we will not make any claims regarding the possible structures for generating pre-verbal or post-verbal clitics. The grammaticality of -*nde* with a pre-verbal clitic in (32), repeated in (46), indicates that -*nde* can be inserted in the vP (47) and not in any other particular position to satisfy features (Agouraki 2010). If verb movement triggers the post-verbal placement in Cypriot Greek, it could be argued that the adjunction of -*nde* to the verb prevents verb movement to a higher position and only proclisis is allowed. Future research can address the question regarding the kind of features that could possibly trigger this.

(46) *θeloume na to dume-nde.*
want-1PL to it-CLI.ACC see.nde-1PL
'We want to see it' (CG)

(47) [CP…[FP it[TP $(we)_i$ [*v*P $[we]_i$ see-*nde*]]]]

Last, and with respect to the other environments imposing restrictions on post-verbal clitic placement, we argue that the existence of -*nde* in the clause differs substantially from the obligatory procliclis environments, such as *wh*-questions, *na*-clause and negative environments, and rather emphasize the arguments previously mentioned. This is also evident from the observation[7] that all the environments restricting post-verbal clitic placement are found pre-verbally, whereas the *validational* marker -*nde* is found post-verbally.

In this section, we presented data from other clitic languages, showing the possibility of clitic affixation on a host, and we have argued that despite the different discourse properties of the *validational* marker -*nde* and pronominal clitics in CG, the two compete for the same adjacent position with their host.

7. We would like to thank João Costa for his observation and feedback.

5. Conclusion

This paper is a first attempt to describe the morphosyntactic properties of the Cypriot Greek suffix -*nde*. This marker appears to be in a process of 'death' in CG, as it is found more and more rarely in everyday speech. The identification of CG as the low variety (L) in Cyprus suggests that it may undergo a process of 'death' (Rowe & Grohmann 2012) and therefore the most dialectal elements will be the first candidates for loss (see Leivada et al. to appear).

The grammatical distribution of -*nde* classifies it as a suffix, appearing only in 1st person PLURAL and without any tense restrictions. Semantically, -*nde* has been argued to belong in the list of *validational* markers, which assert a truth value on the proposition being expressed (Weber 1986) and are associated with (unspecified) direct experience by the speaker.

Most importantly, the syntactic restriction imposed by -*nde* brings up interesting discussion on the difference between clitics and affixes. Post-verbal object clitics cannot appear in the presence of -*nde*, which may suggest that the clitic property of affixation identified in other languages for enclitics may also appear for the CG enclitics. Pronominal object clitics in CG cannot appear as bound forms, but their ungrammaticality with the *validational* marker -*nde* shows that not only overt bound forms need adjacency with their host in post-verbal positions. We argue that the *validational* marker -*nde* attaches to the verb within the vP domain. Pre-verbal object clitics can appear in the presence of -*nde*, which indicates that -*nde* attaches to the verb, before the verb moves to a higher projection to satisfy any strong features (Terzi 1999a, 1999b), as commonly assumed for null-subject languages.

This study has provided a first sketch of the distribution of the suffix -*nde* in CG. The purpose was to provide initial insights into the ungrammaticality observed with post-verbal clitics by analyzing the properties of -*nde* and searching for findings or relevant phenomena in other languages. The detailed analysis provided has shown that phenomena like this enhance the possibility of the appearance of gaps in the knowledge of the characteristics of affixed elements and clitics. Mavrogiorgos (2010) identifies the 'highly hybrid status of clitics' and points out that 'the hallmark of clitics is that they are both word-like and affix-like.' As pointed out in the previous sections, the case studied here can arise from two possible scenarios. The one is that -*nde* satisfies certain features F, which disallow the movement of the verb to a higher position, and therefore no post-verbal clitics can appear in its presence. The other is that -*nde* and post-verbal clitics 'fight' for position that is adjacent to the verb, but the status of the position is still unclear. If this claim is on the right track, there should be a feature that both -*nde* and post-verbal clitics share.

This study contributed to the evidence that morphological idiosyncrasies are more prominent in affixes than clitics, and that the former can show more complex semantic peculiarities than the latter. It is because of such unexpected grammatical discoveries that we can challenge the nature of each element in the clause and provide comparisons between similar phenomena across languages.

References

Agouraki, Yorgia. 2001. The position of clitics in Cypriot Greek. In *Proceedings of the First International Conference of Modern Greek Dialects and Linguistic Theory*, Angela Ralli, Brian Joseph & Mark Janse (eds), 1–17. Patras: University of Patras.

Agouraki, Yorgia. 2010. It-clefts and stressed operators in the pre-verbal field of Cypriot Greek. *Lingua* 120(3): 527–554.

Anderson, Lloyd B. 1986. Evidentials, paths of change and mental maps: Typologically regular assymetries. In *Evidentiality: The Linguistic Code of Epistemology*, Wallace Chafe & Johanna Nichols (eds), 273–312. Norwood NJ: Ablex.

Archakis, Argiris & Tzanne, Angeliki. 2009. Constructing social identities through storytelling: Tracing Greekness in Greek narratives. *Pragmatics* 19(3): 343–362.

Arvaniti, Amalia. 2002. The maintenance of diglossia in Cyprus and the emergence of Cypriot Standard Greek. Ms, University of California, San Diego.

Auer, Peter. 2005a. The construction of linguistic borders and the linguistic construction of borders. In *Dialects across Borders: Selected Papers from the* 11th *International Conference on Methods in Dialectology (Methods XI)* [Current Issues in Linguistic Theory 273], Markku Filppula, Juhani Klemola, Marjatt Palander & Esa Penttilä (eds), 3–30. Amsterdam: John Benjamins.

Auer, Peter. 2005b. Europe's sociolinguistic unity, or: A typology of European dialect/standard constellations. In *Perspectives on Variation* [Trends in Linguistics 163], Nicole Delbecque, Johan van der Auwera & Dirk Geeraerts (eds), 7–42. Berlin: Mouton de Gruyter.

Bally, Charles. 1932. *Linguistique générale et Linguistique française.* Paris: Leroux, 2nd edn. 1944. Bern: A. Francke.

Bošković, Željko. 2004. On the clitic switch in Greek imperatives. In *Balkan Syntax and Semantics* [Linguistik Aktuell/Linguistics Today 67], Olga Mišeska Tomić (ed.), 285–310. Amsterdam: John Benjamins.

Cornips, Leonie. 2006. Intermediate syntactic variants in a dialect-standard speech repertoire and relative acceptability. In *Gradience in Grammar: Generative Perspectives,* Gisbert Fanselow, Caroline Féry, Ralph Vogel & Matthias Schlesewsky (eds), 85–105. Oxford: OUP.

Courtney, Ellen H. 1999. Child acquisition of the Quechua affirmative suffix. In *Proceedings from the Second Workshop on American Indigenous Languages* [Santa Barbara papers in Linguistics 9], 30–41. ⟨http://works.bepress.com/ellenhcourtney/5⟩

Déchaine, Rose-Marie & Wiltschko, Martina. 2002. Decomposing pronouns. *Linguistic Inquiry* 33(3): 409–442.

Erguvanlı, Eser Emine. 1984. *The Function of Word Order in Turkish Grammar* [University of California Publications in Linguistics 106]. Berkeley CA: University of California Press.

Faller, Martina. 2003. The evidential and *validational* licensing conditions for the Cusco Quechua enclitic -*mi*. *Belgian Journal of Linguistics* 16: 7–21.

Floyd, Rick. 1997. *La estructura categorical de los evidenciales en el quechua wanka*. Lima: Ministerio de Educación (Instituto Linguístico de Verano).

Galves, Charlotte, Ribeiro, Ilza & Moraes, Maria Aparecida Torres. 2005. Syntax and morphology in the placement of clitics in European and Brazilian Portuguese. *Journal of Portuguese Linguistics* 2(4): 143–177.

Galves, Charlotte & Sândalo, Filomena. 2004. Clitic-Placement in European Portuguese and the syntax-phonology interface. In *Collected Papers on Romance Syntax* [MIT Working Papers in Linguistics 47], Ana Castro, Marcello Ferreira, Valentine Hacquard & Andrès P. Salanova (eds),115–128. Cambridge MA: MITWPL.

Göksel, Aslı & Kerslake, Celia. 2005. *Turkish: A Comprehensive Grammar*. London: Routledge.

Göksel, Aslı & Özsoy, A. Sumru. 2003. dA: A focus/topic associated clitic in Turkish. *Lingua* 113: 1143–1167.

Grohmann, Kleanthes K. 2011. Some directions for the systematic investigation of the acquisition of Cypriot Greek: A new perspective on production abilities from object clitic placement. In *The Development of Grammar: Language Acquisition and Diachronic Change* [Hamburg Studies on Multilingualism 11], Esther Rinke & Tanja Kupisch (eds), 179–203. Amsterdam: John Benjamins.

Grohmann, Kleanthes K. & Leivada, Evelina. 2012. Interface ingredients of dialect design: Bi-x, socio-syntax of development, and the grammar of Cypriot Greek. In *Towards a Biolinguistic Understanding of Grammar: Essays on Interfaces* [Linguistik Aktuell/Linguistics Today 194], Anna Maria Di Sciullo (ed.), 239–262. Amsterdam: John Benjamins.

Grohmann, Kleanthes K., Theodorou, Eleni, Pavlou, Natalia, Leivada, Evelina, Papadopoulou, Elena & Martínez-Ferreiro, Silvia. 2012. The development of object clitic placement in Cypriot Greek and the Romance connection. In *Selected Proceedings of the Romance Turn IV*, Sandrine Ferré, Philippe Prévost, Laurie Tuller & Rasha Zebib (eds). Newcastle-upon-Tyne: Cambridge Scholars.

Halpern, Aaron. 1995. *On the Placement and Morphology of Clitics*. Stanford CA: CSLI.

Hill, Virginia. 2009. Pragmatic markers as syntactic heads: A case study from Romanian. In *Selected Papers from the 2006. Cyprus Syntaxfest,* Kleanthes K. Grohmann & Phoevos Panagiotidis (eds), 1–10. Newcastle-upon-Tyne: Cambridge Scholars.

Kiefer, Ferenc. 1998. Morphology and pragmatics. In *The Handbook of Morphology*, Andrew Spencer & Arnold M. Zwicky (eds), 66–84. Oxford: Blackwell.

Leivada, Evelina, Papadopoulou, Elena & Pavlou, Natalia. 2013. The gray area of acceptability judgments: Clefts and exhaustivity in Cypriot Greek. In *Language Contact: A Multidimensional Perspective,* Kelechukwu U. Ihemere (ed.), Newcastle-upon-Tyne: Cambridge Scholars.

Leivada, Evelina, Paraskevi Mavroudi, & Epistithiou, Anna. 2010. Metalanguage or bidialectism? Acquisition of clitic placement by Hellenic Greeks, Greek Cypriots and binationals in the diglossic context of Cyprus. In *Proceedings of the* 3rd *ISCA Workshop ExLing 2010*, Antonis Botinis (ed.), 97–100. Athens: University of Athens.

Lobo, Maria & Costa, João. 2012. Acquisition of Clitic Placement in European Portuguese. Paper presented in the CYCL1A Workshop on the Acquisition of Clitics, University of Cyprus, Nicosia, (25–26 May).

Lotte, Hogeweg, de Hoop, Helen & Malchukov, Andrej. 2009. *Cross-linguistics Semantics of Tense, Aspect and Modality* [Linguistik Aktuell/Linguistics 148]. Amsterdam: John Benjamins.

Maia, Marcus. 2004. Evidential Processes in Karaja. In *Sur le médiatif II,* Zlatka Guentcheva & Jon Landaburu (eds). Paris: CNRS.

Mavrogiorgos, Marios. 2010. *Clitics in Greek. A Minimalist Account of Proclisis and Enclisis* [Linguistik Aktuell/Linguistics Today 160]. Amsterdam: John Benjamins.

Muysken, Pieter. 1995. Focus in Quechua. Discource configurational languages. In *Discourse Configurational Languages*, É. Katalin Kiss (ed.), 375–393. Oxford: OUP.

Muysken, Pieter. 2008. *Functional Categories.* Cambridge: CUP.

Neocleous, Theoni. 2012. Πρώιμα στάδια γλωσσικής ανάπτυξης. Η περίπτωση των κλιτικών αντωνυμιών της Κυπριακής [First stages of language development: The case of Cypriot Greek object clitics]. Σεμινάρια στη Διδακτική της Γλώσσας: Δομή, Ποικιλία και Διδασκαλία. [Seminars in Language Teaching: Structure, Variation and Teaching]. Nicosia: University of Cyprus.

Newton, Brian. 1972. *Cypriot Greek: Its Phonology and Inflections.* The Hague: Mouton.

Nuckolls, Janis B. 1993. The semantics of certainty in Quechua and its implications for a cultural epistemology. *Language in Society* 22: 235–255.

Özbek, Nurdan. 1995. Discourse Markers in Turkish and English: A Comparative Study. Ph.D. dissertation, University of Nottingham.

Papadopoulou, Elena, Leivada, Evelina & Pavlou, Natalia. 2012. Clitic placement in Cypriot Greek: A matter of lexical and syntactic stimulation? Paper presented at the CYCL1A Workshop on the Acquisition of Clitics, University of Cyprus, Nicosia, (25–26 May).

Pavlou, Pavlos & Christodoulou, Niki. 2001. Bidialectism in Cyprus and its impact on the teaching of Greek as a foreign language. *International Journal of Applied Linguistics* 11: 75–91.

Petinou, Kakia & Terzi, Arhonto. 2002. Clitic misplacement among normally developing children and children with specific language impairment and the status of Infl heads. *Language Acquisition* 10: 1–28.

Rowe, Charley & Grohmann, Kleanthes K. 2012. Testing the state of diglossia in Cyprus: Cypriots, binationals, and diglossic shift. Ms, University of Cyprus.

Schiering, René. 2006. Morphologization in Turkish: Implications for phonology in grammaticalization. Paper presented at 13th International Conference on Turkish Linguistics, Uppsala, 16–20 August.

Sifianou, Maria. 1992. *Politeness Phenomena in England and Greece. A Cross-cultural Perspective.* Oxford: OUP.

Terzi, Arhonto. 1999a. Clitic combinations, their hosts and their ordering. *Natural Language and Linguistic Inquiry* 17: 85–121.

Terzi, Arhonto. 1999b. Cypriot Greek clitics and their positioning restrictions. In *Studies in Greek Syntax,* Artemis Alexiadou, Geoffrey Horrocks & Melita Stavrou (eds), 227–240. Dordrecht: Kluwer.

Vassiliou, Elena. 1995. Cypriot as a VOS language. *La Trobe Working Papers in Linguistics* 8: 135–149.

Vogel, Irene. 1997. Prosodic phonology. In *The Dialects of Italy,* Martin Maiden & Mair Parry (eds). London: Routledge.

Weber, David. 1986. Information perspective, profile, and patterns in Quechua. In *Evidentiality: The Linguistic Coding of Epistemology,* Wallace Chafe & Johanna Nichols (eds), 137–155. Norwood NJ: Ablex.

Willet, Thomas L. 1988. A cross-linguistic survey of the grammaticalization of evidentiality. *Studies in Language* 12: 51–97.

Yiakoumetti, Androulla, Evans, Michael & Esch, Eiff. 2005. Language awareness in a bidialectal setting: The oral performance and language attitudes of urban and rural students in Cyprus. *Language Awareness* 14: 254–260.

Zwicky, Arnold M. & Pullum, Geoffrey K. 1983. Cliticization vs. inflection: English N'T. *Language* 59(3): 502–513.

Zwicky, Arnold M. 1985. Clitics and particles. *Language* 61: 283–305.

Acquisition of Italian object clitics by a trilingual child

Acquisition of Italian object clitics

Elizaveta Khachaturyan
University of Oslo

This paper describes the acquisition of Italian object pronouns by a trilingual girl who simultaneously acquires Italian, Russian, and Norwegian. Different processes were distinguished according to the subject's age at the time of acquisition. Italian first- and second-person singular clitics were produced correctly during the first stage (at age 2;2) but were replaced by tonic forms after the age of three, while third-person singular clitics were used in a target-consistent manner. On the basis of these data I shall discuss different approaches to Italian clitics.

1. Introduction[1]

Clitics in Romance languages have been the object of much discussion in linguistics. In studies on child language acquisition, analyses of clitic acquisition in Romance languages are based on experimental and empirical data and raise questions concerning syntactic acquisition and development (e.g. Eisenchlas 2003, for Spanish; Hamann et al. 1995, for French; Tedeschi 2006, for Italian). In particular they describe clitic position and the conditions for clitic omission and clitic climbing.

The focus of this paper is the status of Italian object clitics in child language and the phases of clitic acquisition. Since the question of whether they should be considered affixes or independent syntactic forms is still open (e.g. Monachesi 1999, 2006), my analysis will provide this discussion with further arguments and insights.

1. I would like to express my deep gratitude to two anonymous reviewers (one of whom was even kind enough to comment on the paper a second time). Their stimulating comments and criticism were immensely valuable in helping me to shape the final version of this paper.

Child language and child grammar are important focal points for such an investigation because development proceeds from concepts that children need in order to express themselves to the instruments that different languages offer for this purpose. From this point of view the study of plurilingual, simultaneous acquisition is particularly interesting, since concepts are expressed in a different way in different languages according to different grammatical systems.

The empirical data for this study are taken from a longitudinal case study of a young girl, named 'Esther' here, who is acquiring three languages simultaneously: Italian, Russian, and Norwegian. Among these three languages, only Italian has a clear opposition between object clitic and tonic pronouns.

The paper is organized as follows: after a brief presentation of the child's data for this study (Section 2), I will give an overview of the Italian pronominal system (Section 3). I will then show how this system is acquired, first (briefly) by monolinguals (Section 4), and then by the subject, 'Esther' (Section 5). In the last section, I will discuss the process of clitic acquisition and the status of clitics in the speech of the trilingual child.

2. The child data

The data used in this study consist of diary data[2] and audio recordings (a part of an ongoing longitudinal study) of a girl we will call 'Esther,' who was born in Oslo in September 2007 and who was exposed to two languages from birth (Italian from her father and Russian from her mother) and to a third language from the age of 0;11 – Norwegian (in day care). The family language for the parents was Italian, but when talking to the child the strategy one parent – one language was strictly followed.

Esther was regularly recorded from the age of 1;11, while manual recordings in the form of a diary started earlier, from the age of 1;02. Recordings were made at home with the participation of one or both of the parents during free play sessions or daily routine actions (such as eating dinner or preparing to go to bed or to day care); the recordings were then transcribed by myself using the CHAT format used for CHILDES (MacWhinney 2000). The diary data generally noted the most interesting and/or problematic uses and forms, as well as the first appearance of a given form.

2. This girl is my daughter, so the parent diary was identical in form with those typically used in the analysis of child language acquisition (e.g. Tseitlin 2000, 2007).

For the present study the analyzed period is from the age of 2;00 (when the first forms of pronouns appear) to 4;00.

3. A brief overview of the Italian pronominal system

All major Italian grammars (e.g. Dardano & Trifone 2007; Renzi et al. 1996; Salvi & Vanelli 2004) divide Italian personal pronouns into two groups: clitic forms and tonic forms. Tonic forms have two cases, nominative and oblique (Table 1), while clitic forms have four cases: accusative, dative, locative and partitive-genitive (Table 2).

Table 1. Tonic forms

	Singular	Singular	Singular	Plural	Plural	Plural
	1.	2.	3.	1.	2.	3.
Nominative	*io*	*tu*	*lui* (masc.) *lei* (fem.)	*noi*	*voi*	*loro*
Oblique	*me*	*te*	*lui* (masc.) *lei* (fem.)	*noi*	*voi*	*loro*

Table 2. Clitic forms

	Singular	Singular	Singular	Plural	Plural	Plural
	1.	2.	3.	1.	2.	3.
Accusative	*mi*	*ti*	*lo* (masc.) *la* (fem.) *l'* (masc./fem.)	*ci*	*vi*	*li* (masc.) *le* (fem.)
Dative	*mi*	*ti*	*gli* (masc.) *le* (fem.)	*ci*	*vi*	*gli (loro)*
Locative			*ci/vi*			
Partitive-genitive			*ne*			

As we can see, locative and partitive-genitive cases have only one manifestation each: *ci* (locative) and *ne* (partitive-genitive). There are no occurrences at all in my data of the partitive-genitive *ne*, and the use of the form *ci* is limited to three contexts: *c'è un gatto* 'there is a cat', the so-called *ci* of introduction (*c'e' presentativo*, Berruto 2012); and *ci* used in idiomatic expressions: *ce l'ho* 'I have it' and *non ce la faccio* 'I can't manage', where *ce* is a part of the tripartite verbs *aver=ce=la* 'to have' (litt. 'have there it') and *far=ce=la* 'manage to do something' (litt.'do there it'), composed of *aver[e], far[e]*, the infinitive of the verbs *avere* 'to have,' and *fare* 'to do' (with the apocope of the final *-e*), the clitic *ci*, which becomes *ce* anteposed to another clitic,[3] and the clitics *l'* and *la*). *Ci (ce)* in idiomatic constructions is called an inherent clitic (i-clitic) (Espinal 2009). 'I-clitics share identical formal features with non-inherent clitics, but i-clitics are not coreferential with any discourse referent' (Espinal 2009: 1242). Presumably this feature of i-clitics explains their earlier acquisition compared to the acquisition of non-inherent clitics.

To indicate a direct object (acc.) and indirect object (dat.), both tonic and clitic forms can be used. Grammars provide a clear explanation: in addition to the general rule prescribing the use of tonic forms alone, stressed or with a preposition (1–3), tonic forms are used in specific contexts, such as negation (4), focalization (5), or coordination (6), while clitic forms are considered to be neutral forms and are used in all other contexts (e.g. Salvi & Vanelli 2004).

(1) *Chi stai aspettando? – Lui.*
who are waiting him
'Who are you waiting for? Him.'

(2) *Ha invitato* ***lei?!***
you have invited her
'You have invited her?!'

(3) *Con chi stai parlando? – Con te.*
with whom are you talking – with him
'Whom are you talking to? – To you.'

(4) *Aspetto te e non lui.*
I am waiting you.PR.2S.ACC and not him.PR.3S.M.ACC
'I am waiting for you and not for him.'

(5) *Anche a me è piaciuto.*
Also to me it pleased
'I liked it too.'

(6) *Invito voi e Maria.*
Invite.1S you.PR.2S.ACC and Maria
'I invite you and Maria.'

3. If a pronoun is followed by another one, the vowel *i* changes to *e*. This is a general rule that explains forms such as *Maria me lo dice* (Maria – 1SG.DAT – 3SG.ACC says), where both pronouns have a clitic form: *me* (1SG.DAT) changes its form (*mi* to *me*) because of the position: before another clitic pronoun *lo* (3SG.ACC). Maria tells it to me.

Verbs are the hosts of Italian clitics, which occur in a fixed order and fixed position depending on the verbal form. These basic characteristics of clitics can be described by several formal rules that are codified in grammars:

- Position of clitic forms:
  - Pre-position with finite verbal forms (*Maria mi aspetta* 'Maria is waiting for me') and formal imperative forms (*mi aspetti* 'wait for me'),
  - Post-position with non-finite verbal forms and the second-person singular imperative (the so-called informal imperative), where a clitic pronoun and a verbal form are even written as one word (e.g. *devi aspettar=mi* 'you have to wait for me'; *aspetta=mi* 'wait for me'),
  - both positions are possible with several groups of verbs, such as modal verbs, aspectual verbs, motion verbs, as well as causative and perceptual verbs (e.g. *mi devi aspettare/devi aspettarmi* 'you have to wait for me'). This phenomenon is known as clitic climbing.

- Combination of clitic forms:
  - position: IO precedes DO,
  - formal changes: *i* becomes *e* (e.g. *me lo dici* 'tell it to me'), and the pronoun *le* (3S.F.DAT) becomes *glie* if followed by another pronoun (e.g. *le dico la verità,*'I'll tell her the truth'; *gliela dico* 'I'll tell it to her')

In the next section we will see that in the early stages of acquisition some clitics are positioned correctly, while the most frequent error is the omission of a clitic form.

Italian pronouns (both clitic forms and tonic ones) are often described as contextual inflections of verbal regency or valency (e.g. Scalise & Bisetto 2008: 154: *forme di flessione contestuale per reggenza*), and their acquisition is a part of Italian inflectional morphology (e.g. Pizzuto & Caselli 1992). At the same time, the choice of the correct case form of a pronoun (acc. or dat.) is treated in grammars as one of the syntactic-argumental properties of the verb (e.g. Salvi & Vanelli 2004: 45). The use of a tonic or a clitic form, as we have seen (in 1–6), is often determined by the context.

However, whether clitics are considered a part of verbal inflection (the morphological approach) or arguments of the verb (the syntactic approach), their use is mandatory. They fill the valency of the verb and cannot be omitted. For example, the verb *sapere* 'to know' has two valencies that have to be filled in: the subject (Italian is a pro-drop language since the inflectional system is very rich) and the direct object (DO); likewise, the verb *dare 'to give'* has three valencies (subject, DO, and indirect object (IO)), and so on. Moreover, certain verbs such as *sapere* 'to know' are often used with a clitic pronoun even if a subordinate clause occupies the valency of DO, as in *Lo so che ti piace* 'I know that you like it'. But both uses (with the clitic *lo* and without it) are possible when talking about a past event, as in *So che hai lavorato* 'I know that you have worked' and *Lo so che hai lavorato* 'I know that you have worked.' In the next section we will see the importance of these observations for child language acquisition.

In accordance with the preceding discussion, while the subject pronoun is usually omitted in Italian, the omission of a clitic is considered an error. This property is very important for the present study: by contrast, in Russian (one of Esther's languages) it is common to omit verbal arguments, as we can see in the case of examples (7) and (8) below: *da, znaju* (Yes, know-pres.ind.1S); *da, videl* (yes, see-past).

(7)	*Lo*	*so*
	CL.3S.M	know.1S
	'I know it.'	

(8)	*Hai*	*visto*	*Mario?*	–	*Sì,*	*l'*	*ho*	*visto.*
	have.2s	seen	Mario	–	yes	CL.3S.M/F	have.1s	seen
	'Have you seen Mario? – Yes, I've seen him.'							

(9)	*Chi*	*può*	*accendere*	*la*	*luce?.*	*L'*	*accende*	*Mario.*
	who	can.3s	switch on	the	light.	CL.3S.M/F	switch on	Mario
	'Who can switch on the light? – Mario will switch it on.'							

(10) *Aiuta=mi.*
Help–IMP.2S=CL.1S
'Help me.'

Moreover, in spoken Italian, dislocation occurs frequently (e.g. Berruto 2012: 76–77). In this case, a clitic form repeats a DO (or an IO) expressed by a noun and preposed (left dislocation – ex. 11) or postposed (right dislocation – ex. 12–14) to the verbal form:[4]

(11)	*I*	*guanti*	*li*	*prendi*	(instead of *prendi i guanti*,
	The	gloves	CL.3PL.M.ACC	take.2s.	which is also possible).
	'Take your gloves.'				

4. It seems that this phenomenon is typical for some contexts. For example, the right dislocation is often used in a request for an action, with an indicative form of the 2S/3S (polite form) or the forms of the modal verb *potere* (can). This kind of dislocation merits further in-depth analysis based upon corpus data.

(12) *Lo* *chiudi* *il* *frigo* (instead of *chiudi il frigo*).
CL.3S.M.ACC close.2S the refrigerator
'Can you close the refrigerator?'

(13) *Lo* *puoi* *togliere* *il* *libro* (instead of *puoi togliere il libro*).
CL.3S.M.ACC put.2S away the book
'Can you put away the book?'

(14) *Le* *puoi* *dire* *a* *mamma* *di* *chiudere*
CL.3S.F.DAT can.2S tell to Mommy to close
la *porta.* (instead of *puoi dire a mamma di chiudere la porta*)
the door
'Can you tell Mommy to close the door?'

Based on these features of clitics Monachesi (2006) assumes that 'clitics appear in child grammar as fillers given their functional status' (2006: 32). 'Fillers have clear prosodic properties: in the beginning they are not morphologically differentiated among each other. They usually appear in unstressed position before a stressed item' (2006: 32). Some of the data that I will discuss in the following sections can confirm this hypothesis.

4. Different phases in the acquisition of clitics by monolinguals

In Italian monolingual children, the first sporadic clitic forms typically appear at the age of 20–23 months. In a study led by Cipriani that observed six monolingual children (Cipriani et al. 1993), the first form was noted in one of them at the age of 20 months, namely the clitic pronoun 3S (*l'*, *lo*). In Antelmi's (1997) case study of her daughter, she noticed the first pronouns at the age of 22 months in the enclitic position: *ecco=lo* 'here it (is)', *da=mmi* 'give me', and *da=mme=lo* 'give it to me'.

A study of French monolinguals reports similar results: 'the first genuine object clitic occurs at the age of 2;2,13 in the form of an enclitic: *ateins-le (éteins-le)*' (Hamann et al. 1995: 92). Similar observations have been made about monolingual Spanish children (see, e.g. the analysis of different studies on the acquisition of Spanish in Montrul 2004).

I will use the data from the study by Cipriani et al. to describe the pattern of the acquisition of Italian clitic pronouns by monolinguals. The authors analyze the data from six children in the period from 19 to 36 months (video- and audio-recordings made every two weeks). Based mostly on the MLU, the authors distinguish four phases of acquisition: the presyntactic phase, the primitive syntactic phase, the completion of the nuclear phrase, and the consolidation and generalization of rules in complex structures. The authors provide a quantitative analysis of each child and a summarizing overview (in a table) of the appearance of all clitic forms. The main steps of acquisition in their summary are as follows. The first clitic forms of pronouns appear at the end of the first phase and the beginning of the second phase. During the second phase a high omission rate is registered, but in the third phase the number of omissions declines and the correct use of clitics steadily increases. The principal errors noted by the authors in this phase include the wrong genre (*lo* (M) instead of *la* (F)), the wrong number (*lo* (S) instead of *li* (PL)), and the wrong morphophonemic variant (e.g. *me* instead of *mi*). The authors do not mention any conflict between tonic and clitic forms. But in Esther's case (as we will see), her most frequent error is to use tonic forms where she should use clitic forms.

The acquisition of clitics has also been described by Pizzuto and Caselli (1992) in their study of the acquisition of Italian inflectional morphology. The study analyzes the longitudinal, spontaneous data of three Italian children between the ages of 1;4 and 3;0 and focuses specifically on the development of the morphological paradigms of Italian verbs, but it also explores the acquisition of Italian subject and object pronouns, including clitics. The researchers noticed individual differences in the number of morphemes acquired and their order of acquisition. For example, by the age of 3;0, only one child had fully mastered the second-person clitic *ti,* while another one had achieved productive use of the third-person clitics *lo-la*.

The acquisition of Italian clitics by older children (from the age of 3;00) has been studied by R. Tedeschi (2006), who in a pilot study tested six Italian monolinguals aged 3;02 to 4;02. The children were asked to describe pictures, and the experimenter's questions were formulated in such a way that the answers should involve the obligatory use of a direct object, preferably a clitic (only third-person clitics had to be used). In the children's answers there were few omissions (5.8%) or substitutions (3.3%) using the character's name or a demonstrative pronoun, and clitic pronouns were used in 65% (78 of 120) of the phrases uttered. Two types of errors involving the use of clitic pronouns were attested in these 78 phrases: agreement errors (15.4% – or 12/78) and inversions of agent/subject and patient/object (17.9% – or 14/78) (in this case the verb agrees with the object and not with the subject).

5. Phases of Esther's acquisition

5.1 First phase. Qualitative analysis

Before presenting the data on Esther's language acquisition and use of clitic forms, I should provide a general overview of her language development during the period in question. Between the ages of 2;00 and 2;07, her speech was characterized by the frequent mixing of two or three languages:[5]

(15) *@ru Chitat' @no ikke lov @it va a letto dopo @ru pepe*
@ru to read @no not allowed @it go to bed after @ru cookies
@it latte (Talking to her mother and to her father) (2;04)
@it milk
'Not allowed to read, go to bed after cookies and milk.'

(16) *@ru pechenje @it mangia @no og @ru chut'-chut' @it beve*
@ru cookies @it eats @no and @ru little bit @it
(i)l latte (Talking to her father) (2;04)
drinks milk
'Cookies eats and a little bit of milk drinks.'

(17) *Mamma, @no ikke @it sporchi mani, @no ikke @it andata fuori,*
Mommy @no not @dirty hands @no NEG @it was outside
@ru chistye (Commenting on what her mother is doing) (2;03)
@ru clean
'Mommy, not dirty hands, not was outside, clean.'

(18) *@it Pure @ru moloko @it*
@it also @ru milk @it
compra Esther (Playing with her mother) (2;03)
buys Esther
'Also milk will buy Esther.'

(19) *@no ikke @it toccare @ru botinki @no mine*
@no NEG @it touch @ru shoes @no POSS
'Don't touch my shoes.'
(An utterance addressed to a boy in day care, noted in the diary) (2;07)

It seems that each of the three languages provided different elements to Esther's language (a kind of *koiné*). For example, from Norwegian she took negation (*ikke* 'not'), possessive pronouns (*min* 'my', *din* 'your'), demonstrative pronouns (*denne* 'this', *den* 'that'), and spatial adverbs (*her* 'here', *der* 'there'), and no other

5. In the examples below I am using the format of the transcription proposed in MacWhinney (2000). The following abbreviations have been used: @ru – for Russian, @no – for Norwegian, @it – for Italian.

equivalent element from Russian or Italian appeared until the age of 2;7.[6] As to the interaction between Russian and Italian, I will only note here that she used more Italian verbs and more Russian nouns during this period (for more details, see Khachaturyan 2011).

In this context, the first attestations of Esther's use of Italian object clitics involved the use of enclitic forms with imperatives (note that this was also the case with monolingual Italian children), as well as formulaic uses in other contexts.

(20) *Da=mmi* (2;05)
give -IMP=.2S- CL 1S,
'give me'

(21) *Aiuta=mi* (2;05)
help.IMP.2S=CL 1S,
'help me'

(22) *Tanti auguri a te.* (2;04) (words from a birthday song)
Many wishes to -PR.2S
'Many wishes to you.'

(23) *Masha,*[7] *ti prendo in braccio, @no ja?* (2;04)
Masha, CL.2S take.1S in arms @no yes
'Masha, I'll take you in my arms.'

In the same period, forms of the third-person singular DO emerged. They were used in utterances expressing a request:

(24) ***lo*** *puoi togliere @ru ljagusha* (2;04)
CL.3S.M can 2S take away @ru the frog
'Can you take away the frog?'

(25) ***la***[8] *prendi papà succo* (2;05)
CL.3S.F take.2S Daddy juice
'Can you take some juice, Daddy?'

6. This is an intriguing phenomenon that I would like to examine in more depth in the future.

7. Masha is Esther's favorite doll, while the whole utterance *ti prendo in braccio* is the exact quotation of what Esther's father says whenever she is tired.

8. I use this notation to indicate that the sound "l" in the beginning is sometimes unclear in audio data. The same phenomenon has been observed in the data of Pizzuto and Caselli (1992): they called it "vowel forms," "namely *o, a, e* and *i* forms, used instead of the adult *lo, la, le, li*" (1992: 538).

Esther tried to imitate the construction typical for adult speech in a request for an action to take place: before a verbal form, whether the present indicative (25) or a modal verb (24) with infinitive, she inserted an element (*lo*, ^{l}*a*), without paying attention to agreement. The form she was trying to use corresponds to a clitic form in adult speech and can also have the status of a filler, according to Monachesi's hypothesis. At the same time it seems that the semantic properties of the verb are also important in this case: third-person clitics are used in a request for an action where the focus is on the object, while the first-person clitics are used when the action and its beneficiary are more important.

During this period Esther used the Norwegian demonstrative pronoun *den* 'that'/*denne* 'this' (instead of Italian clitics) with Italian verbal forms (26, 27), and also with Russian forms (28, 29).

(26) *@it Prenni @no den* (Giving a pencil to her father) (2;02)
Take.IMP 2S PR.3S
'Take this one.'

(27) *@no Denne @it mette mamma*
PR 3PL.ACC put.3S.on Mommy.
'Mommy will put these on.' (Talking about who will help her dress) (2;05)

(28) *@ru Eshche kupim @no denne* (2;04)
Some more buy.1PL PRON.3PL
'We'll buy these too.'

(29) *@ru Ostav' @no denne* (2;05)
Leave.IMP.2S PRON 3PL
'Leave these.'

In Examples 26 and 27 there should be an Italian clitic pronoun (*prendi=lo*'take it' – post-position with an imperative form; *li mette mamma* 'mommy will put them on' – pre-position with a finite verbal form).

It is important to note that in the case of mixing, only Norwegian third-person singular and plural pronouns were used with Russian and Italian verbs, and never first- or second-person pronouns. For first or second person the whole verbal form with a pronoun in the same language was introduced (*hjelpe meg* 'help me', but never **aiuta meg* 'help me').

(30) *@it Papà @no kan vaske* ***meg*** *og @ru mama*
Daddy can wash PRON 1S and Mommy
@no kan @it legge (2;08)
can read.
'Daddy can wash me and Mommy can read.'

5.2 First phase. Quantitative analysis

Since the verb in Italian serves as the host for clitics and Esther has never used clitic forms by themselves or mixed with verbal forms from either of her other two languages, it will be necessary to provide quantitative data showing how many Italian verbs of which syntactic category (transitive/non-transitive) and of what morphological form Esther mastered during the period in question. The syntactic category is important insofar as non-transitive verbs do not have any DO; therefore, they do not require any clitic form. We can assume that the morphological form of the verb is also significant, but for different reasons. First of all, the imperative form is often used with clitics, so we can expect to encounter clitics in orders and instructions. These speech acts are often used by 'directive' types of parents when talking to children.[9] Second, clitics have an enclitic position with the Italian imperative of the second-person singular. It is a typically inflectional position, and clitics in such cases can be seen as inflectional affixes. Both reasons can explain the earlier emergence of the imperative with clitics in child's speech, as we have seen in Section 4.

To provide an approximate number of Italian verbs used by Esther, I have analyzed three recordings: one for each month from 2;5 to 2;7, each lasting – respectively – 40, 35, and 34.15 minutes. The situation of the recordings is similar: both parents were present and speaking to Esther; Esther stayed with her mother for the whole period of the recording, while her father went away and then returned to ask about what had happened during his absence. I have not counted instances in which Esther immediately repeats the same verbal form she has just used or plays back the words of her parents (primarily her mother). However, I have counted instances in which she uses the same verbal forms in other contexts. For example, Esther uses the verb *aiutare* 'to help' in two different forms: *aiuta=mi* 'help me' and *mamma aiuta* 'mommy helps'. (One form is always used with a clitic while the other is not.) Where she repeats the same form (e.g. *aiuta=mi*) in another situation, I have counted it as a new verbal form. However, it is worth noting that this kind of repetition was minimal. In Recording 1, only two forms are repeated (each of them twice): *chiama* 'call,' and *ci vediamo* 'we see each other.' In Recording 2, no form is repeated, while in Recording 3, two forms are repeated: *vuole* 'want,' which occurs four times, and *prende* 'take,' which occurs twice.

9. See Tsejtlin (2000) about the distinction between declarative and directive types of parents. Esther's father clearly belongs to the directive type (for more information, see Khachaturyan 2012).

Table 3. Verbal forms from three languages

	Italian verbal forms	Russian verbal forms	Norwegian verbal forms
Recording 1 2;5, 40 min	18 (8)[10]	13	1 (*se* 'look')
Recording 2 2;6, 35 min	17 (11)	12	2 (*vil ha* 'want to have')
Recording 3 2;7, 34.15 min	26 (18)	9	6 (*kommer* 'comes'; *er* 'is'; *kan* 'can'; *vil ha* 'wants to have'; *hjelpe meg* 'help me'; *kom* 'come')

The table below presents the morphological division of the Italian forms attested in Esther's speech.

Table 4. Italian verbal forms

	Present indicative			Imperative	Infinitive	Present perfect[11]	Imperfect
	1 sing.	3 sing.	1 pl.				
Recording 1, age 2;5, 40 min	1	9	2[12]	2		4	
Recording 2, age 2;6, 35 min			7	5	1	4	
Recording 3, age 2;7, 34.15 min		13	2	4	4	2	1

We can see that Esther used mostly third-person forms of the imperative and present indicative. The verbal forms in each recording include, respectively, 10, 8, and 8 non-transitive verbs (e.g. *vieni* 'come,' *va* 'go,' *non cadere* 'don't fall,' *giocare* 'to play'; *balla* 'dance') or verbs that do not need any pronoun object complement, since they already have it (e.g. *accendi luce* 'switch on the light';

10. I put in brackets the number of verbs that, in theory, could have a clitic object pronoun.

11. In Italian there are several past tenses, of which two are currently used: *passato prossimo* (present perfect tense) and *imperfetto* (imperfect). The *passato prossimo* is an analytic tense formed by the auxiliary verb and the past participle. In the early stages of language acquisition children use only the past participle without any auxiliary verb (e.g. Pizzuto & Caselli 1992).

12. Both uses correspond to a formulaic greeting, *ci vediamo* 'see you,' which includes the reflexive clitic form *ci* (1PL).

spegni luce 'switch off the light'). Moreover, often the context does not require the use of a clitic form. So even if the quantitative data seem scarce, they are nevertheless significant.

Table 5 reports the total number of Italian verbs Esther used with clitic forms and of Italian verbs mixed with the Norwegian demonstrative *den* 'that'/*denne* 'this.' These numbers have been calculated for all of the audio recordings from 2;5 to 2;7, with two hours of recordings for each month. In this table the role of the repetition is significant: CL 3S used with present indicative is always the same verb – *prendi* 'take' – uttered in different situations, while the imperative with CL 1S contains three verbs: *aiutare* 'to help,' *dare* 'to give,' and *portare* 'to bring,' used in a following way: *aiuta=mi*, *da=mmi*, and *porta=mi*.

Table 5. Italian verbs used with Norwegian demonstrative pronouns and Italian clitics

	Italian verb + *den/denne*	**Imperative + CL 1S**	**CL 3S + present indicative**	**Idiomatic forms**
2;5	2	6	2	*Ce l'ha* (has it)
2;6	3	5	2	-
2;7	2	5	0	-

5.3 Second phase. Qualitative analysis

In general, the period from 2;08 in Esther's language acquisition can be characterized by the weakening of Italian and the strengthening of Russian lexical and grammatical systems. This period took place in the summer, when Esther spent more time with her mother and spoke more Russian. Russian pronouns emerged in her speech at the age of 2;8, and from the age of 2;10, the majority of the Russian pronoun forms she used were correct. By this time she was no longer omitting pronouns: her errors involved only the incorrect use of case and word position.[13]

From the age of 2;11, Esther began to use Norwegian at home more often. The explanation for this could be the fact that she had left her day care for small children (aged from 1;0 to 3;0) and was now attending a day care center with older children (of 4;0–5;0 years). The result was increased Norwegian input from her peers.

13. Using the wrong position is a very interesting error and one that merits more discussion, but since it concerns the information structure of the phrase and not the acquisition of clitics, it lies beyond the scope of this analysis.

For comparison with the previous period (Table 3), Table 6 provides the correlation of verbal forms from all three languages used at the age of 3;0. The conditions of the recording are similar to the previous ones. In this period (from 3;01 onward), the degree to which Esther mixed two or three languages decreased.

Table 6. Verbal forms from three languages

	Italian verbal forms	Russian verbal forms	Norwegian verbal forms
Recording 1, age 3;0, 31 min	8	17	6
Recording 2, age 3;0, 15 min	4	5	7

The weakening of Italian in Esther's speech from the age of 2;08 can also be illustrated by the following syntactic errors:

– The subject pronoun was always used, whereas Italian is a pro-drop language:

(31) *Dove* ***noi*** *andiamo oggi?* (3;00)
where we go today
'Where are we going today?'

(32) *Quando* ***tu*** *bevi tutto?* (3;1)
when you drink all
'When will you drink it all?'

(33) *Quando dici* ***tu*** *'Esther'* ***io*** *non rispondo* (3;7)
when say you 'Esther' I NEG answer
'When you say 'Esther' I don't answer.'

– An adjective is anteposed to a noun, whereas in Italian the adjective is postposed to the noun:

(34) *Masha è in grande stanza* (3;3) (target: *Masha è nella stanza grande*)
Masha is in big room
'Masha is in the big room.'

– The verb is often omitted:

(35) *Dove io? (i.e. on the photo)* (3;4) (target: *Dove sono*?)
Where I? (Target: Where is.1s)
'Where am I?'

– The article is often omitted (see Examples 36–39).

Whereas most monolingual children are becoming fairly systematic in their use of clitic pronouns by the age of 3;00 (e.g. Tedeschi 2006), Esther's use of clitic forms at this age was still sporadic.[14] Moreover, her most frequent error became the substitution of tonic forms for clitic forms. Clitics that she had been using in the previous phase with imperative forms were now replaced by tonic pronouns: instead of *aiuta=mi* 'help me', she consistently used the phrase *aiuta me*, and instead of *guarda=mi* 'look at me' she used *guarda me*.[15]

(36) *Papa', fai treccine* ***a me***
Daddy, do.IMP.2S braids to PRON.1S.DAT
'Daddy, can you do my braids?' (4;00) (Target: *Papa', fa=mmi le treccine.*)

The same usage occurred with other verbal forms:

(37) *F: Metti le calze. C: Mamma mette le calze* ***a me.***
put on the socks. – Mommy put on the socks to PRON.1S.M.DAT.
'F: Put on your socks. E: Mommy will put the socks on me.'
(3;01) (Target: *Mamma mi mette le calze.*)

(38) *Cagnolino mio non capisce* ***te***
little dog my NEG understand.3S – PRON.2S.ACC
'My little dog doesn't understand you.'
(3;9) (Target: *Il mio cagnolino non ti capisce.*)

(39) *Devi aspettare* ***noi*** (4;00) (Target: *Devi aspettar=ci*)
must.2S wait PR.1PL.ACC
'You have to wait for us.'

In this phase, first- and second-person clitic forms were never attested in Esther's speech, with the exception of one occurrence: *mi ha detto a me* '(he) has said it to me,' where the clitic form is repeated with a tonic one. This kind of dislocation is possible in spoken language.

14. Though I am using data from monolinguals in order to have a point of reference and a contrastive aspect in the analysis, I completely agree with the idea introduced by Grosjean (1998, 2010) and often discussed in the literature that a bilingual is not the "sum of two monolinguals." Following the same logic, I would say that a trilingual is not the sum of three monolinguals or of three bilinguals.

15. I have no quantitative data on this particular usage since the target was never used and these two phrases are among the most frequent phrases Esther uttered.

5.4 Second phase. Quantitative analysis

Table 7 provides a quantitative illustration of the observations in Section 5.3. For each month 80 minutes of recordings have been transcribed. The age of 3;5 is skipped because there were not enough recordings in Italian for that month. No plural column appears in the table because Esther did not use plural pronoun forms during this period.[16] The correct use of tonic forms occurs almost exclusively in combination with prepositions (*con* 'with,' *per* 'for,' *di* 'of'); only one occurrence has been attested in the context of contrast:

(40) *a te uno, a mamma uno* (distributes toys): (3;4)
to you one, to Mommy one
'One to you, one to Mommy.'

The erroneous usage indicated in Table 7 was the replacement of a clitic form with a tonic form where the context required a clitic. For example:

(41) *vuole toccare lui* (3;3) Target: *vuole toccar=lo*
wants to touch him
'He wants to touch him.'

(42) *a me piace gelato* (3;7) Target: mi piace il gelato
to me pleases ice-cream
'I like ice cream.'

Table 7. The use of Italian object pronouns

	Tonic forms		Tonic forms				Clitic forms				
	Correct use		Erroneous use								
Age	1 sing.	2 sing.	1 sing.	2 sing.	3 masc.	3 fem.	1 sing.	2 sing.	3 masc.	3 fem.	L′
3;3	-	2	-	-	1	-	-	-	-	-	-
3;4	-	1	1	1	-	-	-	-	1?[17]	-	1
3;6	2	1	2	-	-	-	1	-	1+ 2?	2	1
3;7	2	1	2	1	-	-	1	-	2?	-	-
3;8	-	2	3	3	-	-	1	-	1?	1	-

16. Pizzuto and Caselli make a similar observation about the language used by one of the children in their study: "in the adult's production, as in the child's, singular forms of verbs, pronouns and articles largely predominated over plural forms" (1992: 541).

17. Clitics are not always clearly enunciated, especially when they occur at the end of a verb. I have indicated such cases with a question mark.

As we can see from Table 7, in the period from 3;3 to 3;8, Esther mostly uses clitic forms in the third person. The only occurrence of the first person clitic is with the imperative of *aiutare* 'to help,' in which she uses the wrong inflection: *aiuti=mi* instead of the target *aiuta=mi* (which she had correctly used in the previous phase). The first – and second-person forms she uses are mostly tonic; she never uses combined pronouns.

6. Implications for phases of acquisition

Esther's acquisition of clitics occurred in two phases that can be correlated with two stages of morphological acquisition. In the first phase, when the first clitic forms appeared, they were used correctly with certain verbal forms. As we noted, the majority of clitics in her speech were used in the enclitic position with the imperative. Moreover, Esther never mixed verbal forms with first – or second-person deictic forms from another language. This phase corresponds to the premorphological stage, 'where only few morphological operators occur' (Dressler & Voeikova 2002: 4). The clitic forms Esther used are examples of such operators.

More errors in the use of clitics occur during the transition to a new, protomorphological stage, when 'children discover morphology and start to construct creatively morphological patterns; some by analogy, which may lead to the production of neologisms' (Dressler & Voeikova 2002: 4). In this new stage, Esther reanalyzed the whole verbal form: she distinguished between the root morpheme and the inflectional morpheme and created new imperative and indicative forms. The imperative forms that in the previous period had had the correct inflection were now changed to incorrect forms. Esther was conscious about the form she was using, and in one of the recordings she even explained this to her father: in her mind the ending *i* corresponded to the second-person singular – the form associated to the auditor.

(43) *Aiuti* ***me.*** (*Target: Aiuta=mi*)
help-Pres.Ind-2s PR-1s
'Help me.'

(44) *Guardi* ***me.*** (*Target: Guarda=mi.*)
look-Pres.Ind.-2s. PR-1s
'Look at me.'

During this period Esther applied the principle of analogy Dressler and Voeikova describe when she started to derive Italian first-person singular verbal forms of the present indicative from the second – and third-person forms by adding the correct ending of the first-person singular. But in Italian this kind of formation often does not work, since many verbs have two or three different root morphemes. Table 8 presents the incorrect forms for the first-person singular present indicative that were attested in Esther's recordings from 3;7 to 3;8. During that period, no correct form of these verbs was attested in either the recordings or the diary. Pizzuto and Caselli (1992) note the same phenomenon and call it 'stem regularization errors,' but in their data this type of error occurs very infrequently: 'less than 1% in Claudia and Francesco's production, not found in Marco' (1992: 534).

Table 8. Verbal forms

Infinitive form	2S used as derivative base by Esther	Wrong form of the 1S produced by Esther	Target of the 1S
Venire 'to come'	*vieni*	*vieno*	*vengo*
Tenere 'to hold'	*tieni*	*tieno*	*tengo*
Rimanere 'to stay'	*rimani*	*rimano*	*rimango*
Uscire 'to go out'	*esci*	*escio*	*esco*
Fare 'to do'	*fai*	*fo*	*faccio*

In the same period, Esther used affixes to change the semantics of words. The Italian suffix – *issimo* appeared frequently in her speech, and she added it not only to adjectives (as is correct when creating superlative forms) but also to adverbs and nouns.

(45) *Sono quasi pronta, quasissimo.*
am almost ready, almost+issimo
'I am almost ready, almost+issimo.'

(46) *Sono sorella maggiore, sorellissima.*
am sister big, sister+issima
'I am the big sister, sister+issima.'

All of these observations lead me to assume that during this period Esther discovered different morphological operators. The acquisition of clitics appears to have been part of this process. But, as we can see from Table 7, in this second phase of acquisition, starting at age 3;00, Esther acquired clitics in two different ways that depended on the person of the given clitic. Third-person clitics were either used correctly or omitted. The dislocation often typical of spoken language also occurred.

(47) *La sogno la principessa* (3;5)
CL-3S-F dream-1S the princess
'I am dreaming of the princess.'

In Table 7, of the 15 attested clitic forms, four occur in utterances with dislocation, and only one of these corresponds to the first-person clitic (*mi ha detto a me* '(s/he) has told me.' Two other first-person clitics are used with the imperative of the verb *aiutare* 'help.'

At the same time, acquisition of first- and second-person clitics, whose referential semantics are much more in evidence than third-person clitics, is not complete: they were replaced with tonic forms. The latter clearly had more expressive potential because they could be stressed. That might explain Esther's preference for tonic forms in these instances. In Table 7, of 14 erroneous uses of tonic forms, 13 occurrences involve first- and second-person pronouns. I have not found any description of a similar substitution in monolingual children, so I would be inclined to attribute this phenomenon to the influence of Russian and Norwegian on Esther's use of the Italian pronominal system.[18] An important reason for this incomplete acquisition appears to be the semantics of these forms: in Esther's speech first-person clitics are clearly connected with the speaker and second-person clitics – with the auditor.

7. Conclusion

To sum up, Esther's acquisition of Italian object clitics can be broken down into the following phases. In the first phase the use of a clitic form is tightly connected to the verbal morphological form: imperatives are used with first-person clitics and third-person clitics are attested in requests with modal verbs or with imperatives. In the second phase, pragmatic and syntactic features become more important for the use of clitics. First- and second-person clitics are replaced by tonic forms; third-person clitics remain and are mostly used in the right dislocation contexts. This replacement of the first- and second-person clitics can be explained by analogy with the two other languages Esther acquires, which regularly require the use of tonic forms. Moreover, the fact that the tonic form is post-posed to the verb may also be important in this case: as we have seen, the word order in Esther's Italian is influenced by Russian and Norwegian (e.g. the adjective is often pre-posed to the noun).

At the same time, although she uses third-person clitic forms rarely, she uses them correctly. Surprisingly, no analogy with Russian and/or Norwegian works in this case. There could be several reasons for this fact. First, presumably third-person clitics are easily replaced with nominative constructions. Thus they

18. At the same time, my personal observations as a teacher of Italian to adult learners show that this kind of error is very rare among L2 subjects learning Italian.

appear infrequently in the input and are acquired later. It is worth noting that the first forms appear within the context of a dislocation, where a clitic repeats a nominative construction. Second, clitic forms could be seen by the child as a first part of the construction (a kind of 'filler,' to use Monachesi's terminology) with a finite verbal form whose semantic focus is the object (e.g. as in 47). This use of clitics corresponds to two phenomena described above: the mandatory use with several verbs (like *sapere* – to know, for example) and the use in the dislocation contexts.

The present study opens up two directions for further investigation. One of them concerns the status of clitics: we have seen that the semantic properties of the verb and of the clitic itself (first-/second-person clitics vs. third-person clitics) are important and should be taken into consideration. The other direction is the analysis of the underlying mechanisms behind grammar acquisition by trilinguals. These mechanisms appear to differ from those involved in mono- and bilingual grammar acquisition, but their precise nature remains a topic for future study.

References

Antelmi, Donella. 1997. *La prima grammatica dell'italiano*. Bologna: Il Mulino.

Berruto, Gaetano. 2012. *Sociolinguistica dell'italiano contemporaneo*. Nuova edizione. Roma, Carocci.

Cipriani, Paola, Chilosi, Anna Maria, Bottari, Piero & Pfanner, Lucia. 1993. *L'acquisizione della morfosintassi in italiano. Fasi e processi*. Padova: Unipress.

Dardano, Maurizio & Trifone, Pietro. 2007. *La nuova grammatica della lingua italiana*. Bologna: Zanichelli.

Eisenchlas, Susana. 2003. Clitics in child Spanish. *First Language* 23(2): 193–211.

Espinal, Maria Teresa. 2009. Clitic incorporation and abstract semantic objects in idiomatic constructions. *Linguistics* 47(6): 1221–1271.

Hamann, Cornelia, Rizzi, Luigi & Frauenfelder, Uli. 1995. On the acquisition of the pronominal system in French. *Recherches Linguistiques de Vincennes* 24: 83–101.

Khachaturyan, Elizaveta. 2011. The acquisition of verbs and their grammar (Italian-Russian-Norwegian case). Paper delivered at the 8th International Symposium on Bilingualism (ISB 8), held at the University of Oslo.

Khachaturyan, Elizaveta. 2012. Dva jazyka – dva mira: Usvoenie leksiki v uslovijax rannego detskogo mnogojazychija (Two languages – two worlds: Acquisition of lexis in the context of early child plurilingualism). *Proceedings of the International workshop "Social and cultural integration of Russian immigrants"*: 381–389.

MacWhinney, Brian. 2000. *The CHILDES Project: Tools for Analyzing Talk*, 3rd edn. Mahwah NJ: Lawrence Erlbaum Associates.

Monachesi, Paola. 1999. *A Lexical Approach to Italian Cliticization*. Stanford CA: CSLI.

Monachesi, Paola. 2006. Clitics, pronouns, noun phrases and the head-complement parameter. *Annali Online di Ferrara – Lettere* 2: 15–30.

Montrul, Silvina A. 2004. *The Acquisition of Spanish. Morphosyntactic Development in Monolingual and Bilingual L1 Acquisition and Adult L2 acquisition* [Language Acquisition and Language Disorders 37]. Amsterdam: John Benjamins.

Perez-Leroux, Ana Teresa, Cuza, Alejandro & Thomas, Danielle. 2011. Clitic placement in Spanish-English bilingual children. *Bilingualism: Language and Cognition* 14(2): 221–232.

Pizzuto, Elena & Caselli, Maria Cristina. 1992. The acquisition of Italian morphology: Implications for models of language development. *Child Language* 19: 491–557.

Salvi, Giampaolo & Vanelli, Laura. 2004. *Nuova grammatica italiana*. Bologna: il Mulino.

Scalise, Sergio & Bisetto, Antonietta. 2008. *La struttura delle parole*. Bologna: il Mulino.

Tedeschi, Roberta. 2006. The acquisition of object clitics in Italian: Data from an elicited production task. *Annali Online di Ferrara - Lettere* 2: 31–42.

Tsejtlin, Stella N. 2000. *Jazyk i rebenok: Lingvistika detskoj rechi* (The Language and a Child. Linguistics of Child Language). Moscow: Vlados.

Tsejtlin, Stella N. (ed.) 2007. *Semanticheskie kategorii v detskoj rechi* (Semantic Categories in Child Language). Sankt-Peterburg: Nestor-Istorija.

Voeikova, Maria D. & Dressler, Wolfgang U. (eds). 2002. *Pre- and Protomorphology. Early Phases of Morphological Development in Nouns and Verbs*. Munich: Lincom.

Clitic clusters in early Italo-Romance and the syntax/phonology interface

Diego Pescarini
University of Padua

This paper deals with the morpho-phonology of Italo-Romance clitic clusters. It argues that morpho-phonological processes (i.e. apocope, prosthesis, etc.) are sensitive to both the syntactic make-up of clitic clusters and their prosodic structure. The first part of the paper aims to support the hypothesis that a clitic cluster is a Foot, daughter to a recursive Prosodic Word (Peperkamp 1995, 1996, 1997). The second part of the paper accounts for the distribution of the apocopated clitic *l* (< *lo* 'it/him'/'the.m.sg') in early Italo-Romance. I show that the distribution of *l* follows from syllabic and alignment constraints compatible with the foot-based analysis. The last section addresses a puzzling vowel alternation which targets the leftmost clitic of certain clusters in Old and Modern Italian.

1. Introduction[1]

Theories of prosodic hierarchies differ with respect to the status of clitics. Nespor and Vogel (1986: 150), on the one hand, claim that clitics are unstressed *Prosodic Words* (PrW)[2] dominated by a *Clitic Group* (C), see (1a), while Selkirk (1995), on the other hand, argues that they are extrametrical syllables and daughters to a recursive PrW as shown in (1b).

---

1. I would like to thank Mair Parry, Paola Benincà, Christine Meklenborg Salvesen and two anonymous reviewers for having provided many helpful comments, which led to a much improved version. This work was supported by the FIRB grant RBFR08KR5A 'A grammatical survey of Italian dialects: fieldwork, data management, and linguistic analysis.'

2. In what follows I use the following abbreviations: PPh = Prosodic Phrase, C = Clitic Group, PrW = Prosodic Word, Ft = Foot, σ = syllable.

(1)

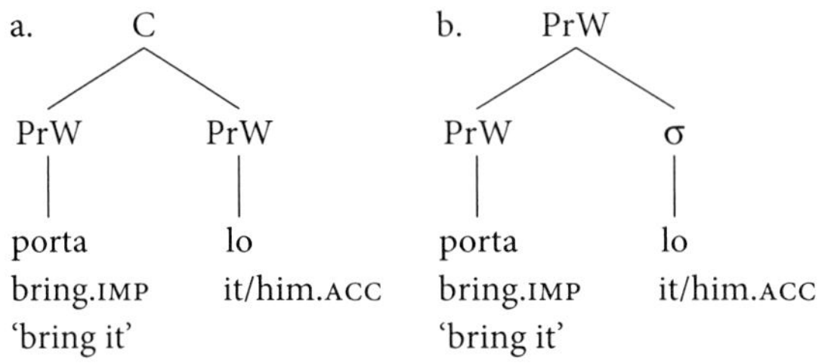

These approaches differ further in the analysis of clitic clusters, i.e. sequences of two or more clitic elements. According to Nespor and Vogel (1986), a clitic cluster is a series of sister PrWs under the same C node (multiple branching is therefore allowed), as shown in (2a). On the contrary, scholars like Peperkamp (1995, 1996, 1997) and Monachesi (1996) have proposed that clusters correspond to an autonomous prosodic constituent. In particular, Peperkamp argues that clitic clusters are Feet, daughters to a recursive PrW as schematized in (2b).

(2)

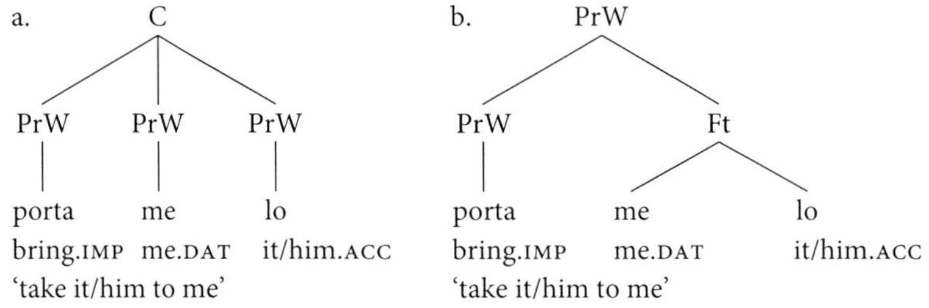

The above geometries show a major distinction between symmetric and asymmetric models. Symmetric representations – like (1a), (2a) – are based on the assumption that clitics and clitic clusters have the same prosodic category as their lexical host, and that prosodic structures are non-recursive and exhaustive (see below). Asymmetric approaches, on the contrary, entail that clitic elements are prosodically 'deficient,' in the sense that they do not correspond to a PrW, and, as a consequence, give rise to prosodic configurations like those in (1b), (2b), which violate basic principles of prosodic hierarchies such as nonrecursivity in (3) and exhaustivity in (4):

(3) Nonrecursivity: no Constituent^{i} dominates Constituent^{j} if j=i, e.g. no PrW dominates another PrW

(4) Exhaustivity: no Constituent^{i} dominates Constituent^{j} if j<i-1, e.g. no PrW directly dominates a syllable

In the following sections I address the distribution of some (morpho)phonological phenomena in various Romance languages, including medieval Italo- and Gallo-Romance, in order to show that asymmetric geometries like those in (1b) and (2b) do in fact account for the majority of the data.

The present work opens with a criticism of symmetric models like Nespor and Vogel's (Section 2): I argue that phenomena like phono-syntactic doubling (*raddoppiamento fonosintattico*), intervocalic *s*-voicing and apocope in modern Italian do not support the claim that clitics are unstressed PrWs and, consequently, that clitic clusters are sequences of PrWs. Rather, Section 3 argues in favour of Peperkamp's claim that clitic clusters are Feet following Bafile's (1992, 1994) analysis of Neapolitan clusters and revising Horne's (1990) account of syncope in Old French.

In Section 4, I turn to medieval vernaculars of northern Italy and, in particular, to the distribution of the apocopated clitic *l* (from *lo* 'him/it'), which is summarized in (5). As Vanelli (1992/1998) pointed out, the apocopated element *l* is found i. enclitically, as in (5a), unless it follows an infinitive, as in (5b); ii. after another clitic element, as in (5c–d). By contrast, *lo* does not undergo apocope when it is proclitic and follows another PrW, as in (5e). (For the sake of consistency, the following examples are taken from texts by the same author, writing in the vernacular spoken in Verona in the 13th/14th century; see Pescarini 2011).

(5) a. *batando=l* *molto* *forto* (Giacomino, Babilonia 83)
beat.GER=him.ACC very hard
'beating him very hard'

b. *per* *far=lo* *tosto* *cosro*
for make.INF=him.ACC immediately cook.INF
'to have him cooked immediately' (Giacomino, Babilonia 123)

c. *voler=ve=l* *dir* *tuto* (Giacomino, Babilonia 89)
want.INF=you.DAT=it.ACC say all
'to want to say it all to you'

d. *ve=l* *poës* *cuitar* (Giacomino, Ierusalem 238)
you.PL.DAT=it.ACC can.3.SG tell.INF
'he can tell it to you'

e. *en* *un'* *aqua* *lo* *meto* (Giacomino, Babilonia 113)
in a water him.ACC put.3.PL
'they put him in some water'

Following the foot-based analysis illustrated in (2b), I show that the distribution of apocope results from syllabic and alignment constraints on the re-syllabification of *l*.

Lastly, Section 5 addresses a puzzling vowel alternation found in Italian clusters: before a 3p accusative clitic (e.g. *lo* 'him', *la* 'her') or the partitive *ne* ('of it/them'), clitics end with *-e* instead of the expected *-i*. For instance, the clitic *mi* '(to) me' becomes *me*, see (6a), and the 3p m.sg clitic *gli* becomes *glie* /ʎe/, see (6b).

(6) a. [*me*] *lo* *porti* [*mi]
me.DAT it.ACC bring.2SG
'You bring it to me'

b. [*ʎe*] *ne* *porti* *due* [*ʎi]
him.DAT of.it bring.2SG two
'You bring him two of it'

In the light of the previous discussion, I speculate on the nature of the *-e/i-* alternation and its correlation with foot-formation and alignment restrictions. I argue that, synchronically, the *-e/i-* alternation is not sensitive to secondary stress, but rather to syntactic edges.

2. Against symmetry

Nespor and Vogel (1986), Nespor (1990, 1993) argue for the analysis of clitics and clitic clusters schematized in (1a)–(2a) on the basis of data from modern Italian.[3] In particular, they focus on three phonological phenomena that, in their opinion, can be considered as constituency tests. Such processes, exemplified later on, are as follows:

i. intervocalic *s*-voicing, which targets word-internal sibilants in northern Italian;
ii. *Raddoppiamento sintattico* (syntactic doubling), which targets word-initial consonants in central-southern Italian;
iii. apocope (or *troncamento*, in Nespor's (1990, 1993) terms), which targets word-final vowels after single sonorants.

In what follows, I will argue that voicing and *raddoppiamento* are not proper diagnostics for the prosodic status of clitics, as they cannot discriminate between the models in (1a) and (1b). With respect to apocope, I will notice that in

3. Part of Nespor & Vogel's analysis is based on data from Modern Greek. For the sake of consistency I will not address these data here.

modern Italian this rule is grammaticalized, as it applies only within a specific morpho-syntactic context, namely infinitive + enclitic.

Intervocalic *s*-voicing is a peculiar feature of northern Italian, where intervocalic sibilants in word-internal position are voiced.

(7) /la susanna/ → [la su'zan:a] lit. 'the Susan' (northern Italian)
*[la su'san:a]
*[la zu'zan:a]

However, voicing is blocked when /s/ is in morpheme-initial position, for instance, after prefixes like Italian *a-*, *anti-*, and between the members of a compound (Nespor & Vogel 1986: 124–129; Oostendorp 1999; Krämer 2009: 207–219 and references therein):

(8) a. a-[s]ociale *[z] 'asocial' (northern Italian)
b. anti-[s]oldato *[z] 'anti-soldier'
c. capo-[s]ala *[z] 'head nurse'

On the contrary, [s] usually undergoes voicing when it is in morpheme-final position:[4]

(9) a. di[z]-armo *[s] 'disarmament' (northern Italian)
b. di[z]-onesto *[s] 'dishonest'
c. bi[z]-avolo *[s] 'great grandparent'

Despite these complications, Nespor and Vogel adopt *s*-voicing as a word-hood test to show that clitics behave like PrWs. As a matter of fact, *s*-voicing is never found between a clitic and its host, as shown in (10):

(10) a. *lo* *[s]aluto* *[z] (northern Italian)
him.ACC greet.1.SG
'(I) greet him'

b. *essendo=[s]i* *salutati* *[z]
be.GER=each.other greet.PART
'having greeted each other'

4. One might object that the prefixed/compound words in (8) have been borrowed from standard Italian as non-adapted loanwords with an unvoiced pronunciation. However, northern dialects display native words with the same feature, e.g. the Veneto adjective *desavío/ desalío* [desa'vio/ desa'lio] < DE SAPITUM 'without salt'.

Since voicing is blocked with both proclitics (11a) and enclitics (11b), they conclude that both the clitic pronoun and its lexical host are PrWs, as schematized in (1a), repeated below with modifications:

(11) (northern Italian)

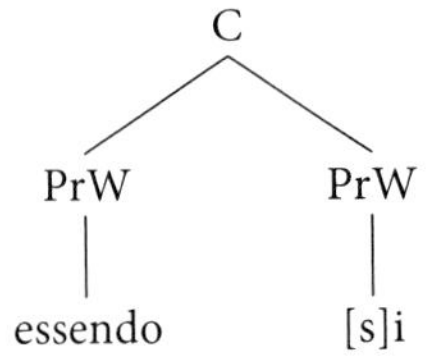

Furthermore, as voicing is not allowed also between clitics, see (12), they argue that each clitic corresponds to a separate PrW, as schematized in (2a), repeated below in (13) with modifications:

(12) *lo* *[s]i* *porta* *[z] (northern Italian)
it/him.ACC one brings
'one brings it'

(13)

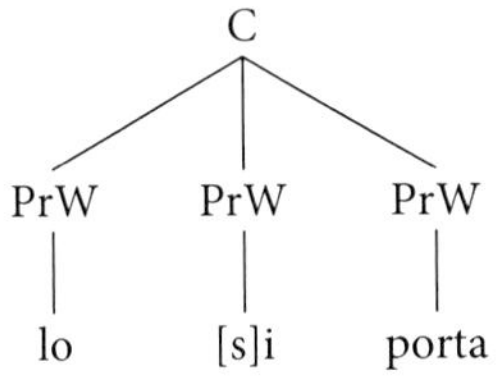

However, as previously mentioned, the absence of voicing within clitic+word and clitic+clitic sequences can be due to the general rule preventing voicing from taking place in morpheme-initial position, as in the case of prefixed words in (8). Hence, the distribution of voicing is not a reliable test to determine the nature of clitics.

After *s*-voicing, Nespor & Vogel turn their attention to a typical word-initial process found in central and southern Italian: *raddoppiamento sintattico*, i.e. consonant gemination after oxytone words or functional elements ending with an etymological consonant, e.g. the preposition *a* 'at/to' < Lat. AD. The conditions triggering *raddoppiamento* are subject to cross-linguistic variation: most southern Italian varieties, for instance, do not display *raddoppiamento* after oxytones (see Loporcaro (1997a) among others), while Tuscan varieties, illustrated below, exhibit both phonologically-conditioned and lexically-conditioned doubling.

(14) a. *farà* *[k:]aldo* *[k] (Tuscan)
be.FUT hot
'it will be hot'

b. *vado* *a* [k:]asa *[k]
go.1.SG to home
'I go home'

Also enclitic elements are subject to *raddoppiamento* after oxytone verbs.

(15) a. *da=[m:]i* *[m] (Italian)
give.IMP=me.DAT
'give me'

b. *amò=[l:]o* *[l] (Old Italian)[5]
love.PAST.3.SG=him/it.ACC
'(he/she) loved him/it'

However, it is worth noting that, in sequences like (15), doubling is mandatory also in northern Italian, which does not allow the general *raddoppiamento* pattern in (14): this means that northern speakers have the context-specific rule responsible for (15), which I will refer to as 'enclitic gemination', although they lack the *raddoppiamento* rule.

A similar distinction between *raddoppiamento* and enclitic gemination can be found also in central and those southern varieties where *raddoppiamento* does not target a following proclitic element, as shown in (16b).

(16) a. *a* *[r:]oma* *[r] (Abruzzese)
at/to Rome
'at/(to) Rome'

b. *a* *[l]a* *casə* *[l:]
at/to the home
'(at) home'

Enclitics, on the contrary, are doubled after imperatives:

(17) *fa* *[l:]ə* *[l] (Abruzzese)
do it.ACC
'do it!'

Again, there is evidence that the rule causing enclitic gemination in (17) is not an instance of *raddoppiamento*, which, as shown in (16b), does not target clitic elements. Hence, *raddoppiamento* cannot be considered a robust test to confirm that clitics are PrWs as enclitics are doubled even in northern varieties, where *raddoppiamento* is not attested, and in southern varieties, where it does not target clitic elements.

5. Modern Italian no longer allows enclitics after finite verbs.

To summarize, I have argued that the absence of *s*-voicing and enclitic gemination do not prove that clitics are PrWs: we have seen that *s*-voicing is blocked whenever it is preceded by a morphological boundary, while enclitic gemination has nothing to do with the word-initial rule of *raddoppiamento sintattico*.[6]

We can now turn to the third phenomenon analysed by Nespor & Vogel, i.e. apocope, which in modern Italian is found only with infinitives when followed by a clitic element, like in (18), or by another infinitive, like in (19); cf. Cardinaletti and Shlonsky (2004) for a syntactic analysis.

(18) *portar(*e)=lo*
bring.INF=it.ACC
'to bring it'

(19) *Lo voglio far(*e) portare*
It/him.ACC want.1.SG make.INF bring.INF
'I want to get somebody to bring it/him'

According to Nespor (1990, 1993), the pattern in (18) depends on a phonological rule having the clitic group as its prosodic domain. Monachesi (1996: 55) and Peperkamp (1996: 109), however, point out that apocope is not allowed when the enclitic pronoun follows finite verbal forms, like in (20a), although the same verbal form allows apocope when it is not followed by an enclitic pronoun, as in (20b):

(20) a. *facciam*(o)=lo veloci*
do.1PL=it.ACC quick
'let'sdo it quickly'

b. *facciam(o) veloci*
do.1PL quick
'let'sdo (it) quickly'

On the basis of these data, we can therefore object that in modern Italian, apocope cannot be treated as a pure phonological rule, as it is nowadays constrained within a specific morpho-syntactic environment. As a consequence,

6. It seems to me that, even leaving these objections aside, Nespor & Vogel's conclusion is logically flawed. Let us assume for the sake of argument that *s*-voicing and *raddoppiamento* are reliable tests showing that a fully-fledged PrW boundary intervenes between the clitic and the preceding/following word. Following this (mistaken) conclusion, one would argue that the PrW boundary blocks word-internal processes (like *s*-voicing) and triggers word-initial ones (like *raddoppiamento)*. However, while a PrW boundary entails that at least one element (either the preceding or the following one) is a PrW, it does not mean that *both* elements – namely, the clitic and its host – are PrWs. The latter is a theoretical assumption which is logically faulty. In fact, the same patterns can be easily accounted for on the basis of both (1a) and (1b), as in both the clitic is preceded by a PrW boundary, even if the clitic itself has a different prosodic status.

a phonological account of apocope in modern Italian ends up being misleading, as the conditions responsible for apocope are ultimately morpho-syntactic in nature, rather than phonological. In early Italian and Italian vernaculars, in contrast, apocope turns out to be rather productive and, consequently, more appealing for a prosodic analysis. I address this point in depth in Section 4, after introducing clitic clusters.

3. Clusters

Symmetric and asymmetric approaches diverge further when clitic clusters are taken into consideration. According to Nespor and Vogel (1986), clitic clusters – i.e. sequences formed by two or more clitic elements – can be represented as a series of sister PrWs under the same C node, as shown in (2a)=(21a). Under Peperkamp's account, in contrast, clusters correspond to Feet (2b)=(21b).

(21)

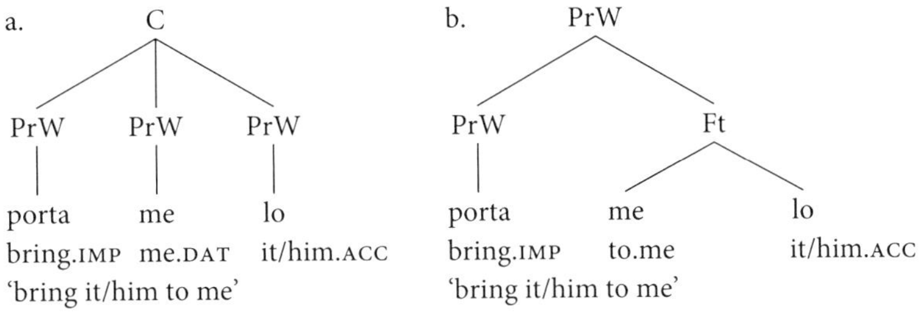

The latter model accounts straightforwardly for languages in which enclitic clusters are stressed. For instance, Bafile (1992, 1994) noticed that in Neapolitan, the penultimate pronoun of an enclitic cluster is stressed, as in (22b), while the same cluster in proclitic position is unstressed, cf. (23b):

(22) a. *Pòrta=tə na bbirrə* single enclitic (Neapolitan)
bring.IMP=you.REFL.DAT a beer
'bring a beer for youself'

b. *pòrta=té=nnə* assaj enclitic cluster
bring.IMP=you.REFL.DAT=of.it a.lot.of
'bring a lot of it (beer) for youself'

(23) a. *tə pòrtə na bbirrə* single proclitic
you.REFL.DAT bring.PRES.1SG a beer
'I'll bring you a beer'

b. *tə nə pòrtə assaj* proclitic cluster
you.REFL.DAT of.it bring.PRES.1SG a.lot.of
'I'll bring you a lot of it (beer)'

According to Bafile's (1992, 1994) description, when stress is assigned to the penultimate clitic, the original stress of the lexical word continues to be primary (the *o* in *pòrtə* is open, and open mid vowels in Neapolitan are allowed only in syllables with primary stress). Furthermore, as a consequence of stress assignment, the inner enclitic is subject to metaphony (which typically affects primary stressed vowels): even if final vowels are reduced to *-ə*, the underlying ending of the rightmost clitic triggers metaphony of the preceding element, whose vowel becomes *-i-* if the following accusative clitic is masculine, and *-e-* if it is feminine:

(24) a. *pòrta=ti=llə* (Neapolitan)
bring.IMP=you.REFL.DAT=him.ACC/them.M.ACC/it.M.ACC
'bring him/it.m/them for you'

b. *pòrta=te=llə*
bring.IMP=you.REFL.DAT=her.ACC/them.F.ACC/it.F.ACC
'bring her/it.f/them.f for you'

According to Peperkamp (1995, 1996, 1997), the above pattern results from a prosodic configuration in which enclitic clusters are grouped under a metrical foot, as shown in (25b), while single enclitics, in (25a), behave like extrametrical syllables:

(25) a. $[[pòrta\ ]_{PrW}\ tə]_{PrW}$ (Neapolitan)
bring.IMP you.REFL.DAT
'Bring … for yourself'

b. $[[pòrta\ ]_{PrW}(té\ .nnə)\ ]_{PrW}$
bring.IMP you.REFL.DAT of-it
'bring some of it for yourself'

The resulting stress pattern – represented in (26) – entails that, in Neapolitan, stress is assigned cyclically, i.e. once the inner PrW has received stress, the outer PrW is subject to a second cycle, assigning stress to the penultimate clitic, i.e. to the foot's head (from now on, Ft/secondary stress is marked by a single asterisk; PrW/primary stress by two asterisks).

```
         *          *
         *          *
(26) [[(por.ta)]PrW (te.nnə)]PrW
```

Proclitic elements, on the contrary, are never stressed.[7] This, however, does not entail that foot formation does not take place proclitically. It only means that, in Neapolitan, proclitic foot-formation is not self-evident.

7. Rather, they are subject to processes of aphaeresis and elision, reducing clitic clusters to a single syllable (see Bafile 2008, 2012):

Evidence for foot formation in proclisis, however, is provided by Old French (Horne 1990),[8] which exhibits two processes targeting unstressed vowels:

i. apocope, deleting final vowels with the exception of *a* (which becomes ə);
ii. syncope, deleting unstressed vowels when they follow a syllable bearing secondary stress.

The syncope rule can be represented as follows:

```
                       *
             *         *
(27)  V → ø/( σ _ ) ( σ ...                          syncope
```

For instance, in case of a word like BONITATE(M), apocope and syncope apply as follows:

```
               *
        *      *
(28)  [(bo.ni)(ta.te)]PrW    >    /bon'te/            (Latin > French)
```

With this in mind, let us turn to clitic clusters, which, in Old French, are subject to a rule deleting the final vowel of the cluster, as illustrated in (29).

(29) *Ne m(e) vidrent* (Old French)
NEG me.ACC see.PAST.3PL
'they did not see me'

In the light of the rule in (27), the pattern in (29) receives a straightforward explanation if one assumes – *à la* Peperkamp – that proclitic clusters are left-headed feet:

```
                                 *
         *                       *
(30)  [(ne   .me)   [(vi.drent)]PrW ]PrW    →    nem vidrent
        NEG  me.ACC  see.PAST.3PL
      'they did not see me'
```

(i) */te la porto/* → [*ta* *'portə*] (Neapolitan)
you.REFL.DAT it.F.ACC bring.PRES.1SG
'I'll bring it to you'

8. Horne's analysis is couched in Nespor and Vogel's (1986) framework. However, it seems to me that the French data are most consistent with the alternative analysis proposed by Peperkamp and supported here. In particular, Selkirk's recursive representation of clitics adopted by Peperkamp accounts straightforwardly for cases in which a lexical rule – like apocope and syncope – is extended to a postlexical domain like clitic + host sequences.

In conclusion, the data above confirm the hypothesis that clusters are feet rather than separate PrWs. Furthermore, the phenomena above also challenge Monachesi's (1996) claim that clusters are PrWs. If this were the case, we would not expect any asymmetry between proclitic and enclitic clusters in terms of stress and syncope, contrary to fact.

4. Apocope in early Italo-Romance

Medieval northern vernaculars (including Old Florentine) share a 'core' rule of apocope, by which word-final *-o*/*-e* are dropped after a single sonorant;[9] see (31).

(31) $[\text{-o/-e}] \rightarrow \text{ø}/[+\text{sonorant}]\ \_\ ]_{\text{PrW}}$

In the 13th/14th century, the rule is optional and subject to intra- and inter-linguistic variation, which I will address later on: for instance, it was active in Old Italian, while it is no longer active in modern Italian, in which apocopated forms sound archaic and can be used only in a poetic register.[10]

9. It is worth noting that, in Italian, apocope cannot be considered a merely phonological process since in many cases it is sensitive to the morpho-syntactic nature of the final vowel: for instance, if *-e* is a feminine plural ending, as in the examples in (i), it never undergoes apocope, while apocope can take place if *-e* derives from the thematic vowel of the Latin 3rd declension, as in (ii).

(i)	a.	suor*(e)	'nuns'
	b.	suol*(e)	'soles'
	c.	le pentol-on*(e) the.F.PL pot-SUFF	'the big pots'
(ii)	a.	cuor(e)	'hearth'
	b.	sol(e)	'sun'
	c.	il pentol-on(e) the.m.sg pot-suff	'the big pot'

As the rule can discriminate between different kinds of inflectional endings, it means that the rule of apocope, even in Early Italo-romance, has a morpho-phonological nature.

10. Although apocopated forms are perceived as archaic or poetic, Benincà (2008:74–76) noticed that speakers are still aware of the distribution of the rule and are therefore able to provide acceptability judgments on truncated forms: they must therefore have an implicit/passive competence of the constraints targeting this rule.

Apocope also targets the *-o* of the clitic element *lo* (< ILLUM), which expresses both the m.sg definite article and the m.sg object pronoun. In this case, however, apocope may be blocked by several phonological factors constraining the resyllabification of the resulting clitic *l*. The following subsections address these constraints on the basis of data from Early Italo-Romance. In particular, I will focus on northern vernaculars, in which the distribution of the apocopated form *l* is much more restricted than in Tuscan varieties.

As Vanelli (1992, 1998: 179–185) pointed out, the distribution of apocope among northern vernaculars is consistent with the following diachronic evolution:

i. Stage 1: apocope is allowed only after another clitic element;
ii. Stage 2: apocope is allowed after every monosyllabic function word;
iii. Stage 3: apocope is allowed everywhere.

In the light of Selkirk's prosodic theory, we might assume that in Stage 1, apocope is allowed when *lo* follows another "affixal clitic", i.e. a function word located within the same recursive PrW, which effectively means another clitic pronoun or a preposition:

(32) $[[\text{X.}l(o)]_{\text{Ft}}\ \text{PrW}]_{\text{PrW}}$ (Stage1)

Later on (Stage 2), we can hypothesize that apocope is allowed when *lo* follows what Selkirk calls a "free clitic," namely, a function word sister to PrW and daughter to the Phonological Phrase (PPh), e.g. complementizers and conjunctions.

(33) $[\text{X}\ [l(o)\ \text{PrW}]_{\text{PrW}}\ ]_{\text{PPh}}$ (stage2)

Lastly, in Stage 3, apocope is allowed also after another PrW, which might be daughter to another PPh:

(34) $[\text{PrW}]_{\text{PPh}}\ [[l(o)\ \text{PrW}]_{\text{PrW}}\ ]_{\text{PPh}}$ (stage3)

Old Florentine, for instance, is representative of Stage 3 as the allomorphs *lo* and *l* are in fact in free variation since the earliest attestations.[11]

11. Modern Italian exhibits a further evolution, as the allomorphs *lo/l'* (plus the epenthetic one, *il*, see below) alternate on the basis of the phonological context. Synchronically, however, this alternation does not result directly from the aforementioned rule of apocope.

4.1 Syllabic constraints

In general, apocope is blocked if the preceding sonorant follows another consonant (e.g. *incontr*(o)* 'meeting') or if it is geminate[12] (e.g. *torr*(e)* 'tower'). Such a restriction follows from a more general principle preventing the formation of complex codas.

Post-lexically, the same restriction prevents the clitic *lo* from undergoing apocope after a word ending with a consonant. In contrast, *-o* can be dropped if the clitic follows a word ending with a vowel, as shown in the examples below, from various medieval vernaculars:

(35) a. *credendo=l* *tener* (Old Aretino, Guittone, Rime, p.109:40)
believe.GER=it.ACC keep.INF
'believing that he was keeping it'

b. *batando=l* *molto* *forto*
beating.GER=him.ACC very hard
'beating him very hard' (Old Veronese, Giacomino, Bab., 83)

c. *farò=l* *se* (Old Fiorentino, Dante,Inferno 15, 36)
do.FUT.1SG=it.ACC if…
'I will do it if…'

Things are more complicated when the enclitic *lo* follows an infinitive. In this case, both elements – namely, the clitic and the preceding verb – are candidates for apocope since they end with a sonorant followed by a thematic vowel. Therefore, a sequence formed by an infinitive, e.g. *fare* 'to make' and *lo* 'it/him,' could display three logically possible patterns of apocope:

(36) a. far(e) lo apocope of the infinitive
b. fare l(o) apocope of the clitic
c. far(e) l(o) apocope of both
do.INF it/him.ACC
'to do it/him'

In fact, only the pattern in (36a) is attested, as illustrated in (37):

(37) *per far-lo* *tosto* *cosro* (Giacomino, Babilonia 123)
for make.INF=him.ACC immediately cook.INF
'to have him cooked immediately'

12. In certain northern dialects, which underwent degemination, final vowels are normally maintained after etymologically geminate sonorants. Zamboni (1976) pointed out that in modern Venetian, word-final consonants are all etymologically single (e.g. *mor* < MORIT 'dies'), while vowels are always found after sonorants due to degemination (e.g. *core* < CURRIT 'runs').

The pattern in (37) follows from Selkirk's hypothesis that clitics are extrametrical syllables, as schematized in (38). If so, apocope takes place cyclically, i.e. from the inner to the outer PrW, targeting the embedded (lexical) word first (e.g. *fare* → *far*). Once the verb has become C-final, apocope of the outer PrW is blocked because the resulting output would be syllabically illicit. In fact, if both the infinitive and the enclitic underwent apocope, an illicit complex coda would result, e.g. **farl*.

(38)

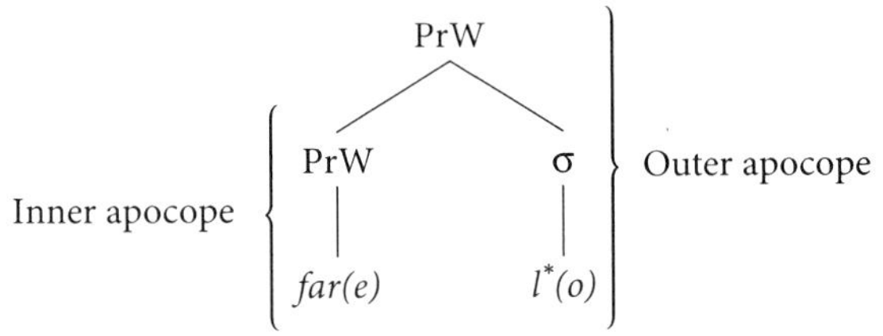

Furthermore, the above analysis accounts straightforwardly for the cases in which the infinitive is followed by two enclitics. In this case, exemplified in (39), the elements subject to apocope are the infinitive and the outmost clitic:

(39) *Voler_=ve=l_* *dir tuto* (Giacomino, Babilonia 89)
want.INF=you.DAT=it.ACC say all
'to want to say it all to you'

According to Peperkamp's analysis of clusters, the representation of the sequence above is as follows:

(40)

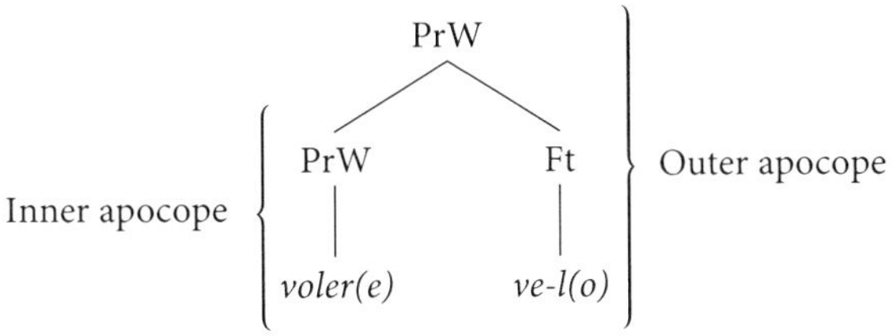

The schema in (40) shows that, in this case, outer apocope can take place as the resulting configuration is syllabically licit: the presence of the 2pl dative clitic *ve* prevents the formation of a complex coda and allows the following clitic *lo* to undergo apocope.

In contrast, a symmetric analysis *à la* Nespor and Vogel (1986), in which each clitic element is a PrW, would be rather problematic as it cannot explain why, among all the possible syllabically licit configurations, only those in (37) and (39) are attested.

4.2 Alignment constraints

Many northern vernaculars exhibit another interesting asymmetry: normally, proclitic *lo* cannot undergo apocope even if it is preceded by a word ending with a vowel, as in (41a) (in the next section, I will account for certain exceptions). Enclitic *lo*, on the contrary, is free to undergo apocope; see (41b):

(41) a. *en un' aqua lo meto* (Giacomino, Babilonia 113)
in a water him.ACC put.3.PL
'they put him in some water'

b. *batando=l molto forto* (Giacomino, Babilonia 83)
beat.GER=him.ACC very hard
'beating him very hard'

This asymmetry cannot result from a syllabic principle, since the proclitic *l* is free to syllabify with the preceding PrW in both (41a) and (41b). The alternative hypothesis is that apocope is blocked because of an *alignment* constraint, namely a requirement demanding "that a designated edge of each prosodic or morphological constituent [...] coincides with a designated edge of some other prosodic or morphological constituent" (McCarthy & Prince 1993). In a nutshell, if apocope applied, as illustrated in (42a), the clitic *l* would end up being phonologically enclitic to the preceding word, although it is syntactically proclitic to the following verb, as illustrated in (42b). This would cause a misalignment between the syntactic and the phonological structure, which is the reason why apocope, at least originally, does not target single proclitics.

(42) a. $[\text{en un'aqua}]_{\text{PPh}}$ $[\textit{lo}\ \text{meto}]_{\text{PPh}}$ → b. $[\text{en un'aqua}\ \textit{l}]_{\text{PPh}}$ $[\text{meto}]_{\text{PPh}}$

Interestingly, apocope is not blocked when *lo* is preceded by another clitic, like a dative clitic pronoun or the negative marker, as in (43):

(43) a. *ve=l poës cuitar* (Giacomino, Ierusalem 238)
you.PL.DAT=it.ACC can.3.SG tell.INF
'he can tell it to you'

b. *cor no 'l po' pensar* (Giacomino, Ierusalem 240)
heart NEG it.ACC can.3SG think.INF
'the heart cannot think it'

In this context, apocope cannot provoke any misalignment as the presence of a preceding clitic prevents the apocopated clitic *l* from "falling off" its original PPh when it resyllabifies with the preceding clitic (rather, it is worth noting that clusters are the first context in which apocope is allowed proclitically, cf. (32)).

4.3 Evidence from prosthesis

Further support to the misalignment hypothesis is provided by the distribution of clitics exhibiting a prosthetic vowel, e.g. *il/el* (< *l*). The diffusion of prosthesis varies across medieval vernaculars and correlates with the diffusion of apocope (Vanelli 1992/1998, see above). In particular, Vanelli shows that prosthetic forms are found in the same phonological context where apocope is allowed, namely V_C. Moreover, she notices that prosthesis is found only in those varieties allowing a wider distribution of apocope, i.e. varieties representative of Stage 2/3.

It is worth noting that, given its distribution in V_C contexts, prosthesis of *l* cannot be triggered by syllabification principles as *l* is always free to syllabify with the preceding vowel.[13] Rather, my hypothesis is that prosthesis is a repair strategy taking place when apocope began to target clitic elements on the left edge of the PPh.

Take, for instance, a variety like the one of Giacomino da Verona, which – as shown in the previous section – is representative of Stage 2. In Giacomino's texts, apocope is usually allowed after function words, but not after lexical words. However, there are a few examples in which apocope has exceptionally targeted a single proclitic following a stressed element, as in (44a-c). Crucially, all these counter-examples exhibit prosthesis:

(44) a. *la scriptura el diso* (Ierusalem 63, 196)
the scripture it.ACC says.3PL
'so scripture says'

b. *li sancti tuti el diso* (Babilonia 34)
the saints all it.ACC say.3PL
'all the saints say that'

c. *enanço k' eli el meta en logo*
before that they it.ACC put.3PL in place
de calura. (Babilonia 115)
of warm
'before they put him in a hot place'

---

13. In many modern northern dialects prosthesis can be regarded as a strategy repairing marked syllabic configurations, which arise as a consequence of vowel deletion processes like apocope. In Gallo-Italic dialects, for instance, apocope determined a systematic loss of final vowels (except *-a*) and, consequently, object clitics were reduced to single consonants like *m* (< ME, 'me'), *t* (< TE, 'you.SG'), *l* (< ILLUM, 'him'), etc. These exponents normally syllabify with either the preceding or the following element. Otherwise, the clitic is syllabified by means of a prosthetic vowel. For instance, in modern Torinese, a prosthetic vowel *a* is inserted when the object clitic follows the 2nd person subject clitic, which is not expressed by a vocalic exponent: e.g. **it m* ('you to-me') → *it am* (Vanelli 1984, 1998: 103).

In these cases, typical of languages evolving from Stage 2 to Stage 3, apocope applies in a non-canonical context (i.e. when *lo* is in PPh-initial position), giving rise to the misalignment illustrated in (45b):

(45) a. [la scriptura]$_{PPh}$ [*l(o)* diso]$_{PPh}$ → b. [la scriptura=*l*]$_{PPh}$ [diso]$_{PPh}$
the scripture it.ACC say.3PL

Prosthesis, as a matter of fact, prevents the misalignment by blocking the syllabification of the accusative pronoun with the preceding PrW.

(46) [la scriptura]$_{PPh}$ [*el* diso]$_{PPh}$

This hypothesis is confirmed by the absence of prosthesis in enclisis, illustrated in (47). In this case – see also Loporcaro (1997) – apocope cannot cause any misalignment because the object clitic follows its host and, as a consequence, prosthesis is never required.

(47) Batando=*l* → batando=(**e*)*l*
beat.GER=him.ACC

Second, this accounts for the absence of prosthesis after unstressed elements like negation markers, as schematized in (48).[14] Again, in this context, prosthesis is blocked because *l* can resyllabify without causing a misalignment.

(48) [*no* (**e*)*l* *pò*]$_{PPh}$
NEG it.ACC can.3SG
'he cannot (do) it'

5. A vowel alternation in Italian clusters

In the preceding sections I have supported Peperkamp's claim that clitic clusters are Feet and argued that morpho-phonological processes are sensitive to the

(i) *It am das an pum.* (Torinese)
You.CL to-me.CL give an apple
'You give me an apple'

14. One might wonder if the negation marker *no* is an affixal clitic or a free clitic (cf. (32) vs (33)), as schematised below:

(i) [[no l]$_{Ft}$ [pò]$_{PrW}$]$_{PrW}$ (if *no* is an affixal clitic)
(ii) [no [l [po]$_{PrW}$]$_{PrW}$]$_{PPh}$ (if *no* is a free clitic)

alignment of prosodic and syntactic edges. In the light of the preceding analysis, in this section I will take into consideration a context-driven alternation targeting the leftmost clitic of certain Italian clusters. As illustrated in (49), before a 3p accusative clitic (e.g. *lo* 'him', *la* 'her') or the partitive *ne* ('of it/them'), clitics end with -*e* instead of -*i*.

(49)	a.	[*me*]	*lo*	*porti*		[*mi]
		me.DAT	it.ACC	bring.2SG		
		'You bring it to me'				
	b.	[*ʎe*]	*ne*	*porti*	*due*	[*ʎi]
		him.DAT	of.it	bring.2SG	two	
		'You bring him two of it'				

This pattern has received a good deal of attention since D'Ovidio (1886: 71), who argues that -*e*- derives from the etymological initial vowel of the second clitic *(e) lo* < ILLUM, *(e)ne* < INDE. According to this reconstruction, the derivation of the above clusters goes as follows:

(50)	a.	ME ĬLLUM	>	M'ĬLLU	>	me lo	'it/him to me'
	b.	ĬLLI ĬNDE	>	ILL'ĬNDE	>	gliene	'of them/it to him/her'

This solution provides a clear and elegant account of the etymology of -*e*- and its synchronic distribution, since -*e*- is found only before clitics deriving from ILLE and INDE. However, D'Ovidio's analysis has three major drawbacks.

First, if -*e*- came from ĭ (< ILLE, INDE), the resulting cluster would be expected to show a geminate sonorant, namely -*ll*- < ILLE, -*nn*- < INDE, as illustrated in (51):

(51)	a.	ME ĬLLUM	>	M'ĬLLU	> *mello	'it/him to me'
	b.	ĬLLI ĬNDE	>	ILL' ĬNDE	> *glienne	'of them/it to him/her'

It is worth noting that in Italian this gemination is shown by sequences of preposition + article (the so-called *preposizioni articolate*, lit. 'article-d prepositions'), illustrated below (see also Formentin (1996)).

(52)	a.	DE ĬLLUM	>	D'ĬLLU	>	dello	'of the'
	b.	IN ĬLLUM	>	(I)N'ĬLLUM	>	nello	'in the'

In these cases, the preservation of the disyllabic form of the determiner (ĬLLU > *ello*) provides a straightforward explanation for both the vowel -*e*- and the following gemination. In light of this, the case of pronoun + pronoun sequences like those in (54) clearly calls for a different explanation, as the absence of gemination is not compatible with D'Ovidio's derivation.

Second, as Parodi (1887: 189–190) pointed out, in the 13th century, the clitics deriving from ILLE, INDE occupied the leftmost position of the cluster and never showed traces of gemination or initial *e*-, as shown by the following examples:

(53) a. *che* [...] *voi* *la* *mi* *concediate*
that [...] you.PL.NOM it.F.ACC me.DAT grant.SUBJ
'that you grant it to me' (Boccaccio, Filocolo 212)

b. *io lo* *vi* *dirò.* (Novellino, p.128)
I it.ACC you.PL.DAT tell.FUT
'I will tell it to you'

The fact that forms like *lo, la, ne* were originally always in first position weakens D'Ovidio's hypothesis as -*e*- cannot derive from ĭ in cluster-internal position.

Third, as shown above, the apocopated allomorph *l* (< *lo*) resyllabifies by means of a prosthetic vowel (Vanelli 1992/1998; Renzi 1993; Renzi & Vanelli 1993). In Florentine, the prosthetic vowel is *i*-, hence *l* → *il*. Crucially, if the etymological *e*- (<ĭ-) had been underlying, the insertion of a prosthetic segment like *i*- would have been unnecessary.

Alternatively, one might wonder whether the -*e*/*i*- alternation is not due to a relic of an etymological segment, but rather to a synchronic pattern of allomorphy exhibited by the leftmost clitic, which has two allomorphs: *mi*/*me*, *ti*/*te*, *ci*/*ce* etc. In what follows, I will elaborate on this proposal in order to account for (i) the origin of the allomorphy (ii) the synchronic distribution of the *e*-forms.

Rohlfs (1966: 178) suggests that the -*e*/*i*- alternation originates from a raising process, which, in Old Florentine, turned final unstressed -*e* into -*i*.

(54) $/e/ \rightarrow [i] / \underset{[\text{-stress}]}{\_\_\_\_}\#$

This rule targeted adverbs and semi-functional words (e.g. *avante* > *avanti* 'before, in front of', *diece* > *dieci* 'ten', *longe* > *lungi* 'far', etc.) and personal pronouns, giving rise to the alternation between strong pronouns, which maintained the etymological vowel (e.g. Lat. ME > strong *me* 'me'), and clitic forms, which underwent raising (e.g. ME > clitic *mi*).

Arguably, such evolution followed from the change that turned strong pronouns (i.e. XPs corresponding to fully-fledged PrWs) into clitic elements (i.e. X^0s corresponding to bare syllables); see Cardinaletti and Starke (1999), Egerland (2005). This change, coupled with the rule in (54), led to the alternation between strong *e*-forms (*me, te, se*, etc.) on the one hand and clitic *i*-forms (*mi, ti, ci*, etc.) on the other.

(55) a. XP (1p.SG strong) b. X^0 (1p.SG clitic)
| |
$[\text{me}]_{\text{PrW}}$ $[\text{mi}]_{\sigma}$

With this in mind, let us turn to the *-e/i-* alternation in clusters. At first sight, one might argue that, in cluster-initial position, the underlying vowel /e/ surfaces as a consequence of secondary stress, which blocks the rule in (54). This hypothesis, however, does not account straightforwardly for the data.

First, take into consideration the 3p dative clitic *gli* ('to him') < Lat. ILLI. Since the original ending of the dative clitic is *-i* (and not *-e*), it is expected to show no alternation as its underlying form /ʎi/ cannot undergo further raising. In fact, Old Italian was consistent with this prediction since 3rd person dative clitics exhibited the etymological vowel *-i*.

(56) a. *che gli le demo p(er) una inpossta* (LibrAmm)
that him.DAT them.F.ACC gave.1PL for a tax
'that we gave them to him for a tax'

b. *ché gli ne potrebbe troppo di*
because him.DAT of.it could too.much of
mal seguire (Boccaccio, Dec.
bad(luck) follow III, 3, p. (197)
'because it could cause him too much misfortune'

Later on, however, the linking vowel of these clusters became *-e-*, which is the only possible form in modern Italian (I repeat below the relevant example):

(57) [*ʎe*] *ne porti due* [*ʎi]
him.DAT of.it bring.2SG two
'You bring him two of it'

Hence, the linking vowel *-e-* cannot be the underlying vowel, surfacing as a consequence of foot formation.

Second, contrary to our expectations, the *-e/i-* alternation is not allowed in several clusters, which display the vowel *-i*:

(58) a. [*mi*] *ci porta Mario* [*me]
me.DAT there bring.3SG Mario
'M. brings me there'

b. [*ʎi*] *si parla dopo* [*ʎe]
him.DAT one speak later
'We'll speak to him later'

The situation is summarized in the following table: the first column reports oblique forms in isolation (*mi, ti, gli*, etc.), in the second and third columns one can see the same oblique form clustered with the 3p accusative *lo* ('him, it') and the partitive *ne* ('of.it/them'), and in the fourth and fifth columns the same oblique clitic appears before the 3p reflexive and impersonal clitic *si* ('himself/herself/themselves/one') and the locative clitic *ci* ('there').

(59)

		with the vowel -*e*-:		with the vowel -*i*-:	
1.SG	(*mi*)	*me lo*	*me ne*	*mi si*	*mi ci*
2.SG	(*ti*)	*te lo*	*te ne*	*ti si*	*ti ci*
3.SG.DAT	(*gli*)	*glielo*	*gliene*	*gli si*	*gli ci*

In order to account for (59) under the phonological analysis (-*e*- is a consequence of secondary stress), we should postulate at least two classes of clitic clusters: one in which the cluster corresponds to a Foot and the other in which the cluster is formed by a sequence of extrametrical syllables. However, such classification is not supported by any independent piece of phonological evidence.

The alternative explanation is that the -*e*/*i*- alternation is syntax-driven, i.e. it is sensitive to the syntactic make-up of the cluster, rather than its prosodic structure. Let us assume that the -*e*/*i*- alternation is triggered by the presence/absence of a morpho-syntactic edge and that the original rule – rewritten in (60a) – has given rise to the morphological alternation represented in (60b).

(60) a. /e/ → [i]/____#

b. -*i*/____#

-*e*

If so, the distribution of -*i*- in clusters is expected to follow from the presence/absence of a morpho-syntactic boundary (#), as illustrated by the following scheme:

(61) a. clusters with the vowel -*e*-, e.g. *me lo, me ne, gliene*, etc.

b. clusters with the vowel -*i*-, e.g. *mi#si, mi#ci, gli#si*, etc.

This amounts to saying that Italian exhibits two types of clitic clusters: one corresponding to a single morpho-syntactic constituent and the other corresponding to a sequence of separate units.

This dichotomy is consistent with Kayne (1994: 19–21), who argues that a combination of clitic elements can correspond to two possible structures: a cluster configuration, where one clitic is incorporated onto the other, and a *split* configuration, where clitics occupy different positions. In the former case, the clitics form a single syntactic unit, while in the latter they are separated by one (or more) maximal projection(s):

(62) a. [[Cl1 Cl2] …] (cluster)

b. [Cl1 … [Cl2 …]] (split)

In the remainder of the section, I will argue that the *-e/i-* alternation correlates with a series of morpho-syntactic phenomena showing that the clusters with the vowel *-i-* are in fact syntactically split, while the others behave like inseparable syntactic units.

First of all, it is worth noting that all the clusters with the vowel *-e-* result from a parametric change reversing the order of clitic elements. As previously mentioned, originally the order of these clusters was accusative > dative, as shown in (63a), while the only possible order in Modern Italian (since the end of the 13th century) is dative > accusative, in (63b).

(63) a. *che* [...] *voi* ***la mi*** *concediate* (Boccaccio, Filocolo 212)
that [...] you.PL it.f to.me grant.subj
'that you grant it to me'

b. *se Egli* ***me la*** *concede* (Boccaccio, Filocolo 72)
if He to.me it.f grants
'if He grants it to me'

Melander (1929) noticed that, since the 13th century, the clusters with the innovative order have always exhibited the linking vowel *-e-*, while the clusters with the archaic order always display *-i-*. Building on Kayne, we can argue that the change from (63a) to (63b) is due to the movement and the consequent left-adjunction of the dative clitic onto the accusative one, illustrated in (64), which gives rise to a cluster configuration.

(64) a. [*la* [*mi* [...]]]
b. [*me-* *la* [t_{me}]]

In the former case, the dative clitic *mi* occupies a dedicated position and is therefore adjacent to a syntactic boundary. Consequently, the allomorph *-i* is selected. In (64b), by contrast, the dative clitic is no longer adjacent to the syntactic boundary, as there is no maximal projection intervening between the two clitics. This triggers the insertion of the allomorph *-e*.

Further support comes from synchronic data. Pescarini (2012) shows that split combinations (with *-i-*) can be marginally separated in restructuring contexts, as illustrated in (65). In contrast, the separation is forbidden with true clusters, i.e. with sequences exhibiting the vowel *-e-*, as shown in (66).

(65) a. %*si può portar=ti domani* (cf. √*ti si* può portare...)
one can take=you tomorrow
'we can take you tomorrow'

b. %*mi ha dovuto portar=ci un'amica*
me has had take=there a friend.F
'A friend of mine had to take me there'
(cf. √*mi ci* ha dovuto portare...)

(66) a. **Carlo si può portar=lo domani*
Carlo for.himself can take=it tomorrow
'Carlo can take it for himself tomorrow' (cf. √Carlo *se lo* può portare...)

b. **lo ha dovuto portar=ci un'amica*
him/it has had take=there a friend.F
'A friend of mine had to take it/him there'
(cf. √*ce l'*ha dovuto portare...)

This confirms that the *e*-clusters count as a single syntactic constituent, while *i*-sequences are syntactically split, i.e. the clitics occupy different syntactic projections.

In conclusion, in this section I have addressed a morphological alternation targeting the leftmost clitic of certain Italian clusters. Even assuming that the alternation originates from a phonological rule (Rohlfs 1966), I showed that, synchronically, this alternation cannot be due to a morpho-phonological process triggered by secondary stress. Rather, I argued for a syntactic analysis on the basis of Kayne's hypothesis that clitic combinations can be either clusters or split sequences. Building on independent syntactic evidence, I showed that the vowel *-i-* appears when a clitic is in a split configuration, while *-e-* is the linking vowel of clitics forming a true cluster.

6. Conclusions

In this paper I have investigated some morpho-phonological aspects of clitic clusters on the basis of data from modern and medieval (Italo)Romance.

First of all, I have argued against Nespor and Vogel's account of the prosodic status of clitics by claiming that intervocalic *s*-voicing, *raddoppiamento sintattico* and apocope do not support a symmetric prosodic model based on exhaustive and non-recursive hierarchies.

On the contrary, evidence for an asymmetric account comes from the analysis of clitic clusters in southern Italian dialects like Neapolitan (Bafile 1992, 1994; Peperkamp 1995, 1996, 1997) and Old French (Horne 1990). These phenomena show that clitic clusters must be conceived of as Feet that are daughters to a recursive PrW, as illustrated below:

(67) [(clitic.clitic) [lexical word $]_{PrW}$ $]_{PrW}$

In light of this analysis, I have addressed the distribution of apocope in medieval Italo-Romance; I have argued that the distribution of the apocopated clitic *l* (< *lo*) depends on syllabic and alignment conditions constraining its re-syllabification.

A syllabic condition blocks apocope if the resulting *l* ends up forming a complex coda. In particular, the syllabic constraint provides a straightforward account of the distribution of apocope in sequences formed by an infinitive and one or two clitic pronoun(s). In this case, the correct distribution results from a recursive application of apocope, as schematized below:

(68)

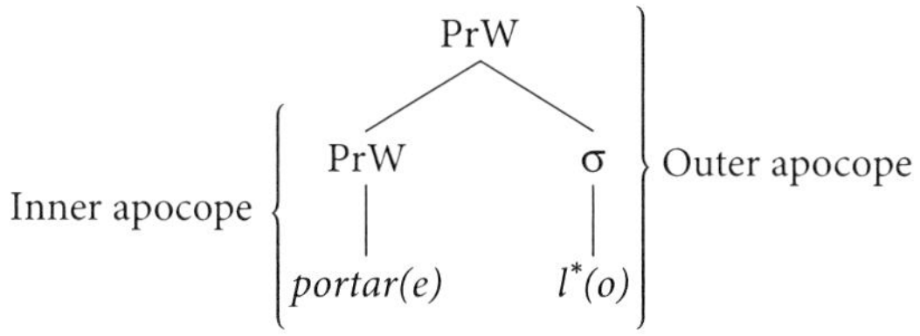

(69)

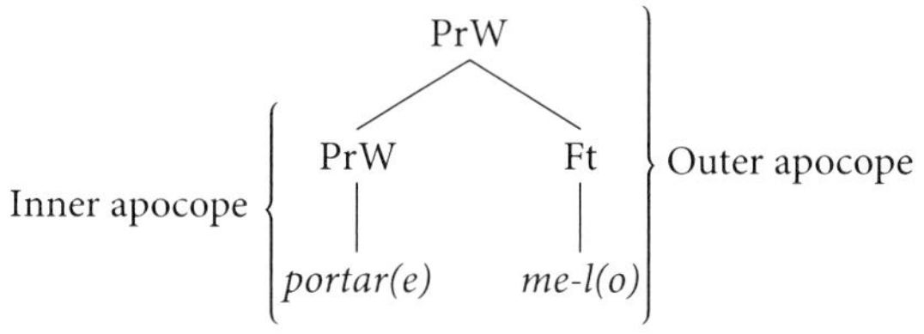

The alignment constraint accounts for the fact that clitics on the left edge of a phrase are not subject to apocope. I have argued that apocope is blocked in order to prevent *l* from syllabifying with the preceding PPh, causing a syntax/prosody misalignment. Otherwise, if apocope targets a proclitic element, a prosthetic vowel is inserted to avoid the syntax/prosody misalignment.

Lastly, I have addressed a puzzling alternation exhibited by the linking vowel of Italian clusters. After an in-depth revision of previous analyses, I have argued that this allomorphy is sensitive to the syntactic make-up of the cluster rather than to its prosodic structure.

References

Bafile, Laura. 1992. Fonologia prosodica e teoria metrica: Accento, cliticizzazione e innalzamento vocalico in napoletano. Ph.D. dissertation, Università di Firenze.

Bafile, Laura. 1994. La riassegnazione postlessicale dell'accento del napoletano. *Quaderni del Dipartimento di Linguistica – Università di Firenze* 5: 1–23.

Benincà, Paola. 2008. Grammatica e stili dell'italiano. In *Didattica della lingua italiana: testo e contesto*, Adam Ledgeway & Anna Laura Lepschy (eds), 73–84. Perugia: Guerra.

Cardinaletti, Anna. 2008. On different types of clitic clusters. In *The Bantu – Romance Connection* [Linguistik Aktuell/Linguistics Today 131], Cécile De Cat & Katherine Demuth (eds), 41–82. Amsterdam: John Benjamins.

Cardinaletti, Anna & Repetti, Lori. 2008. The phonology and syntax of preverbal and postverbal subject clitics in Northern Italian dialects. *Linguistic Inquiry* 39(4): 523–563.
Cardinaletti, Anna & Shlonsky, Ur. 2004. Clitic positions and restructuring in Italian. *Linguistic Inquiry* 35(4): 519–557.
Cardinaletti, Anna & Starke, Michal 1999. The typology of structural deficiency: A case study of the three classes of pronouns. In *Clitics in the Languages of Europe*, Henk van Riemsdijk (ed.), 145–233. Berlin: Mouton de Gruyter.
D'Ovidio, Francesco. 1886. Ricerche sui pronomi personali e possessivi neolatini. *Archivio Glottologico Italiano* 9: 25–101.
Egerland, Verner. 2005. Diachronic change and pronoun status: Italian dative 'loro'. *Linguistics* 43: 1105–1130.
Formentin, Vittorio. 1996. Alcune considerazioni e un'ipotesi sull'articolo determinativo in area romanza. In *Studi offerti a Luigi Blasucci dai colleghi e dagli allievi pisani*, Lucio Lugnani, Marco Santagata & Alfredo Stussi (eds), 275–272. Lucca: Maria Pacini Fazzi editore.
Harris, James. 1991a. The exponence of gender in Spanish. *Linguistic Inquiry* 22(1): 27–62.
Harris, James. 1991b. The form classes of Spanish substantives. *Yearbook of Morphology* 1: 65–88.
Horne, Merle. 1990. The clitic group as a prosodic category in old French. *Lingua* 82(1): 1–13.
Kayne, Richard. 1994. *The Antisymmetry of Syntax*. Cambridge MA: The MIT Press.
Krämer, Martin. 2009. *The Phonology of Italian*. Oxford: OUP.
Loporcaro, Michele. 1997. On vowel epenthesis in Alguer Catalan. In *Certamen Phonologicum III*, Pier Marco Bertinetto, Livio Gaeta, Georgi Jatchev, David Michaels (eds), 205–227. Torino: Rosemberg & Sellier.
McCarthy, John J. & Prince, Alan S. 1993. Generalized alignment. *Yearbook of Morphology 1993*. 79–154. Also in Rutgers Optimality Archive 7: ⟨http://roa.rutgers.edu⟩.
Melander, Johan. 1929. L'origine de l'Italien me ne, me lo, te la, etc. *Studia Neophilologica* 2: 169–203.
Monachesi, Paola. 1996. On the representation of Italian clitics In *Interfaces in Phonology* [Studia Grammatica 41], Ursula Kleinhenz (ed.), 83–101. Berlin: Akademie Verlag.
Nespor, Marina. 1990. Vowel deletion in Italian. The organization of the phonological component. *The Linguistic Review* 7: 375–398.
Nespor, Marina. 1993. *Fonologia*. Bologna: il Mulino.
Nespor, Marina & Vogel, Irene. 1986. *Prosodic Phonology*. Dordrecht: Foris.
van Oostendorp, Marc. 1999. Italian s-voicing and the structure of the phonological word. In *Issues in Phonological Structure* [Current Issues in Linguistic Theory 196], Stephen J. Hannahs & Mike Davenport (eds), 197–214. Amsterdam: John Benjamins.
Parodi, Ernesto Giacomo. 1887. Illustrazioni linguistiche ai suddetti frammenti. *Giornale storco della letteratura italiana* 10: 178–196.
Peperkamp, Sharon. 1995. *Enclitic stress in Romance*. In *Papers from the 31st Regional Meeting of the Chicago Linguistic Society*, Vol. 2: *The Parasession on Clitics*, Audra Dainora, Rachel Hemphill, Barbara Luka, Barbara Need & Sheri Pargman (eds), 234–249. Chicago IL: Chicago Linguistic Society.
Peperkamp, Sharon. 1996. On the prosodic representation of clitics. In *Interfaces in Phonology* [Studia Grammatica 41], Ursula Kleinhenz (ed.), 102–127. Berlin: Akademie Verlag.
Peperkamp, Sharon. 1997. *Prosodic Words* [HIL Dissertations 34]. The Hague: HAG.
Pescarini, Diego. 2011. The evolution of Lat. ILLUM in Old Veronese: Apocope and related phenomena. *Vox Romanica* 70: 63–78.

Pescarini, Diego. 2012. Prosodic restructuring and morphological opacity. The evolution of Italo-Romance clitic clusters. *lingbuzz/001477.*

Renzi, Lorenzo. 1993. Da dove viene l'articolo *il*. In *Verbum Romanicum, Festschrift für Maria Iliescu*, Johannes Kramer & Guntram A. Plangg (eds), 215–230. Hamburg: Buske.

Renzi, Lorenzo & Vanelli, Laura. 1993. Storia e struttura dell'articolo italiano *il*. In *Actes du XXe Congrès International de Linguistique et Philologie Romanes*, III, 293–305. Tübingen: Francke.

Rohlfs, Gerhard. 1966. *Grammatica storica della lingua italiana e dei suoi dialetti*, Vol. I: *Fonetica*. Turin: Einaudi.

Selkirk, Elisabeth. 1995. The prosodic structure of function words. In *Papers in Optimality Theory*, Jill Beckman, Laura Walsh Dickey & Suzanne Urbanczyk (eds), 439–70. Amherst MA: GLSA. Also in *Signal to Syntax: Bootstrapping from Speech to Grammar in Early Acquisition*, James L. Morgan & Katherine Demuth (eds), 187–214. Mahwah NJ: Lawrence Erlbaum Associates.

Vanelli, Laura. 1984. Pronomi e fenomeni di prostesi vocalica nei dialetti italiani settentrionali. *Revue del Linguistique Romane* 48: 281–295.

Vanelli, Laura. 1992. Da "lo" a "il": Storia dell'articolo definito maschile singolare in italiano e nei dialetti settentrionali. *Rivista Italiana di Dialettologia* 16: 29–66.

Vanelli, Laura. 1998. *I dialetti italiani settentrionali nel panorama romanzo.* Roma: Bulzoni.

Zamboni, Alberto. 1976. Alcune osservazioni sull'evoluzione delle geminate romanze. In *Studi di fonetica e fonologia*, Raffaela Simone, Ugo Vignuzzi & Giulanella Ruggiero (eds), 325–336. Roma: Bulzoni.

Texts

Boccaccio, Decameron = Giovanni Boccaccio, *Decameron*, ed. by Vittore Branca, Firenze, Accademia della Crusca, 1976.

Boccaccio, Filocolo = Giovanni Boccaccio, *Filocolo* ed. by Antonio Enzo Quaglio, in *Tutte le opere di Giovanni Boccaccio*, vol. I, Milan, Mondadori, 1967, 61–675.

Dante, Inf = Dante Alighieri, *Commedia*, ed. by Giorgio Petrocchi, vol. II Inferno.

Giacomino, Ierusalem/Babilonia. = Giacomino da Verona, *De Ierusalem Celesti e De Babilonia civitate infernali*, ed. by G. Contini, *Poeti del Duecento*, tomo I, Napoli, 1950, 627–652.

Guittone, Rime, = Guittone d'Arezzo, Rime ed. by Francesco Egidi, Bari, Laterza, 1940.

LibrAmm = Anonymous, Libro d'amministrazione dell'eredità di Baldovino Iacopi Riccomanni, in Arrigo Castellani, *La prosa italiana delle origini: I, Testi toscani di carattere pratico*, Bologna, Pàtron, 1982, 429–64.

LibrCred = Anonymous, Libricciolo di crediti di Bene Bencivenni (Secondo), in Arrigo Castellani, *Nuovi testi fiorentini del Dugento*, Firenze, Sansoni, 1952, 363–458.

Novellino = Anonymous, *Il Novellino*, ed. by Guido Favati, Genova, Bozzi, 1970.

Reflexive verbs and the restructuring of clitic clusters

Christine Meklenborg Salvesen
University of Oslo

In Old French, all clitic clusters containing objects observed the order ACC–DAT. During the 15th and 16th centuries this order was changed into DAT–ACC in cases where objects of the 1st and 2nd person were involved. This change took place rather abruptly. In this paper I will argue that increased use of reflexive forms provoked a change in the order in these clitic clusters. More specifically, I will argue that clusters involving 1st and 2nd person argumental clitics form true clusters in Modern French (in the sense of Pescarini (2012)), whereas they formed split clusters in the old language.

1. Introduction[1]

In the history of the French language, the order of object clitics has changed.[2] In the old language, the accusative clitic always preceded the dative one (ACC–DAT). In Modern French, this is still the order for clitic clusters containing only 3rd person clitics, but in the cases where the 1st and 2nd persons are involved, the dative precedes the accusative (DAT–ACC). The difference between the two orders may be illustrated in (1-a) and (1-b).

(1) a. *et il la me dona.*
and he her.ACC me.DAT gave
'and he gave her to me.' (12th c., Graal, 6677)

b. *Il me la donne.*
he me.DAT her.ACC gives
'He gives her to me.' (Modern French)

---

1. I use the term *clitic* in order to describe an element which does not have any phonological independence and which needs to attach to a host. In Old French the host is always a verb.

2. I would like to thank the following for their comments to the present paper: Terje Lohndal, Marios Mavrogiorgos, Marie Labelle, Hans Petter Helland, and Diego Pescarini. Parts of the data were presented at the XX International Conference on Historical Linguistics in Osaka, July 2011, and I am grateful for the feedback I got from the audience there.

This shift in the internal order of the clitic cluster is not restricted to French. Similar changes have taken place in Northern and Central Italian dialects (Aski 2011; Pescarini 2012), Catalan, Occitan (Brusewitz 1905), and Provençal (see Wanner (1974) for a general overview). Unlike the other languages, French has not undergone a complete change from ACC–DAT to DAT–ACC as clusters involving only 3rd person still display the ACC–DAT order. Nor did the changes take place at the same time in the languages concerned. I will however not look at the other Romance languages in this article, but focus on French.

I will argue that the change in the internal order of the clitic clusters must be seen in relation to the expansion of the reflexive pronoun. As the sequence subject + reflexive pronoun becomes more common, this leads to a reanalysis which requires the form corresponding to the reflexive pronoun to occur in first position. This in turn led to a change of the internal order of clitic clusters. I base my analysis on large electronic corpora and exploit a generative approach in my formal analysis.

In order to investigate the clitic clusters, I have used three different online databases: the *Corpus de la littérature médiévale* (CLM) (Lalou et al. 2001), *Frantext*, and *Base de Français Médiéval* (BMF).[3] The CLM has texts stretching from the 11th to the 16th centuries (approximately 900 texts, number of words unknown), whereas the BFM covers the period from 842 till the end of the 15th century (3,784,304 words). In addition, I've used a subselection of the *Frantext* base for the clitics corpus (selection of 5,862,989 words from the 16th century). References in the CLM and the Frantext base refer to the date the manuscript was originally written, whereas dating in the BFM refers to the manuscript in question.[4]

I have used the *Frantext* database and the CLM in order to establish a database of clitic clusters involving the 1st and 2nd persons, stretching from the 11th to the 16th century. This corpus counts a total of 5136 examples.

The article is organised as follows: First I briefly describe the difference between Old and Modern French in Section 2 before presenting previous research in Section 3. Section 4 presents the quantitative data, whereas Section 5

3. CLM: http://www.classiques-garnier.com/numerique-bases/; Frantext: www.frantext.fr; BMF: http:txm.bfm-corpus.orgbfm/

4. This is especially relevant in the oldest period, as the oldest documents have not been preserved other than in copies. A text such as the *Strasbourg oaths*, will thus be labelled 9th century in the CLP base, but 10th century in the BFM.

investigates the rise of the reflexive. In Section 6 I give a theoretical account of the changes, before concluding in Section 7.

2. Two different systems

Pronominal objects are clitics in all stages of the French language, as far back as we have written sources. In (2), taken from a 9th century poem, the pronouns precede the verb, and the two are written together as one single word: *lafaire* 'her-make' instead of *la faire*. This is a clear graphical reflex of the pronunciation of the time. The pronominal objects occur in the same position they do in later Old French texts.

(2) *Uoldrent la-faire diaule seruir*
would her.ACC-make devil serve
'They wanted to make her serve the devil.' (9th c., Eulalie, 4)

In Old French (OF) (9th–13th c.) the accusative object pronoun preceded the dative one: ACC–DAT. Thus, in (3), the accusative *la* 'her' precedes the dative *te* 'you'.[5]

(3) *Pren la a feme, je la te vuel donner.*
take her.ACC to woman I her.ACC you.DAT will give
'Marry her, I give her to you.' (12th c., Raoul)

The order ACC–DAT is observed also in cases where the clitic is a reflexive pronoun. If the reflexive functions as a dative, it will follow the accusative pronoun.

(4) *onques ne le se pensa*
never NEG it.ACC himself.DAT thought
'He never thought about it.' (13th c., MortArtu, II, 13)

The possible constructions in Old French are represented in Figure 1. Clitics from the first column always precede clitics from the second and are always accusative. Clitics in the second column are either dative or oblique (1st and 2nd persons). In a clitic cluster containing pronominal clitics from both columns, the second clitic must be dative.

5. In Old French, the clitics preceded the modal auxiliary, contrary to Modern French, where they cliticise on the infinitive. I will come back to this later in this section.

Person	1	2	
1st sg		me	'me'
2nd sg		te	'you'
3rd sg	le	li	'him'
3rd sg	la	li	'her'
3rd sg & pl	se	se	reflexive pronoun
1st pl		nos	'us'
2nd pl		vos	'you'
3rd pl	les	lor	'them'

Figure 1. Clitic order in Old French

In addition to this ordering constraint, there is a ban on combinations where a 3rd person dative object is combined with a 1st and 2nd person accusative object (Laenzlinger 1993). In the literature this is known as the Person–Case Constraint (PCC) (see among others Bonet (1991, 1994); Boeckx (2000); Ormazabal and Romero (2007); Manzini (2012)). I have specifically looked for examples that would violate this constraint, without finding any. I thus conclude that the PCC holds also for Old French. There are no examples where both the clitics are in the 1st or 2nd person either, although such examples have been reported in the literature.

In Modern French the system is more complex, as clitics of the 1st and 2nd persons always precede clitics of the 3rd person, while 3rd person clitics have kept the order ACC–DAT. Just as in Old French, the PCC is observed, which essentially implies that clitics of the first column may not be combined with clitics of the third. Emonds (1975) has explained this by proposing that pronouns of the 1st and 3rd columns are base-generated in the same position, and that the pronouns appearing in the first column have been moved in front of ones in the second. I will come back to this line of thought in Section 6.

Person	ACC/DAT	ACC	DAT	
1st sg	me			'me'
2nd sg	te			'you'
3rd sg		le	lui	'him'
3rd sg		la	lui	'her'
3rd sg & pl	se			reflexive pronoun
1st pl	nous			'us'
2nd pl	vous			'you'
3rd pl		les	leur	'them'

Figure 2. Clitic order in Modern French

In addition to the personal pronouns, there are different pronominal adverbials that also function as clitics. I will come back to these in Section 5.

The difference between the two systems becomes clear when we compare examples from the 12th century with their modern counterparts.

(5) **le me > me le**

a. *Se il ne le me tolent, ele ert en*
if they NEG it.ACC me.DAT take-away she be.FUT in
vostre non
your name
'If they don't take it away from me, she [the city] shall carry your name.'
(12th c., Antioche, 4549)

b. *S' ils ne me le volent pas …*
if they NEG me.DAT it.ACC steal NEG
'If they don't steal it away from me …' (Modern French)

(6) **le te > te le**

a. *je le te di*
I it.ACC you.DAT say
'I tell it to you.' (12th c., Renart-II, 3565)

b. *je te le dis*
I you.DAT it.ACC say
'I tell it to you.' (Modern French)

(7) **le nos > nous le**

a. *Damedex le nos dont.*
Lord-God it.ACC us.DAT give
'The Good Lord gives it to us.' (12th c., Aspremont, 5366)

b. *Dieu nous le donne.*
God us.DAT it.ACC gives
'God gives it to us.' (Modern French)

(8) **le vos > vous le**

a. *bien le vos doi conter*
well it.ACC you.DAT shall tell
'I shall tell it to you well.' (12th c., Aliscans, 2942)

b. *Je dois bien vous le conter*
I shall well you.DAT it.ACC tell
'I shall tell it to you well.' (Modern French)

Note that nothing happens in clusters where both clitics are in the 3rd person, as in (9) and (10).

(9) **le li > le lui**

a. *Et cil le li dïent*
et these it.ACC him.DAT say
'And they tell it to him' (12th c., Yvain, 5021)

b. *et ils le lui dient*
and they it.ACC him.DAT tell
'And they tell it to him' (Modern French)

(10) **le lor > le leur**

a. *Ypomedon le leur desfent*
Ipomedon it.ACC them.DAT deny
'Ipomedon refuses it to them.' (12th c., Thèbes, 6617)

b. *Il le leur défend*
he it.ACC them.DAT deny
'He refuses it to them.' (Modern French)

The clitics attach to verbs, much as they do in Modern French. In the oldest texts, clitics obey the Tobler-Mussafia law, which means that they may not occur in the first position of the clause (Hirschbühler & Labelle 2000; Labelle & Hirschbühler 2005). In addition, clitics in the old language cliticised to the modal auxiliary, whereas they cliticise to the infinitive in Modern French.

In the following, I will not discuss the clusters' position in relation to the verb, but focus on the internal order of the clitic clusters.

To sum up: Pronominal objects are always clitics, and they clitisise to the finite verb. In Old French clitic clusters are always ACC–DAT. In Modern French the order ACC–DAT is only observed if both the clitics are in the 3rd person. All other cases are DAT–ACC. The PCC is observed in all stages of the language.

The question is why this change took place. The system in Old French was extremely simple, whereas the modern pronominal system is a lot more complex. Why would a language exchange a simple system for a more complex one? For a child learning the language there must be a strong trigger for the system to change. The question is quite simple: What was this trigger?

3. Previous research

The change in clitic clusters has intrigued researchers since the late 1800s. Most acknowledge that more than one explanation must be evoked in order to account for the change that took place, and why the 3rd person was not affected. Generally researchers point to a combination of phonetic/prosodic principles and syntactic/distributional ones in order to explain the change. In the following section I describe the most influential explanations based on some of the major researchers in the field.

3.1 Phonological explanations

Most researchers seem to agree that the shift has to do with phonological or rhythmical changes. The first one to investigate the phonetic changes was Jung (1887, cited by Brusewitz (1905) and de Kok (1985)), who claimed that the pronouns could be divided into three groups according to their sonority ('Klangfülle'). Their organisation in the sonority hierarchy is as follows (from little sonority to much sonority): *me, te, se, le, la* > *les, nous, vous* > *lui, leur*. According to Jung, the language evolved into a system where more heavy (sonorous) forms would be placed to the right, and lighter ones to the left. According to this analysis, the cluster *les me* should be the ones to change the first. Looking at my data, I find no evidence that would support such a claim. There is no significant difference in the evolutionary pace between *me le*-clusters and *me les*-clusters. An other issue is that it is hard to grasp the notion of *sonority* or *heaviness*. According to Togeby (1979), the final *-s* was lost some time in the 13th and 14th centuries, changing the pronunciation from [les] to [le], [nus] to [nu], and [vus] to [vu]. It is hard to see any substantial difference between *me, le, te,* and *se* on one hand and [le], [nu] and [vu] on the other.

Rhythm is the key-word for several other researchers. Meyer-Lübke (1899: 801) suggests that there was a change in the rhythm of the language which led to a pattern where two short syllables preceded a long, stressed one. This would explain the order *le lui*, and also explain why *le nous* was maintained longer than *le me*. It is, however, difficult to see how stress could relate to the clitic order, as clitics – by definition – must be unstressed (unless they receive secondary stress). It is equally difficult to see why such a change would lead *le me* to change to *me le*, as *le* and *me* are simply a minimal pair. Zink (1997) is also interested in stress, and he proposes that a shift in the accent has played a major role. In the oldest texts, *je* + *le* 'I + him/it' form an enclise: *jol* (11).

(11)	*Jo-l*	*te*	*dirrai*	*tot*	*veirement*
	I-it.ACC	you.DAT	say.FUT	all	truthfully
	'I will tell you it all truthfully.'				(12th c., Adam 145)

There is a syllable boundary between *jol* 'I+it' and *te* 'you'. Towards 1300 this enclisis disappears, and the first clitic becomes proclitic on the second one. This way the syllables are distorted: [*jel*] // [*me*] → [*je*] // [*mle*]. Zink (1997) claims that [*mle*] (or [*tle*] in the case of *te* 'you') represented a phonetic challenge to the speakers, and a way to resolve this was to reorganise the cluster: [*mle*] should be easier to pronounce than [*lme*]. This explanation comes short of explaining what necessitated this shift: Why couldn't the speakers just pronounce the clusters [*lem*] or even [*leme*]? In fact, they may have done so, as we do not know exactly how these clusters were pronounced.

A related approach has been adopted by de Kok (1985). Kok suggests that the clusters originally (prior to Old French) were enclitic to a preceding element. The first change was the one from enclisis to proclisis in the transition to Old French. Then a syntactic principle came into play, requiring that the direct object be closest to the verb (see below). In sum these two changes provoked the change observed in the data. Culbertson (2009), who doesn't comment on the cluster order, also advocates an analysis where the clitics are enclitic to the first element in the clause. It is however necessary to note that in Old French, the pronominal subject is not obligatory, and any XP may precede the verbal cluster. There are however no instances where the clitic seems to cliticise to a preceding adverb or full DP subject, only to pronominal subjects. The question of enclisis in the earliest texts is thus not fully examined.

3.2 Syntactic explanations

The idea that the direct object is more tightly linked to the verb and that this explains the ACC–DAT > DAT–ACC-shift has many adherents (Jung (1889), cited by Zink (1997)), Meyer-Lübke (1899); Wanner (1974); de Kok (1985). Meyer-Lübke (1899) suggests that the change in clitic order took place after a shift from pragmatic to syntactic principles. In the earliest times it was natural to have the accusative pronoun in the first position, as this carried information already mentioned in the context. The dative pronoun would often refer to someone new, possibly accompanied by a gesture. This way it was more natural to have it in second position. When the shift took place, it was the grammatical relation between the verb and its complement that prevailed: as the direct object is more closely linked to the verb than the indirect object, it is natural that it occupies the position closest to the verb, specifically immediately in front of it in declaratives, immediately after it in imperatives. In order to explain why there has been no change in the cases where both clitics are of the 3rd person, Wanner (1974) points to the the language's oxytone intonation which 'requires a 'heavy' element to be placed last in a linear arrangement (…)' (Wanner 1974: 172). It could be argued that the forms *lui*, *lor*, and *leur* are heavier than the others as they are bi-moraic. The form *li* is however mono-moraic, and heaviness cannot explain why it always comes last in a clitic cluster.[6]

6. I thank Marie Labelle for pointing out the difference between bi-moraic and mono-moraic constructions.

The distributional approach begins with Brusewitz (1905:32–35) who pointed out that there is a connection between the emergence of new reflexive verbs and the change of the internal order of clitics. The idea is that the increasing number of constructions of the kind *je me* 'I myself,' *tu te* 'you yourself' and *il se* 'he himself' led to the obligatory fronting of the reflexive clitic in the clitic cluster, which in turn entailed the reorganising of ordinary clitic clusters without reflexives. An argument in favour of this analysis is that the restructuring took place only in the cases where the reflexive pronoun and the dative pronoun have the same form. In the 3rd person, where the reflexive form is distinct (*se* 'himself/herself/themselves'), no restructuring took place. This is the idea that I will explore in Section 5. The strength of my approach compared to previous research is that I combine empirical data exploited from large data bases and use them in a formal analysis.

4. An abrupt change in the 15th century

In the literature, it is not uncommon to see the claim that the change in the order of the clitic clusters in Old French was very slow (Wanner 1974; Zink 1997). Their argument is that there are occurrences of the new clitic order already in the 12th century, but that the change wasn't carried through until the 18th century. I will take the opposite stand: The clitic cluster order was remarkably *stable* until the 15th century. As Figure 3 shows, the use of the new order is marginal from the 11th through the 14th centuries. It suddenly increases in the 15th century, before it becomes the most common clitic order in the 16th.

Century	DAT–ACC		total
	no.	ratio	
11th	0	0.0	27
12th	11	0.02	518
13th	12	0.01	1044
14th	20	0.02	1278
15th	158	0.19	849
16th	835	0.59	1420

Figure 3. The emergence of the new clitic order

4.1 Internal differences

Wanner (1974) provides time charts for the transition in both Old Italian and Old Provençal. He shows that it is clusters which involve the 1st person singular that change first. His claim is however not supported for Old French, which becomes clear when the data in Figure 3 are broken down further, as in Figures 4 and 5. The p-values in the tables have been calculated using a Fisher-test.

	12th century			13th century			14th century		
	New	Total	Ratio	New	Total	Ratio	New	Total	Ratio
ME	3	238	0.013	6	386	0.016	4	427	0.009
TE	1	46	0.022	1	72	0.014	6	169	0.036
NOS	0	26	0	0	57	0	0	144	0.0
VOS	7	208	0.005	5	529	0.009	10	538	0.019
	p = 0.4275			p = 0.6791			p = 0.05273		

Figure 4. The pace of the change

	15th century			16th century		
	New	Total	Ratio	New	Total	Ratio
ME	68	263	0.259	304	408	0.745
TE	34	122	0.279	176	215	0.819
NOS	17	118	0.144	149	254	0.587
VOS	39	346	0.133	206	543	0.379
	p < 0.5			p < 0.5		

Figure 5. The pace of the change

There is no statistically significant difference between the four persons in the 12th, 13th, and 14th centuries.

When we consider Table 5, we see that the ratio of *te*-clusters in the 16th century is higher than the ratio of *me*-clusters. Apparently this contradicts the tendency found in Old Italian and Old Provençal. There is, however, at no point a significant difference between the *te*-clusters and the *me*-clusters. In the 16th century, the p-value is 0.4851, indicating that the difference in ratio may be the result of pure chance, probably because there are a lot more *me*-clusters than *te*-clusters in the corpus. If we compare *me/te*-clusters on the one hand and *nos/vos*-clusters on the other, there is a significant difference between them in the 16th century (p-value < 0.05). We may thus claim that clusters involving the 1st and 2nd person singular change before the 1st and 2nd person plural, but we are not at liberty to claim that the clusters involving the 1st person singular change prior to the 2nd.

We may thus conclude that the internal order of the clitic clusters was quite stable until the 15th century, and the change towards the new order took place within a few generations. The data indicates that clusters involving the 1st and

2nd persons singular started changing prior to clusters involving the plural pronouns.

5. Rise of the reflexive

Brusewitz (1905) was the first to see a link between the increased use of reflexive verbs and the change in the clitic clusters. In the earliest texts, the position of the reflexive was determined by its syntactic role. In (12) the reflexive *se* 'himself' follows the accusative *le* 'it'.

(12) a. *Cil le se tolt et cil le*
that-one.NOM it.ACC REFL.DAT lifted and that-one.NOM it.ACC
s' emble
himself.DAT stole
'One lifted it up before him, and another one stole it.'
(13th c., Coinci, 1725)

b. *onques ne le se pensa*
never NEG it.ACC REFL.DAT thought
'the thought never occurred to him' (13th c., MortArtu, 14)

Consequently, the old system did not distinguish between *form*, only *function*. The function accusative always preceded the function dative, regardless of their form. In this way, Case dictated the position of clitics.

Brusewitz' idea was that an increased use of reflexive forms led to a reanalysis where the sequence subject pronoun + reflexive pronoun became lexicalised, regardless of the syntactic function of the reflexive pronoun. In (13) the reflexive occurs in first position of the cluster, immediately following the subject.

(13) *il me semble que je me le prescry*
it me seems that I REFL.DAT it.ACC prescribe
'It seems to me that I myself require it.' (16th c., Mont-vanité, p 967)

As a next step, the clusters were reanalysed so that all forms of the pronouns which have identical forms as the reflexive pronoun had to come first in the cluster, also in the cases where they did not function as reflexive markers. In the case of the 3rd person, the reflexive has a distinct form, so there was no trigger for a restructuring of the clitic clusters involving the 3rd person. The process is schematised in Figure 6.

Person	REFLEXIVE	ACC	DAT	
1st sg	me	me	~~me~~	'me'
2nd sg	te	te	~~te~~	'you'
3rd sg	se	le	li	'him'
3rd sg	se	la	li	'her'
1st pl	nos	nos	~~nos~~	'us'
2nd pl	vos	vos	~~vos~~	'you'
3rd pl	se	les	lor	'them'

Figure 6. New clitic order

Zink (1997) claims that in order to prove this theory, it is necessary to show that the clitic clusters first changed in the cases where one of the pronouns is a reflexive. In the electronic corpora we have available, we have not found that the first occurrences of the new clitic order appear with reflexive verbs. Obviously, this may be one of the shortcomings of using a corpus, namely that no matter how big a corpus, it only shows fractions of actual or possible utterances. A different way of approaching this problem is to say that the increase in the use of reflexive forms led to an analysis where all forms which were identical to the reflexive form had to come first, regardless of the type of verb. This is the line of reasoning I will follow. A consequence of this is that I will not try to establish strong causality between the two changes. I will rather show how the use of reflexive verbs became more widespread and that this change happened immediately before, and partly overlapping with, the change of the internal order of clitic clusters.

In the next section I will show that both the use of reflexive forms and their frequency increased from the 12th to the 15th century. This increase slightly precedes the change in the clitic clusters, and I will argue that the two changes are linked.

5.1 Reflexive verbs

In order to test Brusewitz' hypothesis, I searched for the sequence *s'en* 'himself'/'herself of-it' from the late 11th and 12th centuries (group 1) and 15th century (group 2) in the BFM base. This is a clear-cut instance of a reflexive pronoun in front of an adverbial pronoun clitic. The reason I chose *s'en* and not just *se* is that *se* may also be the hypothetic subordinator ('if') in Old French, and in Middle French it may also be a particle in the left periphery (corresponding to *si* in the earliest texts). As a reflexive, *se* may be both accusative and dative (with transitive verbs), and it may be an inherent reflexive (with intransitive verbs).

En is what is described as a pronominal adverb in traditional French grammar. Derived from Latin *inde* 'from there,' it may either be an adverbial clitic meaning 'from there' (14-a) or an anaphoric pronoun clitic replacing an indirect object introduced by the preposition *de* 'of' (14-b). As such, *en* may appear with all kinds of verbs: transitive and intransitive.

In all stages of the language *en* must follow *se* in a clitic cluster.

(14) a. *Vait s' en li pople.*
go REFL from-here the people
'The folks leave.' (12th c., Alexis, 601)

b. *Il s' en va*
he REFL from-here go
'He's leaving.' (Modern French)

5.1.1 *Intransitive verbs*

In order to assess the changes that have taken place, it is necessary to make a distinction between the different types of verbs. As Perlmutter (1978) pointed out, there are two different kinds of intransitive verbs, those whose subject is generated as an internal argument and those whose argument is generated as an external argument. The former verb is *unaccusative* (15-a), the latter *unergative* (15-b).

(15) **intranstive structures**

a. unaccusative: $[_{vP} [_{VP} \text{NP V}^0]]$
b. unergative: $[_{vP} \text{NP} [_{VP} \text{V}^0]]$

Être 'be' is the most common auxiliary with unaccusative non-reflexive verbs in French, but a number of them also take *avoir* 'have.' All reflexive verbs take *être* 'be' as their auxiliary, but not all reflexive verbs are unaccusative (Legendre & Sorace 2003). In order to distinguish between unergative and unaccusative reflexive verbs it is therefore necessary to consider their behaviour in different environments. The difference between unaccusative and unergative verbs becomes quite clear when one looks at participial constructions (Helland 2001; Legendre & Sorace 2003). Whereas the past participle of an unaccusative verb may enter into participial constructions such as free predicatives (16-a) or absolute constructions, and as object predicatives, the participles of unergative verbs may not (16-b).

(16) a. *Les Dupont partis, toute la famille se mit à table.*
the Dupont left all the family REFL put at table
'When the Duponts had left, all the family gathered around the table.'
(From Helland (2001))

b. **L' ouvrier travaillé, il est fatigué.*
the worker worked he is tired
'The working man who had worked is tired.'

In addition to the purely syntactic criteria, I have taken semantics into account. This has been particulary important when distinguishing between unaccusative and transitive verbs. Quite a number of verbs can be both transitive and intransitive. Just like unaccusative verbs, transitive verbs can occur in participial constructions. It is thus challenging to determine the nature of a verb such as *torner* 'turn.' Used as a transitive verb, it signifies 'turn,' as in 'turn the page.' Used as an intransitive verb, it signifies 'turn back' or 'return.'

It is common to associate unaccusative and unergative verbs with certain semantic or aspectual features. Cennamo (1999), discussing intransitive verbs in Late Latin, suggests that there is an unaccusativity hierarchy and an unergative hierarchy. At top of the unaccusative hierarchy are the *change of state verbs*, then come the *change of location verbs*, and in the lowest position the *state verbs*. At the top of the unergative hierarchy, one finds the *mental process verbs*, then follow *speech act verbs*, and finally *other activity verbs*.

In the case of a verb such as *torner* 'turn,' it is thus the fact that the verb signifies a change of location that has led me to label it unaccusative. This way *torner* has (at least) two different listings in the lexicon: one as a regular transitive verb, the other as an inherent reflexive unaccusative verb. Discussing Italian data, Burzio notes that 'inherently reflexive alternations would result from alternations in the semantic role of the subject, varying between an external agent, cause or experiencer (transitive), and an internal one (inherent reflexive)' (Burzio 2008). (See also Levin & Rappaport Hovav (1995) for a discussion of this kind of variation.)

In certain cases, such as with *torner*, I have added the reflexive *se* to mark that there is a clear-cut change in meaning between the reflexive and non-reflexive use of the verb in question. Intransitive verbs are listed in Figure 7; transitive verbs in Figure 8.

In order to observe the diachronic change that has taken place, different formatting has been used in the figures. Underlined verbs are only attested in the 12th century; verbs in bold are attested both in the 12th and the 15th centuries; verbs with no special formatting (other than italics) are only attested in the 15th century. The spelling of the verbs and their translations are based on Hindley et al. (2000).

It is characteristic that a large number of unaccusative verbs appear with a reflexive in Old French. The use of a reflexive seems to be paralleled by the use of *sibi* 'himself' with unaccusative verbs in Late Latin (Cennamo 1999). The most dominant unaccusative verb in the 12th century is *se tourner* 'return' (17-a), which is later replaced by the verb *se retourner*. The second most common unaccusative verb is *aller* 'to go' (17-b), which is by far the most frequent in the 15th century. In the 15th century we also find *s'en aller* used as a semi-auxiliary, in front of both gerundives (17-c) and infinitives (17-d).

Unaccusative verbs
afiler 'flow'; ***aler*** 'go'; *atorner* 'turn'; *avancier* 'go forward'; *comovoir* 'move'; ***departir*** 'leave'; *embler* 'vanish'; ***entrer*** 'enter'; *eschapper* 'escape'; *s'esloignier* 'move away'; *espandre* 'spread'; ***fuir*** 'escape'; ***issir*** 'leave'; *mesaller* 'go astray'; ***partir***'leave'; *raler* 'return'; *refuir* 'run back'; ***se repairier*** 'return'; ***retorner*** 'return'; ***revenir***'come back'; *revoler* 'fly off'; *se torner* 'turn'; *se traire*'move'; ***venir*** 'come'; *voler* 'fly'.
Verbal periphrases
aler 'go' + gerundive, *aler* 'go' + infinitiv
Total: 25 different verbs (17 attested in the 12th century; 18 in the 15 th century). 1118 clauses (214 from the 12th century; 904 from the 15th century)

Unergative verbs
abstiner 'abstain'; *apartenir* 'be related to'; *apenser* 'think'; ***apercevoir*** 'perceive'; *cesser* 'cease,' 'end'; *chevauchier* 'ride'; ***corrocier*** 'become angry'; *courir* 'run'; *deporter* 'entertain,' 'behave,' 'be patient'; *desesperer* 'despair'; *desmouvoir* 'refrain from,' 'change'; *disner* 'break one's fast'; *doter* 'doubt,' 'fear'; *entremetre* 'intervene'; *escrier* 'cry out'; *esfreer* 'be alarmed'; *esmovoir* 'move'; *estordre* 'escape'; ***estre*** 'be'; *esveiller* 'awaken'; *gabber* 'joke'; *merveillier* 'marvel'; *movoir* 'move'; *pasmer* 'faint'; *pener* 'suffer'; *plaindre* 'complain'; *recorder* 'remember'; *repentir* 'repent'; *resveillier* 'wake up again'; ***rire*** 'laugh'; *saouler* 'become satisfied'; *se trover* 'find oneself'; *soucier* 'be worried'; ***taire*** 'be silent'; *tarder* 'delay'; *vanter* 'boast'.
Total: 35 different verbs (12 attested in the 12th century; 29 in the 15 th century). 125 clauses (35 from the 12th century; 90 from the 15th century)

Figure 7. Attested intransitive verbs

(17) **Unaccusative verbs**

a. *Tut sul s' en est Eufemien turnét*
all alone REFL from-here is Euphemianus returned
'Euphemianus returned home all by himself.' (12th c., Alexis, 344)

b. *Escrit la cartra tute de sei medisme, cum s' en*
wrote the charter all of him self how REFL from-here
alat e cum il s' en revint.
went and how he REFL from-here came back
'All by himself he wrote down the story about how he went away and how he came back.' (12th c., Alexis, 285)

c. *Jouhanne s' en va riant a sa damme.*
Joanne REFL from-here goes laughing to her lady
'Joanne is laughing as she approaches milady.' (15th c., QJM, p 44)

d. *et puis s' en vont disner.*
and then REFL from-here go dine
'and then they go to dine.' (15th c., Saintre, p 105)

There are about as many different unergative as unaccusative verbs with the sequence *s'en*, but they are less frequent (18).

(18) **Unergative verbs**

a. *Cent mille Francs s' en pasment cuntre tere.*
hundred thousand French REFL from-here faint against earth
'A hundred thousand French fainted and fell to the ground.'
(12th c., Roland, 2932)

b. *Chascun s' en rit, disant: Dieu quelle joye!*
everyone REFL from-here laughed saying God what joy
'Everyone laughed saying: God, what a joy!'
(15th c., CDO, p.100, v.45)

The use of the reflexive with unaccusative verbs is significantly more widespread than with unergative verbs. Even though there is no difference in the number of verbs permitting a reflexive, the total number of clauses with this structure is almost ten times higher with unaccusative verbs (1114) than with unergative ones (120).

5.1.2 *Transitive verbs*

Distinguishing between the three types of verbs runs into methodological problems when looking at the transitive verbs. The question is what happens with a transitive verb when it appears with a reflexive pronoun. Going into a thorough debate on the analysis of reflexive pronouns is too extensive for the present paper. Let me just briefly state that there is a fundamental difference between intrinsic reflexives appearing on unaccusative verbs and those appearing with transitive verbs. A long standing tradition within linguistics has made the claim that a reflexive that appears with a transitive verb absorbs a thematic role (see among others Reinhart and Reuland (1993) and references in Labelle (2008)). A consequence of this line of thought would be that a transitive verb becomes unergative as the the object role is absorbed by the reflexive. A transitive verb such as *doloser* means 'to mourn, lament, bewail.' As a reflexive verb it is intransitive with the meaning 'to suffer, to be in pain'

(Hindley et al. 2000). In Old French, the reflexive occurs in the same position as the corresponding argumental clitic. This is clear when one considers examples such as (4), repeated here as (19).

(19) *onques ne le se pensa*
never NEG it.ACC himself.DAT thought
'He never thought about it.' (13th c., MortArtu, II, 13)

I take this word order as an indication that the reflexive is in fact an argument in the case of transitive verbs. To complicate matters, there are numerous verbs which may have a transitive *and* an intransitive reading at the same time, and it is not always immediately easy to tell what reading the reflexive is derived from. These verbs are also listed under transitive in Figure 9. Figure 8 gives an indication as to the internal composition of the transitive group. Comparing the data from the 12th century to those from the 15th, we see that there is a substantial increase both in the number of clauses attested with transitive verbs and in the number of verbs which appear in such constructions. I build these tables on the listings in Hindley et al. (2000).

From the 12th to the 15th century there is a large expansion in the number of transitive verbs appearing with a reflexive. In some cases the reflexive imposes a passive reading, as in (20-a). In other cases, the reflexive just indicates co-reference with the subject (20-b).

(20) a. *Plus de cent milie s' en adubent ensemble*
more than hundred thousand REFL from-there dubbed together
'More than a hundred thousand [knights] dubbed themselves together.'
(12th c., Roland, 3000)

b. *c' est folie de s' en donner trop grant courroux*
it is madness of REFL from-there give too big rage
'It is madness to get too infuriated.' (15th c., Mélusine, p. 120)

To sum up: The results show that there is a strong increase in the use of reflexive verbs from the 12th to the 15th century. The ratio of *s'en* compared to the total of words in each century reveals an increase from 0.0423 % to 0.1492 %, which in turn gives p-value < 0.05. The increase is thus statistically significant.

Whereas unaccusative verbs account for 79.9 % of the examples in the 12th century, their amount shrinks to 72.9 % in the 15th. Transitive verbs, on the other hand, only account for 7.8 % of the examples in the 12th century. In the 15th century, as much as 20 % of the examples are with transitive verbs. This is a statistically significant change (p-value < 0.05). This increase is compatible with Brusewitz' hypothesis, which states that there is an increase in the use of reflexive verbs.

Transitive verbs
acointier 'make the acquaintance of'; *adober* 'equip (for battle),' 'dub'; *afichier* 'lean against,' 'fasten to something'; *afoler* 'become mad,' 'die,' 'make mad'; *aider* 'help'; ***aquiter*** 'pay (debt),' 'justify,' 'aquit'; *armer* 'arm,' 'equip'; *assembler* 'come together'; *asseurer* 'have faith in,' 'assure'; *atendre* 'wait,' 'expect'; *baignier* 'bath'; *chargier* 'burden,' 'weigh down'; *chastiier* 'improve,' 'warn'; *chaufer* 'heat'; ***clamer*** 'call'; *combatre* 'fight'; *complaindre* 'complain'; *conduire* 'guide'; *conseillier* 'counsel'; *considerer* 'reflect'; *constituir* 'appoint'; *contenter* 'satisfy'; *couchier* 'lie down'; *cuidier* 'believe'; *defendre* 'defend'; *delivrer* 'free'; *deschargier* 'unload'; *desconforter* 'destroy,' 'grieve'; *descovrir* 'reveal'; *desdeigner* 'disdain'; *desdire* 'contradict'; *desjoindre* 'separate'; *despechier* 'free'; *dessaisir* 'disposess'; *destolir* 'go away,' 'remove'; *detenir* 'keep,' 'restrain'; *deviser* 'talk,' 'separate,' 'divide'; *dire* 'say'; *doloir* 'be in pain,' 'regret'; *doloser* 'suffer,' 'mourn'; *doner* 'give'; *donner garde* 'pay attention to'; *donner merveille* 'surprise'; *ensivre* 'follow'; *envoleper* 'envelope'; *esbair* 'trouble'; *esbatre* 'beat,' 'amuse'; *eschiver* 'refrain from'; *escuser* 'apologise'; *esforcier* 'seize'; *esjoir* 'rejoice'; *eslever* 'raise'; *esmerveillier* 'marvel'; *estimer* 'estimate'; *estrangier* 'remove'; *faire* 'do'; *falir* 'be lacking'; *falloir* 'to need'; *feindre* 'hesitate,' 'shape'; ***garder*** 'keep,' 'beware'; *garir* 'cure'; *joir (re-)* 'enjoy'; ***lever*** 'raise'; *loer* 'praise'; *malcontenter* 'not satisfy'; *mesler* 'mingle'; *metre* 'place'; *moquer* 'mock'; *mostrer* 'show'; *obligier* 'oblige'; *parer* 'embellish'; *parjurer* 'break (one's word)'; *passer* 'manage,' 'pass over'; *penser* 'think'; *percoivre* 'perceive'; *perdre* 'lose'; *picquier* 'hack'; *porchacier* 'seek,' 'provide'; *porter* 'carry,' 'behave,' 'be pregnant'; *prendre garde* 'watch out for'; *purgier* 'purge'; *raporter* 'bring back'; *ravoir* 'have again'; *reconforter* 'comfort'; *redouter* 'fear'; *relever* 'raise up'; *rendre* 'give back,' 'surrender'; *retraire* 'withdraw'; *revoir* 'see again'; *saisir* 'seize'; *sauver* 'save'; *savoir* 'know'; *se tirer* 'leave'; *sentir* 'feel'; *sofrir* 'endure'; *sordre* 'rise (up)'; *sormonter* 'surpass'; *tencier* 'quarrel'; *tenir* 'keep'; *vengier* 'avenge'

Verbal periphrases

faire 'make' + infinitive (causative construction).
Total: 100 different verbs (18 attested in the 12th century; 87 in the 15 th century). 262 clauses (19 from the 12th century; 243 from the 15th century)

Figure 8. Attested transitive verbs

The use of reflexive pronouns is spreading to new verbs, but the increase is stronger with transitive verbs than in any other group. Even though we do not find an elevated number of *s'en* constructions with a verb such as *dire* 'say,' we may still claim that the rise of the reflexive forms may have induced a change in

Type	12th century No.	Ratio	15th century No.	Ratio
Unaccusative	214	0.799	900	0.729
Unergative	33	0.123	87	0.07
Transitive	21	0.078	248	0.20
Total	258		1235	
No.words	610,224	0.000423	827,692	0.001492
		p-value < 0.05		

Figure 9. The sequence *s'en*

the clitic clusters. The word order subject–reflexive became so frequent, also with intransitives, that this order was conceived of as natural. Since there is no difference between the reflexive pronoun and the object pronoun of the first and second persons, this induced a change in the internal order of the clitic clusters. This is what I will return to in the next section.

6. Changing the clitic clusters

We have seen that there was a substantial increase in the occurrences of the reflexive pronoun *se* with transitive verbs, something which I interpret as an expansion of the domain of the reflexive. From being first and foremost associated with unaccusative verbs, the reflexive becomes more and more common also with transitive verbs. The idea that I will explore in this section is that this is the trigger for the internal change in the clitic clusters. As the language users used the reflexive more often with transitive verbs, and increasingly with a pronominal subject, the sequence pronominal subject + reflexive was conceived as the natural order. The consequence of this change is that *person*, not *case* (or *syntactic function*) became the major principle of clitic ordering in French. Even though the result relates to syntax, there was a PF-related trigger that created an ambiguous input, which in turn led to a reanalysis.

The exact position of clitics in clusters is not unproblematic. Kayne (1994) points out that it is impossible to adjoin more than one clitic per head as this would mean clitics would c-command each other. He suggests two different solutions:

> "(…) sequences of clitics must not be analyzed as successive adjunctions to the same head but instead should be analyzed as involving either adjunctions to distinct functional heads or as adjunction of one clitic to another, or some combination thereof." (Kayne 1994: 21)

In other words: Clitics either occupy different phrases in some sort of clitic *field*, as has been suggested by different scholars (see Sportiche (1996); Kayne (2000); Poletto and Pollock (2004a,b); Manzini and Savoia (2004)) – or they are incorporated into each other. Pescarini (2012) uses this insight as he proposes two different kinds of clitic clusters. (21-a) is the *split cluster*, where the clitics belong to different but adjacent heads. (21-b) represents the incorporated clitics, which Pescarini refers to as *true clusters*.

(21) a. **Split cluster:** [clitic-ACC [clitic-DAT]]
b. **True cluster:** [clitic-DAT clitic-ACC [~~clitic-~~DAT]]

The idea exemplified in (22-b) strongly resembles the one presented by Emonds (1975) in a very different framework, but where the main idea was that reflexives as well as 1st and 2nd person clitics were base-generated in the same position as 3rd person dative clitics, in other words, in the position following the accusative. In the transformational process, all clitics base-generated in second position, with the noteworthy exception of 3rd person clitics, are moved such that they appear in the first position in the cluster. In addition to explaining the order in which clitics occur, Emonds also very neatly explains the occurrence of the PPC in French.

In order to describe a change from a theoretical point of view, it is necessary to know the starting point and the ending point of a process. We have already seen (Section 2) that clitics are structured in different ways in Old and Modern French. In Old French, the clitic order is ACC – DAT. This way clitics appear in the same order as full DP arguments. What kind of syntactic structures do these word orders reflect? I will first look at Modern French in Section 6.1 before turning to Old French in Section 6.2.

6.1 Clitics in Modern French

Person is the major determining factor when it comes to clitic ordering in Modern French.[7] Clitics of the 1st and 2nd persons always precede 3rd person clitics, regardless of their syntactic role. In addition, the reflexive pronoun also occurs in first position in a clitic cluster. Laenzlinger (1993) suggests that is it necessary to take case-marking into account when explaining the order in which French clitics occur. He distinguishes between case-marked (Cl_{+K}) and non case-marked clitics (Cl_{-K}), exemplified in (22).

7. Of course, case comes into play when both clitics are in the 3rd person, but this is a secondary principle. Note that 3rd person reflexive *se* also comes in first position in the clusters.

(22) a. Cl_{+K}: *le, la, les, lui, leur*
b. Cl_{-K}: *me, te, nous, vous, se*

Clitics lacking case-marking do not distinguish between accusative and dative, whereas clitics with case-marking do. Laenzlinger observes that +K and –K clitics behave in different ways. A +K clitic needs to check its case, which it does by morphological selection. This method of incorporation implies that the clitic head and the verbal head are in a configuration of mutual c-command; in other words: they are sisters. Because the verbal head and the +K clitic must be in a configuration of mutual c-command, they are in complementary distribution.

A –K clitic, on the other hand, has no case to check, and does not take part in such a selectional process. Instead, a –K clitic is free to incorporate into any host that carries a ϕ-feature.

A consequence of these observations is that a +K and a –K clitic may be combined, but that two +K clitics may not. A clause such as *me le* 'me him' in (23) exhibit the combination of a Cl_{-K} and a Cl_{+K}, which is fine. The two clitics are incorporated into the same head, T^0. This way, the clause in (23) has the structure in (24).

(23) *Elle me le donne.*
she me.DAT it.ACC gives
'She has given it to me.'

(24) $[_{TP}$ Elle $[_{T^0}$ me $[_{T^0}$ le $[_{T^0}$ donne$]]]]$.

The reason why it is possible to have clusters combining two Cl_{+K} clitics (e.g. *le lui* 'him him') is that they are not cliticised to the same node. In (25) the clitic *lui* 'of-him' is cliticised to the Aux^0, whereas *le* 'him' is cliticised to T^0.

(25) *Jean le lui a presenté.*
John it.ACC him.DAT has presented
'John has presented it to him.' (from Laenzlinger (1993))

(26) $[_{TP}$ Jean $[_{T^0}$ le $[[_{T^0}$ $[_{AgrO^0}$ $[_{Aux^0}$ lui $[_{Aux^0}$ a $]]]]]]]$ presenté.

Ever since Chomsky (1995) there has been no place for agreement projections in syntax, so the analysis in (26) is rendered somewhat obsolete. I will however retain Laenzlinger's main idea, namely that there are two different kinds of clitic clusters: One where clitics are incorporated into the same head, and one where they cliticise to different heads. Using Pescarini's analysis in (21) I will suggest that clusters involving the 1st and 2nd person are *true clusters*, whereas clusters involving the 3rd person are *split clusters* (27).

(27) a. **Split cluster:** [le.ACC [lui.DAT]]
b. **True cluster:** [me.DAT le.ACC [~~me.~~DAT]]

In the cases where the reflexive *se* is used, it is reasonable to assume that *se* has been moved in front of the accusative, just as in (27).

(28) Il se le dis.
He REFL.DAT it.ACC say
'He tells himself.'

(29) [se.DAT le.ACC [~~se.DAT~~]]

As such, I analyse all clusters involving 1st and 2nd person clitics as well as 3rd person reflexive clitics as true clusters, derived by the same mechanism.

6.2 Clitics in Old French

What was the status of Old French clitic clusters? I will propose that they were all split clusters, as Modern French *le lui*-clusters are still. There are two reasons for assuming this. First and foremost because the *le lui*-cluster is archaic in the sense that it has not been altered. If these clusters are split in Modern French, they must be so in Old French as well. Pescarini (2012) makes the same assumption when he analyses Old Italian clitics, which have undergone a a change similar to the one that affected French clitics.[8] In Italian the shift also has phonological consequences in that the leftmost vowel of the cluster changes from *i* to *e* (30).

(30) [la [mi]] → [me la [~~me~~]]

The vowel does not change as the clitic order is reversed in French. However, in Section 3 we saw that several scholars have suggested that there was some sort of phonological change taking place in Old French simultaneously as the clitic cluster order started changing. Meyer-Lübke (1899) suggested it was a rhytmical change, whereas Zink (1997) discusses what he calls a change in accent. This change implies that the apparent enclitic forms such as *jol* (*jo* + *le*, 'I + it') disappear (31).

(31) jol dis → je le dis

It is however crucial to note that in an example such as the one in (31), the object must still be followed by the finite verb. This is the same observation as

8. The major difference is that also 3rd person clusters are DAT–ACC in Modern Italian.

the one made for Modern Romanian by Miller and Monachesi (2003: 100). In this language a clitic may be enclitic to the preceding element, also when the preceding element is a full DP. Interestingly, Miller & Monachesi suggest that the state of affairs in Romanian is reminiscent of the the cliticisation patterns in Old Romance.

Instead of viewing this as solely the change of a metric pattern (Meyer-Lübke 1899; Zink 1997), it is also a change that may be directly linked to a change in syntax, namely the change from a split to a true cluster.

To sum up: Clitics in Old French form split clusters, whereas clitics in Modern French form either true clusters or split ones. The *me le* type is the instantiation of a true cluster, whereas *le me*-clusters are split ones. We have also seen that clusters involving the reflexive clitic *se* have the reflexive in second position in the oldest texts when it functions as a dative (see example (4) above). This is very interesting, as it shows that syntactic function is the major principle of clitic placement. Other possible criteria, such as person or reflexivehood, do not come into play.

6.2.1 *The clitic field*

In the following I will assume that clitics are heads, and that each clitic head is associated with the head of a particular phrase. This way clitics appear in what may be described as a *clitic field*, perhaps in the way described by Sportiche (1996). I will further assume that clitics that are arguments will occupy designated positions in this hierarchy, and that these positions are defined by their syntactic status. This way there is a slot for accusative clitics and one for dative clitics. I take this order to be universal. The change from a system that is based on case (Old French) into one that is based on person (Modern French) must then affect the operations that take place after the clitics have been merged in their positions.[9]

Furthermore, I will argue that there is a designated slot for inherent reflexives, e.g. clitics that are reflexive and that do not correspond to any argument. I take this position to be situated above the slots for accusative and dative clitics.

A schematic representation of the three clitic positions in Old French is presented in Figure 10. Prior to any restructuring reflexive clitics occur in Cl-1, accusative clitics in Cl-2 and dative clitics in Cl-3.

9. Also note that in the cases of true imperatives, when the clitics are enclitic to the finite verb, they always occur in the order ACC–DAT.

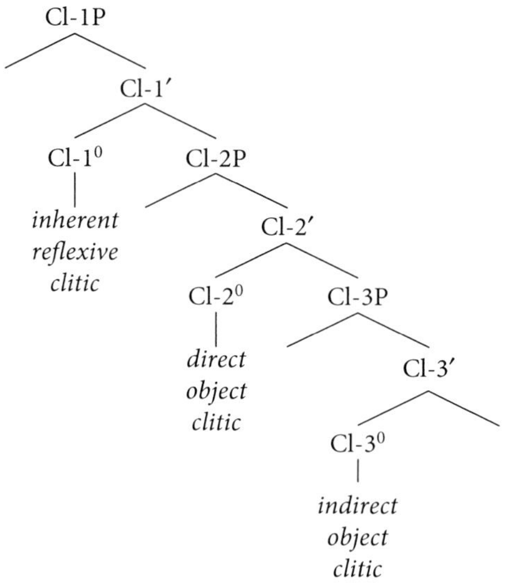

Figure 10. The clitic field in Old French (prior to change)

If what I have proposed is on the right track, namely that the increased use of reflexives led to a reanalysis, we can account for this syntactically. The input dictates that reflexives should occur in first position, which is the only possible position for inherent clitics. As the language does not overtly distinguish between the different functions of the clitics in the 1st and 2nd persons, the analogy then imposes that all syncretic forms occur in first position of the cluster. If, however, the syncretic clitic is a dative, it is merged under Cl-3^0 and would occur in second position of the cluster.[10] In order to occur in the first position in the cluster, it has to move. This way clitics of the 1st and 2nd persons are moved to the first position in the linear order. Also dative *se* has to move as it is a reflexive form and should come first in a cluster, regardless of its syntactic function.

The only way an indirect object may occur in front of a direct object clitic is by moving to the same head and adjoin to the higher head. This is indeed what happens, and we get a true cluster (Figure 11).

This analysis implies that there is a major difference between Old and Modern French when it comes to cluster types. While Old French only displays split clusters, Modern French has both, as exemplified in (32). Note that as reflexives are merged in a higher position, clusters in which they occur must be split clusters.

10. These clusters only contain two elements, so even though it is merged under Cl-3^0, it occurs in second position in the linear order.

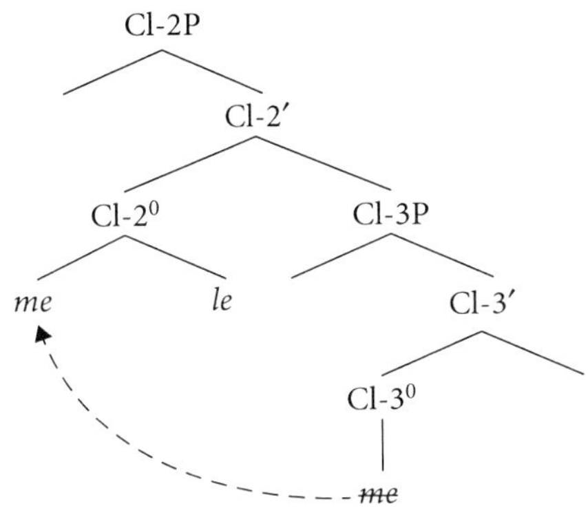

Figure 11. Derivation of a true cluster

(32) **Modern French**

a. **Split clusters:** Clusters involving reflexives, clusters involving 3rd person clitics.

b. **True clusters:** Clusters involving 1st and 2nd person argumental clitics.

Thus, from a derivational point of view, what distinguishes Old French from Modern French is that in Modern French clitics may move after they have been merged. In Old French clitics remain in the position in which they are merged. The trigger for the movement that started taking place in the 15th century was the increased input of reflexive forms.

7. Conclusion

I have shown that the change in clitic clusters in French took place rather quickly, in the 15th and 16th centuries. Clusters including 1st and 2nd person clitics changed from the ACC–DAT order to the DAT–ACC order of Modern French. In the case of 3rd person clitics, no change took place.

I have also shown that from the 11th–12th centuries to the 15th the use of reflexive forms expanded, and that there was an increasing number of transitive verbs which appeared with the reflexive pronoun *se* + the adverbial pronoun *en*. At the same time, the relative proportion of clauses appearing with the reflexive pronoun *se* increased. I have argued that it is the rise of the reflexive pronoun which triggers the change in the clitic clusters in French. As the frequency of the reflexive construction increased, there was a reanalysis which led to a requirement that all reflexives should occur in the first position of a cluster. As the clitics of the 1st and 2nd persons are syncretic, the ambiguity of the input led to place these in the first position, regardless of their syntactic function.

From a formal point of view, I have suggested that clitics in Old French were split clusters, whereas clusters in Modern French involving 1st and 2nd person argumental clusters are true clusters. The change in the linear organisation of the clitic clusters is the reflection of the transfer from a split to a true cluster.

References

Janice M. Aski. 2011. Il vi prometto – ve lo intendo dimostrare: Variable double object clitic clusters in the *Decameron* and Medieval Florentine. In *Accessus ad Auctores, Studies in Honor of Christopher Kleinhenz*, Fabian Alfie & Andrea Dini (eds). Tempe AZ: Center for Medieval & Renaissance Studies.

Boeckx, Cedric. 2000. Quirky agreement. *Studia Linguistica* 54(3): 354–380.

Bonet, Eulàlia. 1991. Morphology after Syntax: Pronominal Clitics in Romance. Ph.D. dissertation, MIT.

Bonet, Eulàlia. 1994. The person-case constraint: A morphological approach. *MIT Working Papers in Linguistics* 22: 33–52.

Brusewitz, Victor. 1905. *Étude historique sur la syntaxe des pronoms personnels* dans la langue des Félibres. Ph.D. dissertation, Uppsala University.

Burzio, Luigi. 2008. The anaphoric and pronominal system. Baltimore MD: Johns Hopkins University. ⟨http://cogsci.jhu.edu/people/files/_pubs-Burzio/ThePronominalSystem.pdf⟩ (January 2013).

Cennamo, Michela. 1999. Late Latin pleonastic reflexives and the unaccusative hypothesis. *Transactions of the Philological Society* 97(1): 103–150.

Chomsky, Noam. 1995. *The Minimalist Program* [Current Studies in Linguistics Series 28]. Cambridge MA: The MIT Press.

Culbertson, Jennifer. 2009. The status of old french clitics in the 12th century. In *Romance Linguistics 2007. Selected papers from the* 37th *Linguistic Symposium on Romance Languages (LSRL), Pittsburgh, 15–18 March 2007*. [Current Issues in Linguistic Theory 304], Pascual José Masullo, Erin O'Rourke & Chia-Hui Huang (eds), 89–104. Amsterdam: John Benjamins.

Emonds, Joseph. 1975. A transformational analysis of French clitics without positive output constraints. *Linguistic Analysis* 1(1): 3–24.

Helland, Hans Petter. 2001. Le participe passé et l'hypothèse inaccusative. In *Langage et référence*, 255–264. Uppsala: Acta Universitatis Upsaliensis.

Hindley, Alan, Langley, Frederick W. & Levy, Brian J. 2000. *Old French–English Dictionary*. Cambridge: CUP.

Hirschbühler, Paul & Labelle, Marie. 2000. Evolving Tobler-Mussafia effects in the placement of French clitics. In *New Approaches to Old Problems. Issues in Romance Historical Linguistics* [Current Issues in Linguistic Theory 210], Steven N. Dworkin & Dieter Wanner (eds), 165–182. Amsterdam: John Benjamins.

Kayne, Richard S. 1994. *The Antisymmetry of Syntax* [Linguistic Inquiry Monographs 25]. Cambridge MA: The MIT Press.

Kayne, Richard S. 2000. Null subjects and clitic climbing. In *Parameters and Universals* [Oxford Studies in Comparative Syntax]. Oxford: OUP.

de Kok, Ans. 1985. *La place du pronom personnel régime conjoint en français; une étude diachronique*. Amsterdam: Rodopi.

Labelle, Marie. 2008. The French reflexive and reciprocal se. *Natural Language and Linguistic Theory* 26(4): 833–876.

Labelle, Marie & Hirschbühler, Paul. 2005. Changes in clausal organization and the position of clitics in Old French. In *Grammaticalization and Parametric Change*, Montse Batllori, Maria-Lluisa Hernanz, Carme Picallo & Francesc Roca (eds), 60–71. Oxford: OUP.

Laenzlinger, Christopher. 1993. A syntactic view of Romance pronominal sequences. *Probus* 5(3): 241–270.

Lalou, Élisabeth, Boutet, Dominique & Gaucher, Elisabeth. 2001. *Corpus de la literature médiévale: En langue d'oil des origines à la fin du XVe siècle: Prose narrative – poésie – théâtre.* Paris: Champion electronique.

Legendre, Géraldine & Sorace, Antonella. 2003. Auxiliaires et intransitivité en français et dans les langues romanes. In *Les langues romanes. Problèmes de la phrase simple,* Danièle Godard (ed.). Paris: CNRS éditions.

Levin, Beth & Rappaport Hovav, Malka. 1995. *Unaccusativity: At the Syntax-Lexical Semantics Interface* [Linguistic Inquiry Monographs 26]. Cambridge MA: The MIT Press.

Manzini, M. Rita. 2012. From Romance clitics to case: Split accusativity and the Person-Case Constraint. In *Romance Languages and Linguistic Theory 2010. Selected papers from 'Going Romance' Leiden 2010.* [Romance Languages and Linguistic Theory 4], Irene Franco, Sara Lusini & Saab Andrés (eds), 1–20. Amsterdam: John Benjamins.

Manzini, M. Rita & Savoia, Leonardo M. 2004. Clitics: Cooccurrence and mutual exclusion patterns. In *The Structure of CP and IP* [Oxford Studies in Comparative Syntax], Luigi Rizzi (ed.). Oxford: OUP.

Meyer-Lübke, Wilhelm. 1899. *Grammatik der Romanischen Sprachen; Romanische Syntax*, Vol. 3. Leipzig: Fues Verlag.

Miller, Philip & Monachesi, Paola. 2003. Les pronoms clitiques dans les langues romanes. In *Les langues romanes. Problèmes de la phrase simple,* Danièle Godard (ed.). Paris: CNRS éditions.

Ormazabal, Jabier & Romero, Juan. 2007. The object agreement constraint. *Natural Language & Linguistic Theory* 25: 315–347.

Perlmutter, David M. 1978. Impersonal passives and the unaccusative hypothesis. In *Proceedings of the Annual Meeting of the Berkeley Linguistics Society* 4: 157–190.

Pescarini, Diego. 2012. Prosodic restructuring and morphological opacity. The evolution of Italo-Romance clitic clusters. *lingBuzz/001477.*

Poletto, Cecilia & Pollock, Jean-Yves. 2004a. On the left periphery of some Romance wh-questions. In *The Structure of CP and IP* [Oxford Studies in Comparative Syntax], Luigi Rizzi (ed.). Oxford: OUP.

Poletto, Cecilia & Pollock, Jean-Yves. 2004b. On wh-clitics and wh-doubling in French and some North Eastern Italian dialects. *Probus* 16(2): 241–272.

Reinhart, Tanya & Reuland, Eric.1993. Reflexivity. *Linguistic Inquiry* 24: 657–720.

Sportiche, Dominique. 1996. Clitic constructions. In *Phrase Structure and the Lexicon* [Studies in Natural Language and Linguistic Theory 33], Johan Rooryck & Laurie Ann Zaring (eds). Dordrecht: Kluwer.

Togeby, Knud. 1979. *Precis historique de grammaire francaise.* Copenhague: Akademisk Forlag.

Wanner, Dieter. 1974. The evolution of Romance clitic order. In *Linguistic Studies in Romance languages: Proceedings*, R. Joe Campbell, Mark G. Goldin & Mary Clayton Wang (eds), 158–177. Washington DC: Georgetown University Press.

Zink, Gaston. 1997. *Morphosyntaxe du pronom personnel (non réfléchi) en moyen français: (XIVe-XVe siècles).* Genève: Librairie Droz.

Appendix: Cited texts

Examples found in the online data bases

CLM = *Corpus de la littérature médiévale: en langue d'oïl des origines à la fin du XVe siècle: prose narrative – poésie – théâtre* (Lalou et al. 2001).
BFM = *la Base de Français Médiéval.*

Adam	Anonymous: *Le Jeu d'Adam* (12 th c.), CLM
Alexis	Anonymous: *Vie de Saint Alexis* (late 11th c., early 12th c.), BFM
Aliscans	Anonymous: *Aliscans* (12 th c.), CLM
Antioche	Anonymous: *Chanson d'Antioche* (12 th c.), CLM
Aspremont	Anonymous: *Chanson d'Aspremont* (12 th c.), CLM
Béroul	Béroul: *Roman de Tristan* (12 th c.), CLM
CDO	Charles d'Orléans: *Songe en complainte* (15 th c.), BFM
Charrete	Chrétien de Troyes: *Chevalier de la charrete* (12 th c.), CLM
Charroi	Anonymous: *Charroi de Nîmes* (12 th c.), CLM
Coinci	Gautier de Coinci: *Miracles de Nostre Dame* (13th c.), BFM
Couci	Chastelain de Couci: *Chansons attribuées au Chastelain de Couci* (12 th c.), CLM
Eulalie	Anonymous: *La Cantilène d'Eulalie* (late 9th c.), CLM
Jouvencel	Jean de Bueil: *Le Jouvencel* (15 th c.), BFM
Mélusine	Jean d'Arras: *Mélusine* (15 th c.), BFM
Mont-Sebond	Michel de Montaigne: *Essais*, t. 1, book 2, Chapter 11: 'Apoogie de Raimond Sebond,' 1592, Frantext
Mont-vanité	Michel de Montaigne: *Essais*, 2. 2, book 3, Chapter 9: 'De la vanité,' 1592, Frantext
Portigal	Anonymous: *Miracle de la femme et du roy de Portigal* (before 1339), CLM
Raoul	Anonymous: *Raoul de Cambrai* (12 th c.), CLM
Renart-I	Anonymous: *Le Roman de Renart* (1175–1250), CLM
QJM	Anonymous: *La Chanson de Roland* (written ca 1080, mauscript from the 12 th c.), BFM
Saintré	Antoine de la Sale: *Jean de Saintré* (15 th c.), BFM
Thèbes	Anonymous: *Le Roman de Thèbes* (12 th c.), CLM
Vieil-T	Anonymous: *Mistére du Vieil Testament* (15 th c.), CLM
Yvain	Chrétien de Troyes: *Yvain* (12 th c.), CLM
QJM	Anonymous: *Quinze joies de mariage* (15 th c.), BFM

Examples retrieved manually

MortArtu	Anonymous: La Mort du roi Arthur (ca 1230), éd David Hult, Paris 2009.

Language index

Subject index